DECISION MATHEMATICS

McGRAW-HILL ACCOUNTING SERIES

NORTON M. BEDFORD, ROBERT K. JAEDICKE, AND
CHARLES E. JOHNSON, *Consulting Editors*

DECISION MATHEMATICS

DENNIS E. GRAWOIG
CHAIRMAN, DEPARTMENT OF QUANTITATIVE METHODS
GEORGIA STATE COLLEGE

McGRAW-HILL BOOK COMPANY
NEW YORK   ST. LOUIS
SAN FRANCISCO   TORONTO   LONDON   SYDNEY

Appendices D through F are from *Handbook of Mathematical Tables and Formulas* 4th ed. by R. S. Burington. Copyright © 1965 by R. S. Burington. McGraw-Hill Book Company. Used by permission.

Problem 15, page 79, is from *Linear Programming* by N. Paul Loomba. Copyright © 1964. McGraw-Hill Book Company. Used by permission.

The following problems are from Mark E. Stern, *Mathematics for Management*, © 1963. Reprinted by permission of Prentice-Hall, Inc., Englewood Cliffs, N.J.:

Problem 5, page 72
Problem 6, page 73
Problem 7, page 74
Problem 9, page 152
Problem 19, page 178
Problem 20, page 179

Problems 1 and 3, page 72, and Problems 11 and 12, page 77, are from Sasieni, Yaspan, and Friedman, *Operations Research: Methods and Problems*, © 1959. Reprinted by permission of John Wiley & Sons, Inc., New York, N.Y.

Problem 14, page 79, is from Daniel Teichroew, *An Introduction to Management Science: Deterministic Models*, © 1954. Reprinted by permission of John Wiley & Sons, Inc., New York, N.Y.

PREFACE

The rapidly changing technology of our generation has created the need for substantial changes in business school curricula. The field of mathematics has become one of the major areas for readjustment. Just a few years ago mathematics for business students was composed of college algebra and mathematics of investment. Algebra was justified as a liberal arts course which broadened the horizons of the student. Mathematics of investment was the only area of application considered generally useful in the fields making up a business curriculum.

Advances in applied mathematics and the increasing accessibility of computers have not only expanded the domain of mathematical applications but have substantially increased its importance as a tools area for business students. Today, mathematics can be used to describe situations, to determine optimal strategies, and to develop plans for securing information. In virtually every business discipline, mathematics is appearing in the literature of the field and underlies the concepts and techniques. The facility of quantitative methods for reducing large batches of data to meaningful information and for concisely representing complex problems will undoubtedly result in an increasing emphasis on these tools in the next few years.

Providing the basic background in mathematics for applied courses in the various business disciplines presents a formidable problem. The time necessary to develop student familiarity with quantitative tools is difficult to secure. This is true both at the undergraduate and graduate levels, but perhaps is most crucial in MBA programs where proficiency in the techniques is necessary within a two-quarter time period if the tools are to be available for use in other courses.

This book will concisely provide a basic familiarity with quantitative tools so that students can rapidly obtain a mathematical foundation. To this end, proofs are eliminated, subject matter is limited to those areas which are currently used in decision models in business and economics, and extensive examples are used. The level of sophistication is intended to be sufficient for students to read the literature in their field and to model and solve basic problems.

I should like to express my appreciation to Professors Eugene Brooks, Catherine Miles, and Charles Bostwick for their suggestions and help in reviewing the initial manuscript. I am also indebted to Dr. Robert Jaedicke, whose encouragement and suggestions have contributed to making this book possible.

Finally, I am most appreciative for the competent and dedicated work of Miss Kathryn Marotte, who typed the manuscript, and Miss Margaret Gammon, who did an exceptionally fine job of proofing and editing.

DENNIS E. GRAWOIG

CONTENTS

PART 1

1 MATRIX ALGEBRA: GENERAL CONCEPTS

INTRODUCTION

Matrix algebra is a branch of algebra where single letters are used to denote groups of data rather than just individual numbers. The rules governing this area of mathematics are different from those which apply to the general algebra with which the reader is already familiar.

Matrix notation is compact and convenient and has already proven to be well adapted to many business problems. Matrix algebra is the basis for linear programming, which at present is the most widely and successfully used technique in the field of mathematical applications for business problem solving. Many other techniques, such as game theory and Markov chains, have wide business applicability and utilize matrix algebra.

VECTORS

A *vector* is a row or column of numbers in which the position of each number within the row or column has a definite, predetermined meaning. For example, quantities of product 1, product 2, and product 3 might be represented by (4, 7, 5), meaning 4 units of product 1, 7 units of product 2, and 5 units of product 3. The same information might

have been conveyed by the vector $\begin{pmatrix} 4 \\ 7 \\ 5 \end{pmatrix}$. Note that if product 1 is to be represented first (as above), then the vector (7, 4, 5) will convey an entirely different set of information, namely, 7 units of product 1, 4 units of product 2, and 5 units of product 3.

If only one type of information is to be represented, then either a column vector or a row vector may be used, as long as the one chosen is used consistently throughout the problem.

Rows versus columns

If in five stores the number of units of product 1, product 2, and product 3 are counted, the results could be shown in vector form as

$$(4, 7, 5) \qquad (3, 1, 2) \qquad (8, 3, 5) \qquad (2, 4, 6) \qquad (3, 1, 9)$$

or

$$\begin{pmatrix} 4 \\ 7 \\ 5 \end{pmatrix} \quad \begin{pmatrix} 3 \\ 1 \\ 2 \end{pmatrix} \quad \begin{pmatrix} 8 \\ 3 \\ 5 \end{pmatrix} \quad \begin{pmatrix} 2 \\ 4 \\ 6 \end{pmatrix} \quad \begin{pmatrix} 3 \\ 1 \\ 9 \end{pmatrix}$$

In the above example, column vectors or row vectors should be used consistently, not intermixed. If, however, two different types of information are to be shown concerning the same data, one type of information must be presented in rows, the other type in columns. For example, if both price and quantity of product 1, product 2, and product 3 are to be shown and if quantity is shown as

$$(4, 7, 5)$$

then price must be shown as

$$\begin{pmatrix} .30 \\ .25 \\ .10 \end{pmatrix}$$

meaning product 1 is $.30 per unit, product 2 is $.25 per unit, and product 3 is $.10 per unit.

Zero entries

If at a particular store 3 units of product 1, 0 units of product 2, and 5 units of product 3 are observed, the vector (3, 0, 5) would be a correct representation. The zero is important and must not be omitted. The vector (3, 5) would have no meaning in the context of product 1, product 2, and product 3.

Addition of vectors

Vectors with the same number of entries and of the same type (row or column) may be added or subtracted by adding or subtracting the corresponding entries.

EXAMPLE 1.1

$$(3, 2, 1) + (4, 3, 7) = (3 + 4, 2 + 3, 1 + 7) = (7, 5, 8)$$

EXAMPLE 1.2

$$(3, 2, 1) - (4, 3, 7) = (3 - 4, 2 - 3, 1 - 7) = (-1, -1, -6)$$

EXAMPLE 1.3

$$\begin{pmatrix} 3 \\ 8 \\ 5 \end{pmatrix} + \begin{pmatrix} 4 \\ 2 \\ 3 \end{pmatrix} = \begin{pmatrix} 3 + 4 \\ 8 + 2 \\ 5 + 3 \end{pmatrix} = \begin{pmatrix} 7 \\ 10 \\ 8 \end{pmatrix}$$

EXAMPLE 1.4

$$\begin{pmatrix} 3 \\ 8 \\ 5 \end{pmatrix} - \begin{pmatrix} 4 \\ 2 \\ 3 \end{pmatrix} = \begin{pmatrix} 3 - 4 \\ 8 - 2 \\ 5 - 3 \end{pmatrix} = \begin{pmatrix} -1 \\ 6 \\ 2 \end{pmatrix}$$

EXAMPLE 1.5

$\begin{pmatrix} 4 \\ 1 \\ 2 \end{pmatrix}$ and (3, 2, 5) cannot be added, since they are not of the same type.

EXAMPLE 1.6

$\begin{pmatrix} 3 \\ 7 \\ 9 \end{pmatrix}$ and $\begin{pmatrix} 2 \\ 3 \end{pmatrix}$ cannot be added, since they do not have the same number of entries.

Vectors are customarily represented by lower case letters. Thus, if **a** is defined as

$$\mathbf{a} = (3, 2, 9)$$

and **b** is defined as

$$\mathbf{b} = (41, 32, 11)$$
$$\mathbf{a} + \mathbf{b} = (3, 2, 9) + (41, 32, 11) = (3 + 41, 2 + 32, 9 + 11)$$
$$= (44, 34, 20)$$
$$\mathbf{b} + \mathbf{a} = (41, 32, 11) + (3, 2, 9) = (41 + 3, 32 + 2, 11 + 9)$$
$$= (44, 34, 20)$$

Note that $\mathbf{a} + \mathbf{b} = \mathbf{b} + \mathbf{a}$ and that the sum (or difference) is always a vector of the same type, either row or column, and with the same number of elements.

Multiplication of a vector by a scalar

Numbers such as 3, 17, .214, -32, and $\frac{3}{8}$ are defined as *scalars*. Any vector can be multiplied by a scalar simply by multiplying each element in the vector by the scalar and forming a new vector of the resulting numbers. Thus if $\mathbf{a} = (2, 7)$, then

$$3\mathbf{a} = 3(2, 7) = (3 \cdot 2, 3 \cdot 7) = (6, 21)$$

and if $\mathbf{b} = \begin{pmatrix} 5 \\ -2 \end{pmatrix}$, then

$$-7\mathbf{b} = -7 \begin{pmatrix} 5 \\ -2 \end{pmatrix} = \begin{pmatrix} -7 \cdot 5 \\ -7 \cdot -2 \end{pmatrix} = \begin{pmatrix} -35 \\ 14 \end{pmatrix}$$

Note that the resulting vector is of the same type and has the same number of elements as the original vector. If $\mathbf{a} = \begin{pmatrix} 5 \\ 0 \end{pmatrix}$ and $\mathbf{b} = \begin{pmatrix} 3 \\ 2 \end{pmatrix}$, then $4(\mathbf{a} + \mathbf{b})$ is found as follows:

$$\mathbf{a} + \mathbf{b} = \begin{pmatrix} 5 \\ 0 \end{pmatrix} + \begin{pmatrix} 3 \\ 2 \end{pmatrix} = \begin{pmatrix} 8 \\ 2 \end{pmatrix}$$

$$4(\mathbf{a} + \mathbf{b}) = 4 \begin{pmatrix} 8 \\ 2 \end{pmatrix} = \begin{pmatrix} 32 \\ 8 \end{pmatrix}$$

$3\mathbf{a} + 2\mathbf{b}$ would be determined as follows:

$$3\mathbf{a} = 3 \begin{pmatrix} 5 \\ 0 \end{pmatrix} = \begin{pmatrix} 15 \\ 0 \end{pmatrix}$$

$$2\mathbf{b} = 2 \begin{pmatrix} 3 \\ 2 \end{pmatrix} = \begin{pmatrix} 6 \\ 4 \end{pmatrix}$$

$$3\mathbf{a} + 2\mathbf{b} = \begin{pmatrix} 15 \\ 0 \end{pmatrix} + \begin{pmatrix} 6 \\ 4 \end{pmatrix} = \begin{pmatrix} 21 \\ 4 \end{pmatrix}$$

Multiplication of a vector by another vector

Two vectors can be multiplied together providing that they each have the same number of entries and that one is a row vector and the other a column vector. (The row vector is placed first, and the resulting product of the two vectors is a scalar number.) Corresponding entries are multiplied and the resulting numbers are added together.

EXAMPLE 1.7

$$(4, 3) \begin{pmatrix} 2 \\ 1 \end{pmatrix} = 4 \cdot 2 + 3 \cdot 1 = 8 + 3 = 11$$

EXAMPLE 1.8

$$(5, 0, -2) \begin{pmatrix} 3 \\ 4 \\ 3 \end{pmatrix} = 5 \cdot 3 + 0 \cdot 4 + (-2) \cdot 3 = 15 + 0 + (-6) = 9$$

EXAMPLE 1.9

$(2, 7)$ and $\begin{pmatrix} 3 \\ 5 \\ 2 \end{pmatrix}$ cannot be multiplied, since they do not have the same number of entries.

Same # entries

EXAMPLE 1.10

(3, 5, 1) and (2, 7, 9) cannot be multiplied, since they are both row vectors.

EXAMPLE 1.11

$\begin{pmatrix} 2 \\ 5 \\ 8 \end{pmatrix}$ and $\begin{pmatrix} 3 \\ 1 \\ 7 \end{pmatrix}$ cannot be multiplied since they are both column vectors.

If **a** and **b** are row and column vectors, respectively, with the same number of elements, and k is a scalar number, then

$$k\mathbf{ab} = (k\mathbf{a})\mathbf{b} = k(\mathbf{ab})$$

EXAMPLE 1.12

Let **a** = (4, 2, 1) and **b** = $\begin{pmatrix} 5 \\ 2 \\ 3 \end{pmatrix}$. Then

$$5\mathbf{a} = 5(4, 2, 1) = (20, 10, 5)$$

and

$$(5\mathbf{a})\mathbf{b} = (20, 10, 5) \begin{pmatrix} 5 \\ 2 \\ 3 \end{pmatrix} = 100 + 20 + 15 = 135$$

The computations could have been performed in a different order with no change in the results. Thus,

$$\mathbf{ab} = (4, 2, 1) \begin{pmatrix} 5 \\ 2 \\ 3 \end{pmatrix} = 20 + 4 + 3 = 27$$

and

$$5(\mathbf{ab}) = 5(27) = 135$$

An example of the use of vectors in a business situation

The Oregon Company sells three fabrics known as Bylon, Crylon, and Donlup. Four yarns are used in the manufacture of these fabrics. To make a yard of Bylon requires 3 units of yarn 1, 5 units of yarn 2, and 1 unit of yarn 4. Crylon requires 2 units of yarn 2 and 3 units of yarn 3 per yard. Donlup requires 2 units of each yarn for a yard. Cost of yarn 1 is $1.00 per unit, yarn 2 is $2.00 per unit, yarn 3 is $5.00 per unit, and yarn 4 is $4.00 per unit. Five hundred yards of Bylon, 200 yards of Crylon, and 100 yards of Donlup will be sold in June.

REQUIRED:

1 Set up a quantity-of-yarn vector for each fabric.
2 Set up a cost-of-yarn vector.
3 Find the quantity of each yarn necessary for June sales.

4 Find the total June costs.

5 Find the cost per yard of each fabric.

SOLUTION:

1 The choice of column or row vectors is arbitrary, except that it must be followed for all three. Let

$\mathbf{a}$ = quantity of yarn 1, 2, 3, and 4, respectively, in 1 yard of Bylon
$\mathbf{b}$ = quantity of yarn 1, 2, 3, and 4, respectively, in 1 yard of Crylon
$\mathbf{c}$ = quantity of yarn 1, 2, 3, and 4, respectively, in 1 yard of Donlup

Then $\mathbf{a} = (3, 5, 0, 1)$ $\mathbf{b} = (0, 2, 3, 0)$ and $\mathbf{c} = (2, 2, 2, 2)$

2 Since row vectors were chosen for the quantity of yarn, a column vector must be chosen for the cost of yarn (this is different information about the same items). Let $\mathbf{d}$ = cost per unit of yarns 1, 2, 3, and 4, respectively. Then

$$\mathbf{d} = \begin{pmatrix} 1.00 \\ 2.00 \\ 5.00 \\ 4.00 \end{pmatrix}$$

3 $500\mathbf{a} + 200\mathbf{b} + 100\mathbf{c}$ = amount of each yarn necessary to cover June sales. Thus,

$500(3, 5, 0, 1) + 200(0, 2, 3, 0) + 100(2, 2, 2, 2)$
$\qquad = (1,500, 2,500, 0, 500) + (0, 400, 600, 0) + (200, 200, 200, 200)$
$\qquad = (1,700, 3,100, 800, 700)$

Let this equal $\mathbf{e}$.

4 Total June costs = cost per yard $\times$ total quantity = $\mathbf{ed}$

$$\mathbf{ed} = (1,700, 3,100, 800, 700) \begin{pmatrix} 1.00 \\ 2.00 \\ 5.00 \\ 4.00 \end{pmatrix}$$
$$= 1,700.00 + 6,200.00 + 4,000.00 + 2,800.00 = \$14,700.00$$

5 Cost per yard of Bylon is

$$\mathbf{ad} = (3, 5, 0, 1) \begin{pmatrix} 1.00 \\ 2.00 \\ 5.00 \\ 4.00 \end{pmatrix} = 3.00 + 10.00 + 0 + 4.00 = \$17.00$$

Cost per yard of Crylon is

$$\mathbf{bd} = (0, 2, 3, 0) \begin{pmatrix} 1.00 \\ 2.00 \\ 5.00 \\ 4.00 \end{pmatrix} = 0 + 4.00 + 15.00 + 0 = \$19.00$$

Cost per yard of Donlup is

$$\mathbf{cd} = (2, 2, 2, 2)\begin{pmatrix}1.00\\2.00\\5.00\\4.00\end{pmatrix} = 2.00 + 4.00 + 10.00 + 8.00 = \$24.00$$

Note that

500 yards of Bylon at $17.00 =	$ 8,500.00
200 yards of Crylon at 19.00 =	3,800.00
100 yards of Donlup at 24.00 =	2,400.00
Total	$14,700.00

which agrees with our earlier calculation of total cost.

MATRICES

A *matrix* is an ordered array of numbers.   As with vectors, the position of a particular entry is very important.   Examples of matrices are

$$\mathbf{A} = \begin{pmatrix}2 & 4\\3 & 5\end{pmatrix} \qquad \mathbf{B} = \begin{pmatrix}3 & 1 & 2\\5 & 6 & -3\end{pmatrix}$$

$$\mathbf{C} = \begin{pmatrix}2 & 15\\4 & 2\\11 & 0\end{pmatrix}$$

A vector is merely a matrix with one row or one column.

The *order* of a matrix refers to the number of rows and columns the matrix contains.   The number of rows is always mentioned first and the number of columns last.

$\begin{pmatrix}2 & 4\\3 & 5\end{pmatrix}$ is a 2 × 2 matrix.

$\begin{pmatrix}3 & 1 & 2\\5 & 6 & -3\end{pmatrix}$ is a 2 × 3 matrix.

$\begin{pmatrix}2 & 15\\4 & 2\\11 & 0\end{pmatrix}$ is a 3 × 2 matrix.

A *square matrix* is one which has the same number of rows as columns. Thus, 2 × 2, 3 × 3, 4 × 4, etc., are square matrices.

Matrix notation

A matrix is usually designated by a capital letter.   Small letters with numerical subscripts are used to designate the elements of the matrix. Subscripts are composed of two numbers, the first referring to the row and the second to the column.

$$\mathbf{X} = \begin{pmatrix} x_{11} & x_{12} & x_{13} \\ x_{21} & x_{22} & x_{23} \\ x_{31} & x_{32} & x_{33} \end{pmatrix}$$

The transpose of a matrix

The *transpose* of a matrix $\mathbf{A}$ is denoted by the symbol $\mathbf{A}^t$. $\mathbf{A}^t$ is a new matrix formed from $\mathbf{A}$ by merely interchanging the numbers making up the subscript of each element of $\mathbf{A}$. The element a_{12} appears in the original $\mathbf{A}$ matrix in the first-row, second-column position. In the transpose, it will appear in the first-column, second-row spot. Thus,

$$\begin{pmatrix} 2 & 5 \\ 4 & 7 \end{pmatrix}^t = \begin{pmatrix} 2 & 4 \\ 5 & 7 \end{pmatrix}$$

$$\begin{pmatrix} 3 & 2 & 9 \\ 4 & 1 & 6 \\ 5 & 7 & 8 \end{pmatrix}^t = \begin{pmatrix} 3 & 4 & 5 \\ 2 & 1 & 7 \\ 9 & 6 & 8 \end{pmatrix}$$

Note that the numbers on the left-to-right diagonal retain their positions, since a_{11}, a_{22}, and a_{33} will appear in the same place whether the first subscript numbers stand for rows or for columns.

Another way to approach the transpose operation is to place each row of the initial matrix as the corresponding column in the transpose. Thus, row 1 in the initial matrix becomes column 1 in the transpose, and so forth.

Matrix addition and subtraction

Matrices can be added if they are of the same order, that is, if they each have the same number of rows and the same number of columns. The result is a new matrix of the same order with elements equal to the sum of the elements in the corresponding positions of the original matrices.

EXAMPLE 1.13

$$\begin{pmatrix} 2 & 1 \\ 5 & 3 \end{pmatrix} + \begin{pmatrix} 3 & 2 \\ 1 & 2 \end{pmatrix} = \begin{pmatrix} 2+3 & 1+2 \\ 5+1 & 3+2 \end{pmatrix} = \begin{pmatrix} 5 & 3 \\ 6 & 5 \end{pmatrix}$$

EXAMPLE 1.14

$$\begin{pmatrix} 3 & 5 \\ 8 & 1 \\ 2 & 8 \end{pmatrix} + \begin{pmatrix} 5 & 6 \\ 2 & -1 \\ -3 & 7 \end{pmatrix} = \begin{pmatrix} 3+5 & 5+6 \\ 8+2 & 1-1 \\ 2-3 & 8+7 \end{pmatrix} = \begin{pmatrix} 8 & 11 \\ 10 & 0 \\ -1 & 15 \end{pmatrix}$$

EXAMPLE 1.15

Note that

$$\begin{pmatrix} 2 & 2 \\ 5 & 4 \\ 1 & 6 \end{pmatrix} \quad \text{and} \quad \begin{pmatrix} 1 & 4 & 7 \\ 2 & 3 & 5 \end{pmatrix}$$

cannot be added, since they are not of the same order.

Subtraction is accomplished in the same manner.

EXAMPLE 1.16

$$\begin{pmatrix} 5 & 2 & 3 \\ 2 & 9 & 5 \end{pmatrix} - \begin{pmatrix} 4 & 3 & 7 \\ 5 & 1 & 1 \end{pmatrix} = \begin{pmatrix} 5-4 & 2-3 & 3-7 \\ 2-5 & 9-1 & 5-1 \end{pmatrix} = \begin{pmatrix} 1 & -1 & -4 \\ -3 & 8 & 4 \end{pmatrix}$$

Multiplication of a matrix by a scalar

A matrix may be multiplied by a scalar by multiplying each element in the original matrix by the scalar. The resulting matrix will be of the same order as the original.

EXAMPLE 1.17

Let $\mathbf{A} = \begin{pmatrix} 2 & 3 \\ 4 & 1 \\ 5 & 2 \end{pmatrix}$. Then

$$-5\mathbf{A} = -5 \begin{pmatrix} 2 & 3 \\ 4 & 1 \\ 5 & 2 \end{pmatrix} = \begin{pmatrix} -5 \cdot 2 & -5 \cdot 3 \\ -5 \cdot 4 & -5 \cdot 1 \\ -5 \cdot 5 & -5 \cdot 2 \end{pmatrix} = \begin{pmatrix} -10 & -15 \\ -20 & -5 \\ -25 & -10 \end{pmatrix}$$

Multiplication of two matrices

Matrices may be multiplied together providing the number of columns of the first is equal to the number of rows of the second. The procedure is to multiply the first row of the first matrix by the first column of the second in the same way that vectors are multiplied to obtain the number appearing in the first row and first column of the resulting matrix. The first row of the first matrix is then multiplied by the second column of the second matrix to obtain the number which appears in row 1 and column 2 of the resulting matrix. The procedure is repeated until each *row* of the first matrix has been multiplied by each *column* of the second matrix. Note that only rows are considered in the matrix which appears first and only columns in the matrix which appears second.

EXAMPLE 1.18

$$\begin{matrix} a \\ b \\ c \end{matrix} \begin{pmatrix} 2 & 3 \\ 3 & 2 \\ 4 & 1 \end{pmatrix} \cdot \begin{matrix} d & e & f \\ \begin{pmatrix} 2 & 5 & 6 \\ 1 & 3 & 4 \end{pmatrix} \end{matrix} = \begin{pmatrix} ad & ae & af \\ bd & be & bf \\ cd & ce & cf \end{pmatrix}$$

The resulting matrix will have the same number of rows as the first matrix and the same number of columns as the second matrix. Therefore, a 3 × 2 matrix times a 2 × 3 matrix will equal a 3 × 3 matrix. The products of the vectors **ad**, **be**, etc. can then be determined.

$$\mathbf{ad} = (2, 3) \begin{pmatrix} 2 \\ 1 \end{pmatrix} = 4 + 3 = 7 \qquad \mathbf{bf} = (3, 2) \begin{pmatrix} 6 \\ 4 \end{pmatrix} = 18 + 8 = 26$$

$$\mathbf{ae} = (2, 3) \begin{pmatrix} 5 \\ 3 \end{pmatrix} = 10 + 9 = 19 \qquad \mathbf{cd} = (4, 1) \begin{pmatrix} 2 \\ 1 \end{pmatrix} = 8 + 1 = 9$$

$$\mathbf{af} = (2, 3) \begin{pmatrix} 6 \\ 4 \end{pmatrix} = 12 + 12 = 24 \qquad \mathbf{ce} = (4, 1) \begin{pmatrix} 5 \\ 3 \end{pmatrix} = 20 + 3 = 23$$

$$\mathbf{bd} = (3, 2) \begin{pmatrix} 2 \\ 1 \end{pmatrix} = 6 + 2 = 8 \qquad \mathbf{cf} = (4, 1) \begin{pmatrix} 6 \\ 4 \end{pmatrix} = 24 + 4 = 28$$

$$\mathbf{be} = (3, 2) \begin{pmatrix} 5 \\ 3 \end{pmatrix} = 15 + 6 = 21$$

Now the final result can be put into matrix form:

$$\begin{pmatrix} 7 & 19 & 24 \\ 8 & 21 & 26 \\ 9 & 23 & 28 \end{pmatrix}$$

EXAMPLE 1.19

$$\begin{matrix} & \mathbf{c} & \mathbf{d} \\ \begin{matrix} \mathbf{a} \\ \mathbf{b} \end{matrix} \begin{pmatrix} 5 & -1 \\ 0 & 3 \end{pmatrix} & \begin{pmatrix} 2 & -3 \\ 4 & -4 \end{pmatrix} = \begin{pmatrix} \mathbf{ac} & \mathbf{ad} \\ \mathbf{bc} & \mathbf{bd} \end{pmatrix} \end{matrix}$$

Note that a 2 × 2 matrix times a 2 × 2 matrix equals a 2 × 2 matrix. The products of the vectors **ac**, **bc**, etc., can then be determined:

$$\mathbf{ac} = (5, -1) \begin{pmatrix} 2 \\ 4 \end{pmatrix} = 10 - 4 = 6$$

$$\mathbf{ad} = (5, -1) \begin{pmatrix} -3 \\ -4 \end{pmatrix} = -15 + 4 = -11$$

$$\mathbf{bc} = (0, 3) \begin{pmatrix} 2 \\ 4 \end{pmatrix} = 0 + 12 = 12$$

$$\mathbf{bd} = (0, 3) \begin{pmatrix} -3 \\ -4 \end{pmatrix} = 0 - 12 = -12$$

Now the final result can be put into matrix form:

$$\begin{pmatrix} 6 & -11 \\ 12 & -12 \end{pmatrix}$$

EXAMPLE 1.20

$$\begin{matrix} & \mathbf{b} & \mathbf{c} & \mathbf{d} \\ \mathbf{a}\ (2, 5) & \begin{pmatrix} 3 & 5 & 7 \\ 1 & 2 & 3 \end{pmatrix} = (\mathbf{ab}, \mathbf{ac}, \mathbf{ad}) \end{matrix}$$

Note that a 1×2 matrix times a 2×3 matrix equals a 1×3 matrix. The products of the vectors **ab**, **ac**, etc., can then be determined:

$$\mathbf{ab} = (2,\ 5) \begin{pmatrix} 3 \\ 1 \end{pmatrix} = 6 + 5 = 11$$

$$\mathbf{ac} = (2,\ 5) \begin{pmatrix} 5 \\ 2 \end{pmatrix} = 10 + 10 = 20$$

$$\mathbf{ad} = (2,\ 5) \begin{pmatrix} 7 \\ 3 \end{pmatrix} = 14 + 15 = 29$$

Now the final result can be put into matrix form:

$$(11,\ 20,\ 29)$$

EXAMPLE 1.21

$\begin{pmatrix} 2 & 7 & 3 \\ 4 & 5 & 6 \end{pmatrix}$ and $\begin{pmatrix} 3 & 5 & 9 \\ 2 & 4 & 4 \end{pmatrix}$ cannot be multiplied, since the number of columns of the first does not equal the number of rows of the second.

EXAMPLE 1.22

If $\mathbf{A} = \begin{pmatrix} 1 & 3 \\ 2 & 4 \end{pmatrix}$ and $\mathbf{B} = \begin{pmatrix} 5 & 1 \\ 2 & 3 \end{pmatrix}$, then

$$\mathbf{AB} = \begin{pmatrix} 1 & 3 \\ 2 & 4 \end{pmatrix} \begin{pmatrix} 5 & 1 \\ 2 & 3 \end{pmatrix} = \begin{pmatrix} 11 & 10 \\ 18 & 14 \end{pmatrix}$$

and
$$\mathbf{BA} = \begin{pmatrix} 5 & 1 \\ 2 & 3 \end{pmatrix} \begin{pmatrix} 1 & 3 \\ 2 & 4 \end{pmatrix} = \begin{pmatrix} 7 & 19 \\ 8 & 18 \end{pmatrix}$$

Note that $\mathbf{AB} \neq \mathbf{BA}$.

Special matrices

A *zero*, or *null*, *matrix*, denoted by the symbol $\emptyset$, is one which has all zero elements:

$$\emptyset = \begin{pmatrix} 0 & 0 \\ 0 & 0 \end{pmatrix} \qquad \emptyset = (0,\ 0,\ 0)$$

An *identity matrix*, denoted by the symbol **I**, is a square matrix which has all zero elements except for the diagonal from left top to right bottom, which is made up of 1s:

$$\mathbf{I} = \begin{pmatrix} 1 & 0 & 0 \\ 0 & 1 & 0 \\ 0 & 0 & 1 \end{pmatrix} \qquad \mathbf{I} = \begin{pmatrix} 1 & 0 \\ 0 & 1 \end{pmatrix}$$

The null matrix is the matrix algebra equivalent of 0, and the identity matrix is the matrix algebra equivalent of 1. Thus, if **A** is any square matrix,

$$\emptyset \mathbf{A} = \mathbf{A} \emptyset = \emptyset$$
$$\mathbf{IA} = \mathbf{AI} = \mathbf{A}$$

Powers of a square matrix

A square matrix may be raised to the second power by multiplying it by itself. Successive multiplications will raise it to higher powers. Thus, if

$$\mathbf{A} = \begin{pmatrix} 3 & 2 \\ 5 & 7 \end{pmatrix}$$

$$\mathbf{A}^2 = \begin{pmatrix} 3 & 2 \\ 5 & 7 \end{pmatrix} \begin{pmatrix} 3 & 2 \\ 5 & 7 \end{pmatrix} = \begin{pmatrix} 19 & 20 \\ 50 & 59 \end{pmatrix}$$

$$\mathbf{A}^3 = \mathbf{A}^2 \cdot \mathbf{A} = \begin{pmatrix} 19 & 20 \\ 50 & 59 \end{pmatrix} \begin{pmatrix} 3 & 2 \\ 5 & 7 \end{pmatrix} = \begin{pmatrix} 157 & 178 \\ 445 & 513 \end{pmatrix}$$

PROBLEMS

1 $(1, 2) + (5, 9) =$

2 $(3, 1, 7) + (4, 2, -9) =$

3 $\begin{pmatrix} 5 \\ -9 \end{pmatrix} + \begin{pmatrix} 3 \\ 7 \end{pmatrix} =$

4 $\begin{pmatrix} 15 \\ 31 \\ 6 \end{pmatrix} + \begin{pmatrix} 5 \\ 19 \\ -8 \end{pmatrix} =$

5 $(18, 9) - (4, 6) =$

6 $(17, 18) - (4, 6) =$

7 $\begin{pmatrix} 2 \\ 3 \end{pmatrix} - \begin{pmatrix} 5 \\ 14 \end{pmatrix} =$

8 $\begin{pmatrix} 13 \\ -4 \\ 6 \end{pmatrix} - \begin{pmatrix} 16 \\ -6 \\ -8 \end{pmatrix} =$

9 $(13, 43) + (18, 1, 9) =$

10 $(12, 7) - \begin{pmatrix} 4 \\ 2 \end{pmatrix} =$

11 $3(2, 1) =$

12 $a(24, 15) =$

13 $5 \begin{pmatrix} 6 \\ -7 \end{pmatrix} =$

14 $-6 \begin{pmatrix} 7 \\ -3 \end{pmatrix} =$

15 $1.4(a, b, -c) =$

16 $(2, 4) \begin{pmatrix} 6 \\ 1 \end{pmatrix} =$

17 $(3, 1, 7) \begin{pmatrix} 2 \\ -1 \\ 6 \end{pmatrix} =$

18 $(2, 4)(6, 1) =$

19 $\begin{pmatrix} 2 \\ 5 \end{pmatrix} (6, 3) =$

20 $(3, 2, 9) \begin{pmatrix} -5 \\ 6 \end{pmatrix} =$

21 $\begin{pmatrix} 3 & 2 \\ 1 & 7 \end{pmatrix} + \begin{pmatrix} 4 & 6 \\ 5 & 3 \end{pmatrix} =$

22 $\begin{pmatrix} 4 & 6 \\ 1 & 9 \end{pmatrix} + \begin{pmatrix} -5 & 6 \\ -2 & -1 \end{pmatrix} =$

23 $\begin{pmatrix} 2 & 3 \\ 1 & 7 \end{pmatrix} - \begin{pmatrix} 3 & 2 \\ -8 & 4 \end{pmatrix} =$

24 $\begin{pmatrix} 1 & 5 \\ 3 & 2 \end{pmatrix} + \begin{pmatrix} 7 & 1 \\ 2 & 8 \end{pmatrix} + \begin{pmatrix} -3 & -2 \\ -8 & -1 \end{pmatrix} =$

25 $\begin{pmatrix} 8 & 1 \\ 4 & 3 \end{pmatrix} + \begin{pmatrix} 1 & 7 \\ -8 & 4 \end{pmatrix} - \begin{pmatrix} -3 & 7 \\ 0 & 6 \end{pmatrix} =$

26 $4 \begin{pmatrix} 3 & 4 \\ 9 & 7 \end{pmatrix} =$

27 $17 \begin{pmatrix} 2 & 3 \\ 4 & -1 \end{pmatrix} =$

28 $-3 \begin{pmatrix} a & 4 \\ b & 6 \end{pmatrix} =$

29 $b \begin{pmatrix} -4 & -7 \\ 3 & -8 \end{pmatrix} =$

30 $\sqrt{9} \begin{pmatrix} 8 & 2 & 3 \\ 7 & 1 & 5 \\ -3 & 6 & 4 \end{pmatrix} =$

31 $\begin{pmatrix} 4 & 1 \\ 6 & 3 \end{pmatrix} \begin{pmatrix} 7 & 3 \\ 1 & 0 \end{pmatrix} =$

32 $\begin{pmatrix} 4 & 3 \\ 1 & 8 \end{pmatrix} \begin{pmatrix} 1 \\ -4 \end{pmatrix} =$

33 $\begin{pmatrix} 5 & 9 & -4 \\ 6 & 1 & 5 \end{pmatrix} \begin{pmatrix} 3 & 2 \\ 8 & 5 \\ 6 & 4 \end{pmatrix} =$

34 $\begin{pmatrix} 3 & 2 \\ 8 & 5 \\ 6 & 4 \end{pmatrix} \begin{pmatrix} 5 & 9 & -4 \\ 6 & 1 & 5 \end{pmatrix} =$

35 $\begin{pmatrix} -4 & -3 \\ -7 & 8 \end{pmatrix} \begin{pmatrix} 14 & 3 & 2 \\ -8 & 6 & 1 \end{pmatrix} =$

36 $(2, 5) \begin{pmatrix} 3 & 6 & 9 & 8 \\ 4 & 2 & -7 & 7 \end{pmatrix} =$

37 $\begin{pmatrix} 9 & 6 \\ 4 & 13 \end{pmatrix} \begin{pmatrix} 2 & 5 \\ 7 & 1 \end{pmatrix} =$

38 $\begin{pmatrix} 2 & 5 \\ 7 & 1 \end{pmatrix} \begin{pmatrix} 9 & 6 \\ 4 & 13 \end{pmatrix} =$

39 $\begin{pmatrix} 14 & 6 & 9 \\ 3 & 1 & 7 \\ -2 & -4 & 6 \end{pmatrix} \begin{pmatrix} 5 & 9 & 18 \\ 4 & -6 & -9 \\ -2 & 1 & 3 \end{pmatrix} =$

40 $\begin{pmatrix} 6 & 5 & 11 \\ 4 & -2 & -2 \\ 3 & 0 & 6 \end{pmatrix} \begin{pmatrix} 0 & 5 & 1 \\ 3 & 0 & 6 \\ 0 & 8 & 9 \end{pmatrix} =$

41 $\begin{pmatrix} 2 & 7 \\ 9 & 4 \end{pmatrix}^t =$

42 $\begin{pmatrix} 3 & -7 \\ -4 & 6 \end{pmatrix}^t =$

43 $\begin{pmatrix} 15 & 31 & -17 \\ 4 & 6 & 9 \\ 2 & 1 & 3 \end{pmatrix}^t =$

44 $\begin{pmatrix} 2 & 7 & -5 \\ 4 & 3 & 9 \end{pmatrix}^t =$

45 $(14, 3, 8)^t =$

46 $\begin{pmatrix} 3 & 4 \\ 7 & 1 \end{pmatrix}^2 =$

47 $\begin{pmatrix} -2 & 1 \\ -4 & 6 \end{pmatrix}^2 =$

48 $\begin{pmatrix} 5 & 5 \\ 4 & 4 \end{pmatrix} \begin{pmatrix} 1 & -1 \\ -1 & 1 \end{pmatrix} =$

49 $\begin{pmatrix} 5 & 5 \\ 4 & 4 \end{pmatrix}^2 \begin{pmatrix} 1 & -1 \\ -1 & 1 \end{pmatrix} =$

50 $\begin{pmatrix} 1 & -1 \\ -1 & 1 \end{pmatrix} \begin{pmatrix} 5 & 5 \\ 4 & 4 \end{pmatrix} =$

51 Let $A = \begin{pmatrix} 2 & 3 \\ 1 & 5 \end{pmatrix}$ and $B = \begin{pmatrix} 4 & 1 \\ 7 & -8 \end{pmatrix}$

Find:

a $A + B$ b $2A - 4B$

c $3(A - 2B)$ d BA

e B^2 f BAB

g AB^2

52 The objective is to find $\mathbf{A}$, which is a 3×4 matrix. The vector which represents the sum of the elements of $\mathbf{A}$ by rows is given by

$$\begin{pmatrix} 4 & 20 & 20 \\ 9 & 10 & 8 \\ 18 & 9 & 8 \end{pmatrix} \begin{pmatrix} 2 \\ 3 \\ 4 \end{pmatrix}$$

The sum of the elements of the first column is 125. The sum of the elements of the second column is 75. The sum of the elements of the third column is given by

$$(4,\ 9) \begin{pmatrix} 8 \\ 2 \end{pmatrix}$$

$$a_{11} = a_{33} \qquad\qquad\qquad\qquad a_{22} = (5,\ 6) \begin{pmatrix} 3 \\ 1 \end{pmatrix}$$

$$a_{23} = (5,\ 3,\ -6,\ 8,\ -12) \begin{pmatrix} 1 \\ 2 \\ 3 \\ -2 \\ -4 \end{pmatrix} \qquad a_{12} = (5,\ 1) \begin{pmatrix} 2 \\ 5 \end{pmatrix}$$

$$a_{13} = a_{23} - a_{31} \qquad\qquad\qquad a_{31} = (8,\ 7) \begin{pmatrix} 4 \\ -6 \end{pmatrix}$$

53 The objective is to form a 4×4 matrix. The sum of the elements of the columns is

$$\text{Column } 1 = 82$$
$$\text{Column } 2 = 70$$
$$\text{Column } 3 = \text{column } 1 + \text{column } 2 - 64$$
$$\text{Column } 4 = 0$$

The sum of the elements of the rows are

$$\text{Row } 1 = \text{column } 1 + \text{column } 2$$
$$\text{Row } 2 = (7,\ 3) \begin{pmatrix} 1 \\ 0 \end{pmatrix}$$
$$\text{Row } 3 = (1,\ 2) \begin{pmatrix} 6 & 3 \\ -4 & -9 \end{pmatrix} \begin{pmatrix} 4 \\ 6 \end{pmatrix}$$

$$a_{11} = a_{33} \qquad\qquad a_{31} = a_{11} + 2a_{33} + a_{43}$$

$$a_{12} = (9,\ 1) \begin{pmatrix} 8 \\ 1 \end{pmatrix} \qquad a_{22} = (1,\ 0,\ -1,\ 0) \begin{pmatrix} 0 \\ 1 \\ 0 \\ -1 \end{pmatrix}$$

$$a_{14} = a_{43} = -a_{21} \qquad a_{42} = a_{31} - a_{33}$$
$$a_{21} = (1,\ 4) \begin{pmatrix} 4 \\ -3 \end{pmatrix} \qquad a_{33} = (5,\ 1) \begin{pmatrix} 4 \\ -10 \end{pmatrix}$$

54 The matrix $\mathbf{A}$ is defined such that

$$a_{ij} = 2i + 3j - 7 \qquad i \neq j$$
$$a_{ij} = (i,\ 3,\ -2j) \begin{pmatrix} j \\ i \\ 2 \end{pmatrix} \qquad i = j$$

The order of the matrix is 3×2. Find $\mathbf{A} \cdot \mathbf{A}^t$ and $\mathbf{A}^t \cdot \mathbf{A}$.

2 MATRIX ALGEBRA: INVERSION METHODS

INTRODUCTION

We covered, in Chap. 1, the matrix algebra methods for addition, subtraction, and multiplication. The reader will recognize the omission of one basic arithmetical technique—division. The reason is that division is the one basic algebraic operation not defined for matrix algebra. When, however, the need for division arises—and it often does—a method is available to produce an equivalent result.

To understand the basis for this alternative to division, let us consider, first, an alternative to division which exists in ordinary arithmetic. The *reciprocal* of a number is 1 divided by the number. Thus, the reciprocal of 5 is $\frac{1}{5}$ and the reciprocal of -147 is $-\frac{1}{147}$. One property of a reciprocal is that multiplication by it produces the same result as division by the original number. Thus, $20 \times \frac{1}{5} = 20 \div 5 = 4$ and $294 \times -\frac{1}{147} = 294 \div -147 = -2$. Since multiplication *is* defined in matrix algebra, if the equivalent of a reciprocal could be found for a matrix, we could multiply by it to provide an operation similar to that of division.

Note that a reciprocal in ordinary arithmetic can be defined in another way. We can say that the reciprocal of the number k is that unique number which when multiplied by k provides the result of 1. Thus, the reciprocal of 5 is $\frac{1}{5}$, since $5 \times \frac{1}{5} = 1$; and the reciprocal of -147 is $-\frac{1}{147}$, since $-147 \times -\frac{1}{147} = 1$. Now, the equivalent of a 1 in matrix algebra is an identity matrix. Thus, if a matrix could be found which when multiplied by another matrix resulted in an identity matrix, it could be expected to provide the same type of result as a reciprocal. Such a matrix is known as an *inverse*. The nomenclature A^{-1} means "the inverse of the matrix A." This is logical, since in ordinary arithmetic a number to the -1 power has the same meaning as 1 over the number.

An inverse in matrix algebra is equivalent to a reciprocal in ordinary arithmetic and when multiplied by another matrix provides the matrix algebra equivalent of division. There *are*, however, differences between a reciprocal and an inverse besides the obvious one that an inverse is a matrix, while a reciprocal is a number. For one thing, every number except zero has a reciprocal, while not every matrix has an inverse. Furthermore, a reciprocal is easy to find, while an inverse is often quite difficult to determine. This chapter will be devoted to developing for the reader two methods for finding the inverses of square matrices when such inverses exist.

Summarizing, we shall define the inverse of a matrix A as a new matrix A^{-1} which has the following relationship with A:

$$AA^{-1} = A^{-1}A = I$$

The product BA^{-1}, if it exists, is the matrix algebra equivalent of dividing the matrix B by the matrix A.

MATRIX INVERSION: THE GAUSSIAN METHOD

The initial setup for the Gaussian inverse method is a tableau of the form $A|I$, where A is the square matrix to be inverted and I is an identity matrix of the same order. For example, if we wish to find the inverse of A, where

$$A = \begin{pmatrix} 3 & 2 \\ 4 & 5 \end{pmatrix}$$

we begin by setting up the initial tableau

$$\begin{pmatrix} 3 & 2 & | & 1 & 0 \\ 4 & 5 & | & 0 & 1 \end{pmatrix}$$

The Gaussian method is to transform this tableau, using any combinations of two operations, so that an identity matrix appears on the left. When this has been accomplished, the inverse of the original matrix will appear on the right. The final tableau, then, will be of the form $I|A^{-1}$.

3.

$$\begin{array}{cc|cc} 3 & 2 & 1 & 0 \\ 4 & 5 & 0 & 1 \\ \hline 1 & \frac{2}{3} & \frac{1}{3} & 0 \end{array}$$

The two operations which are permitted in this transformation procedure are as follows:

1 A row may be multiplied or divided by any scalar number. The row must include all numbers to the left and right of the vertical line. Thus, in our example the first row is made up of the elements 3, 2, 1, 0.

2 A multiple of one row may be added to or subtracted from another row. Thus, in our example we could multiply row 2 by 3 and subtract this from row 1:

$$(3, 2, 1, 0) - 3(4, 5, 0, 1) = (-9, -13, 1, -3)$$

The result in this example would become the new row 1 in the next tableau. This point causes much confusion. The row we actually multiply by a scalar in this operation is *not* the row where the result goes in the new tableau. The row to which we add or subtract the multiple *is* the row, in the next tableau, which must show the result of this operation.

These two operating rules can be followed in any pattern desired in an effort to achieve an identity on the left side of the tableau.   As long as only these operations are used, once an identity appears on the left, the inverse of the initial matrix will appear on the right.

The reader will find worthwhile a suggested sequence of these two operations which will usually result in the most efficient solution routine.   Do not, however, confuse the operating rules and the operating plan.   The rules *must* be followed; the plan is merely a suggestion or a guide.

The plan is to achieve the identity column by column, starting with the left and moving right one column at a time only when the preceding column has its appropriate 1 and zeros.   The idea is to get the 1 in a column first and then proceed to use the 1 in obtaining zeros for the rest of the column.   The plan is to get a 1 in the upper left-hand corner (the a_{11} position), then zeros in the first column, then a 1 in the a_{22} position, then zeros in the second column, continuing with this sequence until every column has been completed.   Furthermore, the plan stipulates that rule 1 should be used to obtain each 1 and rule 2 to obtain the zeros.   Thus, to achieve a 1 in the a_{11} position, we need merely divide the first row by the number in the a_{11} position. Once this has been accomplished, a zero can be achieved in the a_{21} position by multiplying the new row 1 we just developed by the number in the a_{22} position and subtracting this from the second row.   This procedure can be continued until an identity matrix appears to the left of the vertical line.   Let's try some examples.

EXAMPLE 2.1   (Using fractions)

$A = \begin{pmatrix} 3 & 2 \\ 4 & 5 \end{pmatrix}$ Find A^{-1}.

1 Set up the initial tableau $A|I$:

$$\left(\begin{array}{cc|cc} 3 & 2 & 1 & 0 \\ 4 & 5 & 0 & 1 \end{array}\right)$$ Row 1
       Row 2

2 Divide row 1 by a_{11}, which in this example is 3, to put a 1 in the upper left-hand corner:

$$\left(\begin{array}{cc|cc} 1 & \frac{2}{3} & \frac{1}{3} & 0 \\ 4 & 5 & 0 & 1 \end{array}\right)$$ Row 1'
       Row 2

3 Multiply a_{21}, which in this example is 4, by row 1' and subtract from row 2, to put a zero in the lower left-hand corner:

$$\left(\begin{array}{cc|cc} 1 & \frac{2}{3} & \frac{1}{3} & 0 \\ 0 & \frac{7}{3} & -\frac{4}{3} & 1 \end{array}\right)$$ Row 1'
       Row 2'

4 Divide row 2' by a'_{22}, which in this example is $(\frac{7}{3})$, to put a 1 in the a_{22} position:

$$\left(\begin{array}{cc|cc} 1 & \frac{2}{3} & \frac{1}{3} & 0 \\ 0 & 1 & -\frac{4}{7} & \frac{3}{7} \end{array}\right)$$ Row 1'
       Row 2''

5 Multiply a'_{12}, which in this example is $\frac{2}{3}$, by row 2'' and subtract from row 1', to put a zero in the a_{12} position:

$$\left(\begin{array}{cc|cc} 1 & 0 & \frac{5}{7} & -\frac{2}{7} \\ 0 & 1 & -\frac{4}{7} & \frac{3}{7} \end{array}\right)$$ Row 1''
       Row 2''

The tableau has now been transformed to $I|A^{-1}$ and

$$A^{-1} = \begin{pmatrix} \frac{5}{7} & -\frac{2}{7} \\ -\frac{4}{7} & \frac{3}{7} \end{pmatrix}$$

Verify this by proving that $A \cdot A^{-1} = I$.

EXAMPLE 2.2   (Using decimals)

$A = \begin{pmatrix} 4 & -2 & 0 \\ 1 & 3 & 2 \\ 4 & 3 & 7 \end{pmatrix}$ Find A^{-1}.

1 Set up the initial tableau $A|I$:

$$\left(\begin{array}{ccc|ccc} 4 & -2 & 0 & 1 & 0 & 0 \\ 1 & 3 & 2 & 0 & 1 & 0 \\ 4 & 3 & 7 & 0 & 0 & 1 \end{array}\right)$$ Row 1
       Row 2
       Row 3

2 Divide row 1 by a_{11}, which in this example is 4, so a 1 will appear in the a_{11} position:

$$\left(\begin{array}{ccc|ccc} 1 & -.5 & 0 & .25 & 0 & 0 \\ 1 & 3 & 2 & 0 & 1 & 0 \\ 4 & 3 & 7 & 0 & 0 & 1 \end{array}\right)$$ Row 1'
       Row 2
       Row 3

3   Multiply a_{21}, which in this example is 1, by row 1' and subtract from row 2, so a zero will appear in the a_{21} position:

$$\begin{pmatrix} 1 & -.5 & 0 & | & .25 & 0 & 0 \\ 0 & 3.5 & 2 & | & -.25 & 1 & 0 \\ 4 & 3 & 7 & | & 0 & 0 & 1 \end{pmatrix} \quad \begin{matrix} \text{Row 1'} \\ \text{Row 2'} \\ \text{Row 3} \end{matrix}$$

4   Multiply a_{31}, which in this example is 4, by row 1' and subtract from row 3, so a zero will appear in the a_{31} position.

$$\begin{pmatrix} 1 & -.5 & 0 & | & .25 & 0 & 0 \\ 0 & 3.5 & 2 & | & -.25 & 1 & 0 \\ 0 & 5 & 7 & | & -1 & 0 & 1 \end{pmatrix} \quad \begin{matrix} \text{Row 1'} \\ \text{Row 2'} \\ \text{Row 3'} \end{matrix}$$

5   Divide row 2' by a'_{22}, which in this example is 3.5, so a 1 will appear in the a_{22} position:

$$\begin{pmatrix} 1 & -.5 & 0 & | & .25 & 0 & 0 \\ 0 & 1 & .57 & | & -.07 & .29 & 0 \\ 0 & 5 & 7 & | & -1 & 0 & 1 \end{pmatrix} \quad \begin{matrix} \text{Row 1'} \\ \text{Row 2''} \\ \text{Row 3'} \end{matrix}$$

6   Multiply a'_{12}, which in this example is $-.50$, by row 2'' and subtract from row 1', so zero will appear in the a_{12} position:

$$\begin{pmatrix} 1 & 0 & .28 & | & .22 & .14 & 0 \\ 0 & 1 & .57 & | & -.07 & .29 & 0 \\ 0 & 5 & 7 & | & -1 & 0 & 1 \end{pmatrix} \quad \begin{matrix} \text{Row 1''} \\ \text{Row 2''} \\ \text{Row 3'} \end{matrix}$$

7   Multiply a'_{32}, which in this example is 5, by row 2'' and subtract from row 3', so a zero will appear in the a_{32} position:

$$\begin{pmatrix} 1 & 0 & .28 & | & .22 & .14 & 0 \\ 0 & 1 & .57 & | & -.07 & .29 & 0 \\ 0 & 0 & 4.15 & | & -.65 & -1.45 & 1 \end{pmatrix} \quad \begin{matrix} \text{Row 1''} \\ \text{Row 2''} \\ \text{Row 3''} \end{matrix}$$

8   Divide row 3'' by a''_{33}, which in this example is 4.15, so a 1 will appear in the a_{33} position:

$$\begin{pmatrix} 1 & 0 & .28 & | & .22 & .14 & 0 \\ 0 & 1 & .57 & | & -.07 & .29 & 0 \\ 0 & 0 & 1 & | & -.16 & -.35 & .24 \end{pmatrix} \quad \begin{matrix} \text{Row 1''} \\ \text{Row 2''} \\ \text{Row 3'''} \end{matrix}$$

9   Multiply a''_{13}, which in this example is .28, by row 3''' and subtract from row 1'', so a zero will appear in the a_{13} position:

$$\begin{pmatrix} 1 & 0 & 0 & | & .26 & .24 & -.07 \\ 0 & 1 & .57 & | & -.07 & .29 & 0 \\ 0 & 0 & 1 & | & -.16 & -.35 & .24 \end{pmatrix} \quad \begin{matrix} \text{Row 1'''} \\ \text{Row 2''} \\ \text{Row 3'''} \end{matrix}$$

10   Multiply a''_{23}, which in this example is .57, by row 3''' and subtract from row 2'', so that a zero will appear in the a_{23} position:

$$\begin{pmatrix} 1 & 0 & 0 & | & .27 & .24 & -.07 \\ 0 & 1 & 0 & | & .02 & .49 & -.14 \\ 0 & 0 & 1 & | & -.16 & -.35 & .24 \end{pmatrix} \quad \begin{matrix} \text{Row 1'''} \\ \text{Row 2'''} \\ \text{Row 3'''} \end{matrix}$$

The tableau has now been transformed to $I|A^{-1}$, and

$$A^{-1} = \begin{pmatrix} .27 & .24 & -.07 \\ .02 & .49 & -.14 \\ -.16 & -.35 & .24 \end{pmatrix}$$

Verify this by finding $A \cdot A^{-1}$.

Note: The general plan for finding a Gaussian inverse is listed step by step in the appendix to this chapter.

The reader will recall that it was previously mentioned that inverses do not always exist.   If, while trying to solve for an inverse, you find that the entire portion of a row to the left of the vertical line comes out as zeros, no inverse exists.   For example, if you were trying to find the inverse of $\begin{pmatrix} 2 & 4 \\ 3 & 6 \end{pmatrix}$, the initial tableau would be

$$\begin{pmatrix} 2 & 4 & | & 1 & 0 \\ 3 & 6 & | & 0 & 1 \end{pmatrix}$$

the second tableau would be

$$\begin{pmatrix} 1 & 2 & | & \frac{1}{2} & 0 \\ 3 & 6 & | & 0 & 1 \end{pmatrix}$$

and the third tableau would be

$$\begin{pmatrix} 1 & 2 & | & \frac{1}{2} & 0 \\ 0 & 0 & | & -\frac{3}{2} & 1 \end{pmatrix}$$

Note that the portion of the second row to the left of the line is all zeros.   Thus, no inverse exists.   If you were to continue to try to solve the above problem, you would find it impossible to achieve the necessary identity matrix on the left side of the tableau.

DETERMINANTS

The *determinant* of a matrix is a number, or value.   A determinant can be represented by enclosing a matrix with vertical lines rather than parentheses.   In the case of a 2×2 matrix, the determinant is the product of the diagonal from left to right, $a_{11} \cdot a_{22}$, minus the diagonal from right to left, $a_{12} \cdot a_{21}$.

Thus, the determinant $\begin{vmatrix} 3 & 2 \\ 1 & 4 \end{vmatrix}$ has as its value

$$(3 \cdot 4) - (2 \cdot 1) = 12 - 2 = 10$$

and the determinant $\begin{vmatrix} -5 & 1 \\ 0 & 3 \end{vmatrix}$ has as its value

$$(-5 \cdot 3) - (1 \cdot 0) = -15 - 0 = -15$$

In the case of a 3×3 matrix, the value of the determinant may be found by expanding the 3×3 into three 2×2 determinants called *minors*. Any row or column may be used and the procedure is as follows:

1 Select a row or column. (If any zeros are present in the matrix, selection of a row or column containing them will reduce computation.)
2 For each number in the row or column selected, find the minor determinant by eliminating the row and the column containing the selected number and forming a determinant of the remaining numbers.
3 Multiply each of the new 2×2 determinants by the number selected for its formation.
4 In the 3×3 case, three such determinants will be formed. Multiply each determinant value by $+1$ or -1, depending upon the location of each number in the selected row or column of the matrix, as shown in the following chart of cofactors:

$$\begin{vmatrix} +1 & -1 & +1 \\ -1 & +1 & -1 \\ +1 & -1 & +1 \end{vmatrix}$$

5 Add or subtract the three values as indicated.

EXAMPLE 2.3

The value of the determinant $\begin{vmatrix} 1 & 4 & 2 \\ 3 & 5 & 8 \\ 2 & 0 & 6 \end{vmatrix}$ may be found as follows:

1 Select a row or column. We will select the third row.
2 Find the minor determinants:

$$\begin{vmatrix} 1 & 4 & 2 \\ 3 & 5 & 8 \\ 2 & 0 & 6 \end{vmatrix} = \begin{vmatrix} 4 & 2 \\ 5 & 8 \end{vmatrix}$$

$$\begin{vmatrix} 1 & 4 & 2 \\ 3 & 5 & 8 \\ 2 & 0 & 6 \end{vmatrix} = \begin{vmatrix} 1 & 2 \\ 3 & 8 \end{vmatrix}$$

$$\begin{vmatrix} 1 & 4 & 2 \\ 3 & 5 & 8 \\ 2 & 0 & 6 \end{vmatrix} = \begin{vmatrix} 1 & 4 \\ 3 & 5 \end{vmatrix}$$

3 Multiply each determinant by the selected number from which it was formed and by its cofactor, as shown in the following illustration:

$$\begin{vmatrix} +1 & -1 & +1 \\ -1 & +1 & -1 \\ +1 & -1 & +1 \end{vmatrix}$$

$$+2\begin{vmatrix} 4 & 2 \\ 5 & 8 \end{vmatrix} = +2[(4 \cdot 8) - (2 \cdot 5)]$$

$$= +2(32 - 10) = +2(22) = +44$$

$$-0\begin{vmatrix} 1 & 2 \\ 3 & 8 \end{vmatrix} = -0[(1 \cdot 8) - (2 \cdot 3)]$$

$$= -0(8 - 6) = -0(2) = 0$$

$$+6\begin{vmatrix} 1 & 4 \\ 3 & 5 \end{vmatrix} = +6[(1 \cdot 5) - (4 \cdot 3)]$$

$$= +6(5 - 12) = +6(-7) = -42$$

4 Add or subtract:

$$+44 - 0 - 42 = 44 - 42 = 2$$

Note that any row or column could have been selected and would have provided the same determinant value. Take, for example, column 1:

$$\begin{vmatrix} 1 & 4 & 2 \\ 3 & 5 & 8 \\ 2 & 0 & 6 \end{vmatrix} = 1\begin{vmatrix} 5 & 8 \\ 0 & 6 \end{vmatrix} - 3\begin{vmatrix} 4 & 2 \\ 0 & 6 \end{vmatrix} + 2\begin{vmatrix} 4 & 2 \\ 5 & 8 \end{vmatrix}$$

$$= 1(30 - 0) - 3(24 - 0) + 2(32 - 10)$$

$$= 1(30) - 3(24) + 2(22)$$

$$= 30 - 72 + 44 = 2$$

A 4×4 determinant can be reduced to four 3×3s and each 3×3 to three 2×2s for solution by the same method. The cofactors for a 4×4 are

$$\begin{vmatrix} +1 & -1 & +1 & -1 \\ -1 & +1 & -1 & +1 \\ +1 & -1 & +1 & -1 \\ -1 & +1 & -1 & +1 \end{vmatrix}$$

This method can be used for determinants of any order. The cofactor for any position x_{ij} is given by the formula $(-1)^{i+j}$, where i is the row and j the column number. Minus 1 to odd powers, of course, is minus, and to even powers is plus. For matrices of any substantial size, however, the method is unwieldy.

Another method is available for reducing the size of determinants. It is based on the theorem that a multiple of one row or column may be added to, or subtracted from, any other row or column without affecting the value of the determinant. The goal is to transform the determinant so that one row or column has all zeros except for one entry, which should be $+1$ or -1. The steps taken are as follows:

1 Examine the determinant and find two numbers in the same row or column such that a multiple of one of the numbers will, when added to or subtracted from the other, result in $+1$ or -1. This is usually possible.
2 Add or subtract the necessary multiple of either the row or column containing the other number. This will result in $+1$ or -1 appearing somewhere in the determinant. (If a $+1$ or -1 was originally in the determinant, these two steps would, of course, be omitted.)
3 Add or subtract multiples of the row or column containing the 1 from each of the other rows or columns so that a row or column of zeros appears along with the 1.
4 Cross out the row and column containing the 1 and form a new determinant of the remaining numbers (one order smaller than the original). Multiply this new determinant by the $+1$ or -1 and by the cofactor connected with the position of the 1.
5 This procedure may be repeated to reduce the size of the determinant further. Each time it will reduce the order of the determinant by one.

EXAMPLE 2.4

Find the value of $\begin{vmatrix} 2 & 4 & 6 \\ 3 & 9 & 5 \\ 7 & 5 & 3 \end{vmatrix}$.

1 Subtract row 1 from row 2 to obtain a 1 at position x_{21}:

$$
\begin{array}{rrrl}
(3 & 9 & 5) & \text{Row 2} \\
-(2 & 4 & 6) & \text{Row 1} \\
\hline
(1 & 5 & -1) & \text{Row 2}'
\end{array}
$$

The result is

$$\begin{vmatrix} 2 & 4 & 6 \\ 1 & 5 & -1 \\ 7 & 5 & 3 \end{vmatrix}$$

2 Subtract 5 times column 1 from column 2 to obtain a zero at x_{22}:

$$\text{col 2} - 5(\text{col 1}) = \text{col 2}'$$

$$\begin{pmatrix} 4 \\ 5 \\ 5 \end{pmatrix} - \begin{pmatrix} 10 \\ 5 \\ 35 \end{pmatrix} = \begin{pmatrix} -6 \\ 0 \\ -30 \end{pmatrix}$$

The result is

$$\begin{vmatrix} 2 & -6 & 6 \\ 1 & 0 & -1 \\ 7 & -30 & 3 \end{vmatrix}$$

3 Add column 1 to column 3 to obtain a zero at x_{23}:

col 3 + col 1 = col 3'

$$\begin{pmatrix} 6 \\ -1 \\ 3 \end{pmatrix} + \begin{pmatrix} 2 \\ 1 \\ 7 \end{pmatrix} = \begin{pmatrix} 8 \\ 0 \\ 10 \end{pmatrix}$$

The result is

$$\begin{vmatrix} 2 & -6 & 8 \\ 1 & 0 & 0 \\ 7 & -30 & 10 \end{vmatrix}$$

4 Set up the new determinant:

$$\begin{vmatrix} 2 & -6 & 8 \\ 1 & 0 & 0 \\ 7 & -30 & 10 \end{vmatrix} = 1 \begin{vmatrix} -6 & 8 \\ -30 & 10 \end{vmatrix}$$

5 Multiply by the sign of the cofactor:

$$\begin{vmatrix} + & - & + \\ - & + & - \\ + & - & + \end{vmatrix} \qquad -(+1) \begin{vmatrix} -6 & 8 \\ -30 & 10 \end{vmatrix}$$

6 Solve the new determinant:

$$-[-60 - (-240)] = -(180) = -180$$

The reader should ascertain that this value is the same as would have been found by expanding the above determinant into three minor determinants and solving.

MATRIX INVERSION: USING DETERMINANTS

The determinant method for finding inverses of square matrices is often easier than the Gaussian method in the 2 × 2 and 3 × 3 cases in that much fractional addition and multiplication are avoided. However, the Gaussian method is more suitable for computers. The steps to be taken to find the inverse of the square matrix, **A**, using determinants, are as follows:

1 Find the determinant value of the matrix. Label it $|A|$.
2 For each number in the original matrix, to be designated the *pivot number*, find the value of the determinant formed by eliminating the row and column containing the number.
3 Multiply the determinant value by the cofactor ($+1$ or -1) connected with the position of the number selected. The actual sign and value of this number should be disregarded.
4 Divide the resulting number by $|A|$.
5 Set up a new matrix made up of the numbers developed above.
6 The transpose of the matrix developed in step 5 is the inverse of the initial matrix.

EXAMPLE 2.5

$A = \begin{pmatrix} 2 & -1 \\ 5 & 3 \end{pmatrix}$ Find A^{-1}.

1   Find the determinant value of the matrix:

$$|A| = \begin{vmatrix} 2 & -1 \\ 5 & 3 \end{vmatrix} = 6 - (-5) = 11$$

2   Evaluate the determinant remaining after eliminating the row and column containing each number:

$$a_{11} = \begin{vmatrix} 2 & -1 \\ 5 & 3 \end{vmatrix} = 3$$

$$a_{12} = \begin{vmatrix} 2 & -1 \\ 5 & 3 \end{vmatrix} = 5$$

$$a_{21} = \begin{vmatrix} 2 & -1 \\ 5 & 3 \end{vmatrix} = -1$$

$$a_{22} = \begin{vmatrix} 2 & -1 \\ 5 & 3 \end{vmatrix} = 2$$

3   Multiply by the cofactor of the pivot position:

$$\begin{vmatrix} +1 & -1 \\ -1 & +1 \end{vmatrix}$$

$a_{11} = +(+3)$ $a_{12} = -(+5)$ $a_{21} = -(-1)$ $a_{22} = +(+2)$
$a_{11} = 3$ $a_{12} = -5$ $a_{21} = 1$ $a_{22} = 2$

4   Divide by $|A|$:

$$a_{11} = \tfrac{3}{11} \qquad a_{12} = -\tfrac{5}{11} \qquad a_{21} = \tfrac{1}{11} \qquad a_{22} = \tfrac{2}{11}$$

5   Set up a new matrix:

$$\begin{pmatrix} \tfrac{3}{11} & -\tfrac{5}{11} \\ \tfrac{1}{11} & \tfrac{2}{11} \end{pmatrix}$$

6   Transpose to complete the inverse:

$$A^{-1} = \begin{pmatrix} \tfrac{3}{11} & \tfrac{1}{11} \\ -\tfrac{5}{11} & \tfrac{2}{11} \end{pmatrix}$$

The reader should prove that this is the inverse.

EXAMPLE 2.6

Find the inverse of $\begin{pmatrix} 2 & 3 & 0 \\ 7 & 5 & 9 \\ -4 & -6 & 1 \end{pmatrix}$.

1   Find the determinant value of the matrix:
   a   Subtract $9 \cdot$ (row 3) from row 2:

$$\begin{vmatrix} 2 & 3 & 0 \\ 43 & 59 & 0 \\ -4 & -6 & 1 \end{vmatrix}$$

b Find reduced determinant:

$$\begin{vmatrix} 2 & 3 & 0 \\ 43 & 59 & 0 \\ -4 & -6 & 1 \end{vmatrix} = +(+1) \begin{vmatrix} 2 & 3 \\ 43 & 59 \end{vmatrix}$$

c Evaluate:

$$(2 \cdot 59) - (3 \cdot 43) = 118 - 129 = -11 = |A|$$

2 Evaluate the determinant remaining after eliminating the row and column containing each number:

$$a_{11} = \begin{vmatrix} 2 & 3 & 0 \\ 7 & 5 & 9 \\ -4 & -6 & 1 \end{vmatrix} = \begin{vmatrix} 5 & 9 \\ -6 & 1 \end{vmatrix} = 5 - (-54) = 59$$

$$a_{12} = \begin{vmatrix} 2 & 3 & 0 \\ 7 & 5 & 9 \\ -4 & -6 & 1 \end{vmatrix} = \begin{vmatrix} 7 & 9 \\ -4 & 1 \end{vmatrix} = 7 - (-36) = 43$$

$$a_{13} = \begin{vmatrix} 2 & 3 & 0 \\ 7 & 5 & 9 \\ -4 & -6 & 1 \end{vmatrix} = \begin{vmatrix} 7 & 5 \\ -4 & -6 \end{vmatrix} = -42 - (-20) = -22$$

$$a_{21} = \begin{vmatrix} 2 & 3 & 0 \\ 7 & 5 & 9 \\ -4 & -6 & 1 \end{vmatrix} = \begin{vmatrix} 3 & 0 \\ -6 & 1 \end{vmatrix} = 3 - (0) = 3$$

$$a_{22} = \begin{vmatrix} 2 & 3 & 0 \\ 7 & 5 & 9 \\ -4 & -6 & 1 \end{vmatrix} = \begin{vmatrix} 2 & 0 \\ -4 & 1 \end{vmatrix} = 2 - (0) = 2$$

$$a_{23} = \begin{vmatrix} 2 & 3 & 0 \\ 7 & 5 & 9 \\ -4 & -6 & 1 \end{vmatrix} = \begin{vmatrix} 2 & 3 \\ -4 & -6 \end{vmatrix} = -12 - (-12) = 0$$

$$a_{31} = \begin{vmatrix} 2 & 3 & 0 \\ 7 & 5 & 9 \\ -4 & -6 & 1 \end{vmatrix} = \begin{vmatrix} 3 & 0 \\ 5 & 9 \end{vmatrix} = 27 - 0 = 27$$

$$a_{32} = \begin{vmatrix} 2 & 3 & 0 \\ 7 & 5 & 9 \\ -4 & -6 & 1 \end{vmatrix} = \begin{vmatrix} 2 & 0 \\ 7 & 9 \end{vmatrix} = 18 - 0 = 18$$

$$a_{33} = \begin{vmatrix} 2 & 3 & 0 \\ 7 & 5 & 9 \\ -4 & -6 & 1 \end{vmatrix} = \begin{vmatrix} 2 & 3 \\ 7 & 5 \end{vmatrix} = 10 - 21 = -11$$

3 Multiply by the sign of the pivot position:

$$\begin{vmatrix} +1 & -1 & +1 \\ -1 & +1 & -1 \\ +1 & -1 & +1 \end{vmatrix}$$

$$a_{11} = +(+59) = 59 \qquad a_{23} = -(0) = 0$$
$$a_{12} = -(+43) = -43 \qquad a_{31} = +(+27) = 27$$
$$a_{13} = +(-22) = -22 \qquad a_{32} = -(+18) = -18$$
$$a_{21} = -(+3) = -3 \qquad a_{33} = +(-11) = -11$$
$$a_{22} = +(+2) = 2$$

4 Divide by $|A|$:

$$a_{11} = -\tfrac{59}{11} \qquad a_{12} = \tfrac{43}{11} \qquad a_{13} = \tfrac{22}{11} \qquad a_{21} = \tfrac{3}{11} \qquad a_{22} = -\tfrac{2}{11}$$
$$a_{23} = 0 \qquad a_{31} = -\tfrac{27}{11} \qquad a_{32} = \tfrac{18}{11} \qquad a_{33} = \tfrac{11}{11}$$

5 Set up a new matrix:

$$\begin{pmatrix} -\tfrac{59}{11} & \tfrac{43}{11} & \tfrac{22}{11} \\ \tfrac{3}{11} & -\tfrac{2}{11} & 0 \\ -\tfrac{27}{11} & \tfrac{18}{11} & \tfrac{11}{11} \end{pmatrix}$$

6 Transpose to complete the inverse:

$$\mathbf{A}^{-1} = \begin{pmatrix} -\tfrac{59}{11} & \tfrac{3}{11} & -\tfrac{27}{11} \\ \tfrac{43}{11} & -\tfrac{2}{11} & \tfrac{18}{11} \\ \tfrac{22}{11} & 0 & \tfrac{11}{11} \end{pmatrix}$$

APPENDIX: STEPS FOR FINDING A GAUSSIAN INVERSE

1 Set up a tableau in the form $\mathbf{A}|\mathbf{I}$, where $\mathbf{I}$ is an identity matrix of the same order as $\mathbf{A}$.

2 Divide row 1 of the tableau by a_{11} and place this as the first row of a second tableau.

3 Multiply a_{21} by row 1 of the second tableau and subtract the resulting row from row 2 of the first tableau. Place this result as row 2 of the second tableau.

4 Multiply a_{31} by row 1 of the second tableau and subtract the resulting row from row 3 of the first tableau. Place this result as row 3 of the second tableau.

5 Continue as in steps 3 and 4 until all rows have been transformed and placed in the second tableau.

6 Divide row 2 of the second tableau by the second entry in the row. Place the resulting row as the second row in a third tableau.

7 Multiply the second entry in the first row of the second tableau by the second row of the third tableau and subtract the components from the first row of the second tableau. Enter this result as row 1 in the third tableau.

8 Multiply the second entry in the third row of the second tableau by the second row of the third tableau and subtract the components from the third row of the second tableau. Enter this result as row 3 in the third tableau.

9 Continue as in steps 7 and 8 until all rows have been transformed and placed in the third tableau.

10 Continue this procedure, starting with the third entry in the third row of the third tableau and transforming to a fourth tableau and so on, until an identity matrix appears on the left side of the tableau. At this point, the inverse appears on the right side of the tableau. Thus $\mathbf{A}|\mathbf{I}$ is transformed into $\mathbf{I}|\mathbf{A}^{-1}$.

PROBLEMS

1 Find the following inverses using the Gaussian method:

a $\begin{pmatrix} 2 & 4 \\ 3 & 7 \end{pmatrix}^{-1}$

b $\begin{pmatrix} 5 & 6 \\ 7 & 8 \end{pmatrix}^{-1}$

c $\begin{pmatrix} 9 & 7 \\ 4 & 3 \end{pmatrix}^{-1}$

d $\begin{pmatrix} 5 & -2 \\ 3 & -1 \end{pmatrix}^{-1}$

e $\begin{pmatrix} 5 & 7 \\ -6 & 8 \end{pmatrix}^{-1}$

f $\begin{pmatrix} 7 & 4 \\ 5 & 3 \end{pmatrix}^{-1}$

g $\begin{pmatrix} 1 & 3 & 0 \\ 2 & 1 & 0 \\ 0 & 6 & 3 \end{pmatrix}^{-1}$

h $\begin{pmatrix} 2 & 4 & 1 \\ 3 & 2 & 5 \\ 2 & 3 & 2 \end{pmatrix}^{-1}$

i $\begin{pmatrix} 1 & 0 & 0 & 0 & 0 \\ -4 & 1 & 0 & 0 & 0 \\ -5 & -3 & 1 & 0 & 0 \\ -3 & -2 & -4 & 1 & 0 \\ -2 & -1 & -6 & -3 & 1 \end{pmatrix}^{-1}$

j $\begin{pmatrix} 1 & 0 & 0 & 0 & 0 & 0 \\ -2 & 1 & 0 & 0 & 0 & 0 \\ 0 & -3 & 1 & 0 & 0 & 0 \\ -3 & -5 & -2 & 1 & 0 & 0 \\ -1 & 0 & -3 & -4 & 1 & 0 \\ -4 & -1 & 0 & -6 & -3 & 1 \end{pmatrix}^{-1}$

2 Evaluate the following determinants:

a $\begin{vmatrix} 3 & 5 \\ 2 & 6 \end{vmatrix}$

b $\begin{vmatrix} 4 & 7 \\ 3 & 9 \end{vmatrix}$

c $\begin{vmatrix} 5 & 7 \\ 8 & 4 \end{vmatrix}$

d $\begin{vmatrix} 2 & 27 \\ 5 & 13 \end{vmatrix}$

e $\begin{vmatrix} -3 & 1 \\ 4 & 6 \end{vmatrix}$

f $\begin{vmatrix} 5 & 13 \\ 8 & -27 \end{vmatrix}$

g $\begin{vmatrix} 4 & 2 \\ -3 & 6 \end{vmatrix}$

h $\begin{vmatrix} -4 & -3 \\ 8 & -6 \end{vmatrix}$

i $\begin{vmatrix} 1 & 0 & 0 \\ 3 & 5 & 7 \\ 9 & 1 & 4 \end{vmatrix}$

j $\begin{vmatrix} 3 & 4 & 6 \\ 0 & 1 & 0 \\ 5 & 6 & 9 \end{vmatrix}$

k $\begin{vmatrix} 2 & 0 & 3 \\ 5 & 7 & 6 \\ 0 & 2 & 0 \end{vmatrix}$

l $\begin{vmatrix} 4 & 1 & 0 \\ 3 & 2 & -9 \\ -4 & 6 & 3 \end{vmatrix}$

m $\begin{vmatrix} 5 & 0 & 3 \\ 7 & 2 & 9 \\ 4 & 0 & 6 \end{vmatrix}$

n $\begin{vmatrix} 2 & 5 & 1 \\ 3 & 2 & 7 \\ 4 & 6 & 5 \end{vmatrix}$

o $\begin{vmatrix} 7 & -3 & 5 \\ -6 & 4 & 9 \\ 2 & 13 & 8 \end{vmatrix}$

p $\begin{vmatrix} -3 & 7 & -3 \\ 6 & -2 & -8 \\ -4 & 9 & 13 \end{vmatrix}$

q $\begin{vmatrix} 5 & 0 & 3 \\ 1 & 0 & 6 \\ 2 & 0 & 9 \end{vmatrix}$

r $\begin{vmatrix} 2 & 4 & 4 \\ 5 & 3 & 10 \\ 6 & 9 & 12 \end{vmatrix}$

s $\begin{vmatrix} 2 & 4 & 3 & 7 \\ 1 & 5 & 6 & 9 \\ 3 & 8 & 4 & 2 \\ 5 & 4 & 7 & 1 \end{vmatrix}$

t $\begin{vmatrix} 4 & 2 & 3 & 9 \\ 5 & 8 & 4 & 1 \\ 2 & 6 & 5 & 3 \\ 2 & 1 & 4 & 1 \end{vmatrix}$

3 Find the following inverses using determinants:

a $\begin{pmatrix} 2 & 3 \\ 5 & 9 \end{pmatrix}^{-1}$
b $\begin{pmatrix} 5 & 2 \\ 4 & 1 \end{pmatrix}^{-1}$

c $\begin{pmatrix} -3 & 7 \\ 4 & 8 \end{pmatrix}^{-1}$
d $\begin{pmatrix} 5 & 16 \\ 13 & -8 \end{pmatrix}^{-1}$

e $\begin{pmatrix} 4 & -7 \\ 3 & 21 \end{pmatrix}^{-1}$
f $\begin{pmatrix} 3 & 7 \\ -14 & 5 \end{pmatrix}^{-1}$

g $\begin{pmatrix} -4 & -7 \\ -3 & -14 \end{pmatrix}^{-1}$
h $\begin{pmatrix} 1 & 0 & 0 \\ 3 & 5 & 6 \\ 7 & 2 & 3 \end{pmatrix}^{-1}$

i $\begin{pmatrix} 3 & 2 & 7 \\ 1 & 0 & 0 \\ 4 & 8 & 5 \end{pmatrix}^{-1}$
j $\begin{pmatrix} -2 & 4 & 6 \\ 0 & 3 & 5 \\ 2 & 0 & 3 \end{pmatrix}^{-1}$

k $\begin{pmatrix} 3 & 0 & 4 \\ 6 & 1 & 0 \\ 7 & 3 & 4 \end{pmatrix}^{-1}$
l $\begin{pmatrix} 2 & 5 & 9 \\ -3 & 4 & 6 \\ 4 & 2 & -2 \end{pmatrix}^{-1}$

m $\begin{pmatrix} 8 & 7 & 6 \\ 3 & 1 & 2 \\ 5 & 6 & 8 \end{pmatrix}^{-1}$
n $\begin{pmatrix} 2 & 0 & 2 & 3 \\ 4 & 2 & 8 & 5 \\ 1 & 6 & 0 & 0 \\ 8 & 0 & 1 & 3 \end{pmatrix}^{-1}$

o $\begin{pmatrix} 5 & 1 & 4 & 0 \\ 0 & 1 & 0 & 3 \\ 4 & 1 & 2 & 0 \\ 0 & 7 & 2 & 8 \end{pmatrix}^{-1}$
p $\begin{pmatrix} -2 & 8 & 4 & 0 \\ 5 & 0 & 0 & 1 \\ -3 & -6 & 0 & 4 \\ 0 & 1 & 0 & 0 \end{pmatrix}^{-1}$

q $\begin{pmatrix} 1 & 0 & 0 & 0 & 0 \\ -4 & 1 & 0 & 0 & 0 \\ -6 & -3 & 1 & 0 & 0 \\ -2 & -8 & -4 & 1 & 0 \\ -6 & -9 & -3 & -4 & 1 \end{pmatrix}^{-1}$
r $\begin{pmatrix} 1 & 0 & 0 & 0 & 0 \\ 0 & 1 & 0 & 0 & 0 \\ -5 & -3 & 1 & 0 & 0 \\ 0 & 0 & -2 & 1 & 0 \\ -4 & -1 & -3 & -4 & 1 \end{pmatrix}^{-1}$

4 $\begin{pmatrix} -4 & 0 \\ 5 & 3 \end{pmatrix}^{t} \begin{pmatrix} 8 & 7 \\ 1 & -2 \end{pmatrix}^{-1}$

5 $\begin{pmatrix} 4 & 2 \\ 5 & 3 \end{pmatrix}^{-1} \begin{pmatrix} 2 & 4 \\ 6 & 3 \end{pmatrix}^{t}$

6 $\begin{pmatrix} 2 & -6 \\ 0 & 1 \end{pmatrix}^{2} \begin{pmatrix} 7 & 6 \\ -1 & 4 \end{pmatrix}^{t}$

7 $\begin{pmatrix} 5 & 9 \\ 3 & -7 \end{pmatrix}^{2} \begin{pmatrix} 3 & 8 \\ 9 & -4 \end{pmatrix}^{t}$

8 Given: $\mathbf{A} = \begin{pmatrix} 1 & -3 \\ 4 & 5 \end{pmatrix}$ Find: $|A| \cdot \mathbf{A}^{-1}$

9 Given: $\mathbf{A} = \begin{pmatrix} 7 & 4 \\ 3 & 11 \end{pmatrix}$ Find $\mathbf{A}^{-1} \cdot |A|$

10 Given: $A = \begin{pmatrix} -2 & 4 \\ 3 & 1 \end{pmatrix}$ $B = \begin{pmatrix} 0 & 4 \\ 1 & 3 \end{pmatrix}$

Find:
a $|A| \cdot |B|$
b $|A \cdot B|$
c $|B \cdot A|$

11 Given: $A = \begin{pmatrix} 7 & 5 \\ -8 & 3 \end{pmatrix}$ $B = \begin{pmatrix} 5 & 2 \\ 7 & -4 \end{pmatrix}$

Find:
a $|A| \cdot |B|$
b $|A \cdot B|$
c $|B \cdot A|$

12 Given: $A = \begin{pmatrix} 4 & -1 \\ 0 & 2 \end{pmatrix}$ $B = \begin{pmatrix} 5 & 3 \\ 2 & 0 \end{pmatrix}$

Find:
a $A^{-1}B^{-1}$
b $(AB)^{-1}$
c $(BA)^{-1}$

13 Given: $A = \begin{pmatrix} 5 & 9 \\ 4 & -3 \end{pmatrix}$ $B = \begin{pmatrix} 7 & 4 \\ 6 & 8 \end{pmatrix}$

Find:
a $B^{-1}A^{-1}$
b $(BA)^{-1}$
c $(AB)^{-1}$

14 Given: $A = \begin{pmatrix} 1 & 0 \\ 3 & 4 \end{pmatrix}$ $B = \begin{pmatrix} 3 & 5 \\ 7 & 1 \end{pmatrix}$ $c = \begin{pmatrix} 3 \\ 1 \end{pmatrix}$

Find:
a $BA^{-1}c$
b $B^{-1}c$

15 Given: $A = \begin{pmatrix} 4 & 7 \\ -3 & 5 \end{pmatrix}$ $B = \begin{pmatrix} 4 & 6 \\ 2 & 8 \end{pmatrix}$ $c = \begin{pmatrix} 5 \\ 3 \end{pmatrix}$

Find:
a $4AB^{-1}$
b $A(Bc)$
c $(AB)c$

16 Let $A = \begin{pmatrix} 1 & 3 \\ 2 & 4 \end{pmatrix}$ $B = \begin{pmatrix} -4 & 1 \\ 0 & 2 \end{pmatrix}$ $C = \begin{pmatrix} 5 & -2 \\ 3 & -1 \end{pmatrix}$ $d = (3, -7)$

$e = (4, a)$ $f = \begin{pmatrix} 5 \\ 3 \end{pmatrix}$ $g = \begin{pmatrix} 7 \\ -1 \end{pmatrix}$ $h = (1, 1)$

$i = \begin{pmatrix} 1 \\ 1 \end{pmatrix}$

Find:

a AB b CB^t
c dC d eBi
e $h(BA)^{-1}i$ f efg
g $|ABC|$ h $[(hi)(dg) + ei]B$
i $hg(dC^{-1} + eA^{-1})$ j $(I - B)^{-1}$

17 $A = \begin{pmatrix} 3 & 2 \\ 7 & 1 \end{pmatrix}$ $B = \begin{pmatrix} 4 & 7 \\ 1 & -3 \end{pmatrix}$ $c = \begin{pmatrix} 1 \\ 1 \end{pmatrix}$

Find: $(3BA)^{-1}(Bc)$

18 Let $A = \begin{pmatrix} 3 & 1 \\ 2 & 4 \end{pmatrix}$ $B = \begin{pmatrix} 2 & -1 \\ 5 & -3 \end{pmatrix}$ $c = (4, 7)$ $d = \begin{pmatrix} 5 \\ -8 \end{pmatrix}$

Find:

a $(A + B)^{-1}$ using the Gaussian method
b $c(BA)^{-1}d$ using determinants

19 A is a 3×3 matrix.   Note that four 2×2 determinants are represented within the matrix which satisfy the conditions that $i_1 - i_2 \leq 1$ for all i's within the determinant, and $j_1 - j_2 \leq 1$ for all j's within the determinant.   Label these determinants as follows:

$$|K|: i's = 1, 2 \qquad j's = 1, 2$$
$$|L|: i's = 1, 2 \qquad j's = 2, 3$$
$$|M|: i's = 2, 3 \qquad j's = 1, 2$$
$$|N|: i's = 2, 3 \qquad j's = 2, 3$$

$|K| = -12$ $|L| = 14$ $|M| = 60$ $|N| = 12$

$a_{22} = 2$ $a_{12} = 5$ $a_{23} = 4$ $a_{11} = 3a_{13}$ $a_{32} = 2a_{31}$

20 Find a 3×3 matrix whose determinant is 4 such that the transpose of the matrix still has a determinant of 4.

21 Find a 3×3 matrix whose determinant is 5 such that the transpose of the matrix has a determinant of -5.

22 In certain manufacturing operations the assembly of a part requires, in addition to raw materials, one or more other parts previously assembled at the plant. For this type of situation, an $m \times m$ matrix, where m represents the number of different parts involved, may be developed, which is generally labeled with the letter **N**.   The elements of **N** are defined as follows:

$n_{ij} =$ quantity of part i which are assembled directly into one part j

A matrix is then developed, usually called **T**, which is the total requirements matrix.   **T** is determined according to the formula $T = (I - N)^{-1}$.

The elements t_{ij} are defined as the total number of part i which will eventually be needed in order to make one part j.   A column vector **s** can also be determined where the components s_i represent the number of part i's which are to be manufactured, exclusive of those required for use in the plant for making other products.

The vector **x** can then be calculated according to the formula $x = Ts$. The elements x_i represent the number of part i which should be produced in order to fill outside *and* plant needs.

The Grove Equipment Company manufactures five products, which, for convenience, we shall label A, B, C, D, and E. In addition to other raw materials each product requires the following components:

One A requires 4 B's and 1 C.
One C requires 2 B's and 3 E's.
One D requires 6 A's, 2 C's, and 1 E.

Grove wants to produce 3 A's, 5 B's, 6 C's, 8 D's, and 4 E's this month for outside delivery.   Determine the number of each part which will have to be produced.   (The Gaussian inversion method will be easiest.)

23 Using the method developed in Prob. 22, solve the following problem:

The Smithsonian Production Company manufactures six products, which, for convenience, we shall label A, B, C, D, E, and F.   In addition to other raw materials, each product requires the following components:

One A requires 2 B's, 3 C's, and 1 F.
One B requires 5 C's, 4 D's, 1 E, and 2 F's.
One C requires 6 D's and 2 E's.
One D requires 3 E's and 2 F's.
One E requires 2 F's.

If the company wishes to market 5 A's, 3 B's, 10 C's, 5 D's, 3 E's, and 4 F's, how many of each component should be produced?

3 LINEAR SYSTEMS

INTRODUCTION

Suppose that the officials of a large department store must wait for a week before the information as to a day's sales is available. They would like to be provided with an approximation of each day's sales on the next day. Your goal is to find a way to predict or estimate each day's sales.

To begin with, you suspect that some relationship may exist between the number of people entering the store and dollar sales figures for the day. For several weeks, you count the number of people entering the store daily and compare it with the sales figure for the respective day. Finally, you come up with the following relationship:

$$y = 3x_1$$

where y = daily sales in dollars

x_1 = number of people entering store

This is a model for predicting daily sales. y is a dependent variable since it is what you are trying to predict. x_1 is an independent variable, since you are using it to predict y. A mathematical model is a description in numerical or algebraic terms of the relationship of some item, in this case daily sales, to other items, which can be more easily determined. The number of different variables in a model is equal to the number of dimensions necessary for graphing it. Thus, our model can be graphed in two dimensions (Figure 3.1).

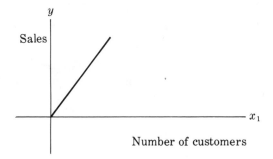

Figure 3.1   **Model for predicting daily sales**

Perhaps after using this model for a while, it occurs to us that weather would also help us to pick dollar sales. As a matter of fact, we notice that sales increase as it gets warmer. Further analysis leads to a new model:

$$y = 2x_1 + .05x_2$$

where x_2 = temperature in Fahrenheit degrees

This is now a three-dimensional model with two independent variables being used to jointly predict a third variable, which is dependent. This model could be graphed as a large sheet of paper in a box where the length and width of the box represented values of x_1 and x_2 and the height represented values of y. Every spot on the bottom of the box is represented uniquely by a pair of x_1 and x_2 values. The height of the piece of paper at any given spot represents the value of y connected with the specific x_1 and x_2 values for the spot.

Although it becomes impossible to graph, the reader should understand that a four-, five-, or six-dimensional model is merely one with four, five, or six different variables. One variable in an equation must always be dependent. Thus, a five-dimensional model has four independent variables and one dependent variable. The dependent variable does not have to be represented by a y. As a matter of fact, it is often true that no variable in an equation is specifically singled out as dependent. For example, if a firm is making two products x_1 and x_2 and we wish to model the restriction that they must make 35 of the two products, we can write $x_1 + x_2 = 35$. Here neither variable is specified as dependent, but note that once a value is set for either one, the other is free to take on only one specific value and is thus dependent.

LINEAR EQUATIONS

A *linear equation* is one which graphs as a straight line or flat plane. For an equation to be linear, not more than one variable can appear in a term, and it must be raised to the first power (if it appears at all). The number of different variables in an equation has no effect on linearity. The *slope* of a line, meaning the increase or decrease in height connected with a one-unit movement to the right, must be the same everywhere if the line is linear.

ONE-VARIABLE LINEAR EQUATIONS

With linear equations of one variable, the value of the variable must be unique, since the equation can be graphed as a point on a line (i.e., as a particular x value).

EXAMPLE 3.1

$$x - 5 = 3$$
$$x = 8$$

See Figure 3.2.

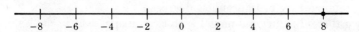

Figure 3.2 Graph of $x - 5 = 3$

EXAMPLE 3.2

$$\frac{x}{10} = 1$$
$$x = 10$$

See Figure 3.3.

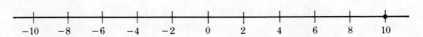

Figure 3.3 Graph of $x/10 = 1$

TWO-VARIABLE LINEAR EQUATIONS: GRAPHING

Two-variable linear equations require two values for graphing. One method for graphing is to convert the equation into the format $y = a + bx$. a, called the y *intercept*, will be the value of y when x is 0. b will be the slope of the line, i.e., the increase in y (or decrease if b is negative) for a one-unit increase in x.

EXAMPLE 3.3

Graph
$$6x + 3y = 12$$
$$3y = 12 - 6x$$
$$y = 4 - 2x \qquad a = 4, b = -2$$

See Figure 3.4.

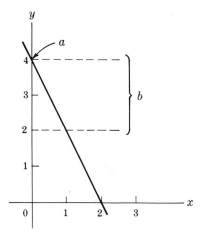

Figure 3.4   Graph of $6x + 3y = 12$

Had the variables been x_1 and x_2, the same method could have been applied (Figure 3.5).

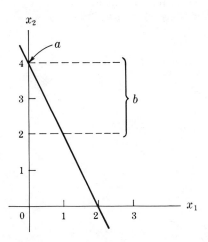

Figure 3.5   Graph of $6x_1 + 3x_2 = 12$

Graph
$$6x_1 + 3x_2 = 12$$
$$3x_2 = 12 - 6x_1$$
$$x_2 = 4 - 2x_1 \qquad a = 4, b = -2$$

A straight line can be uniquely determined if two points are known. Therefore, it is always possible to determine the equation for the straight line passing through two given points. Arbitrarily select one of the points as point 1 and the other as point 2. Label the y values of the two points as y_1 and y_2 and, likewise, label the x values as x_1 and x_2. Be certain that x_1 and y_1 pertain to the same point. First, find b, using the following formula:

$$b = \frac{y_1 - y_2}{x_1 - x_2}$$

then a, the y intercept, can be determined using the x and y value connected with either point by the formula

$$a = y_1 - bx_1 = y_2 - bx_2$$

The equation for the line, once a and b have been determined, is then

$$y = a + bx$$

EXAMPLE 3.4

A line passes through the points (2,3) and (5,7). Graph the line and find its equation.
   (2,3) means the point which is at 2 on the x axis and 3 on the y axis.
   (5,7) means the point which is at 5 on the x axis and 7 on the y axis.
Graphing the equation is simply a matter of plotting the points (Figure 3.6).

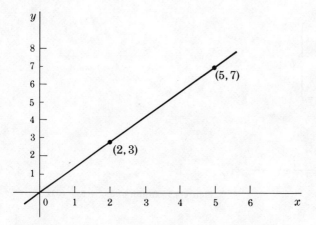

Figure 3.6 Graph of linear equation passing through (2,3) and (5,7)

We next must find a and b. Let (2,3) be point 1 and (5,7) be point 2:

$$b = \frac{y_1 - y_2}{x_1 - x_2} = \frac{3 - 7}{2 - 5} = \frac{-4}{-3} = \frac{4}{3}$$

$$a = y_1 - bx_1 = 3 - \frac{4}{3(2)} = 3 - \frac{8}{3} = \frac{1}{3}$$

The equation, then is

$$y = \frac{1}{3} + \frac{4}{3}x$$

TWO-VARIABLE LINEAR EQUATIONS: SOLUTION

Since the graph of a two-variable linear equation is a line, there is no unique point which represents a solution for the equation. Any pair of values of x and y on the line will provide a solution. If, however, there are two equations in two unknowns, the unique x and y values can be found, if they exist, representing the point of intersection.

If the lines are parallel, no solution will exist. If the lines are identical, every point on each line will represent a point of intersection. Otherwise, the solution can be found in a number of ways.

Substitution

In the substitution method one equation is solved for one variable (in terms of the other), and this solution is substituted in the other equation. The value of one of the variables will thus be found, and this value can be substituted in either equation in order to find the value of the other variable.

EXAMPLE 3.5

$$2x + 4y = 10 \qquad (1)$$
$$3x - 4y = 5 \qquad (2)$$

Solving Eq. (1) for x,

$$2x + 4y = 10$$
$$2x = 10 - 4y$$
$$x = 5 - 2y$$

Substituting in Eq. (2),

$$3x - 4y = 5$$
$$3(5 - 2y) - 4y = 5$$
$$15 - 6y - 4y = 5$$
$$-10y = -10$$
$$y = 1$$

Substituting in Eq. (1),

$$2x + 4y = 10$$
$$2x + 4(1) = 10$$
$$2x = 6$$
$$x = 3$$

The solution is $x = 3$, $y = 1$ (the point of intersection). We could have begun by solving for y in Eq. (1) or by solving for either x or y in Eq. (2).

Elimination

By means of the elimination method, each equation is multiplied by a number, so that when the two equations are added or subtracted, a variable will be eliminated. The variable not eliminated can then be determined. The procedure can be repeated to find the other variable, or the variable found can be substituted into either equation.

EXAMPLE 3.6

$$3x + 2y = 6 \tag{1}$$
$$5x + 7y = 15 \tag{2}$$

Multiply Eq. (1) by 5: $15x + 10y = 30$
Multiply Eq. (2) by 3: $15x + 21y = 45$
Subtract Eq. (2) from Eq. (1): $\overline{0x - 11y = -15}$
$$y = \tfrac{15}{11}$$

Multiply Eq. (1) by 7: $21x + 14y = 42$
Multiply Eq. (2) by 2: $10x + 14y = 30$
Subtract Eq. (2) from Eq. (1): $\overline{11x + 0y = 12}$
$$x = \tfrac{12}{11}$$

$x = \tfrac{12}{11}$, $y = \tfrac{15}{11}$ is the point of intersection.

Gaussian method

A matrix of coefficients of the variables $\mathbf{A}$ is determined, and a vector of constants (the right-hand side of the equations) $\mathbf{b}$ is determined. The tableau $\mathbf{A}|\mathbf{b}$ is then set up and solved as in the Gaussian method for finding inverses. The final tableau will be in the form $\mathbf{I}|\mathbf{x}$, where $\mathbf{I}$ is the identity matrix and $\mathbf{x}$ is the solution vector. (Its first component will be x_1; its second will be x_2.)

EXAMPLE 3.7

$$\begin{array}{l} 5x_1 - 2x_2 = 3 \\ 2x_1 + 5x_2 = 7 \end{array} \qquad \mathbf{A} = \begin{pmatrix} 5 & -2 \\ 2 & 5 \end{pmatrix} \qquad \mathbf{b} = \begin{pmatrix} 3 \\ 7 \end{pmatrix}$$

The initial tableau will be

$$\left(\begin{array}{cc|c} 5 & -2 & 3 \\ 2 & 5 & 7 \end{array} \right)$$

Divide row 1 by 5:

$$\left(\begin{array}{cc|c} 1 & -\tfrac{2}{5} & \tfrac{3}{5} \\ 2 & 5 & 7 \end{array} \right)$$

Subtract 2 times row 1 from row 2:

$$\left(\begin{array}{cc|c} 1 & -\tfrac{2}{5} & \tfrac{3}{5} \\ 0 & \tfrac{29}{5} & \tfrac{29}{5} \end{array} \right)$$

Divide row 2 by $\frac{29}{5}$:

$$\begin{pmatrix} 1 & -\frac{2}{5} & \bigg| & \frac{3}{5} \\ 0 & 1 & \bigg| & 1 \end{pmatrix}$$

Add $\frac{2}{5}$ of row 2 to row 1:

$$\begin{pmatrix} 1 & 0 & \bigg| & 1 \\ 0 & 1 & \bigg| & 1 \end{pmatrix} \quad \begin{matrix} (x_1) \\ (x_2) \end{matrix}$$

Thus, $x_1 = 1$, $x_2 = 1$ is the point of intersection.

If several sets of constants were to be solved for the same set of variables and coefficients, the Gaussian method will permit the solutions to be determined simultaneously. Where $\mathbf{b}_a$, $\mathbf{b}_b$, $\mathbf{b}_c$ are three vectors of constants, the tableau can be set up $\mathbf{A}|\mathbf{b}_a,\ \mathbf{b}_b,\ \mathbf{b}_c$. The Gaussian transformation will convert the tableau to $\mathbf{I}|\mathbf{x}_a,\ \mathbf{x}_b,\ \mathbf{x}_c$, where the $\mathbf{x}$'s represent solution vectors for their respective sets of constants.

EXAMPLE 3.8

If solutions are required for each of the following three sets of simultaneous equations, the Gaussian method can be utilized:

$$\begin{array}{ccc} x_1 + 2x_2 = 2 & x_1 + 2x_2 = 5 & x_1 + 2x_2 = 7 \\ -2x_1 + 3x_2 = 4 & -2x_1 + 3x_2 = 3 & -2x_1 + 3x_2 = 5 \end{array}$$

The initial tableau will be

$$\begin{pmatrix} 1 & 2 & \bigg| & 2 & 5 & 7 \\ -2 & 3 & \bigg| & 4 & 3 & 5 \end{pmatrix}$$

Add 2 times row 1 to row 2:

$$\begin{pmatrix} 1 & 2 & \bigg| & 2 & 5 & 7 \\ 0 & 7 & \bigg| & 8 & 13 & 19 \end{pmatrix}$$

Divide row 2 by 7:

$$\begin{pmatrix} 1 & 2 & \bigg| & 2 & 5 & 7 \\ 0 & 1 & \bigg| & \frac{8}{7} & \frac{13}{7} & \frac{19}{7} \end{pmatrix}$$

Subtract 2 times row 2 from row 1:

$$\begin{pmatrix} 1 & 0 & \bigg| & -\frac{2}{7} & \frac{9}{7} & \frac{11}{7} \\ 0 & 1 & \bigg| & \frac{8}{7} & \frac{13}{7} & \frac{19}{7} \end{pmatrix}$$

The solution, then, to the first set of equations is $x_1 = -\frac{2}{7}$, $x_2 = \frac{8}{7}$. For the second set of equations, the solution is $x_1 = \frac{9}{7}$, $x_2 = \frac{13}{7}$. And for the third set of equations, the solution is $x_1 = \frac{11}{7}$, $x_2 = \frac{19}{7}$. Note that this method is quite efficient when we deal with more than one set of constants.

The Gaussian method for finding inverses and for solving simultaneous equations are procedurally identical. If one begins with an initial tableau which has an identity matrix on the right, an inverse results, while a vector of constants is converted to x values. Had one begun with both an identity matrix and a vector of constants on the right, then both an inverse and an "x vector" would have been obtained, and, the reader will note, the inverse would have been achieved at the cost of only a light to moderate amount of computational effort.

Now, of course, if an inverse were not needed, the additional effort, no matter how small, would be unwarranted. There are, however, certain types of simultaneous equation problems which can be solved with much less effort once an inverse is known.

One approach to the solution of simultaneous linear equations is to find the inverse of the **A** matrix (the same one which occupies the left side of the initial Gaussian tableau) and multiply this inverse by the **b** vector (the constants on the right side of the linear equations). The result is a vector representing the x solution values. This approach would be slower than the Gaussian method for solving the equations directly *if* one had to compute the inverse; but, if the inverse were already known, it would be much faster, since it would involve only the multiplication of a matrix by a vector.

When the problem is of a type where the relationship of the variables remains steady but solutions are needed for different sets of constants, some of which are not known at the time the problem is initially solved, an inverse provides the most effective answer. If all sets of constants are initially known, an inverse is unnecessary, since, as noted previously, the Gaussian method can handle multiple sets of constants directly. An example will illustrate the types of problems where an inverse is useful.

EXAMPLE 3.9

The Clough Manufacturing Company assembles two products which we will label x_1 and x_2. Each product uses the same two parts, which we shall call A and B. Each x_1 is assembled using 1 A and 1 B. Each x_2 uses 2 A's and 3 B's. The supply of parts is limited, and the production department is told at the beginning of each week to quickly determine the number of x_1's and x_2's which will exactly utilize the supply of parts available each week. For the first week, 100 A's and 110 B's are available. At the beginning of the second week, 106 A's and 120 B's are available. To begin with, we must develop equations for the use of parts A and B:

Use of part A, first week: $\quad x_1 + 2x_2 = 100$
Use of part B, first week: $\quad x_1 + 3x_2 = 110$

Now, notice that the left-hand side of these equations will stay the same each week. Only the supply of A and B (the right-hand side of the equation) will change. If we knew the supply of A and B for every week of interest to us, we would develop a tableau of the form $A|b_a, b_b, b_e \ldots$. Since, however, we know the supply of A and B for only one week at a time, an initial tableau of the form $A|Ib$ can be set up, and thereafter A^{-1} will be available for solving the weekly equations. Thus, our initial tableau is

$$\begin{pmatrix} 1 & 2 & 1 & 0 & 100 \\ 1 & 3 & 0 & 1 & 110 \end{pmatrix}$$

Subtract row 1 from row 2:

$$\begin{pmatrix} 1 & 2 & 1 & 0 & 100 \\ 0 & 1 & -1 & 1 & 10 \end{pmatrix}$$

Subtract 2 times row 2 from row 1:

$$\begin{pmatrix} 1 & 0 & \bigm| & 3 & -2 & 80 \\ 0 & 1 & \bigm| & -1 & 1 & 10 \end{pmatrix}$$

The solution, then, for the first week is to assemble 80 x_1's and 10 x_2's.

Also,
$$\mathbf{A}^{-1} = \begin{pmatrix} 3 & -2 \\ -1 & 1 \end{pmatrix}$$

The second week our supply equations are

Use of part A, second week:	$x_1 + 2x_2 = 106$
Use of part B, second week:	$x_1 + 3x_2 = 120$

Now, since $\mathbf{A}^{-1}$ has been determined, we can solve by multiplying $\mathbf{A}^{-1}$ by the new vector of constants:

$$\mathbf{A}^{-1}\mathbf{b} = \begin{pmatrix} 3 & -2 \\ -1 & 1 \end{pmatrix} \begin{pmatrix} 106 \\ 120 \end{pmatrix} = \begin{pmatrix} 318 - 240 \\ -106 + 120 \end{pmatrix} = \begin{pmatrix} 78 \\ 14 \end{pmatrix}$$

The solution, then, for the second week is to assemble $78x_1$'s and $14x_2$'s.

Cramer method

Linear equations may also be solved utilizing determinants. A matrix $\mathbf{A}$ and a vector $\mathbf{b}$ are set up as in the Gaussian method. The determinant of $\mathbf{A}$, which we will call $|A|$, is then evaluated. To find x_1, substitute $\mathbf{b}$ for column 1 of $\mathbf{A}$ and find the determinant value. Divide the value thus found by $|A|$. To find x_2, substitute $\mathbf{b}$ for column 2 of $\mathbf{A}$ and find the determinant value. Divide this by $|A|$.

EXAMPLE 3.10

$$3x_1 + 4x_2 = 10$$
$$2x_1 - 6x_2 = 3$$

$$\mathbf{A} = \begin{pmatrix} 3 & 4 \\ 2 & -6 \end{pmatrix} \qquad \mathbf{b} = \begin{pmatrix} 10 \\ 3 \end{pmatrix}$$

$$|A| = \begin{vmatrix} 3 & 4 \\ 2 & -6 \end{vmatrix} = -18 - 8 = -26$$

$$x_1 = \frac{\begin{vmatrix} 10 & 4 \\ 3 & -6 \end{vmatrix}}{|A|} = \frac{-60 - 12}{-26} = \frac{-72}{-26} = \frac{36}{13}$$

$$x_2 = \frac{\begin{vmatrix} 3 & 10 \\ 2 & 3 \end{vmatrix}}{|A|} = \frac{9 - 20}{-26} = \frac{-11}{-26} = \frac{11}{26}$$

THREE OR MORE VARIABLE LINEAR EQUATIONS: SOLUTION

The number of equations necessary to find a point of intersection is equal to the number of variables present. All of the methods listed in the two variable case except graphing may be utilized when there are three or more variables.

EXAMPLE 3.11 (*Substitution*)

$$x + 2y - 3z = 1 \tag{1}$$
$$2x + 5y + z = 5 \tag{2}$$
$$3x - 2y - z = 3 \tag{3}$$

Solving for x in Eq. (1), we obtain

$$x = 1 - 2y + 3z \tag{1'}$$

Substituting Eq. (1') in Eqs. (2) and (3), we obtain

$$2(1 - 2y + 3z) + 5y + z = 5 \tag{2'}$$
$$2 - 4y + 6z + 5y + z = 5 \tag{2'}$$
$$y + 7z = 3 \tag{2'}$$
$$3(1 - 2y + 3z) - 2y - z = 3 \tag{3'}$$
$$3 - 6y + 9z - 2y - z = 3 \tag{3'}$$
$$-8y + 8z = 0 \tag{3'}$$

Solving Eq. (2') for y, we obtain

$$y = 3 - 7z \tag{2''}$$

Substituting Eq. (2'') in Eq. (3'), we obtain

$$-8(3 - 7z) + 8z = 0 \tag{3''}$$
$$-24 + 56z + 8z = 0 \tag{3''}$$
$$64z = 24 \tag{3''}$$
$$z = \tfrac{24}{64} = \tfrac{3}{8} \tag{3''}$$

Substituting Eq. (3'') in Eq. (2'), we obtain

$$y + 7(\tfrac{3}{8}) = 3 \tag{2'''}$$
$$y + \tfrac{21}{8} = 3 \tag{2'''}$$
$$y = \tfrac{3}{8} \tag{2'''}$$

Substituting y in Eq. (2''') and the z in Eq. (3'') in Eq. (1), we obtain

$$x + 2(\tfrac{3}{8}) - 3(\tfrac{3}{8}) = 1 \tag{1''}$$
$$x + \tfrac{6}{8} - \tfrac{9}{8} = 1 \tag{1''}$$
$$x - \tfrac{3}{8} = 1 \tag{1''}$$
$$x = \tfrac{11}{8} \tag{1''}$$

Thus, we find, by substitution, that the three equations intersect when $x = \tfrac{11}{8}$, $y = \tfrac{3}{8}$, and $z = \tfrac{3}{8}$. Of course, we could have started with any one of the three equations and solved for any variable first.

Substitution becomes difficult, or at least arduous, when the number of variables is greater than 2 or 3.

EXAMPLE 3.12 (*Elimination*)

$$2x - 3y + 4z = 1 \tag{1}$$
$$x - 5y + z = -5 \tag{2}$$
$$-3x + 3y - z = 2 \tag{3}$$

Multiplying Eq. (2) by 2, we obtain

$$2x - 10y + 2z = -10 \tag{2'}$$

and subtracting Eq. (1), $2x - 3y + 4z = 1 \tag{1}$

$$-7y - 2z = -11 \tag{4}$$

Multiplying Eq. (2) by 3, we obtain

$$3x - 15y + 3z = -15 \tag{2''}$$

and adding Eq. (3), $-3x + 3y - z = 2 \tag{3}$

$$-12y + 2z = -13 \tag{5}$$

Then adding Eq. (4) and Eq. (5) gives

$$-7y - 2z = -11 \tag{4}$$
$$-12y + 2z = -13 \tag{5}$$
$$-19y = -24$$
$$y = \tfrac{24}{19}$$

Multiplying Eq. (4) by 12, we obtain

$$-84y - 24z = -132 \tag{4'}$$

and, multiplying Eq. (5) by 7,

$$-84y + 14z = -91 \tag{5'}$$

Subtracting Eq. (4'), $-84y - 24z = -132 \tag{4'}$

$$38z = 41$$
$$z = \tfrac{41}{38}$$

Probably substitution in one of the original equations would provide the easiest method of finding x at this point, but we shall continue by our method of elimination. Adding Eq. (1) and Eq. (3) gives

$$2x - 3y + 4z = 1 \tag{1}$$
$$-3x + 3y - z = 2 \tag{3}$$
$$-x + 3z = 3 \tag{6}$$

Multiplying Eq. (1) by 5, we obtain

$$10x - 15y + 20z = 5 \tag{1'}$$

And, multiplying Eq. (2) by 3,

$$3x - 15y + 3z = -15 \tag{2'''}$$

Subtracting Eq. (1'), $10x - 15y + 20z = 5 \tag{1'}$

$$-7x - 17z = -20 \tag{7}$$

Multiplying Eq. (6) by 17 gives

$$-17x + 51z = 51 \tag{6'}$$

Multiplying Eq. (7) by 3 gives

$$-21x - 51z = -60 \tag{7'}$$

Adding Eq. (6') and Eq. (7'),

$$-17x + 51z = 51 \tag{6'}$$
$$-21x - 51z = -60 \tag{7'}$$
$$-38x = -9$$
$$x = \tfrac{9}{38}$$

The solution to the problem, then, is $x = \tfrac{9}{38}$, $y = \tfrac{24}{19}$, and $z = \tfrac{41}{38}$. The reader should substitute these values in each equation to prove that they are satisfactory.

EXAMPLE 3.13 *(Gaussian method)*

$$3x + z = 10 \qquad (1)$$
$$4y - 2z = 3 \qquad (2)$$
$$3x + y = 5z \qquad (3)$$

Before the Gaussian method can be employed, each equation must be in the form $ax + by + cz = k$.

$$3x + 0y + z = 10 \qquad (1')$$
$$0x + 4y - 2z = 3 \qquad (2')$$
$$3x + y - 5z = 0 \qquad (3')$$

$$\mathbf{A} = \begin{pmatrix} 3 & 0 & 1 \\ 0 & 4 & -2 \\ 3 & 1 & -5 \end{pmatrix} \qquad \mathbf{b} = \begin{pmatrix} 10 \\ 3 \\ 0 \end{pmatrix}$$

The original tableau will be

$$\left(\begin{array}{ccc|c} 3 & 0 & 1 & 10 \\ 0 & 4 & -2 & 3 \\ 3 & 1 & -5 & 0 \end{array} \right)$$

Row 1 ÷ 3 → Row 1:

$$\left(\begin{array}{ccc|c} 1 & 0 & \frac{1}{3} & \frac{10}{3} \\ 0 & 4 & -2 & 3 \\ 3 & 1 & -5 & 0 \end{array} \right)$$

Row 3 − 3 (Row 1) → Row 3

$$\left(\begin{array}{ccc|c} 1 & 0 & \frac{1}{3} & \frac{10}{3} \\ 0 & 4 & -2 & 3 \\ 0 & 1 & -6 & -10 \end{array} \right)$$

Row 2 ÷ 4 → Row 2

$$\left(\begin{array}{ccc|c} 1 & 0 & \frac{1}{3} & \frac{10}{3} \\ 0 & 1 & -\frac{1}{2} & \frac{3}{4} \\ 0 & 1 & -6 & -10 \end{array} \right)$$

Row 3 − Row 2 → Row 3

$$\left(\begin{array}{ccc|c} 1 & 0 & \frac{1}{3} & \frac{10}{3} \\ 0 & 1 & -\frac{1}{2} & \frac{3}{4} \\ 0 & 0 & -\frac{11}{2} & -\frac{43}{4} \end{array} \right)$$

Row 3 ÷ $\left(-\frac{11}{2}\right)$ → Row 3

$$\left(\begin{array}{ccc|c} 1 & 0 & \frac{1}{3} & \frac{10}{3} \\ 0 & 1 & -\frac{1}{2} & \frac{3}{4} \\ 0 & 0 & 1 & \frac{43}{22} \end{array} \right)$$

Row 1 − $\frac{1}{3}$ Row 3 → 1

$$\left(\begin{array}{ccc|c} 1 & 0 & 0 & \frac{177}{66} \\ 0 & 1 & -\frac{1}{2} & \frac{3}{4} \\ 0 & 0 & 1 & \frac{43}{22} \end{array} \right)$$

Row 2 + $\frac{1}{2}$ Row 3 → Row 2

$$\left(\begin{array}{ccc|c} 1 & 0 & 0 & \frac{177}{66} \\ 0 & 1 & 0 & \frac{76}{44} \\ 0 & 0 & 1 & \frac{43}{22} \end{array} \right)$$

The intersection point, then, will be when $x = \frac{177}{66}$, $y = \frac{76}{44}$, and $z = \frac{43}{22}$. As the number of variables increases, this method is particularly well adapted for computer use. Decimals rather than fractions might also be used to simplify calculations, particularly if a calculating machine is available.

EXAMPLE 3.14 (*The Cramer method*)

$$
\begin{aligned}
x + z &= 10y \tag{1}\\
4y &= 8 \tag{2}\\
z - 3x - 4y &= 10 \tag{3}
\end{aligned}
$$

Again, equations must be set up in the form $ax + by + cz = k$ before the Cramer method is used:

$$
\begin{aligned}
x - 10y + z &= 0 \tag{1'}\\
0x + 4y + 0z &= 8 \tag{2'}\\
-3x - 4y + z &= 10 \tag{3'}
\end{aligned}
$$

$$
\mathbf{A} = \begin{pmatrix} 1 & -10 & 1 \\ 0 & 4 & 0 \\ -3 & -4 & 1 \end{pmatrix} \qquad \mathbf{b} = \begin{pmatrix} 0 \\ 8 \\ 10 \end{pmatrix}
$$

then

$$
|A| = \begin{vmatrix} 1 & -10 & 1 \\ 0 & 4 & 0 \\ -3 & -4 & 1 \end{vmatrix} = -0 \begin{vmatrix} -10 & 1 \\ -4 & 1 \end{vmatrix} + 4 \begin{vmatrix} 1 & 1 \\ -3 & 1 \end{vmatrix} - 0 \begin{vmatrix} 1 & -10 \\ -3 & -4 \end{vmatrix}
$$

$$
= 4 \begin{vmatrix} 1 & 1 \\ -3 & 1 \end{vmatrix} = 4[1 - (-3)] = 4(4) = 16
$$

$$
x = \frac{\begin{vmatrix} 0 & -10 & 1 \\ 8 & 4 & 0 \\ 10 & -4 & 1 \end{vmatrix}}{|A|} = \frac{0 \begin{vmatrix} 4 & 0 \\ -4 & 1 \end{vmatrix} - (-10) \begin{vmatrix} 8 & 0 \\ 10 & 1 \end{vmatrix} + 1 \begin{vmatrix} 8 & 4 \\ 10 & -4 \end{vmatrix}}{16}
$$

$$
= \frac{10(8) + 1(-32 - 40)}{16} = \frac{80 - 72}{16} = \frac{8}{16} = \frac{1}{2}
$$

$$
y = \frac{\begin{vmatrix} 1 & 0 & 1 \\ 0 & 8 & 0 \\ -3 & 10 & 1 \end{vmatrix}}{|A|} = \frac{-0 \begin{vmatrix} 0 & 1 \\ 10 & 1 \end{vmatrix} + 8 \begin{vmatrix} 1 & 1 \\ -3 & 1 \end{vmatrix} - 0 \begin{vmatrix} 1 & 0 \\ -3 & 10 \end{vmatrix}}{16}
$$

$$
= \frac{8[1 - (-3)]}{16} = \frac{8(4)}{16} = \frac{32}{16} = 2
$$

$$
z = \frac{\begin{vmatrix} 1 & -10 & 0 \\ 0 & 4 & 8 \\ -3 & -4 & 10 \end{vmatrix}}{|A|} = \frac{1 \begin{vmatrix} 4 & 8 \\ -4 & 10 \end{vmatrix} - (-10) \begin{vmatrix} 0 & 8 \\ -3 & 10 \end{vmatrix} + 0 \begin{vmatrix} 0 & 4 \\ -3 & -4 \end{vmatrix}}{16}
$$

$$
= \frac{1[40 - (-32)] + 10[0 - (-24)]}{16} = \frac{72 + 240}{16}
$$

$$
= \frac{312}{16} = 19.5
$$

The solution of the set of linear equations, then, is $x = \frac{1}{2}$, $y = 2$, and $z = 19.5$.

PROBLEMS

1 Graph each of the lines whose equation is given:
  a $4x + 2y = 8$
  b $-9x + 2y = 14$
  c $.5x = .2y + 2$

2 Find the slope and y intercept of each line in Prob. 1.

3 Find the equation of the line passing through the following points:
  a $(4,7), (-1,-3)$
  b $(5,3), (4,-8)$
  c $(7,-2), (3,14)$

4 Find the equation of the line
  a with slope 7 and y intercept -2
  b with slope $-\frac{3}{2}$ and passing through $(2,4)$
  c with x intercept -2 and y intercept $\frac{5}{2}$

5 Graph each pair on the same axes and estimate the point of intersection:
  a $3x + 4y = 1$
     $2x - 6y = 18$
  b $x = 2 - .25y$
     $9x + 1.25y = 15$

6 Solve by the Cramer method:
  a $4x + 3y = 12$
     $24x + 7y = 6$
  b $-2x_1 - 4x_2 = -8$
     $4x_1 + 7x_2 = 10$

  c $3x + 5y = 18$
     $-21x + 15y = 24$
  d $x = 5 + 3y$
     $-3y - 4x - 7 = 0$

  e $3x - y + 2z = 4$
     $2x + 3y = z + 14$
     $7x - 4y + 3z = -4$
  f $r = 3(s - t)$
       $t = 4(s - r)$
     $r + 5 = 2s - 5$

7 Solve by the Gaussian method:
  a $4x - 5y = 7$
     $2x + 7y = 13$
  b $3x + 4y = 13$
     $-2x + 4 = 2y$

  c $x_2 = x_1$
     $4x_1 = 7 + x_2$
  d $y - 2x = 4$
     $4x + y = 37$

  e $2x + 3y + 2z = 6$
     $3z + 5y = 2x - 16$
     $4y = 3x - 15$
  f $x_3 - x_2 = x_1 + 5$
     $x_2 + 50 = x_3 + x_1 + 2x_2$
     $x_1 = 7x_2 + 7$

and

     $x_3 - x_2 = x_1 + 10$
     $x_2 + 20 = x_3 + x_1 + 2x_2$
     $x_1 = 7x_2 + 15$

8 Solve by any method:
  a $.5x + 1.2y = 1.4$
     $.6x - 7.0y = 5.9$
  b $.5x + .2y = 1.65$
     $.7x - .3y = 2.6$

c $t - u = 5$

$$\frac{4}{u + 5} = \frac{10}{u - t}$$

d $x + y = 3$
$y - 12 = z$
$z + x = 7$

e $x + 2y = 1 - 3z$
$4x - 4y = 3$
$4y - 1 = 6z$

f $24x - 10y = 23$
$12x + 30y = -6$

and

$24x - 10y = 23$
$12x + 30y = 4$

Problems 9 to 14 are designed for practice in the use of variables and in the writing of equations.

9 A rectangle is x feet wide and $x + 3$ feet long.   Between it and an outer rectangle is a border which is 2 ft wide on each side.
   a Write the dimensions of the outer rectangle.
   b Obtain the area of the border in terms of x in simplest form.
   c Find the value of x for which the area of the border is 172 sq ft.

10 To make 50 lb of a certain fiber, a textile mill uses 10 lb of a fiber costing 60 cents/lb, and 40 lb of a fiber costing 90 cents/lb.
   a Find the cost per pound of the mixed fiber.
   b If x pounds of the 60-cent fiber are mixed with $50 - x$ pounds of the 90-cent fiber, express in terms of x in simplest form the cost of 1 lb of the mixed fiber; 30 lb; $22\frac{1}{2}$ lb.
   c Find the value of x for which the cost of 1 lb of the mixed fiber is 69 cents.

11 a Write an expression for the total value of x pounds of tea at 65 cents/lb and y pounds of tea at 80 cents/lb.
   b The tea in part a is mixed and sold at a profit of 25 percent.   Find an expression for the total selling price.
   c Work part b if the profit is 25 percent of the total selling price.

12 The Jones Company wants to erect a shipping room by erecting partitions in the middle of a storage room floor, using available materials.   They have decided to make either a rectangle or a square and to use all of the available materials.   Show that they will obtain a larger area by using a square.   (*Hint:* Work with the perimeters of the two figures.)

13 a A dealer buys x dozen eggs for $\$d$.   Two dozen are bad, but he sells the remainder at a profit of 50 percent of the cost.   Express in terms of x and d the difference between the cost and selling price of one dozen eggs.
   b If b dozen are bad, express in terms of x, d, and b the difference between the selling price and cost price of a dozen eggs in order to make a profit of 40 percent of the cost price.

14 A wholesaler buys n pounds of coffee at c cents per pound and mixes this with $2n$ pounds of coffee costing $1.25c$ cents per pound.   Express in terms of c the selling price per pound in order to obtain a profit of 20 percent of the cost.

15 A plant has 3,200 production line hours and 220 packaging hours available in a week.   Product X requires 2 production hours and .25 packaging hour per unit. Product Y requires 4 production line hours and .20 packaging hour per unit.   How many units of X and how many units of Y will exactly utilize the available capacity?

16 A dealer bought a number of eggs at 40 cents/dozen and two dozen less than this number at 50 cents/dozen. He sold all of the eggs at 60 cents/dozen and made a 35 percent profit. How many dozen eggs of each kind did he buy?

17 The Black and Blue Company estimates that profits are 12 percent of costs. Their costs are presently $24,000. By how much, in dollars, can costs increase, if profit dollars remain constant and profits drop to 10 percent of cost?

18 A company has invested $50,000 at 3 percent and $30,000 at $4\frac{1}{2}$ percent. How much additional money should they invest at 8 percent to make the annual income 5 percent of the total investment?

19 The PQR Corp. makes three products, P, Q, and R. One unit of P requires 8 production hours, 4 painting hours, and .6 packaging hour; one unit of Q requires 12 production hours, 6 painting hours, and .4 packaging hour; one unit of R requires 15 production hours, 3 painting hours and .2 packaging hour. The company makes all three products at each of two plants. In one plant they have available, per week, 11,900 production hours, 4,600 painting hours, and 390 packaging hours. In the other plant they have available 7,100 production hours, 2,200 painting hours, and 180 packaging hours. How many units of P, Q, and R should they produce in each plant in order exactly to utilize the capacity?

20 Company A owns 70 percent of Company B.
Company B owns 30 percent of Company A and 70 percent of Company C.
Company C owns 20 percent of Company B.
The net income for Company A was $20,000 (plus its interest in B's income).
The net income for Company B was $10,000 (plus its interest in A and C).
The net income for company C was $15,000 (plus its interest in B's income).
You own 20 percent of Company C. What is your share of the three companies' income?

21 Pierce, Inc. manufactures two products, which each utilize two scarce parts, sleeves and bearings. Early each morning, a shipment is received representing the day's supply of sleeves and bearings. The company desires to use all of these during the day in making the appropriate quantities of their two products. Each unit of the first product requires 4 sleeves and 13 bearings. Units of the second product use 3 bearings and 10 sleeves. Develop a fast method which they can use to determine how many of each product to make each day. Try it out on the following week (shown in the table below).

Day	Sleeves	Bearings
1	1,831	5,992
2	1,840	6,000
3	1,860	6,030
4	1,850	6,030
5	1,890	6,150

22 The Hollister Corporation sells four products, I, II, III, and IV, in each of two geographical areas, U and V, to three classes of customers: consumers, wholesalers, and retailers. Sales, in 1,000's of units for last year, appear as follows:

Sales in 1,000 Units

Geographical area U

Sold to	Product			
	I	II	III	IV
Consumers	3	4	4	3
Retailers	6	2	6	3
Wholesalers	7	1	5	1
Total	16	7	15	7

Geographical area V

Consumers	4	5	3	6
Retailers	7	2	8	0
Wholesalers	7	2	4	1
Total	18	9	15	7

The firm pays a commission or bonus to salesmen, territory managers, and division managers. The rates vary by geographical areas as follows:

	Salesmen	Territory managers	Division managers
Area U	.06	.05	.02
Area V	.04	.03	.03

The selling price is:

Product	Selling price, in dollars, per 1,000 units
I	$ 200
II	1,000
III	500
IV	700

Find:

  a Total sales in units by product and customer type.

  b Difference between geographical areas in sales in units by product and customer type.

  c Sales for the next period by geographical area, product, and customer type based on a forecast of 10 percent increase in sales.

  d Total sales in dollars by geographical area.

  e Sales in dollars by customer type for each geographical area.

  f Total amount of commission to be paid by type of commission and type of customer.

4 LINEAR PROGRAMMING

INTRODUCTION

Linear programming is regarded by many mathematicians and businessmen as the most successfully and frequently used method resulting from the application of mathematics to business problems. Certainly, all knowledgeable people will agree that linear programming has proven to be of significant value to industry.

Linear programming is a technique for maximizing or minimizing a linear function of any number of variables subject to one or more linear constraints or restrictions. The situation which prompts the use of linear programming for maximizing is one in which the decision-maker is dealing with one or more scarce resources such as time, money, or plant capacity. He has two or more products or items, each of which requires some of the scarce resources, and he is thereby prevented from producing an infinite number of each one. Hence, he uses linear programming to determine how many of each item to produce to maximize revenue, profit, or some quantifiable goal and still keep within the restrictions of the scarce resources.

The minimizing problem which can be solved by linear programming is usually a situation in which one or more restrictions prevent zero activity, which generally results in a minimum for everything.

LINEAR PROGRAMMING TECHNIQUES: IDENTIFICATION OF VARIABLES

One of the first steps in the setup and solution of any linear programming problem is the identification of the variables. The variables in a linear programming problem can be identified by asking the question "What items in this problem does the decision-maker have control over?" The further question might be asked, "If these are the variables, and if I were to find a number to attach to each one, would sufficient information be obtained to solve the problem?"

EXAMPLE 4.1

The T. E. Evans Company manufactures barbecue grills in three styles which we shall label A, B, and C. Each grill is processed in two departments. Time requirements for each department as well as available time in each department are itemized in Table 4.1. Profit per unit is calculated as $2.00 for A, $3.00 for B, and $1.50 for C. What are the controllable variables in the problem?

Table 4.1

Department	Man-hours available	Man-hours necessary per unit		
		A	B	C
1	280	2	3	1
2	336	2	2	3

What items in the problem does the decision-maker have control over? The number of grills of type A, type B, and type C to manufacture is under the control of the decision-maker.

Let
X_1 = number of A grills to manufacture
X_2 = number of B grills to manufacture
X_3 = number of C grills to manufacture

EXAMPLE 4.2

The Syntax Corporation manufactures two types of hair tonics, type A and type B. Three ingredients are common to the two hair tonics and the necessary amounts of each are listed in Table 4.2 along with the cost of the ingredients. The sales price per gallon of A is $30.00 and per gallon of B is $40.00. What are the controllable variables in the problem?

Table 4.2

Ingredient	Amount in 5 gal of A	Amount in 5 gal of B	Cost per gallon	Amount available
1	At least 2 gal	No more than 3 gal	$ 5.00	100 gal
2	No more than 4 gal	At least 3 gal	$ 6.00	150 gal
3	Any amount	Any amount	$10.00	75 gal

Notice that if we were to select amounts of A and B as the variables, this would not tell us how to mix them. Thus, we must look further for the controllable variables. What items in the problem does the decision-maker have control over? He has control, within limits, on how much of each ingredient to put into each product. He also has control over how much of each product to make.

Let us define as the variables

$$X_1 = \text{amount of ingredient 1 in } A \text{ in gallons}$$
$$X_2 = \text{amount of ingredient 2 in } A \text{ in gallons}$$
$$X_3 = \text{amount of ingredient 3 in } A \text{ in gallons}$$
$$X_4 = \text{amount of ingredient 1 in } B \text{ in gallons}$$
$$X_5 = \text{amount of ingredient 2 in } B \text{ in gallons}$$
$$X_6 = \text{amount of ingredient 3 in } B \text{ in gallons}$$
$$X_1 + X_2 + X_3 = \text{amount of product } A$$
$$X_4 + X_5 + X_6 = \text{amount of product } B$$

Notice that by defining the variables in this manner, the amount of each ingredient in each product is left to be determined; and that once this is determined, the amount of each product is also determined, since each product is made up of the sum of its ingredients.

OBJECTIVE FUNCTIONS

The objective function in a linear programming problem is a function of the type

$$A_1X_1 + A_2X_2 + \cdots + A_nX_n$$

where X_1, X_2, . . , X_n represent all the variables in the problem. A_1, A_2, . . . , A_n are scalar coefficients representing the amount to be gained or lost by a one-unit increase in the accompanying variable. The objective function represents what is to be maximized or minimized. Note that linearity is assumed; i.e., a one-unit change in a variable produces the same effect on the objective function whether the value under consideration is 20 or 200.

EXAMPLE 4.3

Returning to Example 4.1, let us determine the objective function to maximize profit.

Note that three variables were identified as

$$X_1 = \text{number of type } A \text{ grills to manufacture}$$
$$X_2 = \text{number of type } B \text{ grills to manufacture}$$
$$X_3 = \text{number of type } C \text{ grills to manufacture}$$

Thus, the objective function must be of the form $A_1X_1 + A_2X_2 + A_3X_3$. The problem also includes the profit for each type of grill, and since our goal is to maximize profit, the function can easily be identified as

$$2X_1 + 3X_2 + 1.5X_3 \qquad \text{Maximize}$$

EXAMPLE 4.4

Set up the objective function for Example 4.2 if the goal is to maximize profit.
Six variables were defined, so our objective function must be of the form

$$A_1X_1 + A_2X_2 + A_3X_3 + A_4X_4 + A_5X_5 + A_6X_6$$

We are concerned with the maximization of profit, so our next step should be to
determine profit using our variables.   Note that profit is equal to revenue less cost.
Since revenue is equal to sales price times quantity, we know that

Price of product A = \$30.00 per gallon   Amount of $A = X_1 + X_2 + X_3$
Price of product B = \$40.00 per gallon   Amount of $B = X_4 + X_5 + X_6$

Thus   Revenue $= 30(X_1 + X_2 + X_3) + 40(X_4 + X_5 + X_6)$

Likewise, cost is equal to quantity times cost per unit.

Cost of ingredient 1 = \$5.00 per gallon   Amount of 1 $= X_1 + X_4$
Cost of ingredient 2 = \$6.00 per gallon   Amount of 2 $= X_2 + X_5$
Cost of ingredient 3 = \$10.00 per gallon   Amount of 3 $= X_3 + X_6$

Thus   Cost $= 5(X_1 + X_4) + 6(X_2 + X_5) + 10(X_3 + X_6)$
and   Profit $= 30(X_1 + X_2 + X_3) + 40(X_4 + X_5 + X_6)$
$\qquad - [5(X_1 + X_4) + 6(X_2 + X_5) + 10(X_3 + X_6)]$

We next must put this into standard form:

$$30(X_1 + X_2 + X_3) + 40(X_4 + X_5 + X_6) - 5(X_1 + X_4)$$
$$- 6(X_2 + X_5) - 10(X_3 - X_6)$$
$$30X_1 + 30X_2 + 30X_3 + 40X_4 + 40X_5 + 40X_6 - 5X_1 - 5X_4$$
$$- 6X_2 - 6X_5 - 10X_3 - 10X_6$$
$$25X_1 + 24X_2 + 20X_3 + 35X_4 + 34X_5 + 30X_6 \qquad \text{Maximize}$$

This is now in general form and is the objective function.

CONSTRAINTS

Constraints are restrictions which prohibit our maximizing by
making 100 million of each item or our minimizing by producing zero
of each item.   They are usually in the form of inequalities rather than
equalities.   This means that situations which give rise to the constraints are usually in the form "X must be at least so much," or "X
may be no more than so much," rather than "X must be exactly so
much."   For a maximizing problem constraints are written in the form

$$B_1X_1 + B_2X_2 + \cdots + B_nX_n \leq C$$

where X_1, X_2, . . . , X_n represent all the controllable variables in
the problem. B_1, B_2, . . . , B_n represent the amount of the restriction used up by one unit of the related variable. C is the amount of
the restricted item available.

In a minimizing problem, the general form for constraints is

$$B_1X_1 + B_2X_2 + \cdots + B_nX_n \geq C$$

If the inequality sign is going the wrong way on a particular constraint for the type of problem, multiplying the entire inequality by -1 will reverse the direction of the inequality sign. The constraint $X_1, X_2, \ldots, X_n \geq 0$ is automatically assumed and provided for in all linear programming problems, and it does not need to be explicitly stated.

EXAMPLE 4.5

Returning again to Example 4.1, let us set up the constraints.
The first restriction which appears in the problem is that only 280 hours are available in department 1.
Man-hours department 1:

$$2X_1 + 3X_2 + 1X_3 \leq 280$$

Note that 2 hours are used up for each unit of product A produced, 3 hours per unit of product B, and 1 hour per unit of product C. Note, also, that the total used must be less than or equal to 280. The inequality sign is going in the proper direction for a maximizing problem.
The second restriction is the number of man-hours available for department 2. Thus,
Man-hours department 2:

$$2X_1 + 2X_2 + 3X_3 \leq 336$$

These are the only constraints appearing in the problem.

EXAMPLE 4.6

Set up the constraint equations for Example 4.2.
We must have at least 2 gal of ingredient 1 in 5 gal of A. This can be written in constraint form as

$$X_1 \geq \tfrac{2}{5}(X_1 + X_2 + X_3)$$

Simplifying,

$$X_1 \geq \tfrac{2}{5}X_1 + \tfrac{2}{5}X_2 + \tfrac{2}{5}X_3$$
$$X_1 - \tfrac{2}{5}X_1 - \tfrac{2}{5}X_2 - \tfrac{2}{5}X_3 \geq 0$$
$$\tfrac{3}{5}X_1 - \tfrac{2}{5}X_2 - \tfrac{2}{5}X_3 \geq 0$$

Multiplying through by -1,

$$-\tfrac{3}{5}X_1 + \tfrac{2}{5}X_2 + \tfrac{2}{5}X_3 + 0X_4 + 0X_5 + 0X_6 \leq 0$$
$$-3X_1 + 2X_2 + 2X_3 + 0X_4 + 0X_5 + 0X_6 \leq 0 \qquad \text{(amount of 1 in } A)$$

Also, the amount of 2 in A is a constraint:

$$X_2 \leq \tfrac{4}{5}(X_1 + X_2 + X_3)$$

Simplifying,

$$X_2 \leq \tfrac{4}{5}X_1 + \tfrac{4}{5}X_2 + \tfrac{4}{5}X_3$$
$$-\tfrac{4}{5}X_1 + \tfrac{1}{5}X_2 - \tfrac{4}{5}X_3 \leq 0$$
$$-\tfrac{4}{5}X_1 + \tfrac{1}{5}X_2 - \tfrac{4}{5}X_3 + 0X_4 + 0X_5 + 0X_6 \leq 0$$
$$-4X_1 + X_2 - 4X_3 + 0X_4 + 0X_5 + 0X_6 \leq 0 \qquad \text{(amount of 2 in } A\text{)}$$

Likewise, the amount of 1 in B is a constraint. Thus,

$$X_4 \leq \tfrac{3}{5}(X_4 + X_5 + X_6)$$
$$X_4 \leq \tfrac{3}{5}X_4 + \tfrac{3}{5}X_5 + \tfrac{3}{5}X_6$$
$$\tfrac{2}{5}X_4 - \tfrac{3}{5}X_5 - \tfrac{3}{5}X_6 \leq 0$$
$$0X_1 + 0X_2 + 0X_3 + \tfrac{2}{5}X_4 - \tfrac{3}{5}X_5 - \tfrac{3}{5}X_6 \leq 0$$
$$0X_1 + 0X_2 + 0X_3 + 2X_4 - 3X_5 - 3X_6 \leq 0 \qquad \text{(amount of 1 in } B\text{)}$$

Also, the amount of 2 in B is a constraint. Thus,

$$X_5 \geq \tfrac{3}{5}(X_4 + X_5 + X_6)$$

Simplifying,

$$X_5 \geq \tfrac{3}{5}X_4 + \tfrac{3}{5}X_5 + \tfrac{3}{5}X_6$$
$$-\tfrac{3}{5}X_4 + \tfrac{2}{5}X_5 - \tfrac{3}{5}X_6 \geq 0$$

Multiplying by -1,

$$0X_1 + 0X_2 + 0X_3 + \tfrac{3}{5}X_4 - \tfrac{2}{5}X_5 + \tfrac{3}{5}X \leq 0$$
$$0X_1 + 0X_2 + 0X_3 + 3X_4 - 2X_5 + 3X_6 \leq 0 \qquad \text{(amount of 2 in } B\text{)}$$

A further constraint is necessary, since only 100 gallons of ingredient 1 are available:

$$X_1 + X_4 \leq 100$$

is the amount of 1 available, or

$$X_1 + 0X_2 + 0X_3 + X_4 + 0X_5 + 0X_6 \leq 100$$

The amount of 2 and 3 available can also be put into constraint form. Thus,

$$X_2 + X_5 \leq 150$$

is the amount of 2 available, or

$$0X_1 + X_2 + 0X_3 + 0X_4 + X_5 + 0X_6 \leq 150 \qquad \text{and} \qquad X_3 + X_6 \leq 75$$

is the amount of 3 available, or

$$0X_1 + 0X_2 + X_3 + 0X_4 + 0X_5 + X_6 \leq 75$$

All the constraints listed in the problem are now set up in the proper form.

THE SIMPLEX METHOD

One of the most generally usable techniques for the solution of linear programming problems is the simplex method. Most, although not all, linear programming problems can be solved through the use of this method. The simplex method will appear rather similar for the reader to the Gaussian method for finding inverses.

The steps to be followed for solving a linear programming problem through the use of the simplex method are easily programmed onto a computer. This method, therefore, is very popular when the solution is to be completed through the help of a computer.

Construction of the tableau

A linear programming maximizing problem is set up differently for solution from a minimizing problem. Let us first discuss the setup for a maximizing problem.

The initial maximizing tableau is

x_i labels E_i labels

E_i labels $\Big\{$	**A**	**I**	**b**
	$-\mathbf{c}$	**0**	**0**

$\mathbf{A}$ is a matrix representing the coefficients of the constraint inequations. Thus, if the constraints are

$$a_{11}x_1 + a_{12}x_2 + \cdots + a_{1n}x_n \leq b_1$$
$$a_{21}x_2 + a_{22}x_2 + \cdots + a_{2n}x_n \leq b_2$$
$$\cdot \qquad \cdot \qquad \qquad \cdot \qquad \cdot$$
$$\cdot \qquad \cdot \qquad \qquad \cdot \qquad \cdot$$
$$\cdot \qquad \cdot \qquad \qquad \cdot \qquad \cdot$$
$$a_{m1}x_1 + a_{m2}x_2 + \cdots + a_{mn}x_n \leq b_m$$

then

$$\mathbf{A} = \begin{pmatrix} a_{11} & a_{12} & \cdots & a_{1n} \\ a_{21} & a_{22} & \cdots & a_{2n} \\ \cdot & \cdot & & \cdot \\ \cdot & \cdot & & \cdot \\ a_{m1} & a_{m2} & \cdots & a_{mn} \end{pmatrix}$$

Note that $\mathbf{A}$ is an $m \times n$ matrix where the problem has m constraints and n controllable variables. $\mathbf{b}$ is a column vector of the constants on the right-hand side of the constraint inequations. Thus,

$$\mathbf{b} = \begin{pmatrix} b_1 \\ b_2 \\ \cdot \\ \cdot \\ \cdot \\ b_m \end{pmatrix}$$

$\mathbf{c}$ is a row vector representing the coefficients of the objective function. Thus, if the objective function is in the form

$$c_1x_1 + c_2x_2 + \cdots + c_nx_n \qquad \text{Maximize}$$

then $\mathbf{c} = c_1, c_2, \ldots, c_n$ and $-\mathbf{c} = -c_1, -c_2, \ldots, -c_n$

$\mathbf{I}$ is an $m \times m$ identity matrix. Note that it is a square matrix and its size is determined by the number of constraints, *not* the number of variables.

$\mathbf{0}$ in the lower center is a zero row vector with m components.

0 in the lower right is simply the number zero.

Let us investigate the basis for the initial tableau structure. Each constraint inequation describes a region on a graph bounded by the inequation. The feasible solution area is the area bounded by these inequations. This can be visualized graphically as shown in Figure 4.1.

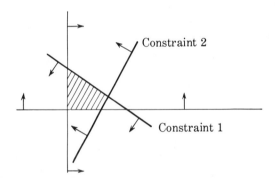

Figure 4.1   Solution space of a two-constraint linear programming problem

Note that the constraint $x_1 \geq 0$ and $x_2 \geq 0$ is always implicitly assumed. Since all functions are linear in this type of model, there could be no advantage in not moving to a corner for the best solution. In other words, it is advantageous to move in this direction, and we shall continue to get better and better solutions as we move. The corners represent the potential "best points." Put another way, no point in the feasible solution space could possibly be any better than a corner. Thus, by investigating only the corners, we are searching all the places necessary to locate the best point. Now the corners are those places where two or more lines intersect, and we have already covered ways in which to solve for points of intersection. But one necessary characteristic of a system for the solution methods which we have learned is that it must be a system of equations, not inequations. So we define a new set of variables, one for each constraint, and define them as the quantity necessary to equate the left and right sides of the inequations. Since no variable is permitted to be negative in linear programming problems, this assures us that the other variables in a constraint will not add up to more than the right side limit. But, since each variable must be listed in every constraint, we include all of those variables in each constraint, giving each variable except the one for the particular constraint a coefficient of zero. This, then, is the reason for the identity matrix in the initial tableau.

These variables which we add in this manner are called "slack" variables, and, in the final solution, the values assigned to them represent the portion of the scarce resources on constraints which are unused in the optimal solution.

Each tableau in a linear programming problem must represent a feasible (though not necessarily optimal) solution to the problem. Generally we begin by giving every variable the value zero, and the zero in the lower right-hand corner stands for the value of the objective function for the solution where all x's are equal to zero.

For a minimizing problem, the tableau is set up somewhat differently. The diagram for a minimizing tableau is

A^t	I	c
$-b$	0	0

Let us define A^t as the transpose of A. This means that the two numbers forming the subscript are interchanged for each element of the new matrix. For example, let

$$A = \begin{pmatrix} a_{11} & a_{12} & a_{13} \\ a_{21} & a_{22} & a_{23} \\ a_{31} & a_{32} & a_{33} \end{pmatrix} \quad \text{then } A^t = \begin{pmatrix} a_{11} & a_{21} & a_{31} \\ a_{12} & a_{22} & a_{32} \\ a_{13} & a_{23} & a_{33} \end{pmatrix}$$

If, for example,

$$A = \begin{pmatrix} 2 & 9 & 7 \\ 4 & 5 & 1 \\ 6 & 3 & 4 \end{pmatrix} \quad \text{then } A^t = \begin{pmatrix} 2 & 4 & 6 \\ 9 & 5 & 3 \\ 7 & 1 & 4 \end{pmatrix}$$

Also, note that the positions of the vectors b and c are exchanged. This necessitates b becoming a row vector and c a column vector. I will still be a square identity matrix, but this time the number of rows (and columns) will be determined by the number of controllable variables, i.e., the number of rows of $\mathbf{A}^t$.

EXAMPLE 4.7

Returning to Example 4.1 again, set up the initial simplex tableau.   Note that this is a maximizing problem.   The constraints are

$$2X_1 + 3X_2 + X_3 \leq 280$$
$$2X_1 + 2X_2 + 3X_3 \leq 336$$

Thus $\mathbf{A} = \begin{pmatrix} 2 & 3 & 1 \\ 2 & 2 & 3 \end{pmatrix}$ and $\mathbf{b} = \begin{pmatrix} 280 \\ 336 \end{pmatrix}$

The objective function is

$$2X_1 + 3X_2 + 1.5X_3 \qquad\qquad \text{Maximize}$$

so $\mathbf{c} = (2, 3, 1.5)$ and $-\mathbf{c} = (-2, -3, -1.5)$

The initial tableau is

	X_1	X_2	X_3	E_1	E_2	
E_1	2	3	1	1	0	280
E_2	2	2	3	0	1	336
	-2	-3	-1.5	0	0	0

where E_1 and E_2 are defined as slack variables and will be discussed later.

EXAMPLE 4.8

Set up the initial simplex tableau for Example 4.2.   This is also a maximizing problem.   The constraints are

$$-3X_1 + 2X_2 + 2X_3 + 0X_4 + 0X_5 + 0X_6 \leq 0$$
$$-4X_1 + X_2 - 4X_3 + 0X_4 + 0X_5 + 0X_6 \leq 0$$
$$0X_1 + 0X_2 + 0X_3 + 2X_4 - 3X_5 - 3X_6 \leq 0$$
$$0X_1 + 0X_2 + 0X_3 + 3X_4 - 2X_5 + 3X_6 \leq 0$$
$$X_1 + 0X_2 + 0X_3 + X_4 + 0X_5 + 0X_6 \leq 100$$
$$0X_1 + X_2 + 0X_3 + 0X_4 + X_5 + 0X_6 \leq 150$$
$$0X_1 + 0X_2 + X_3 + 0X_4 + 0X_5 + X_6 \leq 75$$

and $\mathbf{A} = \begin{pmatrix} -3 & 2 & 2 & 0 & 0 & 0 \\ -4 & 1 & -4 & 0 & 0 & 0 \\ 0 & 0 & 0 & 2 & -3 & -3 \\ 0 & 0 & 0 & 3 & -2 & 3 \\ 1 & 0 & 0 & 1 & 0 & 0 \\ 0 & 1 & 0 & 0 & 1 & 0 \\ 0 & 0 & 1 & 0 & 0 & 1 \end{pmatrix}$ $\mathbf{b} = \begin{pmatrix} 0 \\ 0 \\ 0 \\ 0 \\ 100 \\ 150 \\ 75 \end{pmatrix}$

The objective function is

$$25X_1 + 24X_2 + 20X_3 + 35X_4 + 34X_5 + 30X_6 \qquad\qquad \text{Maximize}$$

so $\mathbf{c} = (25, 24, 20, 35, 34, 30)$
and $-\mathbf{c} = (-25, -24, -20, -35, -34, -30)$

The initial tableau is

	X_1	X_2	X_3	X_4	X_5	X_6	E_1	E_2	E_3	E_4	E_5	E_6	E_7	
E_1	-3	2	2	0	0	0	1	0	0	0	0	0	0	0
E_2	-4	1	-4	0	0	0	0	1	0	0	0	0	0	0
E_3	0	0	0	2	-3	-3	0	0	1	0	0	0	0	0
E_4	0	0	0	3	-2	3	0	0	0	1	0	0	0	0
E_5	1	0	0	1	0	0	0	0	0	0	1	0	0	100
E_6	0	1	0	0	1	0	0	0	0	0	0	1	0	150
E_7	0	0	1	0	0	1	0	0	0	0	0	0	1	75
	-25	-24	-20	-35	-34	-30	0	0	0	0	0	0	0	0

EXAMPLE 4.9

The Armstrong Company is faced with the problem of minimizing the cost of storage of their two products, A and B. A requires twice as much space as B. At least 3 A's must be stored for each B. 50 B's are required to be in storage at all times. The cost of the space necessary to store one B is \$4.00. Set up the tableau for minimizing cost.

First, identifying the controllable variables, we can let

$$X_1 = \text{amount of product } A \text{ to store}$$
$$X_2 = \text{amount of product } B \text{ to store}$$

Then, the objective function for minimizing storage cost is

$$8X_1 + 4X_2 \qquad\qquad \text{Minimize}$$

To determine the constraints, note that if three A's are required for each B, then $X_1 \geq 3X_2$. If this does not seem correct, try substituting some values for A and B.

Simplifying,
$$X_1 \geq 3X_2$$
$$X_1 - 3X_2 \geq 0$$

which is in proper form for a minimizing problem.

The other constraint is

$$X_2 \geq 50 \qquad \text{or} \qquad 0X_1 + X_2 \geq 50$$

Then $\quad \mathbf{A} = \begin{pmatrix} 1 & -3 \\ 0 & 1 \end{pmatrix} \quad \mathbf{b} = (0,50) \quad \text{and} \quad -\mathbf{b} = (0,-50)$

$$\mathbf{c} = \begin{pmatrix} 8 \\ 4 \end{pmatrix} \quad \text{and} \quad \mathbf{A}^t = \begin{pmatrix} 1 & 0 \\ -3 & 1 \end{pmatrix}$$

The initial tableau is

	E_1	E_2	X_1	X_2	
X_1	1	0	1	0	8
X_2	-3	1	0	1	4
	0	-50	0	0	0

Operation of the tableau

The method of solving a linear programming problem using a simplex tableau is identical for either a maximizing or a minimizing problem:

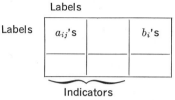

The diagram above explains the location of the key numbers for the tableau operation.

1 Select the largest negative indicator. Let us assume it is in column j.
2 For each positive a_i in column j, find the quotient b_i/a_{ij}. Select the a_{ij} which provides the smallest quotient. Call this the pivot number.
3 Divide the pivot row by the pivot number, and insert the new row in the corresponding position to the original row in a new tableau. Label this row with the label of the pivot column.
4 To determine each other row of the new tableau, take the number in the pivot column position in that row, multiply it by the new pivot row and subtract the resulting vector from the old row being replaced. Enter the result in the new tableau in the corresponding position to the old row being replaced.
5 If, after all rows have been thus inserted into the new tableau, any negative indicators remain, select the largest negative indicator and proceed to repeat the steps outlined above. When no negative indicators remain, the process is complete.

Let us look a little more closely at these five steps. First, concentrating on step 1, why do we select the most negative indicator? You will recognize that the numbers in this section of the initial tableau represent the contribution toward our objective of one unit of the variables in the problem with minus signs attached. Thus, by selecting the most negative one of these numbers, we are, in fact, selecting that variable which has the largest contribution per unit. We could, without affecting the final answer, select any negative number for our pivot column. In the interest of finding the optimal solution in as few steps as possible, however, we generally select the largest negative indicator, since most of the time this will lead us to the optimal solution more rapidly than any other selection would. The answer will not be wrong, however, if an indicator other than the most negative is chosen.

Now, let's look more closely at the second step. The column label for the pivot column represents the variable which we are going to make as large as possible in the tableau we are about to develop. The column of numbers on the right side of the tableau represents the number of unused units of each scarce resource. The numbers in the pivot column represent the number of scarce resource units consumed by one unit of the variable heading the column. The ratio represents the number of units of the variable permissible without exceeding the available quantity of the constraint or scarce resource. We select the smallest ratio because we can't have a solution where we produce more of an item than the most limiting scarce resource will permit. In other words, that constraint which permits us to produce the fewest of one variable must be the controlling or key constraint, and the number which that constraint allows us to produce is the number which we select to produce in the new tableau. Notice that to select a ratio other than the smallest will actually result in a *wrong* answer to the problem, since we will be determining whether an impossible solution is best. Care must be taken to assure the selection of the smallest ratio.

In determining the smallest ratio, we ignore numbers in the pivot column which are not positive. This should be understandable in the above context. A negative number indicates that a decision to increase the size of the variable will actually increase the number of constraint units available. This may be hard to visualize at first, but the situation is usually that a decision to increase the size of the variable under consideration carries with it a decision to decrease the size of another variable in the problem (since, for example, another constraint is already fully utilized), and the variable which must be decreased provides more units of the resource under consideration than the variable being increased uses up.

A zero in the pivot column indicates that an increase in the size of the variable under consideration will have no effect at all on the available quantity of the constraint, and thus the constraint is not a limiting factor in how large we can make the variable under consideration.

The one exception to the rule that a negative number should not be chosen as an indicator is when *both* the pivot column number and the corresponding number in the far right column are negative. This method for solving linear programming problems assumes that each solution, including that portrayed by the initial tableau (make 0 of everything) is feasible. If the right-hand column number is negative, this is not a feasible solution, since it indicates that fewer than zero units of the scarce resource are available. In this case, the negative indicator *must* be chosen as the pivot number in order to arrive at a first feasible solution. This situation will arise when a constraint, such as x must be greater than or equal to 100, is included in the tableau. In order to have the inequality going in the right direction for maximization, this is written $-x \leq -500$.

If a number in the right-hand column is negative while the corresponding number in the pivot column is positive, this indicates the selection of the wrong pivot number in the preceding tableau, since a constraint must have been exceeded to produce the negative number. Table 4.3 summarizes the above discussion.

Table 4.3

Pivot column	Column of C's	Indication
+	+	A candidate for consideration
+	0	Automatically the smallest ratio (if two pairs in the column are like this, pick either one)
+	−	Mistake in preceding tableau
0	+	Do not consider
0	0	Do not consider
0	−	Mistake in preceding tableau
−	+	Do not consider
−	0	Do not consider
−	−	Automatically choose (if two pairs in the column are like this, pick either one)

Steps 3 and 4 are analogous to the Gaussian method for solving simultaneous equations. You are finding the coordinates of a particular corner of the solution space and the value of the objective function at that corner.

Each negative number appearing in the bottom row of the tableau indicates the profit potential yet untapped for the item in the column. For example, the -2 appearing in the lower left-hand corner of the tableau indicates that we can contribute two units to our objective function by increasing x_1 one unit. The most negative indicator thus represents the greatest untapped profit potential.

EXAMPLE 4.10

Solve the tableau developed as Example 4.7. The initial tableau is

	X_1	X_2	X_3	E_1	E_2	
E_1	2	3	1	1	0	280
E_2	2	2	3	0	1	336
	−2	−3	−1.5	0	0	0

Note that the most negative indicator is the -3 in column 2. The two quotients $\frac{280}{3}$ and $\frac{336}{2}$ must be noted. $\frac{280}{3}$ is the smaller, so $a_{12} = 3$ is the pivot number. Divide the pivot row by the pivot number and insert the new row in a new tableau labeled with the label of the pivot column. Next multiply another number in the pivot column, $a_{22} = 2$ by the new pivot row, and subtract this from the old row 2. Thus,

$$-2(\tfrac{2}{3}, 1, \tfrac{1}{3}, \tfrac{1}{3}, 0, \tfrac{280}{3}) + (2, 2, 3, 0, 1, 336) = (\tfrac{2}{3}, 0, \tfrac{7}{3}, -\tfrac{2}{3}, 1, \tfrac{448}{3})$$

Repeat this procedure for row 3. Thus,

	X_1	X_2	X_3	E_1	E_2	
X_2	$\frac{2}{3}$	1	$\frac{1}{3}$	$\frac{1}{3}$	0	$\frac{280}{3}$
E_2	$\frac{2}{3}$	0	$\frac{7}{3}$	$-\frac{2}{3}$	1	$\frac{448}{3}$
	0	0	$-.5$	1	0	280

$$-(-3)(\tfrac{2}{3}, 1, \tfrac{1}{3}, \tfrac{1}{3}, 0, \tfrac{280}{3}) + (-2, -3, -1.5, 0, 0, 0) = (0, 0, -.5, 1, 0, 280)$$

Note that a negative indicator remains, so the procedure must be repeated. Selecting column 3 as the pivot column, examine the quotients $\frac{280}{3} \div \frac{1}{3}$ and $\frac{448}{3} \div \frac{7}{3}$. The latter results in the smaller quotient. Therefore, $a_{23} = \frac{7}{3}$ becomes the pivot number. Divide the pivot row by $\frac{7}{3}$. Now determine the other rows as follows:

Row 1: $-\frac{1}{3}(\frac{2}{7}, 0, 1, -\frac{2}{7}, \frac{3}{7}, \frac{448}{7}) + (\frac{2}{3}, 1, \frac{1}{3}, \frac{1}{3}, 0, \frac{280}{3}) = (\frac{4}{7}, 1, 0, \frac{3}{7}, -\frac{1}{7}, 72)$
Row 3: $-(-.5)(\frac{2}{7}, 0, 1, -\frac{2}{7}, \frac{3}{7}, \frac{448}{7}) + (0, 0, -.5, 1, 0, 280) = (\frac{1}{7}, 0, 0, \frac{6}{7}, \frac{3}{14}, 312)$

	X_1	X_2	X_3	E_1	E_2	
X_2	$\frac{4}{7}$	1	0	$\frac{3}{7}$	$-\frac{1}{7}$	72
X_3	$\frac{2}{7}$	0	1	$-\frac{2}{7}$	$\frac{3}{7}$	64
	$\frac{1}{7}$	0	0	$\frac{6}{7}$	$\frac{3}{14}$	312

Since no negative indicators remain, the solution is completed.

EXAMPLE 4.11

Solve the tableau developed in Example 4.9. The initial tableau is

	E_1	E_2	X_1	X_2	
X_1	1	0	1	0	8
X_2	-3	1	0	1	4
	0	-50	0	0	0

$\uparrow$

Note that the most negative indicator is -50. Since negative and zero numbers are not considered when selecting a pivot row, we must select $a = 1$ as the pivot number.   The tableau is filled in as before:

$$-0(-3, 1, 0, 1, 4) + (1, 0, 1, 0, 8) = (1, 0, 1, 0, 8)$$
$$-(-50)(-3, 1, 0, 1, 4) + (0, -50, 0, 0, 0) = (-15C, 0, 0, 50, 200)$$

	E_1	E_2	X_1	X_2	
X_1	1	0	1	0	8
E_2	-3	1	0	1	4
	-150	0	0	50	200

And continuing as before,

$$-(-3)(1, 0, 1, 0, 8) + (-3, 1, 0, 1, 4) = (0, 1, 3, 1, 28)$$
$$-(-150)(1, 0, 1, 0, 8) + (-150, 0, 0, 50, 200) = (0, 0, 150, 50, 1400)$$

	E_1	E_2	X_1	X_2	
E_1	1	0	1	0	8
E_2	0	1	3	1	28
	0	0	150	50	1400

Since no negative indicators remain, the solution is completed.

Interpretation of a maximization tableau

The following illustration shows the important interpretation areas for a simplex tableau for maximization:

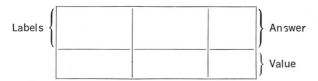

The answers appear in the box on the upper part of the right-hand side of the tableau.   They apply to the corresponding variables as listed on the left side of the tableau.   The value of the objective function for the optimum solution is shown in the box at the lower right-hand corner of the tableau.

EXAMPLE 4.12

Interpret the solution tableau for Example 4.10.   The solution tableau is given as

	X_1	X_2	X_3	E_1	E_2	
X_2	$\frac{4}{7}$	1	0	$\frac{3}{7}$	$-\frac{1}{7}$	72
X_3	$\frac{2}{7}$	0	1	$-\frac{2}{7}$	$\frac{3}{7}$	64
	$\frac{1}{7}$	0	0	$\frac{6}{7}$	$\frac{3}{14}$	312

This can be interpreted as "produce 72 X_2's and 64 X_3's, or 72 type B grills and 64 type C grills (no type A grills)." The value of 312 given in the lower right-hand corner is the optimal value of the objective function. Thus, the objective function in this problem was

$$2X_1 + 3X_2 + 1.5X_3$$

With the values of X_1, X_2, and X_3 from the solution substituted, the function has a value of

$$2(0) + 3(72) + 1.5(64) = 312$$

which is the highest possible value of this function within the limits of the constraints.

Note that the labels on the left-hand side of the tableau were X_2 and X_3. If one of the labels had been E_1, the accompanying answer on the right-hand side of the tableau would have represented the amount of constraint 1 which was not utilized in the optimal solution. Likewise, an answer for E_2 would indicate the amount of constraint 2 not utilized. Variables such as E_1 and E_2 are termed slack variables.

Also observe that in this problem only two positions were available for answers even though there were three variables in the problem. It is a proven theorem of linear programming that the number of variables which will be utilized in any maximization problem will never exceed the number of constraints.

Interpretation of a minimization tableau

The illustration below shows the important interpretation areas for a minimization tableau.

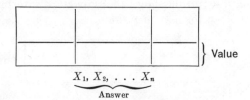

Note that in a minimization problem the answer appears in the lower middle box in the tableau. Also, unlike a maximization answer, it is already in order. Thus the value of variable X_1 is shown first, X_2 is shown second, and so on. The optimal value of the objective function is again shown in the box in the lower right-hand corner.

EXAMPLE 4.13

Interpret the tableau for Example 4.9. (*Note:* This example was continued as Example 4.11.) The solution tableau for this example was determined to be

	E_1	E_2	X_1	X_2	
E_1	1	0	1	0	8
E_2	0	1	3	1	28
	0	0	150	50	1400

Since this is a minimization problem, the optimal values of X_1 and X_2 are 150 and 50, respectively. The objective function was

$$8X_1 + 4X_2$$

Substituting the optimal values, we obtain

$$8(150) + 4(50) = 1200 + 200 = 1400$$

which appears in the box in the lower right-hand corner of the tableau and is the minimum value for this objective function subject to the constraints.

WHEN SHOULD LINEARITY BE ASSUMED?

The linear programming technique assumes a straight-line function for each constraint and for the objective function. Objective functions are rarely linear, and constraints are quite often not linear either. The question often arises as to when linearity should be assumed, specifically in those cases where it is not literally applicable.

Curving lines over short distances can often be reasonably well approximated by straight lines. For example, see Figure 4.2. Note that AB is a much closer approximation to the curve than AC. In those situations where the range of the permissible values for the function is relatively small or where the curve of the function is reasonably well approximated by a straight line, a strong case can be advanced for linear programming.

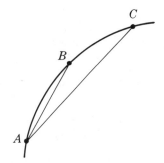

Figure 4.2 Straight line approximation of curvilinear function

First, the precision of the available information is not so sharp that it will adversely be affected by the assumption of linearity. Second, the time savings and procedural simplification resulting from the assumption of linearity will usually be far more significant and valuable than the small additional accuracy.

In short, the effect of assuming linearity should be considered for each new problem. For most cases the assumption will not result in gross misstatements, and linear programming can advantageously be used. If the assumption of linearity is untenable, other methods for solving the problem must be sought.

PROBLEMS

1 A company makes two kinds of leather belts. Belt A is a high-quality belt and Belt B is of lower quality. The respective profits are $.40 and $.30 per belt. Each belt of type A requires twice as much time as a belt of type B, and if all belts were of type B, the company could make 1,000 per day. The supply of leather is sufficient for only 800 belts per day (both A and B combined). Belt A requires a fancy buckle, and only 400 per day are available for Belt A. How many of each type should be made?

2 A plant has 3,200 production line hours and 220 packaging hours available in a week. Product X requires 2 production line hours per unit and .25 packaging hour. Product Y requires 4 production line hours and .20 packaging hour per unit. Product X sells for $5.00 per unit and has costs of $2.00 per unit connected with its manufacture. Product Y sells for $3.00 per unit and has costs of $1.00 per unit connected with its manufacture. Find the optimum quantity of each product which should be produced. Explain your results.

3 A trucking company with $400,000 to spend on new equipment is contemplating three types of vehicles. Vehicle A has a 10-ton payload and is expected to average 35 miles per hour. It costs $8,000. Vehicle B has a 20-ton payload and is expected to average 30 miles per hour. It costs $13,000. Vehicle C is a modified form of B; it carries sleeping quarters for one driver, and this reduces its capacity to 18 tons and raises the cost to $15,000.

Vehicle A requires a crew of one man, and, if driven on three shifts per day, could be run for an average of 18 hours per day. Vehicles B and C require a crew of two men each, but, whereas B would be driven 18 hours per day with three shifts, C could average 21 hours per day. The company has 150 drivers available each day and would find it very difficult to obtain further crews. Maintenance facilities are such that the total number of vehicles must not exceed 30. How many vehicles of each type should be purchased if the company wishes to maximize its capacity in ton-miles per day? Explain meaning of the answer.

4 A farmer has a 100-acre farm. He can sell all the tomatoes, lettuce, or radishes he can raise. The price he can obtain is 19 cents a pound for tomatoes, 10 cents a head for lettuce, and 25 cents a pound for radishes. The average yield per acre is 2,000 lb of tomatoes, 3,000 heads of lettuce, and 1,000 lb of radishes. Fertilizer is available at 10 cents per pound, and the amount required per acre is 100 lb for tomatoes and lettuce and 50 lb for radishes. Labor required for sowing, cultivating, and harvesting per acre is 5 man-days for tomatoes and radishes and 6 man-days for lettuce. A total of 400 man-days of labor are available at $20 per man-day. Formulate the linear programming model for this situation.

5 The Home Products Company has recently experienced such an increase in sales that its plant capacity is not sufficient to manufacture its three products in large enough quantities to meet the current demand. Thus, the company has obtained estimates for subcontracting parts of the manufacturing processes. Since the products are sold at fixed prices and it appears as if everything produced could be sold, Home Products is, naturally, anxious to supply its merchandise in the quantities that would yield the most profit. Each of the three products requires molding, assembly, and packaging.   Although the molding operation for products 1 and 2 could be subcontracted, the molding for product 3 requires special equipment that precludes the use of a subcontractor.   Furthermore, the other two operations of assembly and packaging have to be done on the company's premises.   The direct costs of these operations and the fixed price of each product are shown in the accompanying table.

Each unit of product 1 requires 6 min of molding time (if done at Home Products), 7 min of assembly time, and 3 min of packaging time, whereas for product 2 the times are 10 min, 3 min, and 2 min, respectively.   A unit of product 3 takes 8 min for molding, 8 min for assembly, and 2 min for packaging.   Owing to capacity limitations, there are only 8,000 min of molding time, 12,000 min of assembly time, and 10,000 min of packaging time per week available at the company's plant. Management feels that sales would be limited if production were restricted to the capacities that Home Products has available.   Thus, it is necessary to construct a production schedule that relies upon some holding work being subcontracted. The basis or scheduling production and allocating subcontract work has the simple criterion of maximizing company profits, assuming that all units produced could be sold.

Price	Product 1 $1.50	Product 2 $1.80	Product 3 $1.97
Cost of molding:			
Home products	$.30	$.50	$.40
Subcontracted	.50	.60	
Cost of assembly	.20	.10	.27
Cost of packaging	.30	.20	.20

6   The Pacific Specialities Company of San Francisco manufactures a wide variety of Oriental souvenirs that are sold to tourist shops in Chinatown.   Recently, the firm received a notice from its supplier that listed several basic rubber and plastic materials that would be available in limited supply for an indefinite period.   The purchasing manager of Pacific immediately telephoned the supplier to determine the reason for the notice on restricted materials.   He was told that some manufacturing equipment had broken down and was in the process of being replaced. However, for the next several weeks, production was to be at reduced level and the supplier had been forced to limit his customers' purchases.

Pacific's purchasing and production managers examined the list of restricted materials and noted that only two of the current products use any of the scarce inputs.   Product No. 153 contains materials A and B in amounts that depend upon the manufacturing processes used.   If No. 153 is made by process P, then 6 lb of A and 2 gal of B are consumed, whereas if process Q is used, the required inputs are 4 lb of A and 6 gal of B.   Also, product No. 297 requires 10 lb of A and 1 gallon of B if the product is manufactured by process R; the inputs are 7 lb and 4 gal if alternate process S is used.   Furthermore, each process requires different amounts of labor.   In fact, processes P, Q, R, and S use 10, 3, 15, and 12 man-hours of labor, respectively, to yield one unit of a product.

The profits accruing from each product depend upon the process and are given in the following table.

Product	Process	Profit/unit
No. 153	P	$ 6.50
	Q	5.00
No. 297	R	10.00
	S	6.30

Pacific is restricted to 150 lb per week of material A and 130 gal per week of material B. Further, management will allocate no more than 400 man-hours per week to the combined production of No. 153 and No. 297.

How many units per week of each product should be manufactured by each process in order to maximize profits? What is the total profit per week?

7 The Millwood Metals Corporation uses nickel and tin in the manufacture of many of its products. Rather than purchase the metals in pure form, Millwood buys old automobiles and appliances, melts them down, retains the nickel and tin, and disposes of any other by-products at a nominal price. The company has found this an economical method of procuring its raw materials but has recently been somewhat disturbed with what it considers an inordinate amount of time being spent by its purchasing department in deciding upon the quantities of scrap automobiles and appliances that must be bought each day to satisfy the material requirements for the manufacturing schedule. Specifically, production is scheduled two days in advance and the minimum requirements for nickel and tin are known at that time so that it is the purchasing department's problem to decide how many tons of scrap automobiles and appliances should be bought in order to satisfy the requirements at the least cost to the company. Although it is permissible to buy more than the minimum amounts if particularly low prices prevail, Millwood generally desires to spend a minimum amount of money on any given day to obtain the required metals for its production two days hence. At present, the purchasing department analyzes the price of scrap two hours per day to determine the amounts of each type to buy. Management contends that this cost of analysis substantially reduces the savings accruing from buying scrap as opposed to purchasing the metals in their pure form from a supplier. Thus, the purchasing department has been charged with the responsibility of finding a quick and efficient method of making the daily purchasing decisions for nickel and tin. The method must be fast and yet guarantee that the minimum requirements of nickel and tin will be met at a minimum cost. Although subject to some variation, Millwood has found over the last year that, on the average, each ton of scrap automobiles yields 200 lb of nickel and 200 lb of tin, whereas each ton of old appliances produces 200 lb of nickel and 300 lb of tin. As an illustration of the type of decision that must be made each day, consider yesterday's problem. The minimum requirements for nickel and tin were 3 and 4 tons, respectively. Each ton of scrap automobiles cost $60, and each ton of old appliances sold at $100. Simply stated, the problem was to determine how many tons of each of the two types of scrap should be purchased in order to yield the minimum requirements of nickel and tin at a minimum cost.

8 The Lambda Fertilizer Company will have available to it in the coming month 1,000 tons of nitrates, 1,800 tons of phosphates, and 1,200 tons of potash. These quantities are on hand or have already been ordered, and no more can be received until after the next thirty days have passed.   The firm is interested in mixing these active ingredients together with certain inert ingredients, which are available in unlimited supply, into three basic fertilizer mixes in whatever way will maximize profits in the coming month.

The three basic fertilizers are 5–10–5, 5–10–10, and 10–10–10, the numbers representing in each case the percentage (by weight) of nitrates, phosphates, and potash, respectively, in each of the mixes.

Costs of the fertilizer ingredients per ton are shown below.   Costs of mixing, packaging, and selling are identical for all three mixes and amount to $15 per ton.

Nitrates	$160
Phosphates	40
Potash	100
Inert ingredients	5

Prices for the mixed fertilizer are set competitively, and the Lambda Company cannot control them.   At present these prices are as shown below.   All fertilizer produced can be sold at these prices, but there is a sales commitment to deliver 6,000 tons of 5–10–5 within the month.

5–10–5	$40
5–10–10	50
10–10–10	60

How much fertilizer of each type should be produced this month?

9   The Moon Oil Corporation markets three grades of gasoline: Quosi-flit, Flit, and Super-flit.   All of their sales are made to an intermediary company which distributes the three grades of gasoline to service stations.   Deliveries are made daily to the distributor in Moon's one delivery truck.   Since the driving and delivery take about an hour to complete, the truck is able to make eight deliveries a day. It holds up to 1,000 gal but can deliver only one grade at a time.   It cost $2,141.60 three years ago, and company officials estimate it will last about seven more years. Delivery costs are as follows: the driver is paid $100 per week; gas, oil, repairs, etc., cost about $3 per trip.   Quosi-flit is an 80-octane gasoline made by mixing equal parts of zip and sludge.   Super-flit is 100 octane and is made completely out of zip.   Flit is a rather exciting gasoline for the user.   It has a mysterious quality. This is explained, perhaps, by the formula which states that it must be at least 85 octane.   It also uses the two ingredients, zip and sludge.   Sludge costs the company 50 cents for each 5 gal, and zip costs $1.80 for 10 gal.   Selling prices for the three gases are as follows:

	Less than 5,000 gal	5,000–10,000 gal	Over 10,000 gal
Quosi-flit	$.25 per gal	$.23 per gal	$.22 per gal
Flit	.29 per gal	.27 per gal	.26 per gal
Super-flit	.35 per gal	.33 per gal	.32 per gal

Sludge is available in quantities of 30,000 gal per week and zip is available in quantities of 35,000 gal per week. The company knows from experience that no more than 20,000 gal of any one gasoline should be marketed and that no one gasoline should make up more than half of the total market.

Set up as few initial tableaus as possible in order to determine the maximum profit solution to this problem.

10   Last month the Collier Company sold 5,000 units of A and 4,000 units of B (net); 2,000 direct labor hours were expended on A and 3,000 on B.

The company has been unable to maintain any inventory of either finished product. The sales manager estimates that in the foreseeable future, all items which can be manufactured of either product can be sold. Workers are able to shift between the two products. It isn't feasible to hire any additional labor for the plant, however. Raw material for product B is difficult to obtain presently, and it is estimated that only enough for 3,000 units will be available next month. How

Collier Company Income Statement for the Month Ended January 31, 1965

	Product	Product
Sales	$30,500	$40,800
Less: Returns and allowances	$ 300	$ 1,000
Discounts	500	800
	$ 800	$ 1,800
Net sales	$29,700	$39,000
Raw material inventory, January 1, 1965 (FIFO)	$ 2,000	$ 3,000
Purchases	18,000	10,000
Less: Purchase returns and allowances	(2,500)	
Purchase discounts	(1,000)	(500)
	$16,500	$12,500
Raw material inventory, January 31, 1965 (FIFO)	8,500	
Raw material cost	$ 8,000	$12,500
Direct labor	3,000	5,000
Indirect labor (based on direct labor hours)	200	300
Depreciation—machinery (based on direct labor hours)	2,000	3,000
Depreciation—building (based on # of units sold)	5,000	4,000
Insurance (based on per unit sales price of product)	300	500
Taxes (based on per unit sales price of product)	600	1,000
Utilities (based on direct labor hours)	200	300
Cost of sales	$19,300	$26,600
Gross profit	$10,400	$12,400
General and administrative expenses—variable	$ 2,500	$ 4,000
General and administrative expenses—fixed	429	571
Commissions	2,970	5,850
Advertising	1,000	
Total operating expenses	$ 6,899	$10,421
Income from operations	$ 3,501	$ 1,979
Income taxes	1,050	594
Net income from operations	$ 2,451	$ 1,385

many units of product A and B would you recommend that the company manufacture next month?   Prepare a projected income statement.

11   A blender of whiskey imports three grades, A, B, and C.   He mixes them according to recipes which specify the maximum or minimum percentages of grades A and C in each blend.

Specification of Blends

Blend	Specification	Price per fifth
Blue Dot	Not less than 60% of A Not more than 20% of C	$6.80
Highland Fling	Not more than 60% of C Not less than 15% of A	5.70
Old Frenzy	Not more than 50% of C	4.50

Supplies of the three basic whiskeys together with their costs are shown in the following table.

Availability and Cost of Ingredients

Whiskey	Maximum quantity available, fifths per day	Cost per fifth
A	2,000	$7.50
B	2,500	5.00
C	1,200	4.00

Set up the objective function and constraints necessary to obtain the production policy that will maximize profits.

12   A plant makes two products, A and B, which are routed through four processing centers, 1, 2, 3, 4, as shown by the solid lines in the figure below.   If there is spare capacity in center 3, it is possible to route product A through 3 instead of going through 2 twice, but this is more expensive.

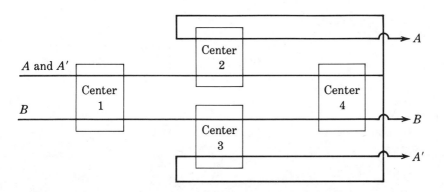

Given the information in the table below, how should production be scheduled to maximize profits?

Product	Center	Input, gal per hour	Percent recovery	Running cost per hour
	1	300	90	$150
	2(1st pass)	450	95	200
A	4	250	85	180
	2(2d pass)	400	80	220
	3	350	75	250
	1	500	90	300
B	3	480	85	250
	4	400	80	240

Product	Raw material, cost per gal	Sales price per finished gal	Maximum daily sales, gal of finished goods
A	$5	$20	1,700
B	6	18	1,500

13 The Zeus Company manufactures a deluxe and a standard model. All production is to stock rather than to customer order.

At the present time a seller's market exists for the company's products. Although the Zeus Company has made no attempt to charge prices other than those that they have charged for several years, they are concerned with the profitability of their product mix. The profit contribution of the deluxe model is $3.00 per unit and that of the standard model is $1.00 per unit.

The manufacture of the product is relatively simple. Both models require a machining operation, and the deluxe model requires an additional painting operation. The same machines are used for machining either model. Since all units are placed in inventory before being sold, warehouse capacity as well as equipment capacities must be considered in making product mix decisions.

The technical requirements and restrictions, on a monthly basis, are as follows:

Resource Requirements

	Machining, machine-hours per piece	Warehousing, sq ft per piece	Painting, man-hours per piece
Standard	2	4	0
Deluxe	3	3	1
Total capacities available	24,000	36,000	6,000

Solve using the simplex method.

14 The Party Nut Company has on hand 550 lb of peanuts, 150 lb of cashew nuts, 50 lb of brazil nuts, and 70 lb of hazel nuts. It packages and sells nuts in the following varieties of standard 8-oz cans and at the indicated net wholesale price: Party Peanuts, 26 cents per can; Party Mix, consisting of 50 percent peanuts, 20 percent cashew nuts, 15 percent brazil nuts, and 15 percent hazel nuts, at 38 cents per can; Cashew Nuts (only) at 51 cents per can; and Luxury Mix, consisting of 40 percent cashew nuts, 25 percent brazil nuts, and 35 percent hazel nuts, at 54 cents per can. The company desires to mix these nuts in a way which will yield maximum revenue. Set up the initial simplex tableau.

15 The Wild Horses Oil Company makes three brands of gasoline: Man o'War, Trigger, and Swayback. Wild Horses makes its products by blending two grades of gasoline, each with a different octane rating. Each brand of gas must have an octane rating greater than a predetermined minimum. In gasoline blending, final octane rating is linearly proportional to component octanes (i.e., a blend of 50 percent 100-octane and 50 percent 200-octane gasoline is 150 octane). The other relevant data are given in Tables 1 and 2. There is no limit on the amount of each gasoline that may be sold.

Table 1

Blending component	Octane	Cost per gallon	Supply per week, gal
A	200	\$.10	20,000
B	130	.08	10,000

Table 2

Brand	Minimum octane	Sales price per gallon
Man o'War	180	\$.24
Trigger	160	.21
Swayback	140	.12

Set up the initial simplex tableau.

16 The Suez Company sells three products, which we shall call A, B, and C. Not only are these products sold separately, but, in addition, certain gift packs are available. Gift pack 1 contains 1 A, 2 B's, and 1 C. Gift pack 2 contains 1 B and 1 C. Gift pack 3 contains 2 A's and 1 C. A's and B's come to the company monthly in a boxcar. The car can hold twice as many B's as A's. If the car was filled so that half of the space in the car was devoted to A's and the other half to B's, 750 units could be accommodated. The boxcar delivery costs \$912.00. C's are delivered by a truck that holds 100. The trucks can make any number of deliveries at a cost of \$40 per delivery made. The supply of A's is limited to 1,400 per month, B's to 800, and C's to 900. Three hundred type 3 gift packs are on standing order for next month. The firm feels that at least twice as many A's should be made as the number of C's. A's are purchased for \$50, B's for \$30, and C's for \$40 (all FOB shipping point). Packages for A cost \$2, for B \$4, and for C \$3.50. Gift package 1 costs \$14, pack 2 costs \$12, and pack 3 costs \$8. Advertising costs are presently being incurred to keep demand at the supply level. The firm believes that the likely relationship of advertising cost to demand is as shown for each product:

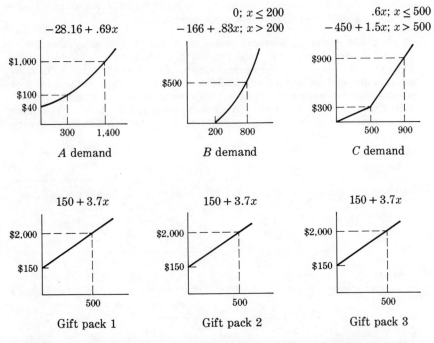

$-28.16 + .69x$

A demand

$\begin{matrix} 0; & x \le 200 \\ -166 + .83x; & x > 200 \end{matrix}$

B demand

$\begin{matrix} .6x; & x \le 500 \\ -450 + 1.5x; & x > 500 \end{matrix}$

C demand

$150 + 3.7x$

Gift pack 1

$150 + 3.7x$

Gift pack 2

$150 + 3.7x$

Gift pack 3

The above formulas represent the closest approximation of linearity which the company believes can be tolerated. Present sales prices are as follows:

$$A—\$60 \qquad 1—\$195$$
$$B—\$40 \qquad 2—\$120$$
$$C—\$50 \qquad 3—\$190$$

With the objective of profit maximization, build as many simplex tableaus as you believe will be necessary to solve this problem and explain how you will select the proper one to go by.

5 GAME THEORY

INTRODUCTION

Game theory is the general title for a body of knowledge which has recently evolved concerning the determination of optimal strategies or courses of action in competitive situations.

ONE-PERSON GAMES AGAINST NATURE

Any game in which the player is competing against a disinterested or impartial party such as nature is defined as a *one-person game*. The main distinguishing characteristic of a game of this type is that the response to any action is in no way connected with the action itself. Thus nature does not choose good or poor weather on the basis of which crop a farmer plants.

One-person games are similar to conditional-value situations where a firm is deciding between several alternative strategies. The difference is that no probability can be assigned to the likelihood of one event or another. Thus, expected value cannot be determined. Several methods are available for determining strategies in this type of situation.

Maximax: the criterion of optimism

If the player feels optimistic, that is, if he feels that whatever he decides to do, nature will be good to him and will provide the best possible response, he may use the maximax rule. Maximax is a short way of writing "Maximize the maximums." If the payoffs for the strategies, or conditional values, are listed in rows, he will compare the maximum values of each of the rows and will select that row, or strategy, which provides the largest maximum. Thus, he will be selecting the strategy which has the possibility of providing the highest payoff.

EXAMPLE 5.1

A player has three possible strategies: S_1, S_2, and S_3. The conditional values associated with these strategies and each of the two possible events which could occur are

	E_1	E_2
S_1	-8	10
S_2	3	15
S_3	24	-800

Which strategy should the player select under the criterion of optimism?
   Note that the three maximums are

$$S_1 = 10$$
$$S_2 = 15$$
$$S_3 = 24$$

The largest of these is $S_3 = 24$. Therefore, S_3 should be selected if maximax is to be employed.

EXAMPLE 5.2

The costs connected with each of the corresponding strategies and events for a given situation are

	E_1	E_2	E_3	E_4
S_1	15	-2	25	3
S_2	8	3	12	2
S_3	22	35	10	-15

Select the maximax strategy.
   Notice that this table represents costs rather than values. Therefore, an optimistic strategy would involve selection of the lowest number rather than the highest. The lowest numbers, by rows, are

$$S_1 = -2$$
$$S_2 = 2$$
$$S_3 = -15$$

Since -15 is the lowest cost, S_3 will be the maximax choice.

Maximin: the criterion of pessimism

Assume, now, that the player is in a pessimistic frame of mind.   For example, he suspects that whatever course of action he follows, the worst possible event will take place.   The strategy which answers this type of outlook is known as maximin, an abbreviation for "Maximize the minimums."   The procedure to follow is to locate the minimum conditional value for each strategy, and to select that strategy for which this minimum is highest, or least low.

EXAMPLE 5.3

For the following payoff matrix, find the maximin strategy:

	E_1	E_2
S_1	-8	10
S_2	3	15
S_3	24	-800

Note that the minimum payoffs, by strategy are

$$S_1 = -8$$
$$S_2 = 3$$
$$S_3 = -800$$

The maximum minimum is 3; therefore, S_2 will provide the maximin solution.

EXAMPLE 5.4

For the following cost matrix, find the maximin strategy:

	E_1	E_2	E_3	E_4
S_1	15	-2	25	3
S_2	8	3	12	2
S_3	22	35	10	-15

Since these are costs, we are interested in isolating the highest possible costs. Thus,

$$S_1 = 25$$
$$S_2 = 12$$
$$S_3 = 35$$

Note that 12 is the least objectionable loss.   Therefore, the maximin strategy is S_2.

Another way to approach cost matrices is to multiply the matrix by -1, converting it, thereby, into a payoff matrix.   Then the standard procedure of finding the smallest minimum will apply.

Minimax: the criterion of regret

The objective of a minimax strategy is to minimize regret. *Regret* is defined as the difference between the conditional values of the best strategy which could have been chosen for a given event and the strategy actually chosen. The first step in the determination of a minimax strategy is the determination of a regret matrix. A payoff matrix is converted to a regret matrix by the following steps:

1 For the column representing the first *event*, select the maximum payoff. In the regret matrix this position is assigned the value zero.
2 Each other entry in the column representing this event is assigned the value representing the positive difference between its payoff and the maximum payoff for the column.
3 These steps are repeated for each remaining column.

Note that each column will have a zero entry and that all entries in a column will be greater than or equal to zero. The minimax can be determined by selecting the strategy that will minimize the maximum regret. Thus, the largest number in each row (each strategy) is examined and the strategy is selected for which that value is a minimum.

EXAMPLE 5.5

Find the minimax strategy for the following payoff matrix:

	E_1	E_2	
S_1	-8	10	
S_2	3	15	Payoff
S_3	24	-800	

If event 1 did occur, the strategy the player would most likely have selected is S_3, since the payoff is the largest possible for event 1. Thus, the regret matrix has a zero regret listed for E_1S_3. The regret for the other two strategies is determined for event 1 by subtracting their payoffs from the best payoff, 24. A similar procedure is followed to find the regret column for event 2. The regret matrix for this problem, then, is

	E_1	E_2	
S_1	32	5	
S_2	21	0	Regret
S_3	0	815	

The maximum regret for each strategy is

$$S_1 = 32$$
$$S_2 = 21$$
$$S_3 = 815$$

The selection of strategy S_2 minimizes the maximum regret.

EXAMPLE 5.6

Find the minimax strategy for the following cost matrix:

	E_1	E_2	E_3	E_4	
S_1	15	-2	25	3	
S_2	8	3	12	2	Cost
S_3	22	35	10	-15	

Either of two approaches may be followed in this problem. The matrix may be multiplied by -1 and then treated precisely as the matrix in Example 5.5. The other alternative is to select the smallest number in a column as the zero entry and subtract it from all other numbers in the column. Note that the smallest number in terms of costs produces minimum regret just as does the largest number in terms of payoffs. The latter method will be demonstrated.

The smallest number (zero regret) for each event is

$$E_1 = 8$$
$$E_2 = -2$$
$$E_3 = 10$$
$$E_4 = -15$$

and the regret matrix is given by

	E_1	E_2	E_3	E_4
S_1	7	0	15	18
S_2	0	5	2	17
S_3	14	37	0	0

The maximum regret for each strategy is

$$S_1 = 18$$
$$S_2 = 17$$
$$S_3 = 37$$

Minimizing the maximum regret, we will select S_2 as the solution.

The criterion of rationality

The reader will notice that each of the three previous methods for selecting strategies in one-person games depended on a particular number in each row. With maximax, we selected the strategy with the largest maximum, even if this strategy had an enormous negative payoff connected with another possible event. Maximin, where we selected the least objectionable of the minimums, might bypass a strategy with an enormous possible positive payoff. When minimax is utilized, an enormous payoff might be forsaken in the course of minimizing regret.

The criterion of rationality considers all possible events for each strategy and is thus influenced by highs and lows rather than just one or the other. The procedure is similar to that used for determining expected value in those cases where probabilities are known. Since in games against nature probabilities for events are unknown, the assumption is made that each event is equally probable. Then, accepting this assumption, the expected value for each strategy is determined. The strategy with the highest expected value is selected.

EXAMPLE 5.7

For the following payoff matrix, find the optimal strategy using the criterion of rationality:

	E_1	E_2
S_1	-8	10
S_2	3	15
S_3	24	-800

Since there are two possible events, each of which must be assigned an equal probability,

$$P(E_1) = \tfrac{1}{2}$$
$$P(E_2) = \tfrac{1}{2}$$

then

$$E(S_1) = \tfrac{1}{2}(-8) + \tfrac{1}{2}(10) = -4 + 5 = 1$$
$$E(S_2) = \tfrac{1}{2}(3) + \tfrac{1}{2}(15) = 1.5 + 7.5 = 9$$
$$E(S_3) = \tfrac{1}{2}(24) + \tfrac{1}{2}(-800) = 12 - 400 = -388$$

Strategy 2 will be selected, since it has the highest expected value.

EXAMPLE 5.8

Select the optimal strategy using the criterion of rationality for the *cost* matrix illustrated:

	E_1	E_2	E_3	E_4
S_1	15	-2	25	3
S_2	8	3	12	2
S_3	22	25	10	-15

Since there are four possible events, each must be assigned the probability $\frac{1}{4}$. Thus,

$$E(S_1) = \tfrac{1}{4}(15) + \tfrac{1}{4}(-2) + \tfrac{1}{4}(25) + \tfrac{1}{4}(3)$$
$$= \tfrac{15}{4} - \tfrac{2}{4} + \tfrac{25}{4} + \tfrac{3}{4} = \tfrac{41}{4}$$
$$E(S_2) = \tfrac{1}{4}(8) + \tfrac{1}{4}(3) + \tfrac{1}{4}(12) + \tfrac{1}{4}(2)$$
$$= \tfrac{8}{4} + \tfrac{3}{4} + \tfrac{12}{4} + \tfrac{2}{4} = \tfrac{25}{4}$$
$$E(S_3) = \tfrac{1}{4}(22) + \tfrac{1}{4}(25) + \tfrac{1}{4}(10) + \tfrac{1}{4}(-15)$$
$$= \tfrac{22}{4} + \tfrac{25}{4} + \tfrac{10}{4} - \tfrac{15}{4} = \tfrac{42}{4}$$

Strategy 2 has the lowest expected *cost* and will be selected.

TWO-PERSON GAMES

Two-person games are games or competitive situations between two active, interested players. The basic assumption underlying two-person games is that each player will act rationally in his best interests. This is the point of contrast between one- and two-person games. Nature reacts unpredictably, while a competitor tries to maximize his own gain.

Zero-sum versus nonzero-sum games

A game can be classified as either zero-sum or nonzero-sum. It is zero-sum if whatever amount A wins, B loses, or conversely, whatever amount B wins, A loses. A nonzero-sum game is one where this condition does not hold. In a nonzero-sum game, for example, both A and B may win simultaneously, or lose simultaneously, or one may win one amount, while the other loses a different amount.

EXAMPLE 5.9 (A zero-sum game)

	B_1	B_2			B_1	B_2
A_1	5	8		A_1	-5	-8
A_2	-2	3		A_2	2	-3
	Payoffs to A				Payoffs to B	

Note that B loses the same amount that A wins for each possible outcome. One matrix is generally used to portray zero-sum games. The numbers represent payoffs to A. The payoffs to B are equal to -1 times the matrix. Thus, the game above would be shown as

	B_1	B_2
A_1	5	8
A_2	-2	3

where $A_1B_1 = 5$ means A wins 5 and B loses 5 if each play strategy 1.

EXAMPLE 5.10 (*A nonzero-sum game*)

	B_1	B_2
A_1	4	−3
A_2	7	5

Payoffs to A

	B_1	B_2
A_1	4	−8
A_2	−3	−10

Payoffs to B

Nonzero-sum games are usually portrayed with separate payoff matrices for each player.

Strictly determined zero-sum 2 × 2 games

Unlike the one-person game, two-person zero-sum games do not present a choice of optimal solutions. The maximin criterion is always best if the same number is the maximin for both players. A game for which the maximins coincide is called a *strictly determined game,* and the number which is the common maximin is known as the *saddle point* of the game. The optimal strategy for each player is the one which includes the saddle point.

EXAMPLE 5.11

Find the optimal strategy for each player:

	B_1	B_2
A_1	5	7
A_2	3	2

Payoffs to A

	B_1	B_2
A_1	−5	−7
A_2	−3	−2

Payoffs to B

This game possesses a saddle point, since each player has a maximin at A_1B_1. Therefore, the optimal strategy for A is A_1, and the optimal strategy for B is B_1, since these strategies include the saddlepoint.

This game could have been solved without the use of a second matrix. Since the game is zero sum, it could have been portrayed simply as

	B_1	B_2
A_1	5	7
A_2	3	2

The maximin for A would be $A_1B_1 = 5$ as before. To find the maximin for B, remember that from B's point of view this is a cost matrix rather than a payoff matrix. Therefore, a minimum as far as B is concerned is the largest number in the matrix, and the maximum minimum is the smallest of the group of "largest" numbers. In terms of procedures, if we look for the minimax for B using the matrix portraying payoffs to A, we shall find the same number as by converting the matrix to a payoff matrix for B and finding the maximin. For example, to find B's minimax for

	B_1	B_2
A_1	5	7
A_2	3	2

we note that the maximum for column B_1 is 5 and B_2 is 7.   The minimum maximum is 5, which is the same position we determined using a separate payoff matrix for B.

Value of a strictly determined game

The value of a strictly determined game is the saddle-point number. This means that if A plays his best strategy, he can expect on the average to win the value of the game each time the game is played, assuming B plays his best strategy. If B plays any strategy other than his best, A will win more than the value of the game. Likewise, if A and B each play their best strategies, B can expect, on the average, to lose the value of the game each time it is played. Any move on the part of A away from the optimum strategy will result in B's losing less than the value of the game.

EXAMPLE 5.12

Using the game from Example 5.11, determine its value.   The game was

	B_1	B_2
A_1	5	7
A_2	3	2

where 5 is the saddle point.   Thus, $V = 5$.   If A plays A_1, the best that B can do is play B_1, which provides A with 5 each time the game is played.   If B were to play B_2, A would win 7 rather than 5.   Using the same reasoning, if B plays B_1, and A plays A_1, B will lose 5.   If A switches to A_2, B will lose only 3.   Thus, each player is motivated to play the optimal strategy, and the game is likely to pay A 5 each time it is played.

Nonstrictly determined games

A game is nonstrictly determined if it has no saddle point, that is, if A's maximin and B's maximin do not coincide.   The optimal strategy for a strictly determined game is called a *pure strategy*.   A pure strategy is one in which a player is to play one strategy all the time.   Thus, in the previous example, the optimal strategy for A was A_1 all the time, and the optimal strategy for B was B_1 all the time.   For a nonstrictly determined game, the optimal strategy for each player will be a *mixed strategy*. This means that the best strategy will be to play one strategy part of the time and the other strategy part of the time. Usually, a mixed strategy is written in vector form as a row vector for A and a column vector for B. The first component in either case is a number between 0 and 1 representing the percentage of the time which strategy 1 should be played. The second component represents the percentage of time which strategy 2 should be played. The sum of all the components of a strategy vector must equal 1.

If we define a, b, c, and d as

	B_1	B_2
A_1	a	b
A_2	c	d

$$A^0 = (p_1^0, p_2^0) = \text{strategy vector for } A$$
$$B^0 = (q_1^0, q_2^0) = \text{strategy vector for } B$$
$$V = \text{value of game}$$

then
$$p_1^0 = \frac{d - c}{a + d - b - c}, \qquad p_2^0 = \frac{a - b}{a + d - b - c}$$
$$q_1^0 = \frac{d - b}{a + d - b - c}, \qquad q_2^0 = \frac{a - c}{a + d - b - c}$$
$$V = \frac{ad - bc}{a + d - b - c}$$

EXAMPLE 5.13

The outcomes for a zero-sum game are

	B_1	B_2
A_1	10	3
A_2	4	15

Find the optimal strategies for A and B and the value of the game. First we note that the maximin for A is $A_2 B_1 = 4$ and the maximin for B is $A_1 B_1 = 10$. Therefore, this game is nonstrictly determined and has no saddle point. To find the optimal mixed strategy for A, that is, $A^0 = (p_1^0, p_2^0)$, we solve

$$p_1^0 = \frac{d - c}{a + d - b - c} \qquad p_2^0 = \frac{a - b}{a + d - b - c}$$
$$p_1^0 = \frac{15 - 4}{10 + 15 - 3 - 4} = \frac{11}{18} = .61$$
$$p_2^0 = \frac{10 - 3}{10 + 15 - 3 - 4} = \frac{7}{18} = .39$$

Thus, the optimal strategy for A is $A^0 = (.61, .39)$ which means that A should play A_1 61 percent of the time and A_2 39 percent of the time.

For B, we must find

$$B^0 = \begin{pmatrix} q_1^0 \\ q_2^0 \end{pmatrix}$$

$$q_1^0 = \frac{d - b}{a + d - b - c} \qquad q_2^0 = \frac{a - c}{a + d - b - c}$$

$$q_1^0 = \frac{15 - 3}{10 + 15 - 3 - 4} = \frac{12}{18} = .67$$

$$q_2^0 = \frac{10 - 4}{10 + 15 - 3 - 4} = \frac{6}{18} = .33$$

The optimal strategy for B, then, is $B^0 = \begin{pmatrix} .67 \\ .33 \end{pmatrix}$, which means that B should follow B_1 67 percent of the time and B_2 33 percent of the time.

The value of the game is

$$V = \frac{ad - bc}{a + d - b - c}$$

$$= \frac{(10)(15) - (3)(4)}{10 + 15 - 3 - 4} = \frac{150 - 12}{18} = \frac{138}{18} = 7.67$$

This means that in the long run, if each player uses his optimal mixed strategy, A will win an average of 7.67 each time the game is played and B will lose the same amount. Failure on the part of either player to utilize his optimal strategy will result in a less-advantageous value for that player.

Playing mixed strategies

An important precaution when playing mixed strategies is to make certain that the opponent is unable to see a pattern in the selection of the strategy for each play. If a pattern is discernible and the opponent can predict each move, he will be able to use this knowledge and to plan his own moves more advantageously. Thus, the preceding game has a value of 7.67, but if B were to know when A would play A_1, he would counter with B_2 and lose only 3. In addition, if B knew when A were going to play A_2, he would counter with B_1 and lose only 4. As can be seen, the value of the game is thereby reduced much below 7.67.

The best way to assume that the opponent will not find a player's pattern is to find a way to avoid any pattern. For example, if A's strategy vector were $A^0 = (.5, .5)$, A should not play A_1, then A_2, etc. One way for A to avoid a pattern is to flip a coin. Heads means play A_1; tails means play A_2. This will result in A_1 and A_2 being played about the same number of times in the long run but will not produce any pattern from play to play.

Another way of keeping a pattern from appearing is to use a random-number table. Random numbers follow no pattern or sequence. Every number, however, has an equal probability of appearing in any given position. Thus, for a column of random numbers, each of the digits 0 through 9 is equally likely to appear in a given place in the column. Assign 5 of these digits, say 0 through 4, to "play strategy A_1" and the other 5, 5 through 9, to "play strategy A_2." Then, for A's first move, he will look at the first number in the table and select A_1 if the number is 0, 1, 2, 3, or 4. If the number is 5, 6, 7, 8, or 9, he will select strategy A_2. For the second move he will look at the second number in the table and play accordingly. In the long run he will play A_1 about half the time, but no pattern will be discernible

EXAMPLE 5.14

If the optimal strategy vector for A is $A^0 = (.67, .33)$, how should A play this strategy?

Using two columns of a random-number table, let us assign the numbers 00 through 66 as "play A_1" and 67 through 99 as "play A_2." Note that 67 of the 100 possible numbers are, in this way, assigned to A_1; and A_1 will thus be played about 67 percent of the time. Using the random-number table in Appendix A, we can show the first 20 plays as

Random number	Play	Random number	Play
62	A_1	62	A_1
32	A_1	24	A_1
53	A_1	08	A_1
15	A_1	38	A_1
90	A_2	88	A_2
78	A_2	74	A_2
67	A_2	47	A_1
75	A_2	00	A_1
38	A_1	49	A_1
62	A_1	49	A_1

Note that in these 20 plays, A_2 has been played 6 times, or 30 percent of the time, which is close to 33 percent, but there is no pattern.

$m \times n$ **games: dominance**

If more than two strategies are available to one or both players, the game will require a matrix of a higher order than 2×2 for its portrayal. Such a game, usually referred to as an $m \times n$ game, is strictly determined and is solved exactly as a 2×2 strictly determined game if it has a saddle point. If no saddle point is present, the next step should be to eliminate rows and columns which are unnecessary for the solution of the game. Hopefully, this will reduce the game to a 2×2 case.

A row or column may be eliminated if it is dominated by another row or column. A row dominates another row if each element in the row is as large or larger than the corresponding element in the other row. A column dominates another column if each element in the column is as small or smaller than the corresponding element in the other column.

If enough rows and/or columns can be eliminated to reduce the game to a 2×2 case, then the method used in the preceding section can be applied. The final strategy vector, however, must have as many elements as the player has strategies available (before elimination). Each strategy eliminated is assigned a zero in the final strategy vector.

EXAMPLE 5.15

Find the optimal strategies for A and B and the value of the game:

	B_1	B_2	B_3
A_1	5	4	15
A_2	7	6	9
A_3	2	4	10

First check for a saddle point. The maximin for A is $A_2B_2 = 6$ and for B is $A_2B_2 = 6$. Therefore, A_2B_2 is a saddle point, and the optimum strategies are

$$A^0 = (0, 1, 0) \qquad B^0 = \begin{pmatrix} 0 \\ 1 \\ 0 \end{pmatrix}$$

The value of the game is 6.

EXAMPLE 5.16

Find the optimal strategies for A and B and the value of the game:

	B_1	B_2	B_3
A_1	3	7	10
A_2	2	5	8
A_3	14	4	5

First, checking for a saddle point, we find the maximin for A is $A_3B_2 = 4$ and for B is $A_1B_2 = 7$. Therefore, no saddle point exists.

We can eliminate column 3, since it is dominated by column 2. Also, row 1 dominates row 2, so row 2 can be eliminated:

	B_1	B_2	B_3
A_1	3	7	10
A_2	2	5	8
A_3	14	4	5

$=$

	B_1	B_2
A_1	3	7
A_3	14	4

The game is now 2×2 and can be solved as a nonstrictly determined game:

$$p_1{}^0 = \frac{4 - 14}{3 + 4 - 7 - 14} = \frac{-10}{-14} = .71$$

$$p_3{}^0 = \frac{3 - 7}{3 + 4 - 7 - 14} = \frac{-4}{-14} = .29$$

Thus, $A^0 = (.71, 0, .29)$, and

$$q_1{}^0 = \frac{4 - 7}{3 + 4 - 7 - 14} = \frac{-3}{-14} = .21$$

$$q_2{}^0 = \frac{3 - 14}{3 + 4 - 7 - 14} = \frac{-11}{-14} = .79$$

Thus,

$$B^0 = \begin{pmatrix} .21 \\ .79 \\ 0 \end{pmatrix}$$

The value of the game is

$$V = \frac{3(4) - 7(14)}{3 + 4 - 7 - 14} = \frac{12 - 98}{-14} = \frac{-86}{-14} = 6.14$$

$m \times n$ games: simplex solutions

If a game is two-person zero-sum and cannot be reduced to the 2×2 form, the simplex method can be used to find an optimal strategy for the game. Let

A = an $m \times n$ payoff matrix for the game from A's point of view
b = an n-component row vector composed entirely of 1's
c = an m-component column vector composed entirely of 1's

If any components of A are negative, add 1 plus the most negative component to every element in the matrix. Let k = the most negative element $+ 1$, and let A_k be the revised matrix.

Then, the initial tableau is

$B_1 B_2 \cdots B_n$

A_k	I	c
$-b$	0	0

The tableau is operated exactly as in linear programming problems, until all indicators are non-negative. The final tableau will be in form

as follows

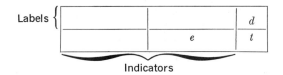

Labels

		d
	e	t

Indicators

A's optimal strategy is $A^0 = \dfrac{1}{t}\,(e)$.

B's optimal strategy is $B^0 = \dfrac{1}{t}\,(d)$.

Value of game is $V = \dfrac{1}{t} - k$.

Note that the components of B's strategy must be put in order according to the labels appearing to the left of the final tableau. A's strategy appears in the final tableau in proper sequence.

EXAMPLE 5.17

Solve the following game:

	B_1	B_2	B_3
A_1	2	7	3
A_2	1	9	10
A_3	5	4	6

The initial tableau is

B_1	B_2	B_3				
2	7	3	1	0	0	1
1	9	10	0	1	0	1
5	4	6	0	0	1	1
-1	-1	-1	0	0	0	0

Selecting any negative indicator, say the -1 in column B_1, we note that $A_3 B_1 = 5$ produces the smallest quotient $\frac{1}{5}$ and is, therefore, the pivot number:

B_1	B_2	B_3				
0	$\frac{27}{5}$	$\frac{3}{5}$	1	0	$-\frac{2}{5}$	$\frac{3}{5}$
0	$\frac{41}{5}$	$\frac{44}{5}$	0	1	$-\frac{1}{5}$	$\frac{4}{5}$
1	$\frac{4}{5}$	$\frac{6}{5}$	0	0	$\frac{1}{5}$	$\frac{1}{5}$
0	$-\frac{1}{5}$	$\frac{1}{5}$	0	0	$\frac{1}{5}$	$\frac{1}{5}$

Row 3, then, is set up in the new tableau, as $\frac{1}{5}(5, 4, 6, 0, 0, 1, 1)$.
Row 1 is

$$-2(1, \tfrac{4}{5}, \tfrac{6}{5}, 0, 0, \tfrac{1}{5}, \tfrac{1}{5}) + (2, 7, 3, 1, 0, 0, 1) = (0, \tfrac{27}{5}, \tfrac{3}{5}, 1, 0, \tfrac{2}{5}, \tfrac{3}{5})$$

Row 2 is

$$-1(1, \tfrac{4}{5}, \tfrac{6}{5}, 0, 0, \tfrac{1}{5}, \tfrac{1}{5}) + (1, 9, 10, 0, 1, 0, 1) = (0, \tfrac{41}{5}, \tfrac{44}{5}, 0, 1, -\tfrac{1}{5}, \tfrac{4}{5})$$

Row 4 is

$$-(-1)(1, \tfrac{4}{5}, \tfrac{6}{5}, 0, 0, \tfrac{1}{5}, \tfrac{1}{5}) + (-1, -1, -1, 0, 0, 0, 0) = (0, -\tfrac{1}{5}, \tfrac{1}{5}, 0, 0, \tfrac{1}{5}, \tfrac{1}{5})$$

Repeating the process, we note that column B_2 has a negative indicator. $A_2 B_2$ provides the smallest quotient and is, therefore, the pivot number. The rows are computed as follows:
Row 2 is

$$\tfrac{5}{41}(0, \tfrac{41}{5}, \tfrac{44}{5}, 0, 1, -\tfrac{1}{5}, \tfrac{4}{5}) = (0, 1, \tfrac{44}{41}, 0, \tfrac{5}{41}, -\tfrac{1}{41}, \tfrac{4}{41})$$

Row 1 is

$$-\tfrac{27}{5}(0, 1, \tfrac{44}{41}, 0, \tfrac{5}{41}, -\tfrac{1}{41}, \tfrac{4}{41}) + (0, \tfrac{27}{5}, \tfrac{3}{5}, 1, 0, -\tfrac{2}{5}, \tfrac{3}{5})$$
$$= (0, 0, -\tfrac{213}{41}, 1, -\tfrac{27}{41}, -\tfrac{11}{41}, \tfrac{3}{41})$$

Row 3 is

$$-\tfrac{4}{5}(0, 1, \tfrac{44}{41}, 0, \tfrac{5}{41}, -\tfrac{1}{41}, \tfrac{4}{41}) + (1, \tfrac{4}{5}, \tfrac{6}{5}, 0, 0, \tfrac{1}{5}, \tfrac{1}{5}) = (1, 0, \tfrac{14}{41}, 0, -\tfrac{4}{41}, \tfrac{9}{41}, \tfrac{5}{41})$$

Row 4 is

$$-(-\tfrac{1}{5})(0, 1, \tfrac{44}{41}, 0, \tfrac{5}{41}, -\tfrac{1}{41}, \tfrac{4}{41}) + (0, -\tfrac{1}{5}, \tfrac{1}{5}, 0, 0, \tfrac{1}{5}, \tfrac{1}{5}) = (0, 0, \tfrac{17}{41}, 0, \tfrac{1}{41}, \tfrac{8}{41}, \tfrac{9}{41})$$

Thus, the tableau is

	0	0	$-\frac{213}{41}$	1	$-\frac{27}{41}$	$-\frac{11}{41}$	$\frac{3}{41}$
B_2	0	1	$\frac{44}{41}$	0	$\frac{5}{41}$	$-\frac{1}{41}$	$\frac{4}{41}$
B_1	1	0	$\frac{14}{41}$	0	$-\frac{4}{41}$	$\frac{9}{41}$	$\frac{5}{41}$
	0	0	$\frac{17}{41}$	0	$\frac{1}{41}$	$\frac{8}{41}$	$\frac{9}{41}$

Since all indicators are positive, this is the final solution. Then

$$A^0 = \tfrac{41}{9}(0, \tfrac{1}{41}, \tfrac{8}{41}) = (0, \tfrac{1}{9}, \tfrac{8}{9})$$

To determine B^0, note the labels which apply to the B strategies. The vector can be arranged as $\begin{pmatrix} \frac{5}{41} \\ \frac{4}{41} \\ 0 \end{pmatrix}$, and this can be multiplied by $\frac{41}{9}$. Thus

$$B^0 = \tfrac{41}{9}\begin{pmatrix} \frac{5}{41} \\ \frac{4}{41} \\ 0 \end{pmatrix} = \begin{pmatrix} \frac{5}{9} \\ \frac{4}{9} \\ 0 \end{pmatrix}$$

The value of the game is

$$V = \frac{1}{\frac{9}{41}} - 0 = \tfrac{41}{9}$$

EXAMPLE 5.18

Solve the following game:

	B_1	B_2	B_3
A_1	-1	2	4
A_2	0	1	-2
A_3	2	-2	3

First, note that negative numbers appear in the matrix. In order to make all entries positive, let $k = 2 + 1 = 3$, since -2 is the most negative entry. Next, add k to each element in the matrix:

$$A_k = \begin{pmatrix} 2 & 5 & 7 \\ 3 & 4 & 1 \\ 5 & 1 & 6 \end{pmatrix}$$

Now set up the initial tableau:

	B_1	B_2	B_3				
	2	5	7	1	0	0	1
	3	4	1	0	1	0	1
	5	1	6	0	0	1	1
	-1	-1	-1	0	0	0	0

Since all the indicators are equally negative, any one may be selected, and the example will arbitrarily select column 1. The 5 in this column produces the minimum quotient and, thus, is our pivot number. The second tableau is determined as follows:

Row 3 is

$$\tfrac{1}{5}(5, 1, 6, 0, 0, 1, 1) = (1, \tfrac{1}{5}, \tfrac{6}{5}, 0, 0, \tfrac{1}{5}, \tfrac{1}{5})$$

This row is given the column label of the pivot number B_1:

Row 1 is

$$-2(1, \tfrac{1}{5}, \tfrac{6}{5}, 0, 0, \tfrac{1}{5}, \tfrac{1}{5}) + (2, 5, 7, 1, 0, 0, 1) = (0, \tfrac{23}{5}, \tfrac{23}{5}, 1, 0, -\tfrac{2}{5}, \tfrac{3}{5})$$

Row 2 is

$$-3(1, \tfrac{1}{5}, \tfrac{6}{5}, 0, 0, \tfrac{1}{5}, \tfrac{1}{5}) + (3, 4, 1, 0, 1, 0, 1) = (0, \tfrac{17}{5}, -\tfrac{13}{5}, 0, 1, -\tfrac{3}{5}, \tfrac{2}{5})$$

Row 4 is

$$1(1, \tfrac{1}{5}, \tfrac{6}{5}, 0, 0, \tfrac{1}{5}, \tfrac{1}{5}) + (-1, -1, -1, 0, 0, 0, 0) = (0, -\tfrac{4}{5}, \tfrac{1}{5}, 0, 0, \tfrac{1}{5}, \tfrac{1}{5})$$

The second tableau can then be filled in:

	B_1	B_2	B_3				
	0	$\frac{23}{5}$	$\frac{23}{5}$	1	0	$-\frac{2}{5}$	$\frac{3}{5}$
	0	$\frac{17}{5}$	$-\frac{13}{5}$	0	1	$-\frac{3}{5}$	$\frac{2}{5}$
B_1	1	$\frac{1}{5}$	$\frac{6}{5}$	0	0	$\frac{1}{5}$	$\frac{1}{5}$
	0	$-\frac{4}{5}$	$\frac{1}{5}$	0	0	$\frac{1}{5}$	$\frac{1}{5}$

Since the indicator for column 2 is negative, this becomes the new pivot column. $\frac{17}{5}$ provides the minimum quotient and, therefore, is the pivot number. The rows in the third tableau can now be computed:
   Row 2 is

$$\tfrac{5}{17}(0, \tfrac{17}{5}, -\tfrac{13}{5}, 0, 1, -\tfrac{3}{5}, \tfrac{2}{5}) = (0, 1, -\tfrac{13}{17}, 0, \tfrac{5}{17}, -\tfrac{3}{17}, \tfrac{2}{17})$$

This row is given the label B_2.
   Row 1 is

$$-\tfrac{23}{5}(0, 1, -\tfrac{13}{17}, 0, \tfrac{5}{17}, -\tfrac{3}{17}, \tfrac{2}{17}) + (0, \tfrac{23}{5}, \tfrac{23}{5}, 1, 0, -\tfrac{2}{5}, \tfrac{3}{5})$$
$$= (0, 0, \tfrac{138}{17}, 1, -\tfrac{23}{17}, \tfrac{7}{17}, \tfrac{1}{17})$$

   Row 3 is

$$-\tfrac{1}{5}(0, 1, -\tfrac{13}{17}, 0, \tfrac{5}{17}, -\tfrac{3}{17}, \tfrac{2}{17}) + (1, \tfrac{1}{5}, \tfrac{6}{5}, 0, 0, \tfrac{1}{5}, \tfrac{1}{5}) = (1, 0, \tfrac{23}{17}, 0, -\tfrac{1}{17}, \tfrac{4}{17}, \tfrac{3}{17})$$

   Row 4 is

$$\tfrac{4}{5}(0, 1, -\tfrac{13}{17}, 0, \tfrac{5}{17}, -\tfrac{3}{17}, \tfrac{2}{17}) + (0, -\tfrac{4}{5}, \tfrac{1}{5}, 0, 0, \tfrac{1}{5}, \tfrac{1}{5}) = (0, 0, -\tfrac{7}{17}, 0, \tfrac{4}{17}, \tfrac{1}{17}, \tfrac{5}{17})$$

The third tableau can then be filled in:

	B_1	B_2	B_3				
	0	0	$\frac{138}{17}$	1	$-\frac{23}{17}$	$\frac{7}{17}$	$\frac{1}{17}$
B_2	0	1	$-\frac{13}{17}$	0	$\frac{5}{17}$	$-\frac{3}{17}$	$\frac{2}{17}$
B_1	1	0	$\frac{23}{17}$	0	$-\frac{1}{17}$	$\frac{4}{17}$	$\frac{3}{17}$
	0	0	$-\frac{7}{17}$	0	$\frac{4}{17}$	$\frac{1}{17}$	$\frac{5}{17}$

The indicator for column 3 is now negative, and the process must be continued. Only positive values are considered for minimum quotient, and the smallest such value is given by $\frac{138}{17}$. This becomes the pivot number, and the computations for the fourth tableau may now be undertaken:
   Row 1 is

$$\tfrac{17}{138}(0, 0, \tfrac{138}{17}, 1, -\tfrac{23}{17}, \tfrac{7}{17}, \tfrac{1}{17}) = (0, 0, 1, \tfrac{17}{138}, -\tfrac{23}{138}, \tfrac{7}{138}, \tfrac{1}{138})$$

This row is given the pivot column label of B_3.
   Row 2 is

$$\tfrac{13}{17}(0, 0, \tfrac{17}{138}, 1, -\tfrac{23}{138}, \tfrac{7}{138}, \tfrac{1}{138}) + (0, 1, -\tfrac{13}{17}, 0, \tfrac{5}{17}, -\tfrac{3}{17}, \tfrac{2}{17})$$
$$= (0, 1, 0, \tfrac{13}{138}, \tfrac{23}{138}, -\tfrac{19}{138}, \tfrac{17}{138})$$

   Row 3 is

$$-\tfrac{23}{17}(0, 0, 1, \tfrac{17}{138}, -\tfrac{23}{138}, \tfrac{7}{138}, \tfrac{1}{138}) + (1, 0, \tfrac{23}{17}, 0, -\tfrac{1}{17}, \tfrac{4}{17}, \tfrac{3}{17})$$
$$= (1, 0, 0, -\tfrac{23}{138}, \tfrac{23}{138}, \tfrac{23}{138}, \tfrac{23}{138})$$

   Row 4 is

$$\tfrac{7}{17}, (0, 0, 1, \tfrac{17}{138}, -\tfrac{23}{138}, \tfrac{7}{138}, \tfrac{1}{138}) + (0, 0, -\tfrac{7}{17}, 0, \tfrac{4}{17}, \tfrac{1}{17}, \tfrac{5}{17})$$
$$= (0, 0, 0, \tfrac{7}{138}, \tfrac{23}{138}, \tfrac{11}{138}, \tfrac{41}{138})$$

The fourth tableau can now be written:

	B_1	B_2	B_3				
B_3	0	0	1	$\frac{17}{138}$	$-\frac{23}{138}$	$\frac{7}{138}$	$\frac{1}{138}$
B_2	0	1	0	$\frac{13}{138}$	$\frac{23}{138}$	$-\frac{19}{138}$	$\frac{17}{138}$
B_1	1	0	0	$-\frac{23}{138}$	$\frac{23}{138}$	$\frac{23}{138}$	$\frac{23}{138}$
	0	0	0	$\frac{7}{138}$	$\frac{23}{138}$	$\frac{11}{138}$	$\frac{41}{138}$

Since no negative indicators now remain, the process is finished:

$$A^0 = \frac{138}{41} \cdot \left(\frac{7}{138}, \frac{23}{138}, \frac{11}{138}\right) = \left(\frac{7}{41}, \frac{23}{41}, \frac{11}{41}\right)$$

$$B^0 = \frac{138}{41} \begin{pmatrix} \frac{23}{138} \\ \frac{17}{138} \\ \frac{1}{138} \end{pmatrix} = \begin{pmatrix} \frac{23}{41} \\ \frac{17}{41} \\ \frac{1}{41} \end{pmatrix}$$

$m \times n$ games: the iterative method

It will probably be found that the simplex method is exceptionally laborious and time-consuming. A method is available which will supply an approximate solution much more quickly and more easily.

The payoff matrix is placed in the upper left-hand corner of a piece of paper. First A arbitrarily selects a row and places it in the first row underneath the payoff matrix. B then examines the row A has chosen and selects the column corresponding to the position of the minimum number in the row. B then writes this column in the first position to the right of the matrix. A examines the column and selects the row corresponding to the largest number in B's column. He adds this to the row he has previously written down and places the result in the next row position. B examines this new row and selects the column corresponding to the smallest entry. B adds this to his previous column and places it in the next column position. This process is repeated a number of times, depending upon the time available. Then A circles the smallest number in each of his rows and B circles the largest number in each of his columns. If ties occur, some method should be used to make certain that each row or column containing the tie has an equal chance of being chosen, or if more than one tie occurs, that the allocations are spread among the rows or columns. The optimal strategy vector is determined by counting the number of circled entries in a row (or column) and dividing by the total number of circled entries in all rows (or columns). The value of the game can be approximated as being greater than the last circled value in the rows divided by the number of iterations and as being less than the last circled number in the columns divided by the number of iterations.

If closer bounds can be found by dividing any preceding circled numbers by the number of rows or columns up to and including the one selected, the closer approximation may be used as an indication of value.

EXAMPLE 5.19

Using 20 iterations, approximate the solution to the game:

	B_1	B_2	B_3
A_1	2	7	3
A_2	1	9	10
A_3	5	4	6

Note how similar the results in Figure 5.1 are to the simplex solution to this game.

EXAMPLE 5.20

Solve the following game by the iteration method using 20 iterations (see Figure 5.2):

	B_1	B_2	B_3
A_1	−1	2	4
A_2	0	1	−2
A_3	2	−2	3

N-PERSON AND NONZERO-SUM GAMES

The theory of games is much less developed when the number of players exceeds two or when the games are nonzero sum. Games within each of these two classifications can be differentiated as *cooperative* or *noncooperative*. The important difference is whether a player has access to the payoff matrices of other players.

If the game is noncooperative, that is, if each player is unaware of the opponent's payoff matrices, then the game is identical to a one-person game against nature. It is impossible to determine the probable moves of the competitors, and, therefore, the choice of strategy depends upon the criterion followed, i.e., optimism, pessimism, regret, or rationality.

If the game is cooperative, that is, if each player is aware of the payoff matrix of each competitor as well as his own, other problems arise. Principally, the major problems are:

1 More than one saddle point may exist.

2 Collusion may be practiced where two players agree on a particular strategy which will benefit them more than the saddle point.

Figure 5.1 (Iterative solution of Example 5.19)

	B																				A's strategy
	2	7	3	2†	4	6	8	10	17	24	31	38†	40	42	44	46	48	50	57	64	71	78	85	
A	1	9	10	(1)	2	3	4	5	14	23	32	(41)	42	43	44	45	46	47	56	65	74	83	(87)	(92)	91
	5	4	6	(5)	(10)	(15)	(20)	(25)	(29)	(33)	(37)	41§	(46)	(51)	(56)	(61)	(66)	(71)	(75)	(79)	(83)		

A's strategy: $\frac{0}{20}$, $\frac{2}{20}$, $\frac{18}{20}$

B's table (selected at random):

B		
2	7	3
(2)	3	3
(7)	7	(9)‡
(12)	11	15
(17)	15	21
(22)	19	27
27	23	(33)§
32	(27)	39
37	(31)	45
42	(35)	51
(43)	(39)	61
(48)	48	67
(53)	52	73
(58)	56	79
(63)	60	85
(68)	64	(91)§
73	(68)	97
78	(72)	103
83	(76)	109
88	(80)	115
93	(84)	121
	(88)	

B's strategy: $\frac{11}{20}$ $\frac{9}{20}$ $\frac{0}{20}$ $\qquad \frac{88}{20} < V < \frac{88}{20}$

† The column corresponding to the minimum number in A's selected row.

‡ The row corresponding to the maximum number in B's selected column plus the preceding row.

§ Since a tie occurs, either column (or row) may be selected.

Figure 5.1 Iterative solution of Example 5.19

101

Figure 5.2 Iterative solution of Example 5.20

Payoff matrix:

	B_1	B_2	B_3
A_1	-1	2	4
A_2	0	1	-2
A_3	2	-2	3

A's strategy: $\frac{7}{20}$, $\frac{8}{20}$, $\frac{5}{20}$

B's strategy: $\frac{12}{20}$, $\frac{8}{20}$, $\frac{0}{20}$

$$\frac{2}{20} \le V \le \frac{8}{20}$$

† Tie. Selection is arbitrary.

3 Side payments may be made between players in order to undertake strategies which are advantageous overall, but slight one of the players.

Therefore, the techniques of game theory are not easily applied to n-person or nonzero-sum games. We shall not go into further detail in this area, since it is beyond the scope of this book.

PROBLEMS

1 For each of the following find the maximax, maximin, minimax, and criterion of rationality strategies. (Strategies are listed as rows and states of nature as columns.)

Events

a Strategies $\begin{array}{c} \\ A \\ B \end{array} \begin{pmatrix} 1 & 2 \\ 5 & 3 \\ 9 & 6 \end{pmatrix}$
    b $\begin{array}{c} \\ A \\ B \end{array} \begin{pmatrix} 1 & 2 \\ 4 & 13 \\ 7 & 2 \end{pmatrix}$

c $\begin{array}{c} \\ A \\ B \end{array} \begin{pmatrix} 1 & 2 \\ 10 & -4 \\ 6 & -8 \end{pmatrix}$
    d $\begin{array}{c} \\ A \\ B \end{array} \begin{pmatrix} 1 & 2 \\ 5 & -24 \\ 13 & -1 \end{pmatrix}$

e $\begin{array}{c} \\ A \\ B \end{array} \begin{pmatrix} 1 & 2 \\ -6 & -8 \\ -4 & -12 \end{pmatrix}$
    f $\begin{array}{c} \\ A \\ B \end{array} \begin{pmatrix} 1 & 2 \\ -15 & -4 \\ -7 & -3 \end{pmatrix}$

g $\begin{array}{c} \\ A \\ B \\ C \end{array} \begin{pmatrix} 1 & 2 & 3 \\ 5 & -7 & 6 \\ 3 & 9 & 5 \\ 4 & 2 & 1 \end{pmatrix}$
    h $\begin{array}{c} \\ A \\ B \\ C \end{array} \begin{pmatrix} 1 & 2 & 3 \\ 15 & 12 & -5 \\ -6 & 8 & 3 \\ 2 & 5 & 1 \end{pmatrix}$

i $\begin{array}{c} \\ A \\ B \\ C \end{array} \begin{pmatrix} 1 & 2 & 3 \\ 1 & 0 & 0 \\ 0 & 15 & 0 \\ -30 & 0 & 100 \end{pmatrix}$
    j $\begin{array}{c} \\ A \\ B \\ C \end{array} \begin{pmatrix} 1 & 2 & 3 \\ 80 & -80 & 0 \\ 40 & 0 & 0 \\ 10 & 10 & 10 \end{pmatrix}$

2 For each of the following two-person games, find the optimal strategies and the value of the game:

a $\begin{array}{c} \\ A_1 \\ A_2 \end{array} \begin{pmatrix} B_1 & B_2 \\ 3 & 6 \\ 5 & 10 \end{pmatrix}$
    b $\begin{array}{c} \\ A_1 \\ A_2 \end{array} \begin{pmatrix} B_1 & B_2 \\ 4 & 8 \\ 11 & 20 \end{pmatrix}$

c $\begin{array}{c} \\ A_1 \\ A_2 \end{array} \begin{pmatrix} B_1 & B_2 \\ 15 & 10 \\ 12 & 8 \end{pmatrix}$
    d $\begin{array}{c} \\ A_1 \\ A_2 \end{array} \begin{pmatrix} B_1 & B_2 \\ 20 & 6 \\ 9 & 5 \end{pmatrix}$

e $\begin{array}{c} \\ A_1 \\ A_2 \\ A_3 \end{array} \begin{pmatrix} B_1 & B_2 & B_3 \\ 2 & 5 & 4 \\ 3 & 8 & 6 \\ 2 & 4 & 5 \end{pmatrix}$
    f $\begin{array}{c} \\ A_1 \\ A_2 \\ A_3 \end{array} \begin{pmatrix} B_1 & B_2 & B_3 \\ 7 & 15 & 9 \\ 4 & 11 & 6 \\ 12 & 19 & 15 \end{pmatrix}$

g $\begin{array}{c} \\ A_1 \\ A_2 \\ A_3 \end{array} \begin{pmatrix} B_1 & B_2 & B_3 \\ 4 & 2 & 6 \\ 20 & 16 & 18 \\ 2 & 1 & 5 \end{pmatrix}$
    h $\begin{array}{c} \\ A_1 \\ A_2 \\ A_3 \end{array} \begin{pmatrix} B_1 & B_2 & B_3 \\ 28 & 29 & 26 \\ 40 & 30 & 28 \\ 46 & 37 & 31 \end{pmatrix}$

$$
\begin{array}{cc}
& B_1 \ B_2 \\
\text{j} & \begin{array}{c} A_1 \\ A_2 \\ A_3 \\ A_4 \end{array}
\begin{pmatrix} 25 & 42 \\ 18 & 27 \\ 36 & 40 \\ 48 & 51 \end{pmatrix}
\end{array}
$$

$$
\begin{array}{cc}
& B_1 \ B_2 \ B_3 \ B_4 \\
\text{i} & \begin{array}{c} A_1 \\ A_2 \end{array}
\begin{pmatrix} 10 & 21 & 42 & 57 \\ 80 & 91 & 100 & 105 \end{pmatrix}
\end{array}
$$

3   For each of the following two-person games, find the optimal strategies and the value of the game:

a
$$
\begin{array}{c}
B_1 \ B_2 \\
\begin{array}{c} A_1 \\ A_2 \end{array}
\begin{pmatrix} 10 & 14 \\ 17 & 5 \end{pmatrix}
\end{array}
$$

b
$$
\begin{array}{c}
B_1 \ B_2 \\
\begin{array}{c} A_1 \\ A_2 \end{array}
\begin{pmatrix} 18 & 15 \\ 3 & 25 \end{pmatrix}
\end{array}
$$

c
$$
\begin{array}{c}
B_1 \ B_2 \\
\begin{array}{c} A_1 \\ A_2 \end{array}
\begin{pmatrix} 15 & 12 \\ 2 & 18 \end{pmatrix}
\end{array}
$$

d
$$
\begin{array}{c}
B_1 \ B_2 \\
\begin{array}{c} A_1 \\ A_2 \end{array}
\begin{pmatrix} 24 & 6 \\ 6 & 10 \end{pmatrix}
\end{array}
$$

e
$$
\begin{array}{c}
B_1 \quad B_2 \\
\begin{array}{c} A_1 \\ A_2 \end{array}
\begin{pmatrix} -15 & -3 \\ -8 & -10 \end{pmatrix}
\end{array}
$$

f
$$
\begin{array}{c}
B_1 \quad B_2 \\
\begin{array}{c} A_1 \\ A_2 \end{array}
\begin{pmatrix} -21 & -15 \\ -4 & -20 \end{pmatrix}
\end{array}
$$

g
$$
\begin{array}{c}
B_1 \quad B_2 \\
\begin{array}{c} A_1 \\ A_2 \end{array}
\begin{pmatrix} -35 & -2 \\ 30 & -15 \end{pmatrix}
\end{array}
$$

h
$$
\begin{array}{c}
B_1 \quad B_2 \\
\begin{array}{c} A_1 \\ A_2 \end{array}
\begin{pmatrix} -28 & -20 \\ 12 & -26 \end{pmatrix}
\end{array}
$$

4   For each of the following two-person games, find the optimal strategies and the value of the game using the simplex method:

a
$$
\begin{array}{c}
B_1 \ B_2 \ B_3 \\
\begin{array}{c} A_1 \\ A_2 \\ A_3 \end{array}
\begin{pmatrix} 10 & 15 & 25 \\ 15 & 8 & 33 \\ 25 & 10 & 5 \end{pmatrix}
\end{array}
$$

b
$$
\begin{array}{c}
B_1 \ B_2 \ B_3 \\
\begin{array}{c} A_1 \\ A_2 \\ A_3 \end{array}
\begin{pmatrix} 2 & 1 & 5 \\ 3 & 4 & 2 \\ 6 & 0 & 0 \end{pmatrix}
\end{array}
$$

c
$$
\begin{array}{c}
B_1 \quad B_2 \quad B_3 \\
\begin{array}{c} A_1 \\ A_2 \\ A_3 \end{array}
\begin{pmatrix} 4 & 0 & 1 \\ 6 & -2 & 0 \\ 3 & 5 & 6 \end{pmatrix}
\end{array}
$$

d
$$
\begin{array}{c}
B_1 \quad B_2 \quad B_3 \\
\begin{array}{c} A_1 \\ A_2 \\ A_3 \end{array}
\begin{pmatrix} 0 & -3 & 4 \\ 5 & 6 & 1 \\ 2 & 8 & 5 \end{pmatrix}
\end{array}
$$

5   Solve the games in Prob. 4 using the iterative method.

PART 2

6 DIFFERENTIAL CALCULUS: BASIC METHODOLOGY

INTRODUCTION

Most people find the thought of beginning the study of calculus disquieting. This is difficult to understand, because the basic concepts and operations involved in the calculus are not particularly complex. Few areas of mathematics turn out to be as intriguing, and, for that matter, few areas appear as impressive. In addition to this, calculus is an area with obvious potential for business. Calculus helps one to describe complex relationships pictorially. This in itself would make it worth studying, since the business environment is filled with situations too involved and complex for an administrator to comprehend and assess without the help of calculus. In addition, calculus can be used to locate maximum and minimum values of functions, and in a multitude of problems one is seeking to maximize profit or to minimize cost. Furthermore, calculus can be used to convert total cost (or revenue or profit) to marginal cost (or revenue or profit), and for many purposes marginal data is the relevant data for decision-making. Calculus is a basis for probability theory, which provides the means for decision-making in an uncertain environment. Calculus can find the total amount of profit expected in a changing environment. The techniques comprising calculus will serve well the business administrator's constant need of converting myriads of data into useful information for decision-making.

Calculus is divided into two distinct sections—differential and integral. Since integral calculus is the reverse process of differential calculus, a thorough understanding of the former is basic to both. The next three chapters will develop the concepts and techniques of differential calculus.

Differential calculus is concerned with the slope of curving lines. The *derivative* is a term meaning slope, and finding the derivative of a curved line is similar in meaning to finding the slope of a straight line. Thus, let us begin our exploration of differential calculus by examining more closely the concept of slope.

SLOPE: LINEAR VERSUS NONLINEAR

We have already defined the *slope* of a straight line as the increase or decrease in y (the vertical axis) for a unit increase in x (the horizontal axis). Thus, if $y = 3$ when $x = 1$ and $y = 5$ when $x = 2$, the slope of the line will be 2, since the height of the line has increased 2 units for a one unit increase in x.

If the line is straight, the slope at one place on the line will be identical to the slope at any other point on the line (Figure 6.1). Note that the line in Figure 6.1 increases 2 units for each unit change

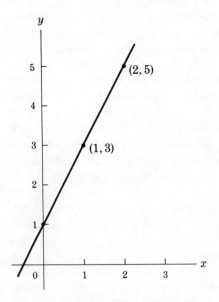

Figure 6.1 Graph of line going through (1,3) and (2,5)

of x. The slope, then, of a straight line can be represented by a constant number such as 2, or -5, or 10.123.

A curving line, however, does not have the same slope at every point.

As a matter of fact, for a 1-unit change in x, say from 0 to 1, many different slopes may be present.   Hence, the concept of slope becomes more complicated when curving lines are under consideration.

We define the slope at a particular point on a curving line in terms of a straight line which passes through the point for which we wish to find the slope and the point "right next" to it.   This is somewhat oversimplified, since, theoretically, whatever point, no matter how close, we choose as the one "right next" to our starting point, an infinite number of points are closer.   If, however, we make the distance between the points very tiny, thinner than the thickness of a piece of paper, our definition will be satisfactory.   When we are dealing with very short distances, a straight line will come very close to describing a curved line.   Remember that the slope of a straight line can be defined as

$$b = \frac{y_2 - y_1}{x_2 - x_1}$$

If the points are 1 unit apart on the x axis, then

$$b = \frac{y_2 - y_1}{1} = y_2 - y_1$$

If, however, the points are less than 1 unit apart, the same result will be obtained by taking the two y values which are, say, $\frac{1}{2}$ unit apart on the x axis and dividing by $\frac{1}{2}$.

For example, our line passing through $(1,3)$ and $(0,1)$ has the slope

$$\frac{3 - 1}{1 - 0} = 2$$

This line also passes through the point $(\frac{1}{2},2)$.   Using $(\frac{1}{2},2)$ and $(0,1)$, the slope will be the same:

$$\frac{2 - 1}{\frac{1}{2} - 0} = \frac{1}{\frac{1}{2}} = 2$$

Since the distance between our points is very small when we are finding slopes for curved lines, we introduce a new symbol h to describe the denominator of the slope formula.   Note that rather than being 1 or $\frac{1}{2}$ it will be closer to $1/1,000,000,000$.   The slope, then, of a curved line is simply the change in height between two very close points divided by the horizontal distance between them.   Looking through a magnifying glass, we can more easily visualize the meaning of the symbols.   Pretend that the magnifying glass is so powerful that only a few points of our curved line are under it (Figure 6.2). The slope, then, is $\dfrac{y_2 - y_1}{h}$.

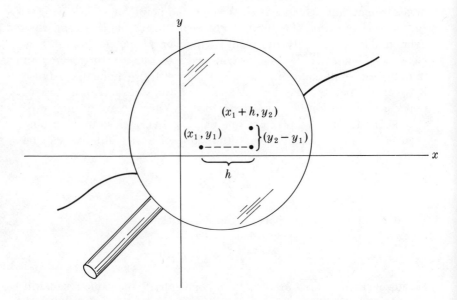

Figure 6.2   Magnification of two adjacent points on a curved line

More precisely, since we really can't find two adjoining points or two points next to one another, we introduce the mathematical concept of *limit*, which means very very close but not at. The formal formula for slope, then, becomes

$$\text{Slope} = \lim_{h \to 0} \frac{y_2 - y_1}{h}$$

where y_1 is the y value connected with a point x, and y_2 is the y value connected with the point $x + h$. Limit means that this formula becomes the formula for slope when h is very close to but not at zero.

THE DERIVATIVE

The slope of a curve is called the *derivative*. The study of differential calculus is concerned with the finding and interpreting of derivatives. Unlike a straight line, the slope of a curved line cannot be represented by a single number such as 10 or -4. The slope is different at different points on the line. Therefore, the derivative is in terms of a formula.   The formula has an x in it, and, for any x value on the graph, the formula provides the numerical value of the slope at that point.   Thus, if the derivative of a particular line were $x + 3$, this would indicate that the slope of the line is 4 when x is 1 and 5 when x is 2.

NECESSARY TERMINOLOGY AND CONCEPTS

Functions

Often a more convenient labeling is effected by utilization of the notation $f(x)$, read "f of x," instead of y.   Graphically, x will be the horizontal axis and $f(x)$ the vertical axis (Figure 6.3).

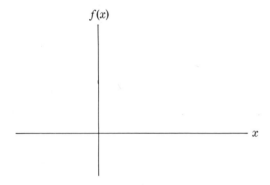

Figure 6.3   Graph illustrating the $f(x)$ axis

Using this terminology, if

$$f(x) = 3x^2 + 5$$
then
$$f(2) = 3(2)^2 + 5$$
and
$$f(a) = 3(a)^2 + 5$$
If
$$f(x) = 2x^2 + 4x - 1$$
then
$$f(3) = 2(3)^2 + 4(3) - 1$$
and
$$f(x + h) = 2(x + h)^2 + 4(x + h) - 1$$

Thus, the replacing of the x in $f(x)$ with another number or symbol is a signal to replace all x's in the function with that number or symbol.

Derivatives

The derivative of $f(x)$ is often denoted $f'(x)$ and is read "f prime of x". $D_x f(x)$ has the identical meaning, and it is read "the derivative with respect to x of the function $f(x)$."   A third symbol, also with the identical meaning, is dy/dx. This is read "the derivative of the function y with respect to x," or "the change in y per change in x."

Effect of the power of variables

Equations which have variables raised to the first power only are *linear*, or *straight-line*, equations. The number of variables determines the number of dimensions necessary for graphing the equation. When an equation has variables raised to powers higher than 1, the graph of the function is curved rather than straight. Thus, $f(x) = 3x + 5$ will be a straight line when graphed (Figure 6.4), while $f(x) = 3x^2 + 5$ will be a curved line when graphed (Figure 6.5).

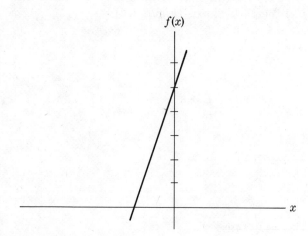

Figure 6.4   Graph of $f(x) = 3x + 5$

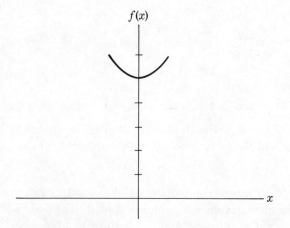

Figure 6.5   Graph of $f(x) = 3x^2 + 5$

Differential calculus is concerned with equations containing at least one term with a power other than 1 for the variable, since it is used to describe the slope of curves.

FINDING DERIVATIVES

A number of rules are available which reduce the time and effort necessary for finding the derivatives of functions. Often several different rules will apply interchangeably in a given situation. In these cases each will result in the same answer, and the solver can take his choice. Often, also, two or more rules will have to be used in combination in order to solve a problem.

DERIVATIVES OF CONSTANTS

A constant, when graphed, will always appear as a horizontal line. Thus, $f(x) = 3$ will graph as shown in Figure 6.6, and $f(x) = -5$ will graph as shown in Figure 6.7.

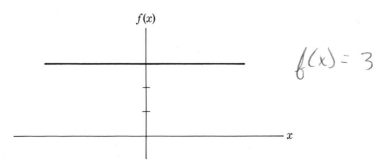

Figure 6.6   Graph of $f(x) = 3$

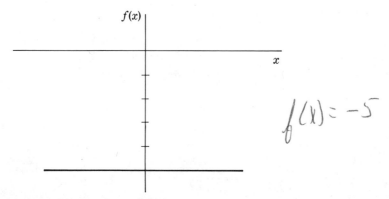

Figure 6.7   Graph of $f(x) = -5$

The derivative of any constant is 0. Since the derivative of an equation is the equation's slope, it can readily be seen that the slope of any constant is zero.

$$Dx\ k = 0$$

where k = any constant

EXAMPLE 6.1

$$f(x) = 5$$
$$f'(x) = 0$$

EXAMPLE 6.2

$$f(x) = a \quad \text{where } a \text{ is a constant}$$
$$f'(x) = 0$$

EXAMPLE 6.3

$$f(x) = -8$$
$$f'(x) = 0$$

EXAMPLE 6.4

$$f(x) = \frac{3}{28}$$
$$f'(x) = 0$$

The derivative of any constant is 0.

EXAMPLE 6.5

$$f(x) = 100k$$
$$f'(x) = 0$$

$f(x) = 100k$
$f'(x) = 0$

EXAMPLE 6.6

$$f(x) = \frac{a}{b} \quad \text{where } a \text{ and } b \text{ are constants}$$
$$f'(x) = 0$$

POWER FUNCTIONS

A rule which is utilized in almost every problem in differential calculus is the rule for derivatives of power functions. The rule states that if $f(x) = x^n$, where n is a constant, then $f'(x) = nx^{n-1}$.

EXAMPLE 6.7

$$f(x) = x^3$$
$$f'(x) = 3x^2$$

$f(x) = x^3$
$f'(x) = 3x^2$

EXAMPLE 6.8

$$f(x) = x^8$$
$$f'(x) = 8x^7$$

$f(x) = x^8$
$f'(x) = 8x^7$

$f(x) = x^{40}$
$f'(x) = 40x^{39}$

EXAMPLE 6.9

$$f(x) = x^{-7}\dagger$$
$$f'(x) = -7x^{-8}$$

EXAMPLE 6.10

$$f(x) = x$$
$$f'(x) = 1$$

EXAMPLE 6.11

$$f(x) = x^a$$
$$f'(x) = ax^{a-1}$$

CONSTANTS MULTIPLIED BY FUNCTIONS

The derivative of a constant times a function is equal to the constant times the derivative of the function. Thus when a constant number is multiplied by a term containing a variable, the constant is brought into the derivative unchanged. This is different from the derivative of a constant not attached to (multiplied by) a variable, where the derivative is zero.

Formally then, $Dx\ kf(x) = k\ Dx\ f(x)$, where k is a constant.

EXAMPLE 6.12

$$f(x) = 3x$$
$$f'(x) = 3\ Dx\ (x) = 3 \cdot 1 = 3$$

EXAMPLE 6.13

$$f(x) = 3x^3$$
$$f'(x) = 3\ Dx\ (x^3) = 3(3x^2) = 9x^2$$

EXAMPLE 6.14

$$f(x) = 7x^{-4}$$
$$f'(x) = 7\ Dx\ (x^{-4}) = 7(-4x^{-5}) = -28x^{-5}$$

EXAMPLE 6.15

$$f(x) = -x^3$$
$$f'(x) = -Dx\ (x^3) = -(3x^2) = -3x^2$$

EXAMPLE 6.16

$$f(x) = ax^{-2} \quad \text{where } a \text{ is a constant}$$
$$f'(x) = a\ Dx\ (x^{-2}) = a(-2x^{-3}) = -2ax^{-3}$$

† x^{-7} is the same as $1/x^7$. A minus exponent means "Find the reciprocal of the number raised to the positive power."

EXAMPLE 6.17

$$f(x) = \frac{x^5}{7} = \tfrac{1}{7}x^5$$
$$f'(x) = \tfrac{1}{7} Dx\ (x^5) = \tfrac{1}{7}(5x^4) = \tfrac{5}{7}x^4$$

SUMS AND DIFFERENCES OF FUNCTIONS

The derivative of two functions added together (or subtracted from one another) is the same as the two individual derivatives added together (or subtracted):

$$Dx\ [f(x) \pm g(x)] = Dx\ f(x) \pm Dx\ g(x)$$

EXAMPLE 6.18

$$f(x) = 3x^2 + 5x + 6$$
$$f'(x) = Dx\ (3x^2) + Dx\ (5x) + Dx\ (6)$$
$$= 6x + 5 + 0 = 6x + 5$$

EXAMPLE 6.19

$$f(x) = 6x^3 + x^{-3}$$
$$f'(x) = Dx\ (6x^3) + Dx\ (x^{-3})$$
$$= 18x^2 + (-3x^{-4}) = 18x^2 - 3x^{-4}$$

EXAMPLE 6.20

$$f(x) = 7x^5 - 4x^{-4}$$
$$f'(x) = Dx\ (7x^5) - Dx\ (4x^{-4})$$
$$= 35x^4 - (-16x^{-5}) = 35x^4 + 16x^{-5}$$

PRODUCTS OF FUNCTIONS

Where two functions, $f(x)$ and $g(x)$, are multiplied together, the derivative of this product is

$$Dx\ [f(x)g(x)] = f(x)\ Dx\ g(x) + g(x)\ Dx\ f(x)$$

EXAMPLE 6.21

$$f(x) = 4x^2(3x^3 + 5)$$
$$f'(x) = 4x^2\ Dx\ (3x^3 + 5) + (3x^3 + 5)\ Dx\ 4x^2$$
$$= 4x^2(9x^2) + (3x^3 + 5)(8x)$$
$$= 36x^4 + 24x^4 + 40x = 60x^4 + 40x$$

EXAMPLE 6.22

$$f(x) = (5x^2 + 3x)(4x^{-2} + 3x)$$
$$f'(x) = (5x^2 + 3x)\ Dx\ (4x^{-2} + 3x) + (4x^{-2} + 3x)\ Dx\ (5x^2 + 3x)$$
$$= (5x^2 + 3x)(-8x^{-3} + 3) + (4x^{-2} + 3x)(10x + 3)$$
$$= -40x^{-1} + 15x^2 - 24x^{-2} + 9x + 40x^{-1} + 12x^{-2} + 30x^2 + 9x$$
$$= 45x^2 + 18x - 12x^{-2}$$

QUOTIENTS OF FUNCTIONS

The derivative of the quotient of two functions, $f(x)$ and $g(x)$, is

$$Dx \frac{f(x)}{g(x)} = \frac{g(x)\, Dx\, f(x) - f(x)\, Dx\, g(x)}{g^2(x)} \dagger$$

EXAMPLE 6.23

$$f(x) = \frac{x^2}{3x + 5}$$

$$f'(x) = \frac{(3x + 5)\, Dx\, (x^2) - x^2\, Dx\, (3x + 5)}{(3x + 5)^2}$$

$$= \frac{(3x + 5)(2x) - x^2(3)}{(3x + 5)^2} = \frac{6x^2 + 10x - 3x^2}{(3x + 5)^2}$$

$$= \frac{3x^2 + 10x}{(3x + 5)^2}$$

EXAMPLE 6.24

$$f(x) = \frac{4x^2 + 3x}{5x^4 + 4}$$

$$f'(x) = \frac{(5x^4 + 4)\, Dx\, (4x^2 + 3x) - (4x^2 + 3x)\, Dx\, (5x^4 + 4)}{(5x^4 + 4)^2}$$

$$= \frac{(5x^4 + 4)(8x + 3) - (4x^2 + 3x)(20x^3)}{(5x^4 + 4)^2}$$

$$= \frac{(40x^5 + 15x^4 + 32x + 12) - (80x^5 + 60x^4)}{(5x^4 + 4)^2}$$

$$= \frac{-40^5 - 45x^4 + 32x + 12}{(5x^4 + 4)^2}$$

EXAMPLE 6.25

$$f(x) = 10\frac{2x + a}{3x^2 + b} \qquad \text{where } a \text{ and } b \text{ are constants}$$

$$f'(x) = 10\, Dx\, \frac{2x + a}{3x^2 + b}$$

$$= 10\frac{(3x^2 + b)\, Dx\, (2x + a) - (2x + a)\, Dx\, (3x^2 + b)}{(3x^2 + b)^2}$$

$$= 10\frac{(3x^2 + b)(2) - (2x + a)(6x)}{(3x^2 + b)^2}$$

$$= 10\frac{6x^2 + 2b - 12x^2 - 6ax}{(3x^2 + b)^2}$$

$$= 10\frac{-6x^2 - 6ax + 2b}{(3x^2 + b)^2}$$

$\dagger\ g^2(x)$ is the same as $[g(x)]^2$ and means the function $g(x)$ squared.   This is in contrast to $g(x^2)$, which means x^2 substitutes for x in the function $g(x)$.

PROBLEMS

1 Find Dx:

a	x^3	**b**	x^{14}
c	x^5	**d**	x^{201}
e	x^{-4}	**f**	x^{-7}
g	x^{-21}	**h**	x^{-18}
i	$x^{3/2}$	**j**	$x^{5/3}$
k	$x^{-7/5}$	**l**	$x^{-1/2}$
m	$x^{1/4}$	**n**	$x^{1/2}$
o	$x^{5.4}$	**p**	$x^{7.65}$
q	$x^{.3}$	**r**	$x^{.5}$
s	$x^{-1.2}$	**t**	$x^{-4.3}$
u	$\dfrac{1}{x^3}$	**v**	$\dfrac{1}{x^5}$
w	$\sqrt[3]{x^2}$	**x**	$\sqrt[5]{x^3}$
y	x^a	**z**	$x^{a/b}$
aa	b^3	**ab**	$c^{1/2}$

2 Find Dx:

a	$4x^5$	**b**	$7x^4$
c	$5x^3$	**d**	$12x^{10}$
e	$5x^{-3}$	**f**	$4x^{-6}$
g	$-3x^{-4}$	**h**	$-7x^{-8}$
i	$6x^{2/2}$	**j**	$10x^{5/2}$
k	$3x^{.2}$	**l**	$5x^{.7}$
m	$\frac{1}{2}x^{3/2}$	**n**	$\frac{5}{9}x^{9/5}$
o	$\dfrac{x^2}{2}$	**p**	$\dfrac{x^5}{4}$
q	$\dfrac{3x^{-7}}{8}$	**r**	$\dfrac{5x^{-4}}{9}$
s	ax^b	**t**	$-ax^{-b}$
u	$\dfrac{a}{x^b}$	**v**	$\dfrac{a}{x^a}$
w	$\dfrac{3}{5x^7}$	**x**	$\dfrac{15}{2x^2}$

3 Find Dx:

a $2x^3 + 4x^2 + 5x + 6$ **b** $7x^4 + 8x^2 + 9x + 10$

c $15x^8 + 3x^6 + 5x^4 + 9$ **d** $12x^6 + 4x^4 + 14x^2 + 15$

e $3x^{-4} + 5x^{-6}$ **f** $2x^{-7} + 9x^{-8}$

g $3x^{-4} - 4x^{-31}$ **h** $5x^2 - 2x^{-10}$

i $4x^{.3} + 7x^{.6}$ **j** $9x^{.4} + 5x^{.3}$

k $3x^{1/4} - 4x^{3/5}$ **l** $7x^{2/5} - 9x^{3/8}$

m $\frac{3}{5}x^{1/4} - \frac{2}{3}x^{3/2}$ **n** $\frac{2}{3}x^{1/5} - \frac{5}{6}x^{1/8}$

o $x - \dfrac{1}{x}$ **p** $\dfrac{1}{x^2} - x^2$

q $\sqrt{x} - \sqrt[3]{x}$　　　　　　**r** $2\sqrt{x} - 3\sqrt[3]{x}$
s $.3x^{1/2} - .4x^{2/3} + .5x^{3/4}$　　**t** $.73x^{-1/2} - .64x^{-2/3} + .55x^{-3/4}$

4 Find Dx:

a $(x^2 - 3)(2x^5 + 7x)$ 　　　　　　　**b** $(x^5 - 8)(2x^4 + 9x)$

c $(x^7 - 1)(3x^9 + 5x)$ 　　　　　　　**d** $(x^3 - 3)(5x^6 + 4x)$

e $(x^2 - 4x + 8)(3x^2 - 6x + 7)$ 　　　**f** $(4x^2 - 6x + 10)(5x^2 - 8x + 4)$

g $(2x^6 - 4x^2 + 3x)(2x^3 - 4x^2 + 8x)$ 　**h** $(4x^3 - 5x^2 + 2x)(3x^3 + 4x^4 + 5x^5)$

i $(2x - 3x^2)(4x^5 - 7x^{-5})$ 　　　　　**j** $(5x^3 + 6x)(9x^2 - 3x^{-4})$

k $(4x^{1/3} + 5x^{3/4})(2x^2 - x)$ 　　　　**l** $(3x^5 - 4x^2)(6x^{1/2} - 7x^{2/3})$

m $(x + \sqrt{x})(x - \sqrt{x})$ 　　　　　　**n** $(x + \sqrt[3]{x})(\sqrt[3]{x} - x)$

o $x\sqrt{x}$ 　　　　　　　　　　　　　**p** $x^2\sqrt[3]{x}$

q $5(x^2 - 3x)(x^4 + 7x^2)$ 　　　　　　**r** $43(x^9 - 7x^7)(x^8 + 8)$

s $(x^2 - 4)(x^3 - 5)(x^4 - 6)$ 　　　　　**t** $(x^5 - 7)(x^6 - 8)(x^7 - 9)$

u $(x^2 - 4x)^2$ 　　　　　　　　　　　**v** $(x^5 - 5x^2)^2$

w $(2x^3 - 4x)^3$ 　　　　　　　　　　**x** $(3x^5 - 5x^2)^3$

5 Find Dx:

a $\dfrac{x - 1}{x + 1}$ 　　　　　　　　　　**b** $\dfrac{x - 3}{x + 3}$

c $\dfrac{3x - 5}{4x - 7}$ 　　　　　　　　　**d** $\dfrac{5x + 2}{9x - 1}$

e $\dfrac{2x^2 - 5x}{x + 1}$ 　　　　　　　　**f** $\dfrac{3x^3 - 4x^2}{5x + 1}$

g $\dfrac{4x^3 - 5x^2 - 3x}{2x^5 + 7x^3 - x}$ 　　　　**h** $\dfrac{2x^3 - 4x^2 + 8x}{3x^7 - 8x^6 - 4x^2}$

i $\dfrac{11x^3 - 5x^2 + 7x}{7x^6 - 5x^4 + 5x^3}$ 　　　**j** $\dfrac{5x^5 - 4x^3 - 8x}{3x^6 + 7x^3 - 5x^2}$

k $\dfrac{3x^{-3} - 5x}{2x^2 + 3x + 8}$ 　　　　　**l** $\dfrac{4x^3 - 51x^{-3}}{2x^{-4} - 8x}$

m $\dfrac{12x^4 + 7x^{-5}}{-3x^{-3} - 3}$ 　　　　　**n** $\dfrac{x^{-4} - x^{-5}}{-31x^{-1} - 4x}$

o $\dfrac{(2x + 5)(3x + 6)}{4x + 7}$ 　　　　　**p** $\dfrac{(10x - 2)(11x - 1)}{12x - 3}$

q $\dfrac{(3x^2 - 4x)(5x^7 - 4x^2)}{6x - 7}$ 　　　**r** $\dfrac{(4x^2 - 6x^4)(2x^3 - 6x^5)}{2x + 1}$

s $\dfrac{(3x + 5)(6x - 1)}{(7x - 2)(3x + 4)}$ 　　　**t** $\dfrac{(5x - 3)(x - 6)}{(2x - 7)(4x + 3)}$

u $4\dfrac{(2x - 1)(3x - 2)}{(5x - 8)(9x + 7)}$ 　　**v** $10\dfrac{(3x + 8)(5x + 7)}{(4x - 1)(3x + 10)}$

w $a\dfrac{(bx + c)(cx^2 - d)}{(ex - 1)(kx^2 - 8)}$ 　**x** $\left(\dfrac{a}{b}\right)^2\dfrac{(ax^{-1} - 1)(bx^{-2} - 2)}{(cx^{-3} - 3)(dx^{-4} - 4)}$

7 DIFFERENTIAL CALCULUS: ADVANCED METHODOLOGY

INTRODUCTION

In the preceding chapter we explored a number of techniques for differentiation, including the power formula, which is the single most important technique in differential calculus. In this chapter the reader will develop an understanding of the chain rule for differentiating composite functions, which is considered second in importance only to the power formula. The chain rule will permit us to take derivatives of all remaining algebraic functions as well as provide a necessary adjunct for the differentiation of logarithmic and trigonometric functions.

This chapter includes those techniques involving one variable which form the basis for applying differential calculus to decision problems in business and economics.

Before tackling the chain rule, let's review some of the operations involving functions.

COMPOSITE FUNCTIONS

A *composite function* is a function within a function.
For example,

$$(3x + 5)^3 \qquad \text{is a composite function}$$
$$f(x) \qquad \text{is something to the third power } x^3$$
$$g(x) \qquad \text{is } 3x + 5$$
$$f(g(x)) \qquad \text{(read ``}f\text{ of }g\text{ of }x\text{'') is } (3x + 5)^3$$

More difficulty is usually experienced in separating and building up composite functions by the beginning student than in actually performing the operations necessary to differentiate composite functions.

When given two functions, $f(x)$ and $g(x)$ and asked to find $f(g(x))$, write down $f(x)$ without any x's.   Leave space wherever an x would have appeared.   Then place $g(x)$ into each space.   In other words, write down $f(x)$, substituting $g(x)$ for each x.

EXAMPLE 7.1

$$f(g(x)) = (7x + 8)^5$$
$$f(x) = x^5$$
$$g(x) = 7x + 8$$

EXAMPLE 7.2

$$f(g(x)) = (3x^2 + 4x)^{-3}$$
$$f(x) = x^{-3}$$
$$g(x) = 3x^2 + 4x$$

EXAMPLE 7.3

$$f(g(x)) = 5\left(\frac{7x + 5}{2x + 7}\right)^6$$
$$f(x) = 5x^6$$
$$g(x) = \frac{7x + 5}{2x + 7}$$

EXAMPLE 7.4

$$f(x) = x^4$$
$$g(x) = 3x^2 + 5$$
$$f(g(x)) = (3x^2 + 5)^4$$

EXAMPLE 7.5

$$f(x) = 4x^{-5}$$
$$g(x) = 3x^2 + 4x + 7$$
$$f(g(x)) = 4(3x^2 + 4x + 7)^{-5}$$

EXAMPLE 7.6

$$f(x) = 2x^3 + 5x^4$$
$$g(x) = 3x - 7$$
$$f(g(x)) = 2(3x - 7)^3 + 5(3x - 7)^4$$

THE DERIVATIVE OF A COMPOSITE FUNCTION

The derivative of a composite function is found through the use of the chain rule.   The general formula is

$$Dx\, f(g(x)) = f'(g(x))g'(x)$$

This means that the derivative of $f(x)$ must be found and that $g(x)$ must be substituted for x in this $f(x)$ derivative. Then the derivative of $g(x)$ is multiplied by $f'(g(x))$.

EXAMPLE 7.7

$$f(g(x)) = (3x^2 + 4)^4$$

Find $f(x)$, $g(x)$, $f'(x)$, and $g'(x)$ before solving a chain-rule problem:

$$f(x) = x^4 \qquad f'(x) = 4x^3$$
$$g(x) = 3x^2 + 4 \qquad g'(x) = 6x$$

then
$$f'(g(x)) = 4(3x^2 + 4)^3$$

and $\quad Dx\,f(g(x)) = f'(g(x))g'(x) = 4(3x^2 + 4)^3(6x) = 24x(3x^2 + 4)^3$

EXAMPLE 7.8

$$f(g(x)) = 5(2x^2 + 5x)^{-3}$$
$$f(x) = 5x^{-3} \qquad f'(x) = -15x^{-4}$$
$$g(x) = 2x^2 + 5x \qquad g'(x) = 4x + 5$$
$$Dx\,f(g(x)) = -15(2x^2 + 5x)^{-4}(4x + 5)$$

EXAMPLE 7.9

$$f(g(x)) = (3x + 2)^3 - 4(3x + 2)^2$$
$$f(x) = x^3 - 4x^2 \qquad f'(x) = 3x^2 - 8x$$
$$g(x) = 3x + 2 \qquad g'(x) = 3$$
$$Dx\,f(g(x)) = [3(3x + 2)^2 - 8(3x + 2)](3) = 9(3x + 2)^2 - 24(3x + 2)$$

EXAMPLE 7.10

$$f(x) = \frac{3x + 5}{(4x^2 + 3x)^3} = (3x + 5)(4x^2 + 3x)^{-3}$$
$$Dx\,f(x) = (3x + 5)\,Dx\,(4x^2 + 3x)^{-3} + (4x^2 + 3x)^{-3}\,Dx\,(3x + 5)$$
$$f(x) = x^{-3} \qquad f'(x) = -3x^{-4}$$
$$g(x) = 4x^2 + 3x \qquad g'(x) = 8x + 3$$
$$Dx\,(4x^2 + 3x)^{-3} = Dx\,f(g(x))$$
$$Dx\,(4x^2 + 3x)^{-3} = -3(4x^2 + 3x)^{-4}(8x + 3)$$
$$Dx\,f(x) = (3x + 5)(-3)(4x^2 + 3x)^{-4}(8x + 3) + (4x^2 + 3x)^{-3}(3)$$
$$= (24x^2 + 49x + 15)(-3)(4x^2 + 3x)^{-4} + (4x^2 + 3x)^{-3}(3)$$
$$= 3(4x^2 + 3x)^{-3}[(24x^2 + 49x + 15)(-1)(4x^2 + 3x)^{-1} + 1]$$

CHAIN RULE: THREE OR MORE FUNCTIONS

In the case of a composite function containing three or more simple functions, the chain rule may still be used. For three functions, the formula becomes

$$Dx\, f(g(h(x))) = f'(g(h(x)))g'(h(x))h'(x)$$

For four functions the rule is

$$Dx\, f(g(h(i(x)))) = f'(g(h(i(x)))) \cdot g'(h(i(x))) \cdot h'(i(x)) \cdot i'(x)$$

The pattern should be evident and is consistent for any number of functions.

EXAMPLE 7.11

$$f(g(h(x))) = [(3x^2 + 4x)^3]^{-2}$$

$$f(x) = x^{-2} \qquad\qquad f'(x) = -2x^{-3}$$

$$g(x) = x^3 \qquad\qquad g'(x) = 3x^2$$

$$h(x) = 3x^2 + 4x \qquad h'(x) = 6x + 4$$

$$Dx\, f(g(h(x))) = -2[(3x^2 + 4x)^3]^{-3}3(3x^2 + 4x)^2(6x + 4)$$

Note that in constructing $f'(g(h(x)))$, it is easiest if first $f'(x)$ is written

$$f'(x) = -2x^{-3}$$

Then substitute $g(x)$ for all x's in $f'(x)$:

$$f'(g(x)) = -2(x^3)^{-3}$$

then substitute $h(x)$ for all x's in $f'(g(x))$:

$$f'(g(h(x))) = -2[(3x^2 + 4x)^3]^{-3}$$

LOGARITHMS

The equation $x = a^{f(x)}$ may be rewritten as $\log_a x = f(x)$. This latter statement is read "the log of x to the base a is $f(x)$." The statement is interpreted as, "To what power must a be raised so that the result is equal to x?" Any number may serve as the base a, although conventionally either 10 or e will be used. The number 10 is a convenient base, since

$$10^0 = 1$$
$$10^1 = 10$$
$$10^2 = 100$$
$$10^3 = 1000$$

This permits the logarithms to follow an easily interpretable, decimal type of sequence. Generally, if $f(x) = \log x$ is written with no base mentioned, 10 will be the assumed base.

The letter e, much like π, represents a number with important mathematical characteristics and uses. The approximate value of e is 2.718281828. When the base e is used for logarithms, the logarithms are said to be *natural logarithms*. Instead of $\log_e x = f(x)$, this can be abbreviated in the case of natural logarithms to $\ln x = f(x)$. The meaning of $\ln x$, then, is the logarithm of x to the base e, or the natural logarithm of x.

DERIVATIVE OF A CONSTANT TO A VARIABLE POWER

The general formula for the derivative of $a^{f(x)}$, where a is any constant, is given by

$$Dx\ a^{f(x)} = f'(x)\ a^{f(x)} \ln a$$

In words, the derivative of a constant to a variable power is equal to the derivative of the exponent multiplied by the original function multiplied by the natural logarithm of the base.

EXAMPLE 7.12

$$f(x) = 10^x$$
$$f'(x) = (1)(10^x)(\ln 10) = (10^x)(\ln 10)$$

EXAMPLE 7.13

$$f(x) = 3^{x^2}$$
$$f'(x) = (2x)(3^{x^2})(\ln 3)$$

EXAMPLE 7.14

$$f(x) = 7^{3x+5}$$
$$f'(x) = (3)(7^{3x+5})(\ln 7)$$

EXAMPLE 7.15

$$f(x) = 8^{(2x^2+4x)^3}$$
$$f'(x) = Dx\ (2x^2 + 4x)^3 (8^{(2x^2+4x)^3})(\ln 8)$$
$$Dx\ (2x^2 + 4x)^3 = Dx\ f(g(x))$$
$$f(x) = x^3 \qquad\qquad f'(x) = 3x^2$$
$$g(x) = 2x^2 + 4x \qquad g'(x) = 4x + 4$$
$$Dx\ (2x^2 + 4x)^3 = 3(2x^2 + 4x)^2(4x + 4)$$
$$f'(x) = 3(2x^2 + 4x)^2(4x + 4)(8^{(2x^2+4x)^3})(\ln 8)$$

DERIVATIVE OF e TO A VARIABLE POWER

In the special case of e, the formula for the derivative of a constant to a variable power can be reduced somewhat. The formula, as given above, would produce the following for $Dx\ e^{f(x)}$:

$$Dx\ e^{f(x)} = f'(x)e^{f(x)} \ln e$$

By definition $\ln e$ is the power of e which equals e. This, of course, is 1. So $\ln e = 1$ and can be eliminated from the above formula, giving

$$Dx \, e^{f(x)} = f'(x) \, e^{f(x)}$$

Note that using this formula the derivative of $e^x = e^x$. One of the important properties of e^x, then, is that it is the only function that has itself as its derivative.

EXAMPLE 7.16

$$f(x) = e^{4x}$$
$$f'(x) = 4e^{4x}$$

EXAMPLE 7.17

$$f(x) = e^{-3x^2}$$
$$f'(x) = -6xe^{-3x^2}$$

EXAMPLE 7.18

$$f(x) = \frac{1}{e^{2x}} = e^{-2x}$$
$$f'(x) = -2e^{-2x}$$

EXAMPLE 7.19

$$f(x) = \frac{25}{e^{3x+5}} = 25e^{-(3x+5)}$$

$$f'(x) = (25)(-3)e^{-3x-5} = -75e^{-3x-5} = -\frac{75}{e^{3x+5}}$$

DERIVATIVE OF $\log_a f(x)$

The derivative of $\log_a f(x)$ is given by the following formula:

$$Dx \, \log_a f(x) = \frac{f'(x)}{f(x)} \log_a e$$

In words, then, the derivative of the logarithm of a function is equal to the derivative of the function divided by the function, all this multiplied by the logarithm of e to the base a.   (*Note:* This is not a natural logarithm.)

EXAMPLE 7.20

$$f(x) = \log_{10}(3x + 5)$$
$$f'(x) = \frac{3}{3x + 5} \log_{10} e$$

EXAMPLE 7.21

$$f(x) = \log_7(x^2 + 4x)$$
$$f'(x) = \frac{2x + 4}{x^2 + 4x} \log_7 e$$

EXAMPLE 7.22

$$f(x) = \log_5 (3x^2 + 5x)^{-2}$$

$$f'(x) = \frac{Dx\,(3x^2 + 5x)^{-2}}{(3x^2 + 5x)^{-2}} \log_5 e$$

$$Dx\,(3x^2 + 5x)^{-2} = Dx\,f(g(x))$$

$$f(x) = x^{-2} \qquad\qquad f'(x) = -2x^{-3}$$

$$g(x) = 3x^2 + 5x \qquad g'(x) = 6x + 5$$

$$Dx\,(3x^2 + 5x)^{-2} = -2(3x^2 + 5x)^{-3}(6x + 5)$$

$$f'(x) = \frac{-2(3x^2 + 5x)^{-3}(6x + 5)}{(3x^2 + 5x)^{-2}} \log_5 e$$

$$= -2(3x^2 + 5x)^{-1}(6x + 5) \log_5 e$$

DERIVATIVE OF ln $f(x)$

In the special case of the derivative of the natural logarithm of a function, the formula would become

$$Dx \ln f(x) = \frac{f'(x)}{f(x)} \log_e e$$

Since $\log_e e = \ln e = 1$, this simplifies to

$$Dx \ln f(x) = \frac{f'(x)}{f(x)}$$

EXAMPLE 7.23

$$f(x) = \ln x$$

$$f'(x) = \frac{1}{x}$$

EXAMPLE 7.24

$$f(x) = \ln (4x^5 + 5x)$$

$$f'(x) = \frac{20x^4 + 5}{4x^5 + 5x}$$

EXAMPLE 7.25

$$f(x) = [\ln (3x^2 + 4)]^{-2}5x$$

$$f'(x) = [\ln (3x^2 + 4)]^{-2} Dx\,5x + 5x\,Dx\,[\ln (3x^2 + 4)]^{-2}$$

Note that $[\ln (3x^2 + 4)]^{-2}$ is a composite function:

$$f(x) = x^{-2} \qquad\qquad f'(x) = -2x^{-3}$$

$$g(x) = \ln (3x^2 + 4) \qquad g'(x) = \frac{6x}{3x^2 + 4}$$

$$f'(x) = [\ln (3x^2 + 4)]^{-2}(5) + (5x)(-2)[\ln (3x^2 + 4)]^{-3}\left(\frac{6x}{3x^2 + 4}\right)$$

LOGARITHMIC DIFFERENTIATION

We have covered methods for differentiating x^a (power formula) and a^x (constant to a variable power formula).   One more type of function in this general category remains, which is the derivative of x^x.   The method for finding the derivative of a variable to a variable power is called *logarithmic differentiation.*

Begin by setting up the formula to be differentiated in the form $y = f(x)^{g(x)}$.   Then take the natural logarithm of each side of the equation: $\ln y = \ln f(x)^{g(x)}$.   Since $\ln f(x)^{g(x)} = g(x) \ln f(x)$, the next step will be to rewrite the equation as

$$\ln y = g(x) \ln f(x)$$

Now proceed to differentiate each side of the equation.   The derivative with respect to x of $\ln y$ is

$$\frac{1}{y}\frac{dy}{dx}$$

the derivative, then, is

$$\frac{1}{y}\frac{dy}{dx} = g(x)\ Dx \ln f(x) + \ln f(x)\ Dx\ g(x)$$

Multiplying both sides of the equation by y gives

$$\frac{dy}{dx} = y[g(x)\ Dx \ln f(x) + \ln f(x)\ Dx\ g(x)]$$

Since $y = f(x)^{g(x)}$

$$Dx\ f(x)^{g(x)} = \frac{dy}{dx} = f(x)^{g(x)}[g(x)\ Dx \ln f(x) + \ln f(x)\ Dx\ g(x)]$$

EXAMPLE 7.26

$$y = (3x^2)^{4x+5}$$

$$\frac{dy}{dx} = (3x^2)^{4x+5}[(4x + 5)\ Dx \ln 3x^2 + \ln 3x^2\ Dx\ (4x + 5)]$$

$$= (3x^2)^{4x+5}\left[(4x + 5)\frac{6x}{3x^2} + \ln 3x^2(4)\right]$$

EXAMPLE 7.27

$$y = (4x^3 + 5x)^{6x^2+3x^{-3}}$$

$$\frac{dy}{dx} = (4x^3 + 5x)^{6x^2+3x^{-3}}[(6x^2 + 3x^{-3})\ Dx \ln (4x^3 + 5x)$$

$$+ \ln (4x^3 + 5x)\ Dx\ (6x^2 + 3x^{-3})]$$

$$= (4x^3 + 5x)^{6x^2+3x^{-3}}\left[(6x^2 + 3x^{-3})\frac{12x^2 + 5}{4x^3 + 5x} + \ln (4x^3 + 5x)(12x - 9x^{-4})\right]$$

EXAMPLE 7.28

$$y = (\log_6 x^2)^{5x^3}$$

$$\frac{dy}{dx} = (\log_6 x^2)^{5x^3}[(5x^3) \, Dx \ln \log_6 x^2 + \ln \log_6 x^2 \, Dx \, (5x^3)]$$

$$\ln \log_6 x^2 = f(g(x))$$

$$f(x) = \ln x \qquad f'(x) = \frac{1}{x}$$

$$g(x) = \log_6 x^2 \qquad g'(x) = \frac{2x}{x^2} \log_6 e = \frac{2}{x} \log_6 e$$

$$Dx \ln \log_6 x^2 = \frac{1}{\log_6 x^2} \left(\frac{2}{x}\right) \log_6 e = \frac{2 \log_6 e}{x \log_6 x^2}$$

$$\frac{dy}{dx} = (\log_6 x^2)^{5x^3} 5x^3 \frac{2 \log_6 e}{x \log_6 x^2} + (\ln \log_6 x^2)15x^2$$

TRIGONOMETRIC DIFFERENTIATION

Formulas for trigonometric differentiation are:

$$Dx \sin x = \cos x$$
$$Dx \cos x = -\sin x$$
$$Dx \tan x = \sec^2 x = (\sec x)^2$$
$$Dx \cos x = -\csc^2 x = -(\csc x)^2$$
$$Dx \sec x = \sec x \tan x$$
$$Dx \cot x = -\csc x \cot x$$

Note that the derivatives for logarithmic functions were given in terms of $f(x)$, while the formulas for trigonometric differentiation are given in terms of x. Thus, while $Dx \ln f(x) = f'(x)/f(x)$ directly as a result of the formula given, $Dx \sin g(x)$ is a chain-rule function and must be solved as such:

$$f(x) = \sin x \qquad f'(x) = \cos x$$
$$g(x) = g(x) \qquad g'(x) = g'(x)$$
$$Dx \sin g(x) = \cos g(x) \, g'(x)$$

EXAMPLE 7.29

$$f(x) = \sin x^3$$
$$f(x) = \sin x$$
$$f'(x) = \cos x$$
$$g(x) = x^3$$
$$g'(x) = 3x^2$$
$$f'(x) = (\cos x^3)(3x^2)$$

EXAMPLE 7.30

$$f(x) = \sec (5x^2 + 4x)$$
$$f(x) = \sec x$$
$$f'(x) = \sec x \tan x$$
$$g(x) = 5x^2 + 4x$$
$$g'(x) = 10x + 4$$
$$f'(x) = [\sec (5x^2 + 4x) \tan (5x^2 + 4x)](10x + 4)$$

EXAMPLE 7.31

$$f(x) = \cot (\ln x)$$
$$f(x) = \cot x$$
$$f'(x) = -\csc^2 x$$
$$g(x) = \ln x$$
$$g'(x) = \frac{1}{x}$$

$$f'(x) = (-\csc^2 \ln x)\frac{1}{x}$$

HIGHER DERIVATIVES

The derivative of a function $f(x)$ can be more precisely called the *first derivative* of $f(x)$. The *second derivative* of $f(x)$ is defined as the derivative of the first derivative of $f(x)$. The symbol for the second derivative is $f''(x)$. The *third derivative* is the derivative of the second and has for its symbol $f'''(x)$.

EXAMPLE 7.32

$$f(x) = 3x^4 + 5x^3 - 6x^2 - 7x + 6$$
$$f'(x) = 12x^3 + 15x^2 - 12x - 7$$
$$f''(x) = 36x^2 + 30x - 12$$
$$f'''(x) = 72x + 30$$

EXAMPLE 7.33

$$f(x) = 3x(6x + 5)$$
$$f'(x) = 3x(6) + (6x + 5)(3) = 18x + 18x + 15 = 36x + 15$$
$$f''(x) = 36$$
$$f'''(x) = 0$$

PROBLEMS

1 Separate the following composite functions into component parts:

   a $(2x - 1)^4$ **b** $(3x^2 - 8)^5$

   c $(4x - 7)^{10}$ **d** $(15x - 3x^2)^{31}$

   e $(2x^3 - 5)^{-4}$ **f** $(10x - 3x^2)^{-8}$

   g $\dfrac{1}{(2x + 5)^4}$ **h** $\dfrac{1}{(4x + 7)^8}$

   i $3(2x^2 + 7)^5$ **j** $7(15x^5 + 3x^2 + 8)^9$

   k $\sqrt{4x + 5}$ **l** $\sqrt[3]{3x^2 - 1}$

   m $\sqrt{(2x + 1)^3}$ **n** $\sqrt[3]{(5x + 8)^2}$

   o $[(x + 1)^2]^3$ **p** $[(x^2 - 1)^{1/2}]^{1/3}$

   q $[\sqrt{(3x - 4)^3}]^5$ **r** $[\sqrt[3]{(2x + 7)^{-2}}]^8$

   s a^{x^2-1} **t** 7^{3x^3+8}

   u $4^{(x^2-1)^2}$ **v** $5^{\sqrt{3x+8}}$

2 Determine the composite function described:

   a $f(x) = x^8$ **b** $f(x) = x^3$
       $g(x) = 3x + 5$ $g(x) = 4x - 1$

   c $f(x) = x^9$ **d** $f(x) = x^3$
       $g(x) = 5x^2 + 7$ $g(x) = 10x^5 - 2x + 7$

   e $f(x) = 2x + 7$ **f** $f(x) = 4x^5 + 2$
       $g(x) = 4x^3 + 8x + 5$ $g(x) = 3x^2 + 8x - 9$

   g $f(x) = x^2 + 3x$ **h** $f(x) = 3x^3 - 4x$
       $g(x) = 2x + 1$ $g(x) = 3x + 6$

   i $f(x) = 2x^4 - 4x^2 + 8x - 9$ **j** $f(x) = 9x^{-5} - 3x^{-6} - 2x^2 + 1$
       $g(x) = 2x + 5x^2 - 1$ $g(x) = 3x^{-3} - 4x^2 - 5$

   k $f(x) = \sqrt{x}$ **l** $f(x) = \sqrt[3]{x}$
       $g(x) = x^2 - 1$ $g(x) = 4x + 5$

   m $f(x) = \sqrt{x^2 - x}$ **n** $f(x) = \sqrt[3]{2x - 5x^3}$
       $g(x) = 4x + 5x^2 + 8$ $g(x) = 2x - 11x^3$

   o $f(x) = 3^x$ **p** $f(x) = 5^x$
       $g(x) = 4x^2 - 1$ $g(x) = 2x^7 - 7$

   q $f(x) = 3^{x^2} - 1$ **r** $f(x) = 9^{3x^2} + 5$
       $g(x) = 3x^5 - 8$ $g(x) = 4x^4 - 3x$

   s $f(x) = 3x^2 - 1$ **t** $f(x) = 2x^9 - 18$
       $g(x) = 5x^3 - 4x + 8$ $g(x) = 4x^5 + 3x^7 + x$
       $h(x) = 3x + 5$ $h(x) = 2x - 3$

   u $f(x) = x$ **v** $f(x) = x^2$
       $g(x) = x$ $g(x) = x$
       $h(x) = x^2$ $h(x) = x$

3 Find Dx:

   a $(3x + 4)^2$ **b** $(4x + 7)^3$

   c $(2x - 6)^7$ **d** $(3x - 8)^6$

   e $(2x^7 - 5x^3 - 3x)^4$ **f** $(5x^5 - 10x^2 + x)^9$

   g $\sqrt{2x + 1}$ **h** $\sqrt[3]{5x - 2}$

   i $\sqrt{4x^3 - x}$ **j** $\sqrt[4]{10x^2 - x + 1}$

   k $\sqrt{2x - 8}$ **l** $\sqrt[3]{4x + 10}$

m $\sqrt{3x^{1/4} - 6}$ **n** $\sqrt[9]{4x \cdot 2 - .2}$

o $3(4x - 7)^7 \sqrt{2x^3 - 1}$ **p** $9(7x^6 - 6)^3 \sqrt[5]{7x - 6}$

q $\dfrac{(2x - 3)^2}{(4x - 1)^3}$ **r** $\dfrac{(5x^2 - 8)^5}{(9x - 10)^6}$

s $\dfrac{\sqrt{2x + 1}\,(3x - 7)^5}{\sqrt{4x - 6}\,(2x - 9)^5}$ **t** $\dfrac{\sqrt[3]{12x - 8}\,(7x + 8x)^{10}}{\sqrt[3]{3x^2 + 18x}\,(4x^2 - 1)^{10}}$

4 Find Dx:

   a $\sqrt{(3x + 1)^3}$ **b** $\sqrt[3]{(7x - 9)^4}$

   c $(\sqrt{14x + 4})^3$ **d** $(\sqrt[4]{24x - 10})^9$

   e $\sqrt{\sqrt{3x - 1}}$ **f** $\sqrt[3]{\sqrt[3]{7x + 2}}$

   g $\sqrt{5(3x + 7)^2 - 4(3x + 7) + 8}$ **h** $\sqrt[3]{7(7x - 5)^3 - 3(7x - 5)^2 + 10}$

   i $[2(x^5 - 5)^5 - 3(x^5 - 5)^2]^9$ **j** $[3(4x^5 + 3x)^4 + 8(4x^5 + 3x)^3]^{10}$

   k $[(7x + 5)^2 - 7x + 5]^7$ **l** $[(4x^3 + 3x)^3 - \sqrt[3]{4x + 3x}]^5$

   m $\sqrt{\sqrt{(3x + 1)}}$ **n** $\sqrt[3]{\sqrt[3]{(4x + 2)^4}}$

   o $f(x) = 7x^2 - 1$ **p** $f(x) = 5x^4 + x^3 + 8$

      $g(x) = \sqrt{x}$ $g(x) = x^5$

      Find: $Dx\,f(g(x))$ Find: $Dx\,f(g(x))$

            $Dx\,g(f(x))$ $Dx\,g(f(x))$

5   **a** What is the logarithm of 8 to the base 2?

    b What is the logarithm of 256 to the base 4?

    c What is the logarithm of 81 to the base 9?

    d What is the logarithm of 1,000 to the base 10?

    e What is the logarithm of 64 to the base 2?

    f What is the logarithm of 125 to the base 5?

    g What is the logarithm of $\frac{1}{2}$ to the base 2?

    h What is the logarithm of $\frac{1}{4}$ to the base 4?

    i What is the logarithm of $\frac{1}{8}$ to the base 2?

    j What is the logarithm of $\frac{1}{256}$ to the base 2?

    k What number provides a $\log_2 = 3$?

    l What number provides a $\log_2 = 5$?

    m What number provides a $\log_4 = 4$?

    n What number provides a $\log_4 = 1$?

    o What number provides a $\log_{10} = 4$?

    p What number provides a $\log_{10} = 2$?

    q What number provides a $\log_{10} = 0$?

    r What number provides a $\log_5 = 0$?

s What number provides a $\log_6 = -1$?

t What number provides a $\log_8 = -2$?

6 Find Dx:

a 4^x **b** 7^x

c 3^{2x} **d** 9^{5x}

e 10^{x^2} **f** 4^{x^3}

g 5^{x^2-1} **h** 6^{2x^2-3x}

i $4^{(2x+5)^2}$ **j** $9^{(5x^2-1)^3}$

k $2^{(3x^2-1)(4x^2-2)}$ **l** $9^{(6x^3+8)(10x+3)}$

m $43^{(5x^2-1)/(3x^2-x)}$ **n** $56^{(2x^5-x^4)/(6x+8)}$

o $23^{\sqrt{4x^2+5x-6}}$ **p** $18^{\sqrt[3]{2x+5x^2}}$

q $(\sqrt{a})^{3x-1}$ **r** $(b^2)^{4x^5+x}$

s $(b-a)^{cxd}$ **t** $(b+a)^{-cx^{-d}}$

7 Find Dx:

a e^{2x} **b** e^x

c e^{5x-1} **d** e^{4x^2}

e $e^{(3x+5)(2x-1)}$ **f** $e^{(2x+1)(9x-8)}$

g e^{e^x} **h** $e^{e^{e^x}}$

i x^{e^m} **j** $(2x)^e$

k $e^{\sqrt{x-1}}$ **l** $e^{\sqrt[3]{3x}}$

m $e^{x^2}e^{2x^2-1}$ **n** $e^{5x}e^{3x+5}$

o $[(e^{x^2+4})(e^{2x^2-1})]^3$ **p** $[(e^{5x^5+8})(e^{4x^7+10})]^5$

q $e^{x^e}x^e$ **r** $e^x x^e$

8 Find Dx:

a $\log_{10} 5x$ **b** $\log_{10} 8x$

c $\log_{10} 3x^2 - 5$ **d** $\log_{10} 6x^4 - x$

e $\log_5 (4x^5 - 3x)(2x + 5)$ **f** $\log_7 (2x^9 - 4x^3)(7x + 8x^2)$

g $\log_2 \dfrac{x-4}{3x+4}$ **h** $\log_7 \dfrac{2x-1}{x^2+x}$

i $\log_6 \sqrt{x}$ **j** $\log_5 \sqrt{x^2-1}$

k $\log_3 (2x^4 - 8)^5$ **l** $\log_5 (9x^5 - 3x^2 + 1)^{-2}$

m $\log_6 (\sqrt{2x+1})^4$ **n** $\log_2 (\sqrt[3]{x^2+8x})^9$

o $\log_3^2 x$ **p** $\log_2^3 x$

q $\log_3^3 x$ **r** $\log_3^{-3} \sqrt[3]{x}$

s $\log_9 e^x$ **t** $\log_{10} 5^x$

9 Find Dx:

  a $\ln x$ **b** $\ln x^2$

  c $\ln (x^3 - 3x)$ **d** $\ln (5x^4 - 2x^3)$

  e $\ln (2x - 1)^3$ **f** $\ln (25x - 8)^5$

  g $\ln^3 (2x - 1)$ **h** $\ln^5 (25x - 8)$

  i $\ln (3x + 8)(5x^2 - x^3)$ **j** $\ln (4x + 42)(4x^2 + 42x^3)$

  k $\ln \dfrac{2x - 1}{3x + 5}$ **l** $\ln \dfrac{12x^2 - 3x}{10x^2 + 4x}$

  m $\ln \dfrac{(2x + 5)(3x - 2)}{(4x + 6)(5x - 7)}$ **n** $\ln \dfrac{(3x - 4)(15x + 3)}{(6x - 8)(4x + 41)}$

  o $\ln \sqrt{4x + 8}$ **p** $\ln \sqrt[5]{5x}$

  q $\ln \log_3 (x^2 - 1)$ **r** $\log_3 \ln (x^2 - 1)$

  s $\log_5^7 \ln^6 (5x - 1)$ **t** $\log_{10}^2 \ln^2 x$

10 Find Dx:

  a x^x **b** $(x + 1)^x$

  c $(2x - 3)^x$ **d** $(5x + 10)^x$

  e $x^{3x^2 - 1}$ **f** $x^{5x^4 - x}$

  g $(x + 10)^{x+10}$ **h** $(x - 3)^{x-3}$

  i $(2x^2 + 5x)^{x^2 - 4x + 5}$ **j** $(4x^5 - 3x^2)^{2x^4 - 4x^2 - 1}$

  k $(2x - 1)^{x^2}(4x + 5)$ **l** $(3x^2 + 8x)^{2x}(5x + 12)$

  m $\log_3^x x$ **n** $\ln^x (x + 1)$

  o x^{e^x} **p** x^{5x}

  q $\left(\dfrac{3x - 4}{4x^2 - 8}\right)^{x^2}$ **r** $\left(\dfrac{2x + 5}{6x^3 - x}\right)^{x^3 - 1}$

  s $a^x \cdot x^a$ **t** $[(x + a)^{x+a}][\ln^{x+a}(x + a)]$

11 Find Dx:

  a $\sin 2x$ **b** $\cos 5x$

  c $\tan x^2$ **d** $\cot 3x^3$

  e $\sec 2x$ **f** $\csc 5x^4$

  g $\sin (3x^2 - 4x + 5)$ **h** $\tan (2x^5 + 4x^3 + x)$

  i $\sec x \tan x$ **j** $\sin x \csc x$

  k $\tan \dfrac{2x + 5}{3x - 1}$ **l** $\csc \dfrac{4x + 7}{5x + 9}$

  m $\sin \sin x$ **n** $\sin \csc x$

  o $\sin^5 x^2$ **p** $\sec^4 x^5$

  q $5^{\sin x}$ **r** $e^{\cos x}$

  s $x^{\sin x}$ **t** $(3x^2 - \cos x)^{\sin x}$

12 Find first and second derivatives:

   a $x^2 - 4x + 5$ **b** $2x^2 + 7x + 9$

   c $x^4 - 4x^2$ **d** $x^7 - 5x^6$

   e $x^{1/2}$ **f** $x^{.2}$

   g $\sin x$ **h** $\cos 4x$

   i 3^{x^3} **j** 5^{2x^2-1}

   k $\dfrac{2x^2 - 1}{3x + 5}$ **l** $\dfrac{3x + 6}{5x - 4x + 8}$

   m $\ln x^2$ **n** $\log_5 (4x^4 - 3x^2)$

   o $\sec x$ **p** $\csc (3x - 1)$

   q $\sin^3 (x^2 - 1)$ **r** $\cos^4 (3x^5 - x^2)$

   s $(\sqrt{x})^3$ **t** $\sqrt[3]{(3x^2 - 1)^{-7}}$

13 Show the signs of the first and second derivatives for the equation shown in the graph below.

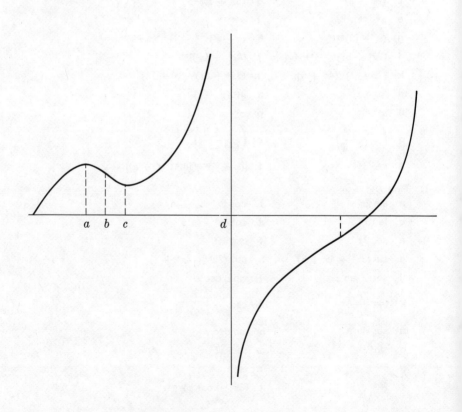

	Sign of derivative	
	1	2
$x < a$		
$x = a$		
$a < x < b$		
$x = b$		
$b < x < c$		
$x = c$		
$c < x < d$		
$x = d$		
$d < x < e$		

8 DIFFERENTIAL CALCULUS: APPLICATIONS

MAXIMA AND MINIMA

Differential calculus provides a method for locating maximal and minimal points of functions. This is of major importance for business problem solving, and herein lies one of the major contributions which calculus has made and can continue to make for business.

Let us begin by defining a *maximum* as a point which is higher than the nearby points on either side of it. Also, we can define a *minimum* as a point which is lower than the nearby points on either side. These definitions can be visualized as peaks and troughs on a graph. Note that they do not include the end points of the curve, which may, in fact, represent maximum or minimum values. Nor do they distinguish one maximum on a curve from another maximum on the same curve. For example, two peaks may appear on the same curve, and one may be higher than the other. Differential calculus can be used to locate both maxima, but it will not distinguish between them. It will not show that one is higher than the other, nor will it consider one of them *the* maximum. Thus, differential calculus can be used to find all peaks and troughs on the graph of a function. In the discussion to follow, maximum or minimum will be considered to mean a peak or trough, respectively, and not necessarily the high value or low value of the function.

Those values of x which produce zero first derivatives are termed *critical values*. If, for one of these critical values, the second derivative is a negative number, then this critical value of x represents a maximum.   If, on the other hand, the second derivative is positive for a particular critical value, then that value represents a minimum of the function.   If the second derivative is zero at a critical value, then the critical value does not represent either a maximum or a minimum point for the function.

In business problem solving, local maxima or minima are usually of more interest than global ones.   For example, the global minimum for costs would always be zero (if the company goes out of business), but this is usually of very little interest.

A zero value of the first derivative must accompany all maximum or minimum points or, more compactly, all extreme points of a function, since a curve is neither rising nor falling at a maximum or minimum point and thus has a zero slope.   This does not mean that all zero first derivatives represent maxima or minima.   A zero derivative can exist without an extreme point, but an extreme point cannot exist without a zero first derivative.

EXAMPLE 8.1

If costs per unit produced for a particular company could be represented by the function $f(x) = 2x^2 - 10x + 50$ when x is thousands of units produced, for what value of x would costs be at a minimum (other than zero)?

First, find the first and second derivatives of the equation

$$f(x) = 2x^2 - 10x + 50$$
$$f'(x) = 4x - 10$$
$$f''(x) = 4$$

Then find the critical values of x by setting the first derivative equal to zero:

$$4x - 10 = 0$$
$$4x = 10$$
$$x = \tfrac{10}{4} = 2.5$$

Note that $f''(x)$ is positive for this value of x (for all values, as a matter of fact) and that $x = 2.5$ is thereby a minimum of the function.   The company can be told that minimum costs, costs per unit produced, will occur when 2,500 units are produced. The cost per unit produced at this volume can be found by substituting 2.5 for x in the original equation.

Thus,
$$f(2.5) = 2(2.5)^2 - 10(2.5) + 50$$
$$= 2(6.25) - 10(2.5) + 50$$
$$= 12.5 - 25 + 50$$
$$= 37.5$$

EXAMPLE 8.2

Assume the profit function for a particular company can be represented by $f(x) = x - .00001x^2$, where x is units sold.   Find the optimal sales volume and the amount of profit to be expected at that volume.

$$f(x) = x - .00001x^2$$
$$f'(x) = 1 - .00002x$$
$$f''(x) = -.00002$$

The critical value occurs when

$$1 - .00002x = 0$$
$$- .00002x = -1$$
$$x = \frac{1}{.00002} = 50,000 \text{ units}$$

Note that the second derivative is negative, and therefore 50,000 unit sales will be a maximum:

$$f(50,000) = 50,000 - .00001(50,000)^2$$
$$= 50,000 - .00001(2,500,000,000)$$
$$= 50,000 - 25,000 = 25,000$$

Sales of 50,000 units then will provide profits of $25,000. The reader should verify that other volumes will always produce lower profits.

EXAMPLE 8.3

After a detailed study, the Worthier Company found a formula, $x^3 - 100x^2 + 3,125x$, where x equals advertising expenditures in thousands of dollars, which would provide a close approximation of expected profit for different advertising volumes. What volume of advertising would produce the maximum profit, and what profit would be expected at this volume? First, we must find the first and second derivatives of the profit function:

$$f(x) = x^3 - 100x^2 + 3,125x$$
$$f'(x) = 3x^2 - 200x + 3,125$$
$$f''(x) = 6x - 200$$

Next, we must locate critical points by setting the first derivative equal to zero:

$$f'(x) = 3x^2 - 200x + 3,125 = 0$$

Recall that equations in the form

$$ax^2 + bx + c = 0$$

can be solved through the use of the quadratic formula, which is

$$x = \frac{-b \pm \sqrt{b^2 - 4ac}}{2a}$$

In our problem

$$a = 3$$
$$b = -200$$
$$c = 3,125$$

$$x = \frac{-(-200) \pm \sqrt{(-200)^2 - 4(3)(3,125)}}{2(3)}$$

$$= \frac{200 \pm \sqrt{40,000 - 37,500}}{6}$$

$$= \frac{200 \pm \sqrt{2,500}}{6}$$

$$= \frac{200 \pm 50}{6}$$

The two solutions, then, are

$$x = \frac{250}{6} = 41\frac{2}{3}$$

and

$$x = \frac{150}{6} = 25$$

each of which will result in a zero first derivative.   Substituting each of these values in the second derivative, we obtain

$$f''(\tfrac{250}{6}) = 6(\tfrac{250}{6}) - 200$$
$$= 250 - 200$$
$$= 50$$
$$f''(25) = 6(25) - 200$$
$$= 150 - 200$$
$$= -50$$

Thus, $x = \frac{250}{6}$ is a minimum, since the second derivative is positive; and $x = 25$ is a maximum, since the second derivative is negative.

Since we are looking for maximum profit, $x = 25$ is the solution to the problem. Substituting 25 for x back in the original equation,

$$f(25) = (25)^3 - 100(25)^2 + 3{,}125(25)$$
$$= 15{,}625 - 62{,}500 + 78{,}125$$
$$= 31{,}250$$

Thus advertising expenditures of $25,000 should result in profits of $31,250, and expenditures on advertising of either more or less will result in smaller profits.

EXAMPLE 8.4

Johnstone, Inc., has developed a logarithmic model which closely resembles the relationship of their profits at different volume levels.   If we allow x to represent volume in thousands of units, the model is

$$\text{Profit} = f(x) = \log_{10}(x^2 - 6x - 1)$$

At what volume is profit maximized?

Again we must begin by finding the first and second derivatives of the profit function:

$$f(x) = \log_{10}(x^2 - 6x - 1)$$
$$f'(x) = \frac{2x - 6}{x^2 - 6x - 1} \log_{10} e$$
$$f''(x) = \frac{(x^2 - 6x - 1)(2) - (2x - 6)^2}{(x^2 - 6x - 1)^2}$$

Next, we must locate the critical points by setting the first derivative equal to zero:

$$f'(x) = \frac{2x - 6}{x^2 - 6x - 1} \log_{10} e = 0$$

The reader will recognize that $\log_{10} e$ is a constant positive number.   Thus, the function $(2x - 6)/(x^2 - 6x - 1) \log_{10} e$ will equal zero if and only if $(2x - 6)/(x^2 - 6x - 1)$ equals zero.   Also, notice that a fraction is equal to zero only if the *numerator* equals zero.   ($a/0$ is *not* zero; it is ∞.)   Thus, $(2x - 6)/(x^2 - 6x - 1)$

will equal zero only when $2x - 6$ equals zero. Solving, we obtain

$$2x - 6 = 0$$
$$x = 3$$

Thus, $\qquad f'(3) = \dfrac{2(3) - 6}{(3)^2 - 6(3) - 1} \log_{10} e = \dfrac{0}{-10} \log_{10} e = 0$

Now, substituting $x = 3$ in the second derivative, we determine

$$f''(3) = \frac{[3^2 - 6(3) - 1](2) - [2(3) - 6]^2}{[3^2 - 6(3) - 1]^2}$$

Note that the second term of the numerator is zero; we had determined the value of x to make it so. Also, note the denominator is positive, since it is a number squared. Therefore, the sign of the first term of the numerator will be the sign of the second derivative:

$$f''(3) = \frac{(-10)(2) - 0}{(-10)^2} = \frac{-20}{100} = \frac{-1}{5}$$

The sign could have been determined just by calculating the -10. Thus, $x = 3$ will produce a maximum profit and the company should plan on 3,000 units of production.

EXAMPLE 8.5

Senora, Ltd., wishes to maximize their extra revenue from advertising. They have found that

$$f(x) = 1,000 - 1,000e^{-3x}$$

where $x =$ thousand dollars of advertising and $f(x) =$ increased revenue from advertising, provides an excellent model. They are prepared to budget up to $5,000.

For the first and second derivatives, we obtain

$$f'(x) = (-3)(-1,000)e^{-3x}$$
$$f''(x) = -3(3,000)e^{-3x} = (-9,000)e^{-3x}$$

The reader will recognize that any exponential function is always positive. Thus, the first derivative will always be positive. There are no critical points. Therefore, the optimal value must occur at an end point. The end points are $x = 0$ and $x = 5$. Since $f'(x)$ is positive for all values of x, the function must be higher at $x = 5$ (the line is always going up). Therefore, increased revenue will be maximized when $x = 5$. The company should budget the entire $5,000.

MARGINAL RATES OF CHANGE

Another interpretation which is of considerable value in business decision making is that the derivative of an aggregate function, such as total cost, total profit, or total revenue, represents marginal cost, marginal profit, or marginal revenue. *Marginal* is defined as the change in the aggregate figure resulting from a small increase in the independent variable. Thus, marginal cost is the additional cost resulting from the manufacture of additional units. The relationship of marginal to aggregate can be seen to correspond to the relationship of derivative to original function.

Marginal information is better than aggregate (or average) data for most purposes. Marginal data is dynamic, whereas total and/or average data is static. One of the major services which mathematics can perform for the businessman is to distinguish among four types of conditions.

1 The return per extra unit expended is diminishing, so that, although profit may be still increasing overall, the effort necessary to affect the increase is too great to be generally practical.

2 The return per unit is increasing, as is profit, so extra units would be profitable and should be considered.

3 The return per unit is increasing, but the situation presently shows an overall loss. Here, also, extra production may quite possibly be advisable.

4 The return per extra unit added is decreasing, as is total profit, so that extra effort quite definitely should not be expended.

EXAMPLE 8.6

Total cost for a particular operation is well modeled by

$$f(x) = 10,000 + 400x - 3x^2 + .2x^3$$

Find the marginal cost of the tenth unit. When is marginal cost at a minimum? What is the marginal cost for the optimal last unit? What is the total cost for the optimal number of units?

The first derivative of the total cost function is the marginal cost function. Thus,

$$f(x) = 10,000 + 400x - 3x^2 + .2x^3$$
$$f'(x) = 400 - 6x + .6x^2$$

The function, then, which describes marginal cost is $f'(x) = 400 - 6x + .6x^2$. The marginal cost of the tenth unit is

$$f'(10) = 400 - 6(10) + .6(10)^2$$
$$= 400 - 60 + 60$$
$$= 400$$

The marginal cost curve is at a minimum when its first derivative is zero and its second derivative is positive. (These are the second and third derivatives of the original function for total cost.)

$$f'(x) = 400 - 6x + .6x^2$$
$$f''(x) = -6 + 1.2x$$
$$f'''(x) = 1.2$$

Finding the critical value of $f''(x)$,

$$f''(x) = -6 + 1.2x = 0$$
$$1.2x = 6$$
$$x = 6/1.2 = 5$$

So, when $x = 5$, the first derivative of the marginal function is zero, and the second derivative is positive.   The marginal cost of the fifth unit produced is

$$f'(5) = 400 - 6(5) + .6(5)^2$$
$$= 400 - 30 + 15$$
$$= 385$$

Total costs for five units will be

$$f(5) = 10,000 + 400(5) - 3(5)^2 + .2(5)^3$$
$$= 10,000 + 2,000 - 75 + 25$$
$$= 11,950$$

Note that this is not a minimum for total costs but, rather, an indication that this operation is being carried on at peak efficiency.

EXAMPLE 8.7

Total profits for a company can be modeled by the function

$$f(x) = 200x - 10x^2 + 1,111e^{-x}$$

When is marginal profit at a maximum?   What is the total profit for the optimal number of units?   What is the marginal profit for the optimal last unit?   Find the marginal profit for the fifth unit.   Find the marginal profit for the third unit.
   Marginal profit is the derivative of total profit:

$$f(x) = 200x - 10x^2 + 1,111e^{-x}$$
$$f'(x) = 200 - 20x - 1,111e^{-x}$$

Marginal profit is at a maximum when its first derivative is zero and its second derivative is negative (the second and third derivative of the total profit function).

$$f''(x) = -20 + 1,111e^{-x}$$
$$f'''(x) = -1,111e^{-x}$$
$$f''(x) = -20 + 1,111e^{-x} = 0$$
$$1,111e^{-x} = 20$$
$$e^{-x} = .018$$

In the table of e^{-x}, we find that $e^{-4} = .018$.   Therefore, $x = 4$ is a critical value. The second derivative of the marginal profit will be

$$f'''(4) = -1,111e^{-4} = -1,111(.018) = -20$$

This is negative, so $x = 4$ provides a maximum.   The total profit for four units will be:

$$f(4) = 200(4) - 10(4)^2 + 1,111e^{-4}$$
$$= 800 - 160 + 20$$
$$= 660$$

The marginal profit for the fourth unit will be

$$f'(x) = 200 - 20(4) - 1{,}111e^{-4}$$
$$= 200 - 80 - 20$$
$$= 100$$

The marginal profit for the fifth unit will be

$$f'(5) = 200 - 20(5) - 1{,}111e^{-5}$$
$$= 200 - 100 - 1{,}111(.0067)$$
$$= 200 - 100 - 7.4$$
$$= 92.6$$

The marginal profit for the third unit will be

$$f'(3) = 200 - 20(3) - 1{,}111e^{-3}$$
$$= 200 - 60 - 1{,}111(.05)$$
$$= 200 - 60 - 55.6$$
$$= 84.4$$

PARTIAL DERIVATIVES

Up to this point, we have considered only equations which have one independent variable and one dependent variable, x and $f(x)$, respectively. A number of optimization problems involve more than two variables, and for these problems an extension of the methods previously covered will be necessary.

If we have a function with two independent variables x and y and the dependent variable $f(x,y)$, the partial derivative with respect to x is the derivative of $f(x,y)$, treating x as a variable and y as a constant. The partial derivative with respect to y is, in the same manner, the derivative of $f(x,y)$, treating y as the variable and x as the constant. Generally, the symbol $f_x(x,y)$ indicates the first derivative of $f(x,y)$ with respect to x, and $f_y(x,y)$ indicates the first derivative with respect to y.

EXAMPLE 8.8

$$f(x,y) = 30x^2y^2 - 4xy^2 + 100y^2 + 5x^2 - 10$$
$$f_x(x,y) = 60y^2x - 4y^2 + 0 + 10x - 0$$
$$f_y(x,y) = 60x^2y - 8xy + 200y + 0 - 0$$

EXAMPLE 8.9

$$f(x,y) = x \ln 2y^3$$
$$f_x(x,y) = \ln 2y^3(1)$$
$$= \ln 2y^3$$
$$f_y(x,y) = x \frac{6y^2}{2y^3}$$
$$= \frac{3x}{y}$$

Note that ln $2y^3$ is a constant just like 10 or -15 when we are differentiating with respect to x. Therefore, this is not a product problem but, rather, a constant times a variable.

EXAMPLE 8.10

$$f(x,y) = \frac{\sin x \csc y}{3x + y}$$

$$f_x(x,y) = \frac{(3x + y)(\csc y \cos x) - (\sin x \csc y)(3)}{(3x + y)^2}$$

$$f_y(x,y) = \frac{(3x + y)(-\csc y \cot y \sin x) - (\sin x \csc y)(1)}{(3x + y)^2}$$

Second partial derivatives are similar to second derivatives in that they are determined simply by taking the derivative of the first derivative. However, there are four second derivatives in the three variable problems. They are

$f_{xx}(x,y)$ is the second derivative, first with respect to x and second with respect to x

$f_{yy}(x,y)$ is the second derivative, first with respect to y and second with respect to y

$f_{xy}(x,y)$ is the second derivative, first with respect to x and second with respect to y

$f_{yx}(x,y)$ is the second derivative, first with respect to y and second with respect to x

EXAMPLE 8.11

$$\left.\begin{array}{l} f(x,y) = 4x^2 + 10xy - 3y^4 \\ f_x(x,y) = 8x + 10y - 0 = 8x + 10y \\ f_y(x,y) = 0 + 10x - 12y^3 = 10x - 12y^3 \end{array}\right\} \text{ First derivatives}$$

$$\left.\begin{array}{l} f_{xx}(x,y) = 8 + 0 = 8 \\ f_{yy}(x,y) = 0 - 36y^2 = -36y^2 \\ f_{xy}(x,y) = 0 + 10 = 10 \\ f_{yx}(x,y) = 10 - 0 = 10 \end{array}\right\} \text{ Second derivatives}$$

EXAMPLE 8.12

$$\left.\begin{array}{l} f(x,y) = e^{x^2y^3} \\ f_x(x,y) = (2y^3x)(e^{x^2y^3}) \\ f_y(x,y) = (3x^2y^2)(e^{x^2y^3}) \end{array}\right\} \text{ First derivatives}$$

$$\left.\begin{array}{l} f_{xx}(x,y) = (2y^3x)(2y^3x)(e^{x^2y^3}) + e^{x^2y^3}(2y^3) \\ f_{yy}(x,y) = (3x^2y^2)(3x^2y^2)(e^{x^2y^3}) + e^{x^2y^3}(6x^2y) \\ f_{xy}(x,y) = (2y^3x)(3x^2y^2)(e^{x^2y^3}) + e^{x^2y^3}(6xy^2) \\ f_{yx}(x,y) = (3x^2y^2)(2y^3x)(e^{x^2y^3}) + e^{x^2y^3}(6y^2x) \end{array}\right\} \text{ Second derivatives}$$

EXAMPLE 8.13

$$f(x,y,z) = 3x^2 - 4y^3 + 7z^4 - 2xy^2z^3$$
$$f_x(x,y,z) = 6x - 0 + 0 - 2y^2z^3 = 6x - 2y^2z^3$$
$$f_y(x,y,z) = 0 - 12y^2 + 0 - 4xz^3y = -12y^2 - 4xz^3y$$
$$f_z(x,y,z) = 0 - 0 + 28z^3 - 6xy^2z^2 = 28z^3 - 6xy^2z^2$$

First derivatives

$$f_{xx}(x,y,z) = 6 - 0 = 6$$
$$f_{yy}(x,y,z) = -24y - 4xz^3$$
$$f_{zz}(x,y,z) = 84z^2 - 12xy^2z$$
$$f_{xy}(x,y,z) = 0 - 4z^3y = -4z^3y$$
$$f_{xz}(x,y,z) = 0 - 6y^2z^2 = -6y^2z^2$$
$$f_{yx}(x,y,z) = 0 - 4z^3y = -4z^3y$$
$$f_{yz}(x,y,z) = 0 - 12xyz^2 = -12xyz^2$$
$$f_{zx}(x,y,z) = 0 - 6y^2z^2 = -6y^2z^2$$
$$f_{zy}(x,y,z) = 0 - 12xz^2y = -12xz^2y$$

Second derivatives

Third and higher partial derivatives are calculated in a similar manner.

Interpretation of partial derivatives

Recall that the number of variables in a problem determined the number of dimensions. Thus, in our one independent variable problems the function could be graphed as a curved line on a piece of paper. The problem was two-dimensional. In this situation, a maximum occurred when the function reached a high spot, and a minimum occurred when the function dropped to a low spot.

A function of two independent variables requires three dimensions for graphing. The partial derivative of this function with respect to one of the two variables can be visualized as the slope of a thin slice. If we visualize the graph area as a cube, the partial derivative with respect to x is the slope of the path of the function on a slice of the cube with near zero thickness as shown in Figure 8.1. It represents the slope of the function from left to right across the graph. By selecting specific y values, we can determine the slope of specific slices algebraically.

The partial derivative with respect to y is the slope of the path of the function on a thin slice of the cube as shown in Figure 8.2. By selecting specific x values, we can determine the slope of specific slices.

Still considering the two-variable problem, the second partial derivatives $f_{xx}(x,y)$ and $f_{yy}(x,y)$ have the same interpretation with

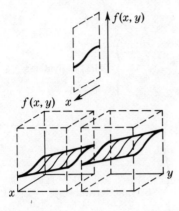

Figure 8.1   Partial with respect to x

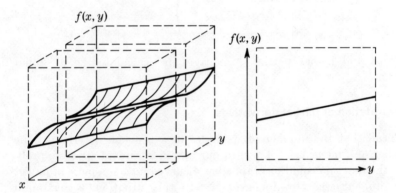

Figure 8.2   Partial with respect to y

respect to their narrow slices as $f''(x)$ has. $f_{xy}(x,y)$ and $f_{yx}(x,y)$ will be equal if the equation is continuous, i.e., if it has no breaks or sudden changes of direction.

Extrema of two-variable functions

Maxima for two-variable functions may be visualized as hilltops. They are points from which the function moves down in any direction. Minima have the opposite interpretation.   To find local maxima and minima within the region being investigated, we must compute $f_x(x,y)$, $f_y(x,y)$, $f_{xx}(x,y)$, $f_{yy}(x,y)$, $f_{xy}(x,y)$, and $f_{yx}(x,y)$.

A maximum or minimum can occur only where $f_x(a,b)$ and $f_y(a,b)$ are zero for a point a on the x axis and a point b on the y axis.   To determine whether a maxima or a minima (or neither) has occurred, we must also solve the equation

$$D(x,y) = f_{xx}(x,y)f_{yy}(x,y) - f_{xy}^2(x,y)$$

and substitute the critical values of $x = a$ and $y = b$.

1 If $D(a,b) > 0$ and $f_{xx}(a,b) < 0$, then $f(a,b)$ is a maximum.
2 If $D(a,b) > 0$ and $f_{xx}(a,b) > 0$, then $f(a,b)$ is a minimum.
3 If $D(a,b) < 0$, then $f(a,b)$ is not an extremum.

Note also that if $f_{xy}(x,y) \neq f_{yx}(x,y)$, the function is not continuous and the above test cannot be used.

EXAMPLE 8.14

If $f(x,y) = 3x^2 - 4xy + 2y$, are there any extrema (except at end points)?   We first must find the partial derivatives with respect to x and y:

$$f_x(x,y) = 6x - 4y$$
$$f_y(x,y) = -4x + 2$$

Solving simultaneously,

$$6x - 4y = 0$$
$$-4x + 2 = 0$$

we find that

$$-4x + 2 = 0 \qquad\qquad 6x - 4y = 0$$
$$-4x = -2 \qquad\qquad 6(\tfrac{1}{2}) - 4y = 0$$
$$x = \tfrac{1}{2} \qquad\qquad\qquad -4y = -3$$
$$y = \tfrac{3}{4}$$

So $x = \tfrac{1}{2}$ and $y = \tfrac{3}{4}$ is a critical point.   Finding the second partial derivatives:

$$f_{xx}(x,y) = 6$$
$$f_{yy}(x,y) = 0$$
$$f_{xy}(x,y) = -4$$
$$f_{yx}(x,y) = -4$$

Note that $f_{xy}(x,y) = f_{yx}(x,y)$.   Next we can find $D(x,y)$:

$$D(x,y) = 6(0) - (-4)^2$$
$$= 0 - 16$$
$$= -16$$
$$D(\tfrac{1}{2},\tfrac{3}{4}) = -16$$

Since $D(x,y) < 0$, no extremum exists at this critical point, and the answer to the question is no.

EXAMPLE 8.15

Find the extreme points of the function

$$f(x,y) = 3x^2 + 5y^2 + 5xy$$

if any exist.   The first partial derivatives are

$$f_x(x,y) = 6x + 5y$$
$$f_y(x,y) = 10y + 5x$$

Setting these equal to zero and solving simultaneously, we obtain

$$6x + 5y = 0$$
$$5x + 10y = 0$$
$$6x = -5y$$
$$x = -\tfrac{5}{6}y$$
$$5(-\tfrac{5}{6}y) + 10y = 0$$
$$-\tfrac{25}{6}y + 10y = 0$$
$$y = 0$$
$$x = 0$$

$x = 0$, $y = 0$, then, is a critical point. The second partial derivatives are

$$f_{xx}(x,y) = 6$$
$$f_{yy}(x,y) = 10$$
$$f_{xy}(x,y) = 5$$
$$f_{yx}(x,y) = 5$$

Note that $f_{xy}(x,y) = f_{yx}(x,y)$

$$D(x,y) = 6(10) - (5)^2$$
$$= 60 - 25$$
$$= 35$$
$$D(0,0) = 35$$

Thus, $D(a,b) > 0$ and $f_{xx}(x,y) > 0$, and $f(0,0)$ is a minimum point for the function $f(x,y)$.

EXAMPLE 8.16

Find the extreme points of the function

$$f(x,y) = 4x^2 + 5y^2 - 8xy + 10x + 15y$$

if any exist.

$$f_x(x,y) = 8x - 8y + 10$$
$$f_y(x,y) = 10y - 8x + 15$$

Any critical points will have to satisfy

$$8x - 8y + 10 = 0$$
$$-8x + 10y + 15 = 0$$

Using the Cramer method,

$$8x - 8y = -10$$
$$-8x + 10y = -15$$

$$\mathbf{A} = \begin{pmatrix} 8 & -8 \\ -8 & 10 \end{pmatrix} \qquad \mathbf{b} = \begin{pmatrix} -10 \\ -15 \end{pmatrix}$$

$$A = \begin{vmatrix} 8 & -8 \\ -8 & 10 \end{vmatrix} = 80 - 64 = 16$$

$$x = \frac{\begin{vmatrix} -10 & -8 \\ -15 & 10 \end{vmatrix}}{16} = \frac{-100 - 120}{16} = \frac{-220}{16} = -13.75$$

$$y = \frac{\begin{vmatrix} 8 & -10 \\ -8 & -15 \end{vmatrix}}{16} = \frac{-120 - 80}{16} = \frac{-200}{16} = -12.5$$

$x = -13.75$ and $y = -12.5$ is, therefore, a critical point.

$$f_{xx}(x,y) = 8$$
$$f_{yy}(x,y) = 10$$
$$f_{xy}(x,y) = -8$$
$$f_{yx}(x,y) = -8$$

and
$$D(x,y) = 8(10) - (-8)^2$$
$$= 80 - 64 = 16$$
$$D(-13.75, -12.5) = 16$$

Thus, $D(a,b) > 0$ and $f_{xx}(a,b) > 0$, so the point $(-13.75, -12.5)$ represents a minimum.

Marginal interpretation of partial derivatives

A marginal interpretation can also be applied to partial derivatives. Given an aggregate or total function in two variables, partial derivatives can be utilized to ascertain the marginal effect of an additional unit of x or one more unit of y.

EXAMPLE 8.17

If the partial derivative of a profit function $f(x,y)$ with respect to x is $75x - 30y$, then, when $y = 2$, the marginal profit associated with the tenth unit is

$$75(10) - 30(2) = 690$$

PROBLEMS

1 Find Dx

a $\dfrac{3x^2}{a}$

b x^{a^4}

c a^{x^4}

d $(3x^3 + 4x + 5)^{10}(3x^2 + 8)$

e $10e^2 - 15e + 10$

f $\ln(3x^4 + 2)$

g $\sin x^5$

h $\dfrac{(4x^{-3} - 2x^{-5})^5}{3x + a}$

i $2x^5 + 3^{\sin 2x^2}$

j $\log_8 4^{x^2}$

k $\cos(\ln e^x)$

l $(x^3 + 4x)^{x^2}$

m $\log_7 e^{3x^2}$

n $\ln \sin \dfrac{x^2 + 4x^5}{3x^2 + 5}$

o $3xy + 4x + 56$

where y is a dependent variable.

2 $f(x)$ passes through $(0,0)$; draw $f(x)$ and $f''(x)$.

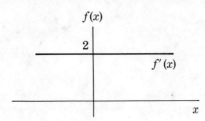

3 Find Dx:

a $4x^3$

b $7x^{-4}$

c $(2x - 5)(x + 1)$

d $5x^8$

e $4x^{-3}$

f $ex^{1/3}$

g 8^{5x^2}

h $(2x - 4)^{23}(4x + 5)$

i $e^{\csc x}$

j $\ln 2x^{-10}$

k $(2x^8 - 4)(5x^5 - 5x^3 + 10)^{24}$

l $\dfrac{2x^2 - 5}{3x + 1}$

m $\cos 20x^8$

n $\sec \ln 5^x$

o $\ln \sec 5^x$

4 Find the first and second derivative of $\ln |-4x^3 + 7x^2 + 4x|$.

5 Locate maxima and minima:

a $f(x) = -x^2 + 6x - 8$

b $f(x) = 3x^2 + 10x + 15$

c $f(x) = -6x^2 - 6x - 6$

d $f(x) = -10x^2 - 3x + 8$

e $f(x) = x^3 - 7x^2 - 5x + 10$

f $f(x) = 2x^3 + 9x^2 + 12x + 25$

g $f(x) = -5x^3 + 6x^2 - 2x - 5$

h $f(x) = -6x^3 + 2x^2 + 14x - 12$

i $f(x) = e^{2x^2 - 8x + 10}$

j $f(x) = e^{-4x^2 + 24x - 3}$

k $f(x) = 8^{3x^2 - 4x - 3}$

l $f(x) = 12^{7x^2 - 98x + 10}$

m $f(x) = e^{x^3 - 8x^2 + 5x - 10}$

n $f(x) = e^{x^3 + 3x^2 - 9x + 5}$

o $f(x) = \ln (x^2 - 4x + 5)$

p $f(x) = \ln (3x^2 + 18x - 1)$

q $f(x) = \log_5 (4x^2 - 40x - 10)$

r $f(x) = \log_3 (6x^2 + 72x + 3)$

s $f(x) = \ln (4x^3 - 7x^2 - 2x + 3)$

t $f(x) = \ln (-6x^3 - 2x^2 + 14x - 1)$

6 Find all first and second derivatives:

a $f(x,y) = 3x - 4y$

b $f(x,y) = -8x + 2y$

c $f(x,y) = x^2 - 3x + y^2 - 3y$

d $f(x,y) = 4x^2 + 5x + 3y^2 - 6y$

e $f(x,y) = 2x^2 + 5x + 7xy + 3y + 2y^2$

f $f(x,y) = 7x^2 - 3xy - 2x - 3y^2 + 2y$

g $f(x,y) = x^3 - 3x + y^{-3} - 4y$

h $f(x,y) = 7x^6 - 5x^{-4} - 3y^2$

i $f(x,y) = e^{xy}$

j $f(x,y) = e^{2x - 3y}$

k $f(x,y) = 4^{x^3 - y^4}$

l $f(x,y) = 11^{5x^2 + 3y^{-4}}$

m $f(x,y) = \ln(x^2 y^2)$ **n** $f(x,y) = \ln(3x^2 y^{-4})$

o $f(x,y) = y \log_3(x^2 - 1)$ **p** $f(x,y) = x^2 \log_7(y^2 + y)$

q $f(x,y) = x^y$ **r** $f(x,y) = (3x)^{4y}$

s $f(x,y) = 2x^2 - 3y^2 + 4z^2$ **t** $f(x,y) = \dfrac{xz}{y}$

7 Find maxima and minima where possible:
  a $f(x,y) = x^2 - 2x + 2y^2 - 8y + 4$
  b $f(x,y) = 3x^2 + 24x + 8y^2 - 16y - 1$
  c $f(x,y) = -5x^2 + 5y^2 + 10x - 15y - 3$
  d $f(x,y) = -8x^2 - 3y^2 - 144x - 12y + 10$
  e $f(x,y) = x^3 - 4x^2 - 3x + y^3 - 2y^2 - 4y$
  f $f(x,y) = 3x^3 + 5x^2 - x - 5x^3 + 6x^2 - 2x$
  g $f(x,y) = x^2 - 4x + 6y^2 - 24y - 4xy$
  h $f(x,y) = 4x^2 - 8x + 16y^2 + 160y + 100xy$
  i $f(x,y) = -6x^2 + 24x + 2y^2 - 100y + 5xy$
  j $f(x,y) = -8x^2 - 16x - 3y^2 + 12y + 24xy$
  k $f(x,y) = x^3 - 3x^2 - 3xy - y^2 + 6y$
  l $f(x,y) = -2x^3 + 5x^2 - 2xy + y^2 - 4y$
  m $f(x,y) = e^{2x^2 - 8x - 3y^2 - 12y}$
  n $f(x,y) = e^{5x^2 + 50x - 6y^2 + 12y}$
  o $f(x,y) = 3^{x^2 - 27x - y^2 + 75y}$
  p $f(x,y) = 9^{-2x^2 + 24x - 3y^2 + 324y}$
  q $f(x,y) = \ln(x^2 - 4x + 2y^2 - 16y)$
  r $f(x,y) = \ln(3x^2 - 21x - 6y^2 + 12y)$
  s $f(x,y) = \log_{10}(5x^3 - 10x^2 + 5x + 3y^3 - 6y^2 + 3y)$
  t $f(x,y) = \log_{15}(9x^3 + 20x^2 + 13x + 8y^3 + 15y^2 + 6y)$

8 a When is the profit rate at a maximum? (Prove you have a maximum.)

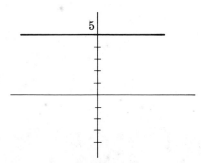

Sales revenue rate

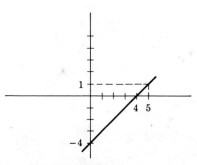

Derivative of cost rate

    b What will the profit be on the 200,000 through 600,000 units sold? (x is in terms of 100,000 units)

9 Total cost is given by $\sqrt[4]{40Q - 160} + 120$, where $Q > 4$ is the level of production. Find the marginal cost and determine whether it increases or decreases as Q increases.

10 The Lakewood Telephone Company is presently bringing lines to rural communities on the following basis: Monthly charges per customer are $8.00 each for up to 8 subscribers. For each additional subscriber the company reduces the monthly rate for all subscribers 20 cents. The president of the company is interested in knowing the number of subscribers which will produce maximum revenue from a community.

11 The Dixie Taxi Company has 25 cars working metropolitan New Rochelle. Each car carries an average of 50 passengers a day. The fare is presently $1.75 for any place in downtown New Rochelle. It has been estimated that a 20-cent decrease in fare will result in an additional 10 passengers per car. What fare should be charged in order to maximize revenue?

12 The Exeter Company is considering a change in the number of salesmen. We have determined their profit function to be $4q^{3/2} - 50q$, where q is the number of salesmen. What number of salesmen will provide a maximum profit? What number of salesmen will provide the maximum rate of profit per salesman?

13 The Taylor Company has determined the following equation which closely relates costs to quantity of production:

$$f(x) = \text{cost in dollars}$$
$$x = \text{quantity in thousands produced and sold}$$
$$f(x) = 29 + 4x + .03x^2$$

Moreover, they have been able to model the relationships of quantity sold to price per unit. Let

$$P = \text{price per 1,000 units charged}$$
$$x = 150 - 5P$$

The government is considering levying a tax on the product which Taylor Company is producing. If we assume the tax will be k dollars per 1,000 units, determine the price and resultant quantity which will maximize profit. How much of the tax did you decide to pass on to the customer? How much of any variable cost would you pass on to the customer?

9 INTEGRAL CALCULUS

INTRODUCTION

Now, having completed our explorations into differential calculus, we are ready to begin studying integral calculus. The reader will quickly recognize that the two branches of the calculus are closely related. The integral, as a matter of fact, is defined in terms of the derivative. The process of integration is merely differentiation in reverse. What will be most amazing to the reader is the wide realm of new business applications and interpretations which are available merely by reversing the differentiation process. Integral calculus is a vital tool in all decision problems involving risk (probabilities). It is a rapid summation device. It can be used to find the area under curved lines. These applications should serve to illustrate the wide difference in application.

Let's clarify the statement that integration is the reverse process of differentiation. The integral is the antiderivative of a function. For example, if

$$f(x) = 3x^2 + 5x$$

then

$$f'(x) = 6x + 5$$

$f'(x)$ would, of course, be the derivative of $f(x)$. At the same time, $f(x)$ is the integral of $f'(x)$. If we were to ask what function was the integral of $6x + 5$, we would be asking what function has $6x + 5$ as its derivative, and the answer would be $3x^2 + 5x$.

INTEGRAL NOTATION

The notation accepted as the sign to integrate a function is

$$\int f(x)\, dx$$

The term $\int dx$ is read "the integral with respect to the variable x."
Thus, $\int f(x)\, dx$ is read "the integral of the function $f(x)$ with respect to the variable x."

THE FINAL TERM FOR EVERY INTEGRAL

When finding the integral for any function, we always add the constant C as the last term. C, in this context, represents any constant, and since the derivative of a constant is zero, the integral of the function could have any constant attached without affecting the function.   As a further clarification, note that the integral of a particular function is defined as any other function having the original as its derivative.   No matter what constant is added to the end of a function, the derivative is unchanged.

EXAMPLE 9.1

$$f(x) = 3x^2 + 5$$
$$f(x) = 3x^2 + 9$$
$$f(x) = 3x^2 - 15$$

all have the same derivative :

$$f'(x) = 6x$$

There , $\int 6x\, dx = 3x^2 + C$, and C can be any constant.

INTEGRATION OF A CONSTANT

The integral of a constant is given by the formula

$$\int k\, dx = kx + C$$

Note that the derivative of $kx + C$ is k.

EXAMPLE 9.2

$$\int 35\, dx = 35x + C$$

EXAMPLE 9.3

$$\int -10\, dx = -10x + C$$

EXAMPLE 9.4

$$\int a \, dx = ax + C$$

EXAMPLE 9.5

$$\int \frac{e}{\sin 10} \, dx = \frac{e}{\sin 10} x + C$$

Note that both e and sin 10 are constants.

EXAMPLE 9.6

$$\int dx = x + C$$

Note that $\int dx$ is identical to $\int 1 \, dx$.

INTEGRATION OF A VARIABLE TO A CONSTANT POWER

The formula for integrating a power function x^n, where n is a constant, is

$$\int x^n \, dx = \left(\frac{1}{n+1} \right) x^{n+1} + C, \quad n \neq -1$$

This integral can be verified by noting that the derivative of $[1/(n+1)]x^{n+1} + C$ is

$$(n+1) \left(\frac{1}{n+1} \right) x^n = x^n$$

EXAMPLE 9.7

$$\int x^3 \, dx = \tfrac{1}{4}x^4 + C$$

EXAMPLE 9.8

$$\int x^a \, dx = \left(\frac{1}{a+1} \right) x^{a+1} + C$$

EXAMPLE 9.9

$$\int x^{-4} \, dx = -\tfrac{1}{3}x^{-3} + C$$

EXAMPLE 9.10

$$\int x^{3/4} \, dx = \tfrac{4}{7}x^{7/4} + C$$

EXAMPLE 9.11

$$\int x^{-2/9} \, dx = \tfrac{9}{7}x^{7/9} + C$$

EXAMPLE 9.12

$$\int x^{-3.5}\,dx = -.4x^{-2.5} + C$$

EXAMPLE 9.13

$$\int x^{e+3/a} = \left(\frac{1}{e + 3/a + 1}\right) x^{e+(3/a)+1} + C$$

INTEGRAL OF A CONSTANT TIMES A FUNCTION

As in differentiation, a constant, when multiplied by any function of the variable, is included unchanged in the final answer when integrating. Mathematically, the relationship may be expressed:

$$\int kf(x)\,dx = k\int f(x)\,dx \qquad \text{for any constant } k$$

EXAMPLE 9.14

$$\int 24x\,dx = 24\int x\,dx = 24(\tfrac{1}{2})x^2 + C = 12x^2 + C$$

EXAMPLE 9.15

$$\int -x^2\,dx = -\int x^2\,dx = -\tfrac{1}{3}x^3 + C$$

EXAMPLE 9.16

$$\int \frac{x^{10}}{23}\,dx = \frac{1}{23}\int x^{10}\,dx = \tfrac{1}{23}(\tfrac{1}{11})x^{11} + C = (\tfrac{1}{253})x^{11} + C$$

EXAMPLE 9.17

$$\int \frac{1}{2x^2}\,dx = \tfrac{1}{2}\int x^{-2}\,dx = \tfrac{1}{2}(-1)x^{-1} + C = -\tfrac{1}{2}x^{-1} + C$$

The reader should compute the derivatives of each of the answers to prove to himself that integration formulas do, in fact, produce the function which has as its derivative the original function.

THE SUM OR DIFFERENCE OF TWO FUNCTIONS

Sums and differences of functions may be treated separately when integrating just as they are when differentiating:

$$\int [f(x) \pm g(x)]\,dx = \int f(x)\,dx \pm \int g(x)\,dx$$

EXAMPLE 9.18

$$\int (x^2 + 3x^3)\,dx = \int x^2\,dx + \int 3x^3\,dx$$
$$= \tfrac{1}{3}x^3 + C_1 + 3(\tfrac{1}{4})x^4 + C_2$$
$$= \frac{x^3}{3} + \frac{3x^4}{4} + C$$

It should be noted that, since C may stand for any number, it is unnecessary to collect C's and show the above result as

$$\frac{x^3}{3} + \frac{3x^4}{4} + 2C \quad \text{or} \quad \frac{x^3}{3} + \frac{3x^4}{4} + C_1 + C_2$$

EXAMPLE 9.19

$$\int (-4x^{-5} - 7x^2)\, dx = \int -4x^{-5}\, dx - \int 7x^2\, dx$$

$$= -4 \int x^{-5}\, dx - 7 \int x^2\, dx$$

$$= [-4(-\tfrac{1}{4})x^{-4} + C_1] - [7(\tfrac{1}{3})x^3 + C_2]$$

$$= x^{-4} - \frac{7x^3}{3} + C$$

EXAMPLE 9.20

$$\int (3x^2 - x^{-2} + 5)\, dx = \int 3x^2\, dx - \int x^{-2}\, dx + \int 5\, dx$$

$$= 3 \int x^2\, dx - \int x^{-2}\, dx + 5 \int dx$$

$$= 3(\tfrac{1}{3})x^3 + C_1 - (-\tfrac{1}{1})x^{-1} + C_2 + 5x + C_3$$

$$= x^3 + x^{-1} + 5x + C$$

THE INTEGRAL OF A CONSTANT TO A VARIABLE POWER

The formula for integrating a function of the form a^{kx}, where a is any constant > 0, is

$$\int a^{kx}\, dx = \frac{1}{\ln a}\frac{1}{k} a^{kx} + C$$

Differentiating $(1/\ln a)(1/k)(a^{kx}) + C$ will show this to be true. Thus,

$$Dx\frac{1}{\ln a}\left(\frac{1}{k}\right) a^{kx} + C = \frac{1}{\ln a}\left(\frac{1}{k}\right) Dx\, a^{kx} + C = \frac{1}{\ln a}\left(\frac{1}{k}\right)$$

$$ka^{kx} \ln a + 0 = a^{kx}$$

Note that this formula provides the integral of a^{kx}, not $a^{f(x)}$. This formula cannot be used if the x in the exponent is raised to a power other than one.

EXAMPLE 9.21

$$\int 10^{3x}\, dx = \frac{1}{\ln 10}(\tfrac{1}{3})10^{3x} + C = \frac{1}{3 \ln 10} 10^{3x} + C$$

EXAMPLE 9.22

$$\int 7^{-2x}\, dx = \frac{1}{\ln 7}(-\tfrac{1}{2})7^{-2x} + C = \frac{-1}{2 \ln 7} 7^{-2x} + C$$

EXAMPLE 9.23

$$\int \tfrac{1}{2}^{4x} + x^2 \, dx = \int \tfrac{1}{2}^{4x} \, dx + \int x^2 \, dx$$

$$= \frac{1}{\ln \frac{1}{2}} \tfrac{1}{4}(\tfrac{1}{2})^{4x} + C_1 + \tfrac{1}{3}x^3 + C_2$$

$$= \frac{1}{4 \ln \frac{1}{2}} (\tfrac{1}{2})^{4x} + \frac{x^3}{3} + C$$

EXAMPLE 9.24

$$\int 3^{4x-5} \, dx = \frac{1}{\ln 3} \tfrac{1}{4}(3^{4x-5}) + C$$

THE INTEGRAL OF e TO A VARIABLE POWER

The integral of e to a variable power is similar to the integral of a to a variable power, except that, since $\ln e = 1$, the formula can be reduced:

$$\int e^{kx} \, dx = \frac{1}{\ln e} \frac{1}{k} e^{kx} + C = \frac{1}{k} e^{kx} + C$$

EXAMPLE 9.25

$$\int e^{5x} \, dx = \tfrac{1}{5}e^{5x} + C$$

EXAMPLE 9.26

$$\int e^{-3x-5} \, dx = -\tfrac{1}{3}e^{-3x-5} + C$$

EXAMPLE 9.27

$$\int e^{4x} - a^{2x} \, dx = \int e^{4x} \, dx - \int a^{2x} \, dx$$

$$= \tfrac{1}{4}e^{4x} + C_1 - \frac{1}{\ln a} \tfrac{1}{2}a^{2x} + C_2$$

$$= \tfrac{1}{4}e^{4x} - \frac{1}{2 \ln a} a^{2x} + C$$

EXAMPLE 9.28

$$\int 3e^{-6x} \, dx = 3 \int e^{-6x} \, dx = 3(-\tfrac{1}{6})e^{-6x} + C = -\tfrac{1}{2}e^{-6x} + C$$

SIMPLE TRIGONOMETRIC INTEGRALS

Most of the trigonometric derivatives are complicated and cannot be easily integrated by the techniques covered in this book. (All can be integrated, however.) The sine and cosine are quite easily integrated, and the formulas are

$$\int \sin x \, dx = -\cos x + C$$
$$\int \cos x \, dx = \sin x + C$$

EXAMPLE 9.29

$$\int 3 \sin x \, dx = 3 \int \sin x \, dx = 3(-\cos x) + C = -3 \cos x + C$$

EXAMPLE 9.30

$$\int 4 \sin x - 5 \cos x \, dx = \int 4 \sin x \, dx - \int 5 \cos x \, dx$$
$$= 4 \int \sin x \, dx - 5 \int \cos x \, dx$$
$$= 4[(-\cos x) + C_1] - 5(\sin x + C_2)$$
$$= -4 \cos x - 5 \sin x + C$$

INTEGRATION BY INSPECTION

Sometimes careful inspection of a function will provide the easiest method for finding its integral. Three integrals, in particular, can often be most easily found in this manner.

If the function is of the form $f'(x)/f(x)$, the integral will be $\ln |f(x)| + C$.

If the function is of the form $f(x)g'(x) + g(x)f'(x)$, the integral will be $f(x)g(x) + C$.

If the function is of the form $[g(x)f'(x) - f(x)g'(x)]/g^2(x)$, the integral will be $f(x)/g(x) + C$.

EXAMPLE 9.31

$$\int \frac{3x^2 + 5}{x^3 + 5x - 4} \, dx = ?$$

Note that $3x^2 + 5$ is the derivative of $x^3 + 5x - 4$, and this is an integral of the form $\int f'(x)/f(x) \, dx$, which is equal to $\ln |f(x)| + C$. So

$$\int \frac{3x^2 + 5}{x^3 + 5x - 4} \, dx = \ln |x^3 + 5x - 4| + C$$

EXAMPLE 9.32

$$\int x^{-1} \, dx = ?$$

This can be rewritten as $\int 1/x \, dx$. Again, the form is $\int f'(x)/f(x) \, dx$, and the answer is $\ln |x| + C$.

EXAMPLE 9.33

$$\int \frac{40x + 100}{2x^2 + 10x} \, dx = ?$$

The derivative of $2x^2 + 10x$ is $4x + 10$. The numerator can be factored to $10(4x + 10)$. Since 10 is a constant, this integral can be rewritten as

$$10 \int \frac{4x + 10}{2x^2 + 10x} \, dx$$

and is now in the form $\int f'(x)/f(x) \, dx$. The solution, then, is

$$10 \ln |2x^2 + 10x| + C$$

EXAMPLE 9.34

$$\int \frac{x}{3x^2} \, dx = ?$$

The derivative of the denominator is $6x$. Without changing the value of the integral, we can multiply it by 6 and by $\frac{1}{6}$ (net effect of 1). So

$$\int \frac{x}{3x^2} \, dx = \int 6(\tfrac{1}{6}) \frac{x}{3x^2} \, dx$$

Since $\frac{1}{6}$ is a constant, we can bring it in front of the integral:

$$\frac{1}{6} \int \frac{6x}{3x^2} \, dx$$

Now the integral is in the form

$$\int \frac{f'(x)}{f(x)} \, dx$$

and the integral is equal to

$$\tfrac{1}{6} \ln |3x^2| + C$$

EXAMPLE 9.35

$$\int (9x^2)(4x + 5) + (18x)(2x^2 + 5x) \, dx$$

This integral is in the form $\int f(x)g'(x) + f'(x)g(x) \, dx$. The answer is the product $f(x)g(x)$ plus a constant. So

$$\int (9x^2)(4x + 5) + (18x)(2x^2 + 5x) \, dx = (9x^2)(2x^2 + 5x) + C$$

EXAMPLE 9.36

$$\int (-3x - 4)(4x^3 + 4x) - 3(x^4 + 2x^2) \, dx$$

First, extracting the minus sign from $(-3x - 4)$, yields

$$-(3x + 4)$$

Then, factoring a -1 from each term yields:

$$\int -1[(3x + 4)(4x^3 + 4x) + (3)(x^4 + 2x^2)]\, dx$$

The -1 is a constant and can be moved out in front of the integral, giving

$$-1 \int (3x + 4)(4x^3 + 4x) + 3(x^4 + 2x^2)\, dx$$

This integral is now in the form of

$$\int f(x)g'(x) + f'(x)g(x)\, dx$$

and $f(x) = 3x + 4$ $\qquad g(x) = x^4 + 2x^2$

$$\int (-3x - 4)(4x^3 + 4x) - 3(x^4 + 2x^2)\, dx = -(3x + 4)(x^4 + 2x^2) + C$$

EXAMPLE 9.37

$$\int \frac{(4x^2 + 5x)(4x) - (2x^2)(8x + 5)}{(4x^2 + 5x)^2}\, dx$$

This integral is easily recognized as a quotient.

$$\int \frac{(4x^2 + 5x)(4x) - (2x^2)(8x + 5)}{(4x^2 + 5x)^2}\, dx = \frac{2x^2}{(4x^2 + 5x)} + C$$

EXAMPLE 9.38

$$\int \frac{(2x^5 + 1)(-3) + (3x - 8)(10x^4)}{(2x^5 + 1)^2}\, dx$$

Extracting a -1 from each term in the numerator yields

$$\int \frac{-1(2x^5 + 1)(3) - (3x - 8)(10x^4)}{(2x^5 + 1)^2}\, dx$$

Since the -1 is a constant, this integral can be written

$$-1 \int \frac{(2x^5 + 1)(3) - (3x - 8)(10x^4)}{(2x^5 + 1)^2}\, dx$$

This will be recognized as a quotient problem with $f(x) = 3x - 8$ and $g(x) = 2x^5 + 1$. Thus,

$$-1 \int \frac{(2x^5 + 1)(3) - (3x - 8)(10x^4)}{(2x^5 + 1)^2}\, dx = -\frac{(3x - 8)}{2x^5 + 1} + C$$

CHANGE OF VARIABLE

If the formula to be integrated is of the chain-rule type, i.e., in the form $\int f'(g(x))\, g'(x)\, dx$, then a technique known as *change of variable* will prove helpful for integrating. The letter u is substituted for $g(x)$ in the original problem, and at the same time du is substituted for $g'(x)\,dx$. The resulting formula is integrated with respect to u. After this has been accomplished, u is replaced by $g(x)$ in the final answer. Thus,

$$\int f'(g(x))\,g'(x)\,dx = \int f'(u)\,du \Big|_{u=g(x)+C}$$
$$= f(u)\Big|_{u=g(x)}$$
$$= f(g(x)) + C$$

EXAMPLE 9.39

Find $\displaystyle\int 2x(x^2+3)^3\,dx$.

Let $\qquad\qquad\qquad u = x^2 + 3$
then $\qquad\qquad\qquad du = 2x\,dx$

Substituting, the integral becomes

$$\int u^3\,du \Big|_{u=x^2+3}$$

Solving this integral,

$$\int u^3\,du \Big|_{u=x^2+3} = \frac{u^4}{4} + C \Big|_{u=x^2+3}$$

Substituting $x^2 + 3$ for u gives the final answer:

$$\frac{u^4}{4} + C \Big|_{u=x^2+3} = \frac{(x^2+3)^4}{4} + C$$

EXAMPLE 9.40

Find $\displaystyle\int (2x+5)(x^2+5x-4)^9\,dx$.

Let $\qquad\qquad\qquad u = x^2 + 5x - 4$
then $\qquad\qquad\qquad du = 2x + 5\,dx$

Substituting,

$$\int (2x+5)(x^2+5x-4)^9\,dx = \int u^9\,du \Big|_{u=x^2+5x-4}$$

Solving the integral,

$$\int u^9\,du \Big|_{u=x^2+5x-4} = \frac{u^{10}}{10} + C \Big|_{u=x^2+5x-4}$$

and replacing u, we obtain

$$\int (2x+5)(x^2+5x-4)^9\,dx = \frac{(x^2+5x-4)^{10}}{10} + C$$

EXAMPLE 9.41

Find $\int 3(6x - 4)^7 \, dx$.

Let $$u = 6x - 4$$
then $$du = 6 \, dx$$

Since the formula to be integrated contains only 3 dx, we must convert this to 6 dx before continuing with change of variable. This can be accomplished by multiplying by 2 and $\frac{1}{2}$ simultaneously:

$$\int (3)(6x - 4)^7 \, dx = \int (2)(\tfrac{1}{2})(3)(6x - 4)^7 \, dx$$

The $\frac{1}{2}$ can be moved out from behind the integral sign, since it is a constant. Thus,

$$\int (2)(\tfrac{1}{2})(3)(6x - 4)^7 \, dx = \tfrac{1}{2} \int (2)(3)(6x - 4)^7 \, dx$$

$$= \tfrac{1}{2} \int 6(6x - 4)^7 \, dx$$

The change of variable may now be executed:

$$\tfrac{1}{2} \int 6(6x - 4)^7 \, dx = \tfrac{1}{2} \int u^7 \, du \Big|_{u = 6x - 4}$$

$$\tfrac{1}{2} \int u^7 \, du \Big|_{u = 6x - 4} = \tfrac{1}{2}(\tfrac{1}{8})u^8 + C \Big|_{u = 6x - 4} = \tfrac{1}{16}(6x - 4)^8 + C$$

EXAMPLE 9.42

Find $\int \dfrac{3}{(x + 10)^4} \, dx$.

Let $$u = x + 10$$
then $$du = dx$$

The 3 in the original formula may be moved in front of the integral, giving

$$3 \int \frac{dx}{(x + 10)^4}$$

Substitution can now be performed:

$$3 \int \frac{dx}{(x + 10)^4} = 3 \int \frac{du}{u^4} \Big|_{u = x + 10} = 3 \int u^{-4} \, du \Big|_{u = x + 10}$$

$$= 3(-\tfrac{1}{3})u^{-3} + C \Big|_{u = x + 10}$$

$$= -(x + 10)^{-3} + C \text{ or } \frac{-1}{(x + 10)^3} + C$$

INTEGRATION BY PARTS

The following identity is often helpful in the evaluation of certain integrals:

$$\int u \, dv = uv - \int v \, du$$

If the integral to be evaluated is in the form of a product, or can be put into this form, it can sometimes be evaluated by integrating one part, finding the derivative of the other part, and applying the above formula. As to which part to integrate and which to differentiate, this is a matter of trial and error; i.e., if it doesn't work one way try the other.

EXAMPLE 9.43

Find $\int x \ln x \, dx$.

Let $\qquad\qquad u = \ln x \qquad$ and $\qquad dv = x \, dx$

then $\qquad\qquad du = \dfrac{1}{x} dx \qquad$ and $\qquad v = \dfrac{x^2}{2}$

$$\int x \ln x \, dx = \frac{x^2}{2} \ln x - \int \frac{x^2}{2} \frac{1}{x} dx = \frac{x^2}{2} \ln x - \int \frac{x}{2} dx$$

$$= \frac{x^2}{2} \ln x - \tfrac{1}{2} \int x \, dx = \frac{x^2}{2} \ln x - (\tfrac{1}{2})(\tfrac{1}{2})x^2 + C$$

$$= \frac{x^2}{2} \ln x - \tfrac{1}{4}x^2 + C = \frac{x^2}{2} \ln x - \frac{x^2}{4} + C$$

$$= \frac{x^2}{2} (\ln x - \tfrac{1}{2}) + C$$

EXAMPLE 9.44

Find $\int \ln x \, dx$.

Let $\qquad\qquad u = \ln x \qquad$ and $\qquad dv = 1 \, dx$

then $\qquad\qquad du = \dfrac{1}{x} dx \qquad$ and $\qquad v = x$

$$\int \ln x \, dx = x \ln x - \int x \frac{1}{x} dx = x \ln x - \int dx$$

$$= x \ln x - x + C$$

$$= x(\ln x - 1) + C$$

EXAMPLE 9.45

Find $\int \dfrac{x}{e^x} dx$.

First, put the integral into product form:

$$\int \frac{x}{e^x} dx = \int x \frac{1}{e^x} dx = \int x e^{-x} dx$$

then, let $\qquad\quad u = x \qquad\quad$ and $\qquad dv = e^{-x} dx$

then $\qquad\qquad du = dx \qquad\quad$ and $\qquad v = -e^{-x}$

Substituting, we obtain

$$\int \frac{x}{e^x} \, dx = -xe^{-x} - \int -e^{-x} \, dx$$
$$= -xe^{-x} - e^{-x} + C$$
$$= \frac{-1}{e^x} (x + 1) + C$$

EXAMPLE 9.46

Find $\int e^x \sin x \, dx$.

Let $\qquad\qquad u = \sin x \qquad$ and $\qquad dv = e^x \, dx$
Then $\qquad\quad\; du = \cos x \, dx \qquad$ and $\qquad v = e^x$
This produces

$$\int e^x \sin x \, dx = e^x \sin x - \int e^x \cos x \, dx$$

To solve this, use integration by parts again on $\int e^x \cos x \, dx$:

Let $\qquad\qquad u = \cos x \qquad$ and $\qquad dv = e^x \, dx$
then $\qquad\quad\; du = - \sin x \, dx \qquad$ and $\qquad v = e^x$

Substituting again, we obtain

$$\int e^x \sin x \, dx = e^x \sin x - \left(e^x \cos x - \int -e^x \sin x \, dx \right)$$
$$\int e^x \sin x \, dx = e^x \sin x - e^x \cos x + \int -e^x \sin x \, dx$$
$$\int e^x \sin x \, dx = e^x \sin x - e^x \cos x - \int e^x \sin x \, dx$$

Collecting the $2 \int e^x \sin x \, dx$'s, we obtain

$$2 \int e^x \sin x \, dx = e^x \sin x - e^x \cos x$$

and, therefore,

$$\int e^x \sin x \, dx = \frac{e^x \sin x - e^x \cos x}{2}$$

TABLE OF INTEGRALS

For the convenience of readers, a table is included at the end of the book which will be useful for integrating functions not covered by the methods on the preceding pages.

THE DEFINITE INTEGRAL

An integral of the form $\int f(x) \, dx$ is said to be an *indefinite integral*. A *definite integral* will include limits or boundaries for integration and will be written in the form $\int_a^b f(x)\,dx$. To solve a definite integral, the indefinite integral is first found. Assuming $F(x)$ to be the indefinite integral of $f(x)$,

$$\int_a^b f(x)\,dx = F(x)\Big|_a^b = F(b) - F(a)$$

EXAMPLE 9.47

Find $\int_3^5 x^2 + 3x - 4\,dx$.

$$\int_3^5 x^2 + 3x - 4\,dx = \tfrac{1}{3}x^3 + \tfrac{3}{2}x^2 - 4x \Big|_3^5 + C$$

$$= \tfrac{1}{3}(5)^3 + \tfrac{3}{2}(5)^2 - 4(5) + C - [\tfrac{1}{3}(3)^3 + \tfrac{3}{2}(3)^2 - 4(3) + C]$$

$$= \tfrac{125}{3} + \tfrac{75}{2} - 20 + C - (9 + \tfrac{27}{2} - 12 + C)$$

$$= 41\tfrac{2}{3} + 37\tfrac{1}{2} - 20 + C - 9 - 13\tfrac{1}{2} + 12 - C$$

$$= 48\tfrac{2}{3}$$

Note that C will cancel out when you are finding a definite integral.

EXAMPLE 9.48

Find $\int_1^2 2x^3 - \dfrac{5}{x^2}\,dx$.

$$\int_1^2 2x^3 - \dfrac{5}{x^2}\,dx = \dfrac{2}{4}x^4 - \dfrac{5}{-1}x^{-1}\Big|_1^2 = \tfrac{1}{2}x^4 + \dfrac{5}{x}\Big|_1^2$$

$$= \tfrac{1}{2}(2)^4 + \tfrac{5}{2} - [\tfrac{1}{2}(1)^4 + \tfrac{5}{1}]$$

$$= (8 + \tfrac{5}{2}) - (\tfrac{1}{2} + 5)$$

$$= 10\tfrac{1}{2} - 5\tfrac{1}{2}$$

$$= 5$$

EXAMPLE 9.49

Find $\int_0^\tau 3t^3 + 4t\,dt$.

$$\int_0^\tau 3t^3 + 4t\,dt = \tfrac{3}{4}t^4 + 2t^2 \Big|_0^\tau = \tfrac{3}{4}\tau^4 + 2\tau^2 - [\tfrac{3}{4}(0)^4 + 2(0)^2]$$

$$= \tfrac{3}{4}\tau^4 + 2\tau^2$$

EXAMPLE 9.50

Find $\int_0^1 \dfrac{x}{x^2 + 3}\,dx$.

Multiply by 2 and $\tfrac{1}{2}$:

$$\int_0^1 2(\tfrac{1}{2}) \dfrac{x}{(x^2 + 3)}\,dx$$

Move the $\frac{1}{2}$ in front of the integral:

$$\tfrac{1}{2} \int_0^1 \frac{2x}{x^2 + 3} \, dx$$

The integral is now in the form

$$\int \frac{f'(x)}{f(x)} \, dx$$

$$\int_0^1 \frac{x}{x^2 + 3} \, dx = \tfrac{1}{2} \ln (x^2 + 3) \Big|_0^1$$

$$= \tfrac{1}{2} \{ \ln [(1)^2 + 3] - \ln [(0)^2 + 3] \}$$

$$= \tfrac{1}{2} (\ln 4 - \ln 3)$$

In the table for ln x we find that ln $4 = 1.386$ and ln $3 = 1.099$.   So,

$$\int_0^1 \frac{x}{x^2 + 3} \, dx = \tfrac{1}{2} (1.386 - 1.099)$$

$$= \tfrac{1}{2} (.287) = .1435$$

THE AREA INTERPRETATION OF THE INTEGRAL

Area, it will be recalled, in terms of a rectangle (Figure 9.1) can be calculated using the formula:

$$A = L \cdot W$$

When we are dealing with a curved surface, however, this method cannot be directly applied.   Integral calculus can be used to deter-

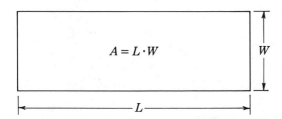

Figure 9.1   Area of a rectangle

mine the area under a curve.   An approximation to the area under the curve $f(x)$ bounded by a,b and the x axis could be obtained by inscribing a rectangle within the curve as shown in Figure 9.2.   The area of this rectangle, given by $f(a) \cdot (b - a)$ would represent the shaded area shown in Fig. 9.2 and would be smaller than the actual area under the curve.

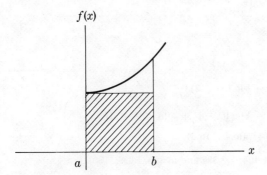

Figure 9.2   First approximation of area under $f(x)$

A closer approximation could be developed by placing two rectangles under the curve as shown in Figure 9.3.   The area within these two rectangles can be determined by multiplying the length by the height for each rectangle and adding the two areas together.

$$f(a) \cdot (c - a) + f(c) \cdot (b - c)$$

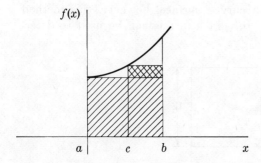

Figure 9.3   Second approximation of area under
$f(x)$

If c is equidistant from a and b, then $c - a = b - c$.   Let the distance represented by either $c - a$ or $b - c$ be represented by k_1.   Then

$$A = f(a)k_1 + f(c)k_1 = k_1[f(a) + f(c)]$$

Note that this area is larger than the area obtained using just one rectangle, by the amount shown in the cross-hatched shading in Figure 9.3, and is, thereby, a closer approximation of the area under the curve.

We can further subdivide the curve into four rectangles as shown in Figure 9.4. This area is an even closer approximation of the area under the curve and is equal to

$$f(a) \cdot (d - a) + f(d) \cdot (c - d) + f(c) \cdot (e - c) + f(e) \cdot (b - e)$$

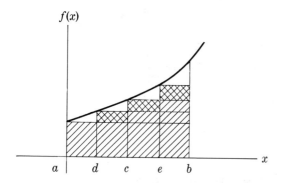

Figure 9.4   Third approximation of area under $f(x)$

If a, b, c, d, and e are chosen so that

$$(d - a) = (c - d) = (e - c) = (b - e) = k_2$$

then
$$A = k_2[f(a) + f(d) + f(c) + f(e)]$$

As we increase the number of rectangles and, thereby, reduce the width of each individual rectangle, the resulting area approximation will be even closer to the area under the curve.

The integral may be thought of as the sum of an enormous number of heights, $f(x)$'s, under the curve, each multiplied by an extremely narrow base dx. The width dx is meant to be much thinner than the thickness of a piece of paper. Thus, the integral takes a height $f(a)$ and multiplies it by a very narrow width dx and then takes the height of the next point on the curve (dx away from a) $f(b)$ and multiplies it by dx, and so on, adding all the results together to give a close approximation to the area under the curve (Figure 9.5):

$$f(a) \cdot dx + f(b) \cdot dx + \cdots + f(n) \cdot dx = [f(a) + f(b) + \cdots \\ + f(n) \; dx]$$

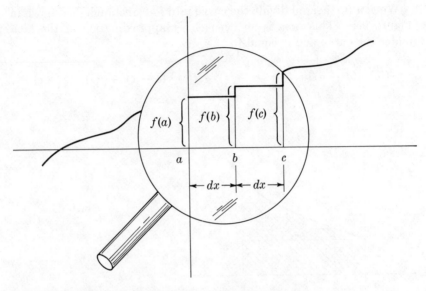

Figure 9.5 Magnification of $f(x)$ to show three adjacent points

$\int_a^b f(x) \; dx$ can be interpreted as the area under the curve $f(x)$ bounded by a, b, and the x axis (assuming $f(x)$ is positive between a and b). If $f(x) < 0$ between a and b, then $- \int_a^b f(x) \; dx$ will be the area bounded by the curve a, b and the x axis (Figures 9.6, 9.7, and 9.8).

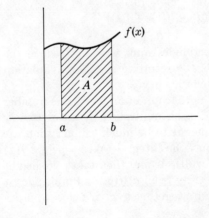

Figure 9.6 $A = \int_a^b f(x) \; dx$

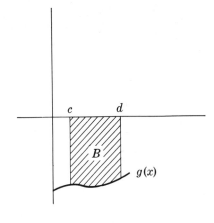

Figure 9.7 $B = -\displaystyle\int_c^d g(x)\,dx$

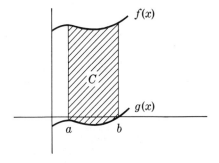

Figure 9.8 $C = \displaystyle\int_a^b f(x)\,dx - \int_a^b g(x)\,dx$

EXAMPLE 9.51

Find the area bounded by $x = 2$, $x = 5$, $f(x) = 0$, and $g(x) = 2x^2 - 3x$:

$$
\begin{aligned}
A &= \int_2^5 2x^2 - 3x\,dx = \tfrac{2}{3}x^3 - \tfrac{3}{2}x^2 \Big|_2^5 \\
&= \tfrac{2}{3}(5)^3 - \tfrac{3}{2}(5)^2 - [\tfrac{2}{3}(2)^3 - \tfrac{3}{2}(2)^2] \\
&= (\tfrac{250}{3} - \tfrac{75}{2}) - (\tfrac{16}{3} - \tfrac{12}{2}) \\
&= \tfrac{250}{3} - \tfrac{75}{2} - \tfrac{16}{3} + \tfrac{12}{2} \\
&= \tfrac{234}{3} - \tfrac{63}{2} \\
&= 78 - 31\tfrac{1}{2} \\
&= 46\tfrac{1}{2}
\end{aligned}
$$

EXAMPLE 9.52

Find the area bounded by $x = 3$, $x = 7$, $f(x) = 5x^2 - 3x$, $f(x) = -x - 10$:

$$A = \int_3^7 5x^2 - 3x \, dx - \int_3^7 - x - 10 \, dx$$

$$= \tfrac{5}{3}x^3 - \tfrac{3}{2}x^2 \Big|_3^7 - (-\tfrac{1}{2}x^2 - 10x) \Big|_3^7$$

$$= \tfrac{5}{3}(7)^3 - \tfrac{3}{2}(7)^2 - [\tfrac{5}{3}(3)^3 - \tfrac{3}{2}(3)^2] - [-\tfrac{1}{2}(7)^2 - 10(7)] + [-\tfrac{1}{2}(3)^2 - 10(3)]$$

$$= \frac{1{,}715}{3} - \frac{147}{2} - \left(45 - \frac{27}{2}\right) + \frac{49}{2} + 70 - \left(\frac{9}{2} + 30\right)$$

$$= \frac{1{,}715}{3} - \frac{147}{2} - 45 + \frac{27}{2} + \frac{49}{2} + 70 - \frac{9}{2} - 30$$

$$= \frac{1{,}715}{3} - \frac{80}{2} - 5$$

$$= 526\tfrac{2}{3}$$

MULTIPLE INTEGRATION

Multiple integration is the reverse process of partial differentiation. In the two-independent-variable case with variables x and y, multiple integration would be performed by integrating from the inside out. Thus,

$$\int_a^b \int_c^d f(x,y) \, dy \, dx = \int_a^b \left[\int_c^d f(x,y) \, dy \right] dx$$

The integration with respect to y would be performed first, since dy is on the inside. The integration with respect to y would be performed as if x were a constant (similar to partial differentiation). After the definite integral with respect to y is found, this is then integrated with respect to x (treating y as a constant).

The multiple integral can be interpreted as the area of the solid bounded by c and d on the y axis and a and b on the x axis and the function.

EXAMPLE 9.53

Find $\int_1^3 \int_2^5 xy - 2x + 4y^2 \, dy \, dx$.

First,

$$\int_2^5 xy - 2x + 4y^2 \, dy = \tfrac{1}{2}xy^2 - 2xy + \tfrac{4}{3}y^3 \Big|_2^5$$

$$= \tfrac{1}{2}x(5)^2 - 2x(5) + \tfrac{4}{3}(5)^3 - [\tfrac{1}{2}x(2)^2 - 2x(2) + \tfrac{4}{3}(2)^3]$$

$$= \tfrac{25}{2}x - 10x + \tfrac{500}{3} - (2x - 4x + \tfrac{32}{3})$$

$$= \tfrac{9}{2}x + \tfrac{468}{3}$$

$$= \tfrac{9}{2}x + 156$$

then

$$\int_1^3 \tfrac{9}{2}x + 156 \; dx = \tfrac{9}{4}x^2 + 156x \Big|_1^3$$

$$= \tfrac{9}{4}(3)^2 + 156(3) - [\tfrac{9}{4}(1)^2 + 156(1)]$$

$$= \tfrac{81}{4} + 468 - (\tfrac{9}{4} + 156)$$

$$= \tfrac{72}{4} + 312$$

$$= 18 + 312$$

$$= 330$$

EXAMPLE 9.54

Find $\displaystyle\int_0^3 \int_1^2 \frac{x}{y+1} \, dy \, dx$.

First

$$\int_1^2 \frac{x}{y+1} \, dy = x \int_1^2 \frac{1}{y+1} \, dy$$

(since x is a constant in this part of the problem)

$$= x[\ln (y+1)] \Big|_1^2 = x[\ln (2+1) - \ln (1+1)]$$

$$= x(\ln 3 - \ln 2)$$

$$= x(1.099 - .693)$$

$$= .406x$$

then

$$\int_0^3 .406x \, dx = \frac{.406}{2} x^2 \Big|_0^3 = .203(3)^2 - .203(0)^2$$

$$= 1.827$$

PROBLEMS

1   Find the following integrals:

a $\displaystyle\int 4 \, dx$ b $\displaystyle\int 5 \, (31) \, dx$

c $\displaystyle\int -7 \, dx$ d $\displaystyle\int \tfrac{2}{9} \, dx$

e $\displaystyle\int a \, dx$ f $\displaystyle\int 5a^2 \, dx$

g $\displaystyle\int (a+b)(c-d) \, dx$ h $\displaystyle\int dx$

i $\displaystyle\int \frac{a^2}{2} \, dx$ j $\displaystyle\int ab^{-1} \, dy$

k $\displaystyle\int a \, dx + \int b \, dy$ l $\displaystyle\int \frac{a^2}{2a-1} \, dx$

2 Find the following integrals:

a $\int x\, dx$ **b** $\int x^2\, dx$

c $\int x^{-4}\, dx$ **d** $\int x^{2/7}\, dx$

e $\int x^{-2}\, dx$ **f** $\int x^{-3/5}\, dx$

g $\int x^{-3}\, dx$ **h** $\int x^{2a}\, dx$

i $\int x^{a^2}\, dx$ **j** $\int x^{a^2}\, dy$

k $\int a^x\, da$ **l** $\int \sqrt{x}\, dx$

3 Find the following integrals:

a $\int 2x\, dx$ **b** $\int 4x^2\, dx$

c $\int -7x^{-3}\, dx$ **d** $\int -3(4x^5)\, dx$

e $\int \dfrac{x^{-3}}{5}\, dx$ **f** $\int -ax^b\, dx$

g $\int -3^a b x^7\, dx$ **h** $\int \dfrac{7x}{a}\, dx$

i $\int \dfrac{2x^a}{b}\, dx$ **j** $\int 8x^{-1/2}\, dx$

k $\int 5^2 \cdot 3^2 \cdot 7^2\, da$ **l** $\int \dfrac{a^2}{x^2}\, dx$

4 Find the following integrals:

a $\int x^2 - x^7\, dx$ **b** $\int x^{-4} + x^{-.4}\, dx$

c $\int 3x^5 - 7x^3\, dx$ **d** $\int \dfrac{4x - 1 + 7x^3}{9}\, dx$

e $\int ax^b - cx^d\, dx$ **f** $\int (x - 1)(k - 2)\, dx$

5 Find the following integrals:

a $\int 5^x\, dx$ **b** $\int 3^x\, dx$

c $\int 7^{-2x}\, dx$ **d** $\int e^{3x}\, dx$

e $\displaystyle\int 5a^{2x}\,dx$ **f** $\displaystyle\int 8(4^{-7x})\,dx$

g $\displaystyle\int a^{bx+c}\,dx$ **h** $\displaystyle\int 8^{4x-1}\,dx$

i $\displaystyle\int 3(5^{-2x+5})\,dx$

6 Find the following integrals:

a $\displaystyle\int e^x\,dx$ **b** $\displaystyle\int e^{2x}\,dx$

c $\displaystyle\int 3e^{4x}\,dx$ **d** $\displaystyle\int 5e^{5/2}\,dx$

e $\displaystyle\int \frac{e^{2x-1}}{3}\,dx$ **f** $\displaystyle\int e^{ax+b}\,dx$

g $\displaystyle\int -8e^{-8}\,dx$ **h** $\displaystyle\int -4e^{-x}\,da$

i $\displaystyle\int e^{\frac{1}{2}x}\,dx$

7 Find the following integrals:

a $\displaystyle\int \sin x\,dx$ **b** $\displaystyle\int \cos x\,dx$

c $\displaystyle\int -4\sin x\,dx$ **d** $\displaystyle\int a\cos x\,dx$

e $\displaystyle\int \sin a\cos x\,dx$ **f** $\displaystyle\int \cos 5(x)\,dx$

g $\displaystyle\int 3\sin 7x\,dx$ **h** $\displaystyle\int a\sin(bx+c)\,dx$

i $\displaystyle\int \cos 5\left(\frac{x}{2}\right)\,dx$

8 Find the following integrals:

a $\displaystyle\int 2(x-1)+2x-2\,dx$ **b** $\displaystyle\int 6x^2(3x^2-4)+(6x)(2x^3+7)\,dx$

c $\displaystyle\int (5x^3-2x)(-8x^{-3}+9x^{-4})+(4x^{-2}-3x^{-3})(15x^2-2)\,dx$

d $\displaystyle\int \frac{4x-3}{2x^2-3x}\,dx$ **e** $\displaystyle\int \frac{-15x^{-4}+14x}{5x^{-3}+7x^2}\,dx$

f $\displaystyle\int \frac{(x+2)-(x-1)}{(x+2)^2}\,dx$ **g** $\displaystyle\int \frac{x^2-2x+3-(x-5)(2x-2)}{(x^2-2x+3)^2}\,dx$

h $\displaystyle\int 3x^2-3x+3(x+5)(2x-1)\,dx$

i $\displaystyle\int \frac{-6x}{3x^2-1}\,dx$ **j** $\displaystyle\int \frac{6(2x-1)-4(3x+2)}{(3x+2)^2}\,dx$

9 Find the following integrals:

a $\displaystyle\int 2x(x^2 - 3)^4 \, dx$ b $\displaystyle\int 3x^2(x^3 - 8)^{-7} \, dx$

c $\displaystyle\int 2x \sin x^2 \, dx$ d $\displaystyle\int 5x^4 \cos (x^5 - 1) \, dx$

e $\displaystyle\int x(x^2 + 8)^2 \, dx$ f $\displaystyle\int 5x(3x^2 - 8)^{1/2} \, dx$

g $\displaystyle\int \cos x \sin^2 x \, dx$ h $\displaystyle\int \cos^2 x \sin x \, dx$

i $\displaystyle\int xe^{x^2} \, dx$ j $\displaystyle\int x^3 a^{5x^4} \, dx$

k $\displaystyle\int x^2 a^{27a^3x^3} \, dx$ l $\displaystyle\int \sin^3 3x \cos 3x \, dx$

10 Find the following integrals:

a $\displaystyle\int x \sin x \, dx$ b $\displaystyle\int x \ln x \, dx$

c $\displaystyle\int x(x - 5)^{15} \, dx$ d $\displaystyle\int 3x^2 \cos 4x \, dx$

e $\displaystyle\int 5x^2 \log_7 (2x - 1) \, dx$ f $\displaystyle\int \ln x \, dx$

g $\displaystyle\int \sin x \cos 2x \, dx$

11 Find the following integrals:

a $\displaystyle\int_1^4 x \, dx$ b $\displaystyle\int_2^7 x^2 - 1 \, dx$

c $\displaystyle\int_a^b \sin x \, dx$ d $\displaystyle\int_0^r x^2 - 3ax \, dx$

e $\displaystyle\int_2^4 \frac{1}{x} \, dx$ f $\displaystyle\int_8^{59} \ln x \, dx$

12 Find the areas under the following curves:

a $x^2 + 4x - 1; \ 3 \leq x \leq 7$ b $x - 7; \ 2 \leq x \leq 10$

c $3x^2 + 7x - 8; \ 0 \leq x \leq 5$ d $x + 3; \ -4 \leq x \leq 5$

e $\displaystyle\frac{4}{x + 5}; \ 2 \leq x \leq 5$

13 Find the following integrals:

a $\displaystyle\int_2^3 \int_0^4 x \, dy \, dx$ b $\displaystyle\int_0^5 \int_1^4 \, dy \, dy \, dx$

c $\displaystyle\int_0^x \int_0^y xy^2 \, dy \, dx$ d $\displaystyle\int_{-2}^2 \int_0^x \frac{y}{x} \, dy \, dx$

e $\displaystyle\int_a^b \int_c^d x(1 - y) \, dx \, dy$ f $\displaystyle\int_0^3 \int_{x-1}^{x^2} x^2 - 3 \, dx \, dx$

14 **a** $\int_1^3 x^2(4x^3 + 5)\,dx$ **b** $\int 2x(4x^2 + 5)^7\,dx$

c $\int x^2 \ln x\,dx$ **d** $\int 3x^2(4x + 5) + (2x^2 + 5x)(6x)\,dx$

e $\int_2^5 x^2 + 2x\,dx$ **f** $\int 2x^2(x^7 + 100)^{50}\,dx$

g $\int x^7 - 3x^{-4}\,dx$ **h** $\int x^4(x^5 - 10)^{14}\,dx$

i $\int_a^f x \sin x\,dx$ **j** $\int_2^4 x^3 \ln^2 x\,dx$

k $\int_1^3 \frac{i}{2x - 7}\,dx$

15 A computer manufacturer wants to include repairs and maintenance as a part of its rental charge for a computer. Repairs and maintenance increase, of course, as the computer gets older. They have modeled the expected costs as follows:

$$f(x) = \text{maintenance cost}$$
$$x = \text{time in years}$$
$$f(x) = 1{,}000 + 5x - .01x^2$$

If the computer is to be rented for 6 years, and if the manufacturer wishes to charge the same rental each year, how much should be added for repairs and maintenance each year?

16 A decision is to be made about whether to buy a new welding machine. The machine would cost $2,000 and would have a life of 3 years with no salvage. If savings are estimated as:

$$f(x) = \frac{3{,}100}{x + 3}$$

where x is time in years, will the machine pay for itself?

17 Mr. Barnes, who is in the masonry business, has been seriously considering the possibility of purchasing an electric mortar mixer. The mixer has an expected useful life of 10 years with $500 scrap value. Costs per year at a rate of 5,000 + $20x - x^2$ are predicted (where x is years after purchase). Mr. Barnes presently employs three helpers. With the new machine he will be able to eliminate one of these men. The wages which would be paid to this helper over the next 10 years are estimated at the rate of 4,000 + 100x. The mixer would cost $18,000 and would be of no use to Mr. Barnes after 10 years. Which alternative would result in the least costs to Mr. Barnes?

18 The Atfan Company sells and distributes a small fan to retailers at a fixed unit price. Owing to increased business activity, Atfan found it necessary to divide the geographical area it covered into two regions that were thought to have equal sales potential. Thus, the $10,000 per period budgeted for selling expenses has been divided equally between region 1 and region 2. However, doubt is growing among Atfan's management that the two regions actually have the same potential. In fact, last period region 1 brought in sales of 55,000 units compared to 45,000 units from region 2. Management is convinced that the salesmen (all of whom are on straight salary) are of equal competence and their efficiency would not be affected by a change of region.   Consequently, an investigation has been undertaken to determine the optimal budgeting of the selling expenses between the regions so that total sales would be maximized.   Since the only selling expenses are the salesmen's salaries and traveling allowances, which are about the same for each man, the task amounts to reapportioning the salesmen in the two regions. Atfan's product is not unique, and there are several competitors working the same territory so that each additional sale is made more difficult and costly than the previous one.   Thus, the marginal selling expense is an increasing function of sales, and it is estimated that the expense of the nth sale is proportional to the square root of n.   Furthermore, Atfan is willing to assume that the sales made during one period do not substantially affect the next period's sales.   Based upon the above information, an analysis must be performed that will yield the optimum allocation for the next period of the budgeted selling expense of $10,000 between regions 1 and 2 so that the total sales revenue will be maximized.

19   The Darby Manufacturing Company is in the home appliance business and recently has been approached by a publisher of women's magazines for the purpose of soliciting advertisements.   The publisher intends to put out a new monthly magazine that presents home appliances to the housewives across the nation. The magazine will be in color and divided into sections, each of which will deal with a specific type of appliance.   Manufacturers will have the opportunity to have one or more pages devoted to their appliance lines, and the features of the appliances will be promoted in the advertisements.

The publisher claims that the magazine will provide an inexpensive means for the smaller manufacturer to gain recognition by housewives who otherwise see only the major brands advertised in the well-known magazines.   The Darby Company had participated in this type of promotion about 5 years ago; at that time, the campaign resulted in an increase in sales of about 4 percent per month during the time of the promotion.   According to the publisher, the advertising cost for the first 12 issues (one year) of the magazine would be $125,000.   At present, company sales are $750,000 per month and profits are 10 percent of sales.   The criterion upon which Darby will decide whether to be a participating advertiser in the magazine is that the additional profits from the increase in sales over the 12-month period must be at least a 10 percent return on the advertising investment.

As a result of Darby's previous experience, it will be assumed that the monthly rate of sales during the campaign can be estimated by the exponential function $750,000e^{.04t}$, where t is the variable of time measured in months.   Thus, the total sales resulting from the first t months of the promotional campaign can be calculated as

$$\text{Total sales for first } t \text{ months } = \int_0^t 750,000e^{.04t}\, dt$$

Assume that Darby continues its normal advertising and marketing during the period of the promotional campaign and that its profits will remain 10 percent of sales.   The $125,000 to be spent for advertising in the new magazine should be considered an additional cost.   Thus, find the net profit accruing from increased sales owing to the special promotional campaign, determine the rate of return on the $125,000 investment, and decide whether the Darby Manufacturing Company should enter into the venture proposed by the magazine publisher.

20 Two years ago Sam Cartwright bought out the owners of the Big Bend Pretzel Company, whose sales had been going steadily downhill for several years. After Cartwright assumed leadership of the company, he introduced scientific management as well as successful promotional campaigns. The Big Bend Pretzel Company is a retailer of pretzels that are purchased from a local manufacturer, packaged in various-sized paper bags, boxed, and distributed by truck to grocery stores. A few days ago, the company's president was looking over the sales records he had achieved since taking over, and he calculated that the seasonally adjusted annual sales rates for this month and the corresponding months of the last two years were 150,000, 120,000, and 100,000 pounds of pretzels per year, respectively. Since Cartwright believes that sales will continue to increase at the same rate for several more years, he feels that he could use these data to predict when he will sell his millionth pound of pretzels. The latter date is important, since he expects to launch a big promotional campaign at that time.

Since sales have been growing in a nonlinear fashion, it is believed that the deseasonalized annual rate of sales should be forecast by a parabola; i.e.,

$$S = A + Bt + Ct^2$$

where A, B, and C are constants to be determined, t is the time in years since Cartwright bought the company, and S is the deseasonalized annual rate of sales in pounds of pretzels. In order to determine the unknown constants, note that, for $t = 0$, $S = 100,000$; for $t = 1$, $S = 120,000$; and for $t = 2$, $S = 150,000$. Substituting these values into the equation gives

$$A = 100,000 \qquad A + B + C = 120,000 \qquad A + 2B + 4C = 150,000$$

so that $A = 100,000$, $B = 15,000$, and $C = 5000$. Therefore, the equation that gives the deseasonalized instantaneous rate of sales at time t is

$$S = 100,000 + 15,000t + 5000t^2$$

Thus, for example, after three years of being in control, Cartwright would expect a sales rate of

$$S = 100,000 + 15,000(3) + 5000(3^2)$$
$$= 190,000 \text{ pounds of pretzels per year}$$

The use to which Cartwright intends to put the sales rate forecasting function is to predict total sales for the coming years. In particular, the predicted sales for the third year of operation S_3 can be found as

$$S_3 = \int_2^3 (100,000 + 15,000t + 5,000t^2) \, dt$$
$$= (100,000t + 7,500t^2 + 1,667t^3) \Big|_2^3$$
$$= 169,173 \text{ pounds of pretzels}$$

Based upon the above discussion, it should be possible to calculate the date when Cartwright will sell his millionth pound of pretzels. Determine the value of t for which this is true and, thus, pinpoint the month in which the "Millionth Pound of Pretzels" campaign will be launched.

PART 3

10 SET THEORY: BASIC CONCEPTS

INTRODUCTION

Each branch of mathematics has its own rules. The rules for set theory produce some interesting results, which can be quite surprising to a person familiar with basic arithmetic and algebra—such as $1 + 1 = 1$, and $A + BC = (A + B)(A + C)$. These results, of course, are meaningful only for those situations where set theory applies, but these situations are more numerous than one might at first imagine. As a rough illustration of the $1 + 1 = 1$ phenomenon, consider all the people in a town with two eyes and add to this all the people in the town with one nose. In most towns the sum would come out the same as each of the parts.

Set theory provides a basis for analyzing a large number of business problems which are not adaptable to conventional algebra. It is also an essential tool for an investigation of probability theory, which, in turn, is necessary for the solution of all business problems dealing with uncertainty.

THE CONCEPT OF A SET

A set is a group of items with a common identifying characteristic. All the items which have the identifying characteristic which defines a particular set are called elements of the set. Any item, of course, can be an element of many different sets. For example, we could establish as the identifying characteristics of three different sets the following criteria:

1 Men under 35.
2 Men with blue eyes.
3 Men who are 5 feet, 6 inches or less.

A man could belong to all three sets as well as many others. However, each of the above sets is different; that is, each has a different identifying characteristic. Also, each set will have a different population of elements. While some elements may belong to all three sets, other elements will belong to only one set or another, and some to two of the three sets.

A set is usually represented by a capital letter, such as A, B, or C, while elements within the set are designated by lowercase letters. For example a_1, a_2, a_3, and a_4, may be elements of the set A. The letter a_i stands for the ith element of the set A.

VENN DIAGRAMS

Venn diagraming is a technique which helps in the visualization of set theory concepts and operations. The diagram is a rectangle with one or more circles drawn within it (Figure 10.1). Within the walls

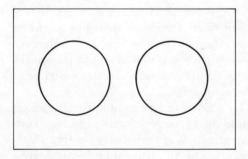

Figure 10.1 A Venn diagram

of the rectangle every item of every set is included. The particular sets of interest are represented by circles drawn within the rectangle. Elements can, if desired, be represented by dots. Whether or not the dots are drawn, we assume that every dot, representing every element of a particular set, is included within the circle of its set. Finally, in a Venn diagram, the area of interest is shaded to set it apart from the rest of the diagram. Thus in Figure 10.2, assuming we wished to diagram the elements which belong to the sets A and B at the same time, we have shaded that area which is common to both A and B.

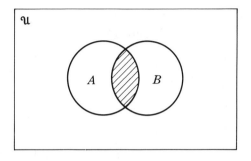

Figure 10.2 Venn diagram illustrating elements common to sets A and B

SPECIAL SETS

The *universal set*, designated $\mathcal{U}$, is the set which contains all elements. In terms of a Venn diagram, the universal set is represented by the entire area within the rectangle (Figure 10.3).

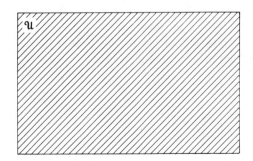

Figure 10.3   Universal set

"All elements" actually refers to all elements under consideration in a particular situation. Thus, if we were interested in sets or classifications of people, the universal set, then, would be the set which contains all the people who could possibly be included in any of the sets being defined for a particular problem.

Another very important set is the null set, designated $\emptyset$. The *null set* is the empty set, the set which contains no elements. If, for example, we are interested in the set of men who are in both sets A

and B and if no men are in both of these sets, we could say that the set representing those men who are in both A and B is the null set.

SET SYMBOLS

The symbol $\in$ means "is an element of." Thus, a quick way of writing "a_1 is an element of A" is $a_1 \in A$ (Figure 10.4).

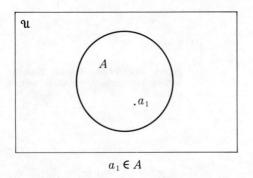

$$a_1 \in A$$

Figure 10.4 Venn diagram illustrating an element of set A

The symbol $\subseteq$ means "is a subset of." Thus, $A \subseteq B$ is read "the set A is a subset of the set B." $A \subseteq B$ is defined as "every element of A is also an element of B." Notice in Figure 10.5 that $A \subseteq B$, since each element in A is also contained in B. We can also define the symbol $\nsubseteq$ as "not a subset of." In this illustration, note that $B \nsubseteq A$, since there are elements in B which are not included in A.

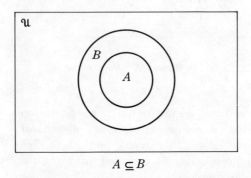

$$A \subseteq B$$

Figure 10.5 Venn diagram illustrating A as a subset of B

In Figure 10.6, A and B contain the same elements. Thus, by our definition, $A \subseteq B$ and $B \subseteq A$.

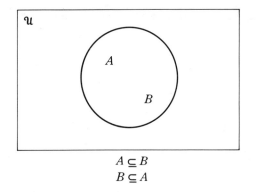

$$A \subseteq B$$
$$B \subseteq A$$

Figure 10.6 Venn diagram illustrating A **as a subset of** B **and** B **as a subset of** A

It is equally correct to write $A \subseteq B$ or $B \supseteq A$. The meaning is identical. An easy way to remember which is a subset of which is to consider the set symbol $\subseteq$ as similar to the already familiar mathematical symbol $\leq$ "less than or equal to." Thus, $A \subseteq B$ means $A \leq B$ and $B \supseteq A$ means $B \geq A$.

Proper subsets

Proper subsets are designated by $A \subset B$, read "A is a proper subset of B." If a set is a proper subset of another, it is also a subset of the other. That is, if $A \subset B$, every element is A must be included also in B. The further restriction is added that A must contain at least one less element than B. Thus, A and B cannot contain exactly the same elements (Figure 10.7).

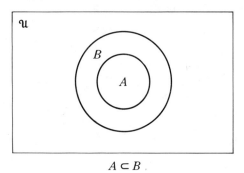

$$A \subset B$$

Figure 10.7 Set A **as a proper subset of set** B

$A \subset B$ can also be written $B \supset A$. As with subsets, the direction of the subset relationship can be determined by substituting the "less than" $<$ or "greater than" $>$ symbols for the proper subset symbols. Thus, $A \subset B$ means that $A < B$.

Whenever a proper subset relationship exists, it should be labeled and interpreted as such, rather than as just a subset, since the meaning is more restrictive and thereby, more exact.

Union

The operation of *union* is designated by the symbol $\cup$. $A \cup B$ is defined as the set of elements in A and the set of elements in B, including those elements in both A and B. Those elements in both A and B, it should be emphasized, are to be included only once, not twice. Examples of union are illustrated by the diagrams (Figures 10.8 to 10.13).

EXAMPLE 10.1

$$A \cup B$$
$$A = (1, 2, 3)$$
$$B = (4, 5, 6)$$
$$A \cup B = (1, 2, 3, 4, 5, 6)$$

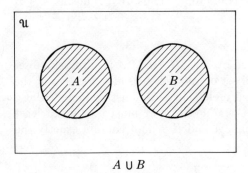

$$A \cup B$$

Figure 10.8 Union of two disjoint sets

EXAMPLE 10.2

$$A \cup B$$
$$A = (1, 2, 3)$$
$$B = (3, 4, 5)$$
$$A \cup B = (1, 2, 3, 4, 5)$$

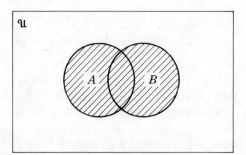

Figure 10.9 Union of two conjoint sets

EXAMPLE 10.3

$$A \cup B \cup C$$
$$A = (1, 2, 3)$$
$$B = (4, 5, 6)$$
$$C = (5, 6, 7)$$
$$A \cup B \cup C = (1, 2, 3, 4, 5, 6, 7)$$

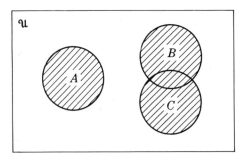

Figure 10.10   Union of three sets

EXAMPLE 10.4

$$A \cup \mathfrak{U}$$
$$A = (1, 2)$$
$$\mathfrak{U} = (1, 2, 3, 4)$$
$$A \cup \mathfrak{U} = (1, 2, 3, 4)$$

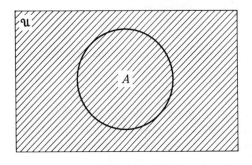

Figure 10.11   Union of set A and the universal set

EXAMPLE 10.5

$$A \cup \varnothing$$
$$A = (1, 2, 3)$$
$$A \cup \varnothing = (1, 2, 3)$$

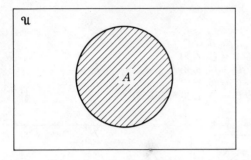

Figure 10.12   Union of set A and the null set

EXAMPLE 10.6

$$A \cup B$$
$$A = (1, 2)$$
$$B = (1, 2, 3)$$
$$A \cup B = (1, 2, 3)$$

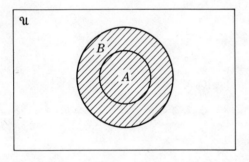

Figure 10.13   Union of a set with a subset

The union of two sets always results in a set as large as or larger than the larger of the two original sets.

Intersection

The operation of *intersection* is designated by the symbol ∩. $A \cap B$ is the set of elements in both A and B at the same time. $A \cap B \cap C$ is the set of elements common to all three sets A, B, and C.   Figures 10.14 to 10.19 illustrate intersection.

EXAMPLE 10.7

$$A \cap B$$
$$A = (1, 2, 3)$$
$$B = (3, 4, 5)$$
$$A \cap B = (3)$$

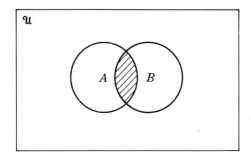

Figure 10.14 Intersection of two conjoint sets

EXAMPLE 10.8

$$A \cap B = \emptyset$$
$$A = (1, 2, 3)$$
$$B = (4, 5, 6)$$
$$A \cap B = \emptyset$$

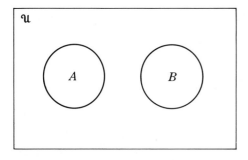

Figure 10.15 Intersection of two disjoint sets

EXAMPLE 10.9

$$A \cap B \cap C = \emptyset$$
$$A = (1, 2, 3)$$
$$B = (4, 5, 6)$$
$$C = (5, 6, 7)$$
$$A \cap B \cap C = \emptyset$$

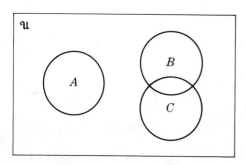

Figure 10.16 Intersection of three sets where one is disjoint

EXAMPLE 10.10

$$A \cap \mathfrak{U}$$
$$A = (1, 2, 3)$$
$$\mathfrak{U} = (1, 2, 3, 4)$$
$$A \cap \mathfrak{U} = (1, 2, 3)$$

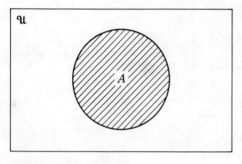

Figure 10.17 Intersection of a set with the universal set

EXAMPLE 10.11

$$A \cap \varnothing = \varnothing$$
$$A = (1, 2, 3)$$
$$A \cap \varnothing = \varnothing$$

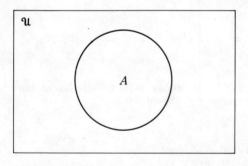

Figure 10.18 Intersection of a set with the null set

EXAMPLE 10.12

$$A \cap B$$
$$A = (1, 2)$$
$$B = (1, 2, 3)$$
$$A \cap B = (1, 2)$$

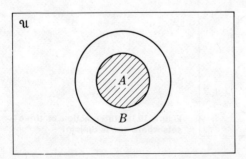

Figure 10.19 Intersection of a set with a subset

The intersection of two sets always results in a set as small as or smaller than the smaller of the two sets.

Complement

The *complement* of the set A is designated either as $\tilde{A}$ or A'. $\tilde{A}$ or A' is the set of items not in A.   The concept of complement is illustrated by the Venn diagrams in Figures 10.20 to 10.29.

EXAMPLE 10.13

$$A'$$
$$\mathfrak{u} = (1, 2, 3, 4)$$
$$A = (1, 2)$$
$$A' = (3, 4)$$

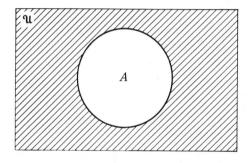

Figure 10.20 Complement of a set

EXAMPLE 10.14

$$A \cup B$$
$$\mathfrak{u} = (1, 2, 3, 4, 5, 6, 7)$$
$$A = (1, 2, 3)$$
$$B = (2, 3, 4)$$
$$(A \cup B)^1 = (5, 6, 7)$$

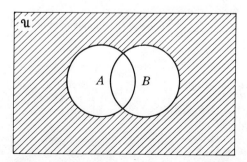

Figure 10.21 Complement of two conjoint sets

EXAMPLE 10.15

$$A \cap B$$
$$\mathfrak{u} = (1, 2, 3, 4, 5, 6, 7)$$
$$A = (1, 2, 3)$$
$$B = (2, 3, 4)$$
$$(A \cap B)^1 = (1, 4, 5, 6, 7)$$

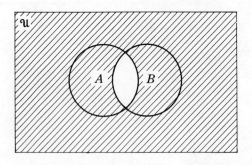

Figure 10.22 Complement of the intersection of two sets

EXAMPLE 10.16

$$A'$$
$$\mathfrak{u} = (1, 2, 3, 4)$$
$$A = (1, 2)$$
$$B = (2, 3)$$
$$A' = (3, 4)$$

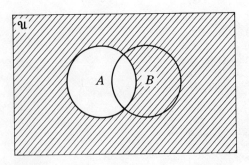

Figure 10.23 Complement of set A

EXAMPLE 10.17

$$B'$$
$$\mathfrak{u} = (1, 2, 3, 4)$$
$$A = (2, 3)$$
$$B = (1, 2, 3)$$
$$B' = (4)$$

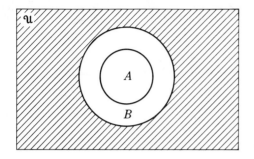

Figure 10.24 Complement of set B

Minus

In set theory terms $A - B$ is the same as $A \cap \tilde{B}$.   Illustrations of minus operations are

EXAMPLE 10.18

$$A - B$$
$$A = (1, 2, 3, 4)$$
$$B = (3, 4, 5, 6)$$
$$A - B = (1, 2)$$

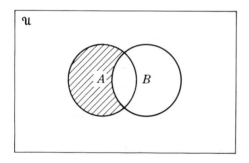

Figure 10.25 Set A **minus set** B
where A **and** B **are conjoint**

EXAMPLE 10.19

$$A - B$$
$$A = (1, 2, 3, 4)$$
$$B = (2, 3)$$
$$A - B = (1, 4)$$

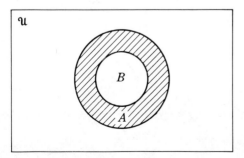

Figure 10.26 Set A **minus set** B
where B **is a subset of** A

EXAMPLE 10.20

$$A - \emptyset = A$$
$$A = (1, 2, 3, 4)$$
$$A - \emptyset = (1, 2, 3, 4)$$

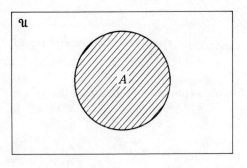

Figure 10.27 Set A minus the null set

EXAMPLE 10.21

$$A - B$$
$$A = (1, 2, 3, 4)$$
$$B = (5, 6, 7, 8)$$
$$A - B = (1, 2, 3, 4)$$

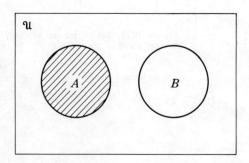

Figure 10.28 Set A minus set B where A and B are disjoint

EXAMPLE 10.22

$$A - \mathfrak{U} = \emptyset$$
$$A = (1, 2)$$
$$\mathfrak{U} = (1, 2, 3, 4)$$
$$A - \mathfrak{U} = \emptyset$$

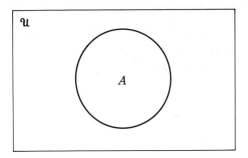

Figure 10.29 Set A minus the universal set

THE ABSTRACT LAWS OF SET OPERATIONS

The abstract laws of set operation are similar to, but not exactly the same as, the laws of mathematical relationships used in ordinary algebra. Each law is shown with a Venn diagram illustrating the relationship.

LAW 1

$$A \cup A = A$$

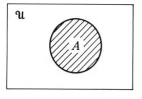

Figure 10.30

EXAMPLE 10.23

Let	$A = (1, 2, 3)$
then	$A \cup A = (1, 2, 3)$
Therefore	$A \cup A = A = (1, 2, 3)$

LAW 2

$$A \cap A = A$$

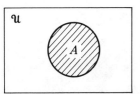

Figure 10.31

EXAMPLE 10.24

Let $\qquad\qquad\qquad\qquad A = (1, 2, 3)$
then $\qquad\qquad\qquad A \cap A = (1, 2, 3)$
Therefore $\qquad\qquad A \cap A = A = (1, 2, 3)$

LAW 3

$$A \cup B = B \cup A$$

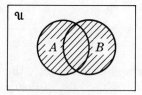

Figure 10.32

EXAMPLE 10.25

Let $\qquad\qquad\qquad\qquad A = (1, 2, 3)$
$\qquad\qquad\qquad\qquad\qquad B = (3, 4, 5)$
then $\qquad\qquad\qquad A \cup B = (1, 2, 3, 4, 5)$
also $\qquad\qquad\qquad B \cup A = (1, 2, 3, 4, 5)$
Therefore $\qquad\qquad A \cup B = B \cup A = (1, 2, 3, 4, 5)$

LAW 4

$$A \cap B = B \cap A$$

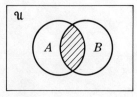

Figure 10.33

EXAMPLE 10.26

Let $\qquad\qquad\qquad\qquad A = (1, 2, 3)$
$\qquad\qquad\qquad\qquad\qquad B = (3, 4, 5)$
then $\qquad\qquad\qquad A \cap B = (3)$
also $\qquad\qquad\qquad B \cap A = (3)$
Therefore $\qquad\qquad A \cap B = B \cap A = (3)$

LAW 5

$$A \cup (B \cup C) = (A \cup B) \cup C$$

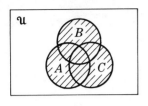

Figure 10.34

EXAMPLE 10.27

Let
$$A = (1, 2, 3, 4)$$
$$B = (3, 4, 5, 6)$$
$$C = (2, 4, 5, 7)$$
then
$$B \cup C = (2, 3, 4, 5, 6, 7)$$
$$A \cup (B \cup C) = (1, 2, 3, 4, 5, 6, 7)$$
also
$$A \cup B = (1, 2, 3, 4, 5, 6)$$
$$(A \cup B) \cup C = (1, 2, 3, 4, 5, 6, 7)$$
Therefore
$$A \cup (B \cup C) = (A \cup B) \cup C = (1, 2, 3, 4, 5, 6, 7)$$

LAW 6

$$A \cap (B \cap C) = (A \cap B) \cap C$$

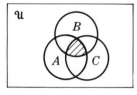

Figure 10.35

EXAMPLE 10.28

Let
$$A = (1, 2, 3, 4)$$
$$B = (3, 4, 5, 6)$$
$$C = (2, 4, 5, 7)$$
then
$$B \cap C = (4, 5)$$
$$A \cap (B \cap C) = (4)$$
also
$$A \cap B = (3, 4)$$
$$(A \cap B) \cap C = (4)$$
Therefore
$$A \cap (B \cap C) = (A \cap B) \cap C = (4)$$

LAW 7

$$A \cap (B \cup C) = (A \cap B) \cup (A \cap C)$$

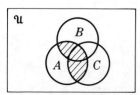

Figure 10.36

EXAMPLE 10.29

Let
$$A = (1, 2, 3, 4)$$
$$B = (3, 4, 5, 6)$$
$$C = (2, 4, 5, 7)$$
then
$$B \cup C = (2, 3, 4, 5, 6, 7)$$
$$A \cap (B \cup C) = (2, 3, 4)$$
also
$$A \cap B = (3, 4)$$
$$A \cap C = (2, 4)$$
$$(A \cap B) \cup (A \cap C) = (2, 3, 4)$$
Therefore
$$A \cap (B \cup C) = (A \cap B) \cup (A \cap C) = (2, 3, 4)$$

LAW 8

$$A \cup (B \cap C) = (A \cup B) \cap (A \cup C)$$

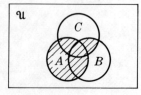

Figure 10.37

EXAMPLE 10.30

Let
$$A = (1, 2, 3, 4)$$
$$B = (3, 4, 5, 6)$$
$$C = (2, 4, 5, 7)$$
then
$$B \cap C = (4, 5)$$
$$A \cup (B \cap C) = (1, 2, 3, 4, 5)$$
also
$$A \cup B = (1, 2, 3, 4, 5, 6)$$
$$A \cup C = (1, 2, 3, 4, 5, 7)$$
$$(A \cup B) \cap (A \cup C) = (1, 2, 3, 4, 5)$$
Therefore
$$A \cup (B \cap C) = (A \cup B) \cap (A \cup C) = (1, 2, 3, 4, 5)$$

LAW 9

$$A \cup \mathfrak{U} = \mathfrak{U}$$

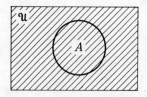

Figure 10.38

EXAMPLE 10.31

Let $$\mathfrak{U} = (1, 2, 3, 4)$$
$$A = (1, 2)$$
then $$A \cup \mathfrak{U} = (1, 2, 3, 4)$$
Therefore $$A \cup \mathfrak{U} = \mathfrak{U} = (1, 2, 3, 4)$$

LAW 10

$$A \cap \mathfrak{U} = A$$

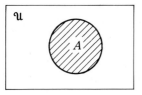

Figure 10.39

EXAMPLE 10.32

Let $$\mathfrak{U} = (1, 2, 3, 4)$$
$$A = (1, 2)$$
then $$A \cap \mathfrak{U} = (1, 2)$$
Therefore $$A \cap \mathfrak{U} = A = (1, 2)$$

LAW 11

$$A \cup \varnothing = A$$

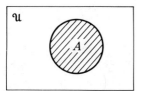

Figure 10.40

EXAMPLE 10.33

Let $$A = (1, 2, 3)$$
then $$A \cup \varnothing = (1, 2, 3)$$
Therefore $$A \cup \varnothing = A = (1, 2, 3)$$

LAW 12

$$A \cap \varnothing = \varnothing$$

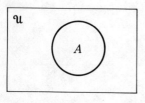

Figure 10.41

EXAMPLE 10.34

Let $\qquad A = (1, 2, 3)$
then $\qquad A \cap \varnothing = \varnothing$
Therefore $\qquad A \cap \varnothing = \varnothing = \varnothing$

LAW 13

$$\widetilde{\widetilde{A}} = A$$

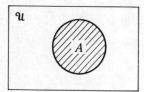

Figure 10.42

EXAMPLE 10.35

Let $\qquad \mathcal{U} = (1, 2, 3, 4)$
$\qquad A = (1, 2, 3)$
then $\qquad \widetilde{A} = (4)$
$\qquad \widetilde{\widetilde{A}} = (1, 2, 3)$
Therefore $\qquad \widetilde{\widetilde{A}} = A = (1, 2, 3)$

LAW 14

$$A \cup \widetilde{A} = \mathcal{U}$$

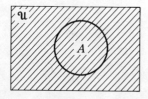

Figure 10.43

EXAMPLE 10.36

Let

$$\mathfrak{U} = (1, 2, 3, 4)$$
$$A = (1, 2, 3)$$

then

$$\tilde{A} = (4)$$
$$A \cup \tilde{A} = (1, 2, 3, 4)$$

Therefore

$$A \cup \tilde{A} = \mathfrak{U} = (1, 2, 3, 4)$$

LAW 15

$$A \cap \tilde{A} = \varnothing$$

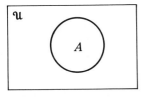

Figure 10.44

EXAMPLE 10.37

Let

$$\mathfrak{U} = (1, 2, 3, 4)$$
$$A = (1, 2, 3)$$

then

$$\tilde{A} = (4)$$
$$A \cap \tilde{A} = \varnothing$$

Therefore

$$A \cap \tilde{A} = \varnothing = \varnothing$$

LAW 16

$$(A \cup B)^1 = \tilde{A} \cap \tilde{B}$$

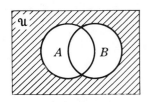

Figure 10.45

EXAMPLE 10.38

Let

$$\mathfrak{U} = (1, 2, 3, 4, 5)$$
$$A = (1, 2, 3)$$
$$B = (2, 3, 4)$$

then

$$A \cup B = (1, 2, 3, 4)$$
$$(A \cup B)^1 = (5)$$

also

$$\tilde{A} = (4, 5)$$
$$\tilde{B} = (1, 5)$$
$$\tilde{A} \cap \tilde{B} = (5)$$

Therefore

$$(A \cup B)^1 = \tilde{A} \cap \tilde{B} = (5)$$

LAW 17

$$(A \cap B)^1 = \tilde{A} \cup \tilde{B}$$

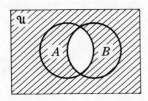

Figure 10.46

EXAMPLE 10.39

Let	$\mathfrak{U} = (1, 2, 3, 4, 5)$
	$A = (1, 2, 3)$
	$B = (2, 3, 4)$
then	$(A \cap B) = (2, 3)$
	$(A \cap B)^1 = (1, 4, 5)$
also	$\tilde{A} = (4, 5)$
	$\tilde{B} = (1, 5)$
	$\tilde{A} \cup \tilde{B} = (1, 4, 5)$
Therefore	$(A \cap B)^1 = \tilde{A} \cup \tilde{B} = (1, 4, 5)$

LAW 18

$$\tilde{\mathfrak{U}} = \varnothing$$

Figure 10.47

EXAMPLE 10.40

Let	$\mathfrak{U} = (1, 2, 3)$
then	$\tilde{\mathfrak{U}} = \varnothing$
Therefore	$\tilde{\mathfrak{U}} = \varnothing = \varnothing$

LAW 19

$$\tilde{\varnothing} = \mathfrak{U}$$

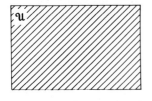

Figure 10.48

EXAMPLE 10.41

Let $\qquad$ $\mathfrak{U} = (1, 2, 3)$

then $\qquad$ $\tilde{\varnothing} = (1, 2, 3)$

Therefore $\qquad$ $\tilde{\varnothing} = \mathfrak{U} = (1, 2, 3)$

LAW 20

$$\mathfrak{U} - A = \tilde{A}$$

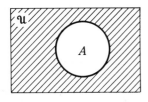

Figure 10.49

EXAMPLE 10.42

Let $\qquad$ $\mathfrak{U} = (1, 2, 3, 4, 5)$

$\qquad$ $A = (1, 2, 3)$

then $\qquad$ $\tilde{A} = (4, 5)$

also $\qquad$ $\mathfrak{U} - A = (4, 5)$

Therefore $\qquad$ $\mathfrak{U} - A = \tilde{A} = (4, 5)$

LAW 21

$$A - \mathfrak{U} = \varnothing$$

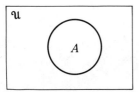

Figure 10.50

EXAMPLE 10.43

Let
$$\mathcal{U} = (1, 2, 3, 4, 5)$$
$$A = (1, 2, 3)$$
then
$$A - \mathcal{U} = \emptyset$$
Therefore
$$A - \mathcal{U} = \emptyset = \emptyset$$

LAW 22

$$A - \emptyset = A$$

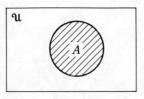

Figure 10.51

EXAMPLE 10.44

Let
$$A = (1, 2, 3)$$
then
$$A - \emptyset = (1, 2, 3)$$
Therefore
$$A - \emptyset = A = (1, 2, 3)$$

LAW 23

$$\emptyset - A = \emptyset$$

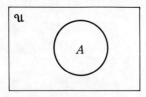

Figure 10.52

EXAMPLE 10.45

Let
$$A = (1, 2, 3)$$
then
$$\emptyset - A = \emptyset$$
Therefore
$$\emptyset - A = \emptyset = \emptyset$$

LAW 24

$$A - A = \emptyset$$

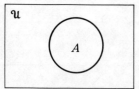

Figure 10.53

EXAMPLE 10.46

Let $\qquad\qquad\qquad\qquad A = (1, 2, 3)$

then $\qquad\qquad\qquad\quad A - A = \varnothing$

Therefore $\qquad\qquad\qquad A - A = \varnothing = \varnothing$

LAW 25

$$(A - B) - C = A - (B \cup C)$$

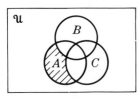

Figure 10.54

EXAMPLE 10.47

Let $\qquad\qquad\qquad\qquad\qquad A = (1, 2, 3, 4)$
$$B = (3, 4, 5, 6)$$
$$C = (2, 4, 5, 7)$$

then $\qquad\qquad\qquad\qquad A - B = (1, 2)$
$$(A - B) - C = (1)$$

also $\qquad\qquad\qquad\qquad B \cup C = (2, 3, 4, 5, 6, 7)$
$$A - (B \cup C) = (1)$$

Therefore $\qquad\quad (A - B) - C = A - (B \cup C) = (1)$

LAW 26

$$A - (B - C) = (A - B) \cup (A \cap C)$$

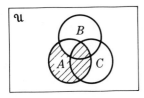

Figure 10.55

EXAMPLE 10.48

Let $\qquad\qquad\qquad\qquad\qquad\qquad A = (1, 2, 3, 4)$
$$B = (3, 4, 5, 6)$$
$$C = (2, 4, 5, 7)$$

then $\qquad\qquad\qquad\qquad\qquad B - C = (3, 6)$
$$A - (B - C) = (1, 2, 4)$$

also $\qquad\qquad\qquad\qquad\qquad A - B = (1, 2)$
$$A \cap C = (2, 4)$$
$$(A - B) \cup (A \cap C) = (1, 2, 4)$$

Therefore $\qquad A - (B - C) = (A - B) \cup (A \cap C) = (1, 2, 4)$

LAW 27

$$A \cup (B - C) = (A \cup B) - (C - A)$$

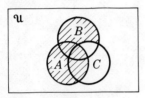

Figure 10.56

EXAMPLE 10.49

Let
$$A = (1, 2, 3, 4)$$
$$B = (3, 4, 5, 6)$$
$$C = (2, 4, 5, 7)$$
then
$$B - C = (3, 6)$$
$$A \cup (B - C) = (1, 2, 3, 4, 6)$$
also
$$(A \cup B) = (1, 2, 3, 4, 5, 6)$$
$$(C - A) = (5, 7)$$
$$(A \cup B) - (C - A) = (1, 2, 3, 4, 6)$$
Therefore $A \cup (B - C) = (A \cup B) - (C - A) = (1, 2, 3, 4, 6)$

LAW 28

$$A \cap (B - C) = (A \cap B) - (A \cap C)$$

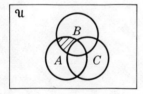

Figure 10.57

EXAMPLE 10.50

Let
$$A = (1, 2, 3, 4)$$
$$B = (3, 4, 5, 6)$$
$$C = (2, 4, 5, 7)$$
then
$$B - C = (3, 6)$$
$$A \cap (B - C) = (3)$$
also
$$(A \cap B) = (3, 4)$$
$$(A \cap C) = (2, 4)$$
$$(A \cap B) - (A \cap C) = (3)$$
Therefore $A \cap (B - C) = (A \cap B) - (A \cap C) = (3)$

LAW 29

$$(A \cap B) \subseteq A \qquad \text{and} \qquad (A \cap B) \subseteq B$$

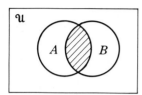

Figure 10.58

EXAMPLE 10.51

Let
$$A = (1, 2, 3)$$
$$B = (3, 4, 5)$$
then
$$A \cap B = (3)$$
also
$$3 \subseteq (3, 4, 5)$$
$$3 \subseteq (1, 2, 3)$$
Therefore
$$(A \cap B) \subseteq A$$

LAW 30

$$A \subseteq (A \cup B) \qquad \text{and} \qquad B \subseteq (A \cup B)$$

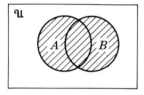

Figure 10.59

EXAMPLE 10.52

Let
$$A = (1, 2, 3)$$
$$B = (3, 4, 5)$$
then
$$A \cup B = (1, 2, 3, 4, 5)$$
$$(1, 2, 3) \subseteq (1, 2, 3, 4, 5)$$
$$(3, 4, 5) \subseteq (1, 2, 3, 4, 5)$$
Therefore
$$A \subseteq (A \cup B)$$

LAW 31

If
$$B \subseteq A, A \cap B = B$$

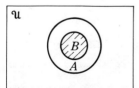

Figure 10.60

EXAMPLE 10.53

Let
$$A = (1, 2, 3, 4)$$
$$B = (2, 3)$$
then
$$A \cap B = (2, 3)$$
Therefore
$$A \cap B = B = (2, 3)$$

LAW 32

$$A \cup (A \cap B) = A$$

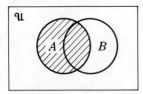

Figure 10.61

EXAMPLE 10.54

Let
$$A = (1, 2, 3)$$
$$B = (3, 4, 5)$$
then
$$A \cap B = (3)$$
$$A \cup (A \cap B) = (1, 2, 3)$$
Therefore
$$A \cup (A \cap B) = A = (1, 2, 3)$$

LAW 33

$$A \cup (A \cup B) = A \cup B$$

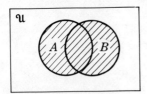

Figure 10.62

EXAMPLE 10.55

Let
$$A = (1, 2, 3)$$
$$B = (3, 4, 5)$$
then
$$A \cup B = (1, 2, 3, 4, 5)$$
$$A \cup (A \cup B) = (1, 2, 3, 4, 5)$$
Therefore
$$A \cup (A \cup B) = A \cup B = (1, 2, 3, 4, 5)$$

LAW 34

$$(A \cup B) \cap (C \cup D) = (A \cap C) \cup (A \cap D) \cup (B \cap C) \cup (B \cap D)$$

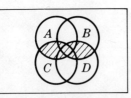

Figure 10.63

EXAMPLE 10.56

Let
$$A = (1, 2, 3, 4, 5, 6)$$
$$B = (4, 5, 6, 7, 8, 9)$$
$$C = (3, 4, 5, 7, 10, 11)$$
$$D = (2, 4, 6, 7, 9, 12)$$

then
$$A \cup B = (1, 2, 3, 4, 5, 6, 7, 8, 9)$$
$$C \cup D = (2, 3, 4, 5, 6, 7, 9, 10, 11, 12)$$
$$(A \cup B) \cap (C \cup D) = (2, 3, 4, 5, 6, 7, 9)$$

also
$$A \cap C = (3, 4, 5)$$
$$A \cap D = (2, 4, 6)$$
$$B \cap C = (4, 5, 7)$$
$$B \cap D = (4, 6, 7, 9)$$
$$(A \cap C) \cup (A \cap D) \cup (B \cap C) \cup (B \cap D) = (2, 3, 4, 5, 6, 7, 9)$$

Therefore $(A \cup B) \cap (C \cup D) = (A \cap C) \cup (A \cap D) \cup (B \cap C) \cup (B \cap D)$
$$= (2, 3, 4, 5, 6, 7, 9)$$

PROBLEMS

1   If $a \in A$ and $B \subset A$, is a necessarily $\in B$?

2   Draw Venn diagrams describing
   a Union   **b** Intersection
   c Subset   **d** Proper Subset
   e Minus   **f** Conjoint
   g Disjoint   **h** Universal Set
   i Null Set   **j** Complement

3   Draw Venn diagrams describing
   a $A \cup B$ **b** $A \cap B$
   c $A \cup B \cup C$ **d** $A \cap B \cap C'$
   e $A \cap (B \cup C)$ **f** $A \cap B'$
   g $A \cup (B \cap C)'$
   h $(A \cap C)' \cup [A' \cap (B \cup C)]$

4   Draw Venn diagrams describing
   a $A \subset B, B \cap C \neq \emptyset, A \cap C = \emptyset, C \not\subset B$
   b $A \cap B \neq \emptyset, A \cap C = \emptyset, B \cap C \neq \emptyset$
   c $A \cap B = \emptyset, A \cap C = \emptyset, B \cap C \neq \emptyset$
   d $A \cap B = \emptyset, A \cap C = \emptyset, B \cap C = \emptyset$
   e $A \cap B = \emptyset, A \subset C, B \subset C$
   f $A \subset B, B \subset C$
   g $A \cap B \cap C \neq \emptyset, A \not\subset B, B \not\subset A, C \not\subset (A \cup B), (A \cup B) \not\subset C$

11 BOOLEAN ALGEBRA

INTRODUCTION

Any algebra having two operations defined, one of which can be substituted for union and the other for intersection, which obeys all the laws in the preceding section, is considered a *Boolean algebra*. Most commonly, the union sign is replaced by a plus sign and the intersection sign by a multiplication sign. Quite often a 0 is used to denote the null set and a 1 to denote the universal set.

As an example, we shall develop a simple Boolean algebra. We shall use two symbols, 0 and 1. The 0 can be interpreted as the null set and the 1 as the universal set. Set A and set B can be used to represent either the 0 or the 1. Now let us define two operations, addition and multiplication. Addition will be defined to coincide with the set-theory operation of union. Multiplication will be defined to coincide with the set-theory operation of intersection. We can develop a table showing the results of addition for all possible combinations of the symbols.

+	0	1
0	0	1
1	1	1

This table is read similarly to the mileage chart on a road map. Thus $1 + 0 = 1$ is found in the table as illustrated:

+	0	1
0	0	1
1	→ 0	1

Another table can be developed for multiplication.

×	0	1
0	0	0
1	0	1

This table is read in the same way as the addition table.   For example, $0 \cdot 1 = 0$ is determined from the table as illustrated:

The reader should satisfy himself that all of the rules for set operation listed in the preceding section are consistent with the operations defined in the two tables.

EXAMPLE 11.1

One of the rules for set operation is:

$$(A \cup B) \cap (A \cup C) = A \cup (B \cap C)$$

Let
$$A = 1$$
$$B = 0$$
$$C = 1$$

Then we can translate the above rule into our Boolean algebra system.

$$(1 + 0) \cdot (1 + 1) = 1 + (0 \cdot 1)$$

According to the addition table
$$1 + 0 = 1$$
$$1 + 1 = 1$$
$$0 \cdot 1 = 0$$

so this reduces to
$$1 \cdot 1 = 1 + 0$$

According to the tables
$$1 \cdot 1 = 1$$
$$1 + 0 = 1$$

and therefore
$$1 = 1$$

All of the set-theory rules will prove consistent no matter which symbols are selected for A, B, C, and D.

CIRCUIT DESCRIPTION THROUGH BOOLEAN ALGEBRA

The design and simplification of electrical circuits is an important use for Boolean algebra and offers a number of possible business applications. The two operations to be defined for circuit-theory Boolean algebra are addition (in place of union) and multiplication (in place of intersection). Two types of switch arrangements are possible, series and parallel. Two switches are set up so that either one, if opened, will stop the electricity flow through the network (Figure 11.1). A multiplication sign is used to denote switches in

Open   Closed   **Figure 11.1 Illustration of open and closed circuits**

series. Thus, the illustration of the series circuit in Figure 11.2 would

Figure 11.2 X and Y **connected in series**

be algebraically represented by $X \cdot Y$ or simply XY. In order for the electricity flow to be halted when switches are connected in parallel, both switches must be opend. A plus sign is used to denote switches in parallel. Thus, Figure 11.3, the illustration of the parallel circuit, would be algebraically represented by $X + Y$.

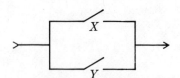

Figure 11.3 X and Y **connected in parallel**

X' is defined as a switch which is closed whenever the switch X is opened and which is opened whenever the switch X is closed. Thus X' is the opposite of X. Furthermore, if two or more X switches appear in the same circuit this means that a master control, labeled X, will open and close all the X switches simultaneously.

CIRCUIT REPRESENTATION

The first step in a study of circuit theory is to develop mathematical or algebraic models to represent the circuits. When formulating the equation for a circuit, look at the overall picture first, and narrow down slowly until the small subcircuits have been represented.

EXAMPLE 11.2

Set up the equation for the circuit pictured in Figure 11.4. The overall picture here is two assemblies connected in series (Figure 11.5). If either assembly is open, the

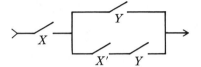

Figure 11.4

electricity will not flow. The formula is $X \cdot (\quad)$. Looking more closely at the second assembly, we can see that there are two separate routes which the electricity

Figure 11.5

would follow, each of which would allow the current to flow through if it was closed. Thus this is a parallel arrangement (Figure 11.6). The formula for this is $Y + (\quad)$, and putting this into its place in the overall formula we obtain $X[Y + (\quad)]$. Now, looking at the bottom part of the parallel circuit, we see two switches connected in series.

They can be algebraically represented by $X' \cdot Y$. If we include this in the overall formula, we have $X[Y + (X'Y)]$, which is an algebraic representation of the circuit illustrated in Figure 11.6.

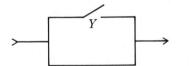

Figure 11.6

EXAMPLE 11.3

Set up the equation for the circuit pictured in Figure 11.7. This circuit is made up of three sections connected in series (Figure 11.8). The formula will be $(\quad)X(\quad)$.

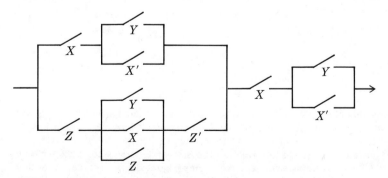

Figure 11.7

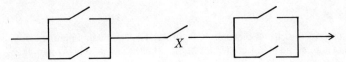

Figure 11.8

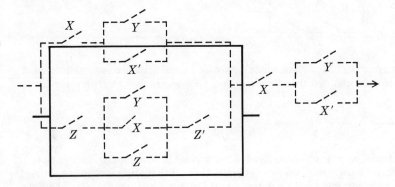

Figure 11.9

The first section is a parallel circuit (Figure 11.9). Therefore, the formula can be further described by $[(\;\;) + (\;\;)]X(\;\;)$. The upper part of the parallel circuit is made up of two groups connected in series (Figure 11.10). The formula can, then,

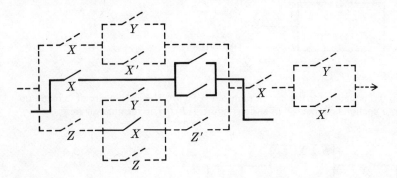

Figure 11.10

be further modified $\{[X \cdot (\;\;)] + (\;\;)\}X(\;\;)$. Looking more closely at the second part of the series subcircuit, it is simply a parallel circuit with the formula $Y + X'$ (Figure 11.11). So, we can expand the formula to $\{[X \cdot (Y + X')] + (\;\;)\}X(\;\;)$. Moving our attention to the lower half of the first large parallel complex, we note three switch subassemblies connected in series (Figure 11.12). This can be added to the formula: $\{[X \cdot (Y + X')] + [Z(\;\;)Z']\}X(\;\;)$. The middle subassembly (Figure

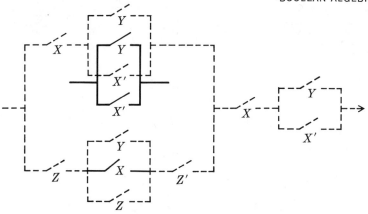

Figure 11.11

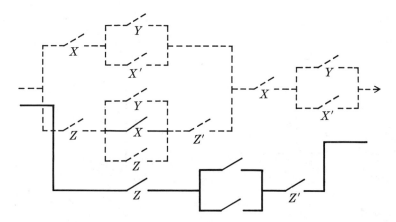

Figure 11.12

11.13) is made up of three switches connected in parallel.   This can also be added to the overall formula.

$$\{[X \cdot (Y + X')] + [Z(Y + X + Z)Z']\}X(\quad)$$

All that remains in formulating the mathematical model of the circuit is to describe the last subassembly on the right-hand side of Figure 11.14.   This will easily be recognized as a parallel circuit $Y + X'$.   The final answer, then, is

$$\{[X(Y + X')] + [Z(Y + X + Z)Z']\}X(Y + X')$$

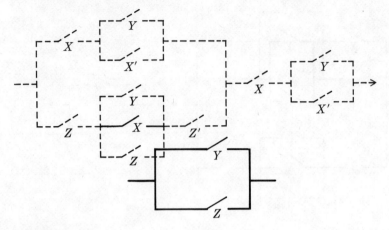

Figure 11.13

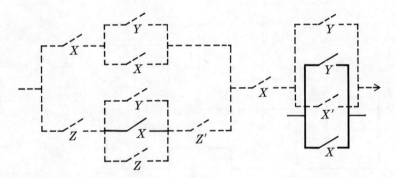

Figure 11.14

CIRCUIT SIMPLIFICATION

Once the mathematical model has been set up, the circuit formula is simplified by using the laws of set theory; remember that a plus sign is analogous to union and a multiplication sign is analogous to intersection. Unfortunately no set pattern or best method can be suggested for this purpose, nor can one tell for certain, in a complicated case, whether he has succeeded in simplifying the circuit as far as possible. Experience and practice are of great value in simplification problems.

EXAMPLE 11.4

Simplify the circuit model: $XY + XZ[(X + Y) + (X + X') + X'] + Z$

Table 11.1

Formula	Rule
$XY + XZ[(X + Y) + (X + X') + X'] + Z$	Given
$XY + XZ[(X + Y) + \mathfrak{U} + X'] + Z$	$A \cup \tilde{A} = \mathfrak{U}$
$XY + XZ(\mathfrak{U} + X') + Z$	$A \cup \mathfrak{U} = \mathfrak{U}$
$XY + XZ(\mathfrak{U}) + Z$	$A \cup \mathfrak{U} = \mathfrak{U}$
$XY + X(Z\mathfrak{U}) + Z$	$(A \cap B) \cap C = A \cap (B \cap C)$
$XY + XZ + Z$	$A \cap \mathfrak{U} = A$
$XY + Z$	$A \cup (A \cap B) = A$

EXAMPLE 11.5

Simplify the circuit model: $XY + X' + (Z + X)(Z' + Y)$

Table 11.2

Formula	Rule
$XY + X' + (Z + X)(Z' + Y)$	Given
$XY + X' + ZZ' + ZY + XZ' + XY$	$(A \cup B) \cap (C \cup D) = (A \cap C)$
	$\cup (A \cap B) \cup (B \cap C) \cup (B \cap D)$
$(XY + X') + ZZ' + ZY + XZ' + XY$	$A \cup (B \cup C) = (A \cup B) \cup C$
$(X + X')(Y + X') + ZZ' + ZY$	$A \cup (B \cap C) = (A \cup B) \cap (A \cup C)$
$\quad + XZ' + XY$	
$\mathfrak{U}(Y + X') + ZZ' + ZY + XZ' + XY$	$A \cup \tilde{A} = \mathfrak{U}$
$(Y + X') + ZZ' + ZY + XZ' + XY$	$A \cap \mathfrak{U} = A$
$Y + X' + ZZ' + ZY + XZ' + XY$	$(A \cup B) \cup C = A \cup (B \cup C)$
$Y + X' + \emptyset + ZY + XZ' + XY$	$A \cap \tilde{A} = \emptyset$
$Y + X' + ZY + XZ' + XY$	$A + \emptyset = A$
$X' + Y + ZY + XZ' + XY$	$A \cup B = B \cup A$
$X' + Y + YZ + XZ' + XY$	$A \cap B = B \cap A$
$X' + Y + XZ' + XY$	$A \cup (A \cap B) = A$
$X' + XZ' + Y + XY$	$A \cup B = B \cup A$
$X' + XZ' + Y + YX$	$A \cap B = B \cap A$
$X' + XZ' + Y$	$A \cup (A \cap B) = A$
$(X' + X)(X' + Z') + Y$	$A \cup (B \cap C) = (A \cup B) \cap (A \cup C)$
$\mathfrak{U}(X' + Z') + Y$	$A \cup \tilde{A} = \mathfrak{U}$
$(X' + Z') + Y$	$A \cap \mathfrak{U} = A$
$X' + Z' + Y$	$A \cup (B \cup C) = (A \cup B) \cup C$

EXAMPLE 11.6

Formulate the model, simplify, and show the simplified circuit for Figure 11.15. The model is $[(YZ + Y')X(Y + Y')ZX(X + Y + Z)] + Z(Z + X)$.

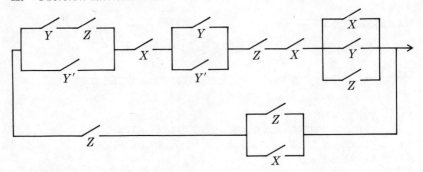

Figure 11.15

Table 11.3

Formula	Rule
$[(YZ + Y')X(Y + Y')ZX(X + Y + Z)]$ $+ Z(Z + X)$	Given
$[(YZ + Y')X\mathfrak{U}ZX(X + Y + Z)]$ $+ Z(Z + X)$	$A \cup \bar{A} = \mathfrak{U}$
$[(YZ + Y')(X\mathfrak{U})ZX(X + Y + Z)]$ $+ Z(Z + X)$	$(A \cap B) \cap C = A \cap (B \cap C)$
$[(YZ + Y')XZX(X + Y + Z)]$ $+ Z(Z + X)$	$A \cap \mathfrak{U} = A$
$[(YZ + Y')XXZ(X + Y + Z)]$ $+ Z(Z + X)$	$A \cap B = B \cap A$
$[(YZ + Y')(XX)Z(X + Y + Z)]$ $+ Z(Z + X)$	$(A \cap B) \cap C = A \cap (B \cap C)$
$[(YZ + Y')XZ(X + Y + Z)]$ $+ Z(Z + X)$	$A \cap A = A$
$(YZ + Y')(XXZ + XZY + XZZ)$ $+ Z(Z + X)$	$A \cap (B \cup C) = (A \cap B) \cup (A \cap C)$
$(YZ + Y')[(XX)Z + XZY + X(ZZ)]$ $+ Z(Z + X)$	$(A \cap B) \cap C = A \cap (B \cap C)$
$(YZ + Y')(XZ + XZY + XZ)$ $+ Z(Z + X)$	$A \cap A = A$
$(YZ + Y')[(XZ) + (XZ)Y + XZ]$ $+ Z(Z + X)$	$(A \cap B) \cap C = A \cap (B \cap C)$
$(YZ + Y')(XZ + XZ) + Z(Z + X)$	$A \cup (A \cap B) = A$
$(XZ + Y')(XZ) + Z(Z + X)$	$A \cup A = A$
$(XZ + Y')(XZ) + ZZ + XZ$	$A \cap (B \cup C) = (A \cap B) \cup (A \cap C)$
$(YZ + Y')(XZ) + Z + XZ$	$A \cap A = A$
$(YZ + Y')(XZ) + Z$	$A \cup (A \cap B) = A$
$XYZZ + XY'Z + Z$	$A \cap (B \cup C) = (A \cap B) \cup (A \cap C)$
$XYZ + XY'Z + Z$	$A \cap A = A$
$XYZ + XZY' + Z$	$A \cap B = B \cap A$
$(XZ)Y + (XZ)Y' + Z$	$(A \cap B) \cap C = A \cap (B \cap C)$
$XZ(Y + Y') + Z$	$(A \cap B) \cup (A \cap C) = A \cap (B \cup C)$.
$XZ + Z$	$A \cup A' = \mathfrak{U}; \quad A \cap \mathfrak{U} = A$
Z	$A \cap B \subseteq A; \quad A \cup B = A$ $\text{if } B \subseteq A$

$$Z \longrightarrow$$

CIRCUIT DESIGN

Our previous discussion has been concerned with circuits already formulated. The purpose was to simplify the circuit without changing the response of the circuit to combinations of open and closed switches.

We can now approach the other part of the problem, namely, formulating circuits which will perform in a specified manner. For example, if we have two master switches, X and Y, there are four combinations possible. Let 0 stand for open and 1 stand for closed. Then the four combinations are:

Table 11.4

X	Y	Operate	Term
1	1	✓	XY
1	0	✓	XY'
0	1		
0	0	✓	$X'Y'$

If we want to design a circuit which will pass current when X and Y are closed, when X is closed and Y is not, or when neither is closed, we begin by checking the positions for which the circuit is to operate on the above chart. For each position checked we list the term representing the operation. If a 1 appears in the column X, an X should be listed, and if a 0 appears in column X, an X' should be listed. Likewise the X or X' will be multiplied by a Y or Y' depending upon whether a 1 or 0 appears in the Y column. After a term has been formulated for each position checked, the terms are added together. Thus

$$XY + XY' + X'Y'$$

is the mathematical representation for a circuit with two master switches, X and Y, which will pass current when both switches are closed, or when X is closed and Y open, or when both switches are open. Next, this formula can be simplified using the techniques of the preceding section. Finally, the simplified circuit may be drawn. Simplifying, we obtain:

Table 11.5

Formula	Rule
$XY + XY' + X'Y'$	Given
$X(Y + Y') + X'Y'$	$A \cap (B \cup C) = (A \cap B) \cup (A \cap C)$
$X(\mathfrak{U}) + X'Y'$	$A \cup \bar{A} = \mathfrak{U}$
$X + X'Y'$	$A \cap \mathfrak{U} = A$
$(X + X')(X + Y')$	$A \cup (B \cap C) = (A \cup B) \cap (A \cup C)$
$(\mathfrak{U})(X + Y')$	$A \cup \bar{A} = \mathfrak{U}$
$X + Y'$	$A \cap \mathfrak{U} = A$

The circuit in Figure 11.16 will operate in the desired manner.

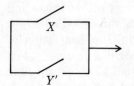

Figure 11.16

EXAMPLE 11.7

If three master switches are to be used, X, Y, and Z, and if the circuit must operate only when X and Y are closed or when X and Z are closed or when Y is closed while Z is open, find and draw the circuit.

First we set up the table, itemizing the eight possible combinations available with three switches. (Note that the number of possible combinations is 2^x where x is the number of master switches.) Then we check these combinations for which the circuit is to operate. The formulation of terms for each position checked is then performed. Finally the terms are added together. The formula is then simplified and drawn.

Table 11.6

X	Y	Z	Operate	Term
1	1	1	✓	XYZ
1	1	0	✓	XYZ'
1	0	1	✓	$XY'Z$
1	0	0		
0	1	1		
0	1	0	✓	$X'YZ'$
0	0	1		
0	0	0		

Model: $$XYZ + XYZ' + XY'Z + X'YZ'$$

Table 11.7 Simplification

Formula	Rule
$XYZ + XYZ' + XY'Z + X'YZ'$	Given
$(XY)Z + (XY)Z' + XY'Z + X'YZ'$	$(A \cap B) \cap C = A \cap (B \cap C)$
$XY(Z + Z') + XY'Z + X'YZ'$	$A \cap (B \cup C) = (A \cap B) \cup (A \cap C)$
$XY(\mathfrak{U}) + XY'Z + X'YZ$	$A \cup \bar{A} = \mathfrak{U}$
$XY + XY'Z + X'YZ'$	$A \cap \mathfrak{U} = A$
$X(Y + Y'Z) + X'YZ'$	$A \cap (B \cup C) = (A \cap B) \cup (A \cap C)$
$X(Y + Y')(Y + Z) + X'YZ'$	$A \cup (B \cap C) = (A \cup B) \cap (A \cup C)$
$X\mathfrak{U}(Y + Z) + X'YZ'$	$A \cup \bar{A} = \mathfrak{U}$
$X(Y + Z) + X'YZ'$	$A \cap \mathfrak{U} = A$
$XY + XZ + X'YZ'$	$A \cap (B \cup C) = (A \cap B) \cup (A \cap C)$
$XY + X'YZ' + XZ$	$A \cup B = B \cup A$
$YX + YX'Z' + XZ$	$A \cap B = B \cap A$
$Y(X + X'Z') + XZ$	$A \cap (B \cup C) = (A \cap B) \cup (A \cap C)$
$Y[(X + X')(X + Z')] + XZ$	$A \cup (B \cap C) = (A \cup B) \cap (A \cap C)$
$X[\mathfrak{U}(X + Z')] + XZ$	$A \cup \bar{A} = \mathfrak{U}$
$Y(X + Z') + XZ$	$A \cap \mathfrak{U} = A$

The simplified formula, then, is

$$Y(X + Z') + XZ$$

(see Figure 11.17)

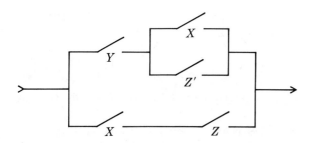

Figure 11.17

PROBLEMS

1   Develop Boolean algebra equations for the following circuits:

a

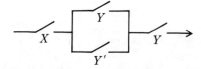

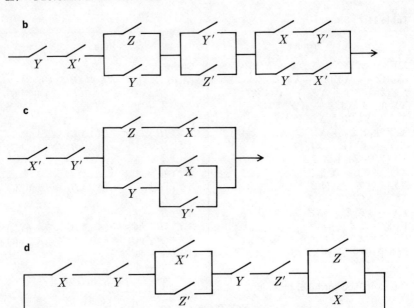

2 Simplify each of the circuits in Problem 4 and draw pictures of the resulting equivalent circuits.

3 Design, simplify, and draw circuits which will accomplish the following:
  a Two switches; current flows when X and Y are both open or both closed.
  b Three switches; current flows when X is open and Y or Z closed, and when Z is open with both X and Y closed.
  c Three switches; current flows when X and Z are either both open or both closed, and when Y is closed with X open and Z closed, and when Z is closed if Y is open.

12 SET THEORY: PARTITIONING AND COUNTING

NUMBER OF ELEMENTS IN A SET

Another important area of set theory deals with the number of elements in a set. The term $n(A)$ is used to represent the number of elements in set A. Algebraically, where two sets are involved

$$n(A \cup B) = n(A) + n(B) - n(A \cap B)$$

This formula is logical, since the number in A includes what is in the intersection of A and B, and the number in B also includes the elements in the intersection, so that when the two sets are added, the elements in the intersection are added twice and a compensating subtraction must be made. Using this formula, any three of the four quantities will be needed to determine the fourth. Thus, if $n(A) = 15$, $n(A \cup B) = 30$, and $n(A \cap B) = 5$, a diagram would be prepared as shown in Figure 12.1.

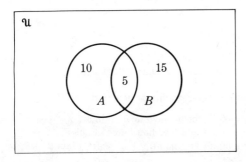

Figure 12.1

Always fill in the intersection first, if the information is given. Note that $n(A) = 15$, and that since 5 of these elements were in the intersection, only 10 are in the part of A not included in B. If the problem had added that fifty elements were in the universal set, this would be taken into account as pictured in Figure 12.2.

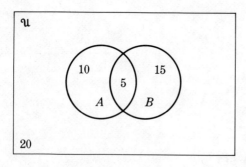

Figure 12.2

Twenty of the fifty elements are in neither A nor B.

If the number of sets is increased to three, the formula for the number of items becomes somewhat more complicated.

$$n(A \cup B \cup C) = n(A) + n(B) + n(C) - n(A \cap B) - n(B \cap C)$$
$$- n(A \cap C) + n(A \cap B \cap C)$$

The reasoning behind the formula is the same as with two sets. Note that any seven items will be sufficient for determining the eighth.

Venn diagrams can be used in the three-set case also. The basic rule is to work from the center of the diagram, wherever possible, outward.

EXAMPLE 12.1

Assume that in a survey of 250 people, it was found that:

1   125 smoked.
2   140 drank liquor.
3   90 had been victims of heart attacks.
4   40 smoked and had been victims of heart attacks.
5   5 smoked, drank liquor, and had been victims of heart attacks.
6   50 of those who smoked did not drink liquor.
7   100 of those who drank liquor had not been victims of heart attacks.

a   How many smoked, but did not drink liquor or have heart attacks?
b   How many did not smoke or drink liquor and had had heart attacks?
c   How many did not smoke or drink liquor and had not had heart attacks?

In Figure 12.3, A = smoked, B = drank liquor, C = victims of heart attacks.

In a problem of this type, try to work from the inside out. The first thing to insert in the Venn diagram (Figure 12.3) is $n(A \cap B \cap C)$ = 5, which is the fifth item on the list of information.

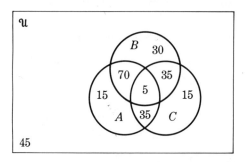

Figure 12.3

Next, note that $n(A \cap C)$ = 40, which is the fourth listed. Observe that $n(A \cap B)$ is divided into two parts, $n(A \cap C \cap B)$ and $n(A \cap C \cap \tilde{B})$. Since $n(A \cap C \cap B)$ = 5, $n(A \cap C \cap \tilde{B})$ must be the remainder, which is 35.

Third, the problem states that $n(A \cap \tilde{B})$ = 50, which is the sixth listed. This must be divided among $n(A \cap \tilde{B} \cap C)$ and $n(A \cap \tilde{B} \cap \tilde{C})$. We have already found that $n(A \cap \tilde{B} \cap C)$ = 35, so $n(A \cap \tilde{B} \cap \tilde{C})$ must be the remainder, which is 15.

Fourth, note that only one more number remains to be filled in for $n(A)$, which is $n(A \cap B \cap \tilde{C})$. Since $n(A)$ = 125, which is the first listed, this last part must be the difference between the total $n(A)$ and the sum of the other parts. Thus $n(A \cap B \cap \tilde{C})$ = 125 − (15 + 35 + 5) = 70.

Fifth, observe the $n(B \cap \tilde{C})$ = 100, which is the seventh listed. This also is divided into two parts, $n(B \cap \tilde{C} \cap A)$ and $n(B \cap \tilde{C} \cap \tilde{A})$. We have already determined that $n(B \cap \tilde{C} \cap A)$ is 70, so $n(B \cap \tilde{C} \cap \tilde{A})$ must be 100 − 70 = 30.

Only one part of $n(B)$ remains to be filled in, $n(B \cap C \cap \tilde{A})$. Since $n(B)$ = 140, which is the second listed, $n(B \cap C \cap \tilde{A})$ must be 140 less the sum of all the other entries in $n(B)$. Thus, $n(B \cap C \cap \tilde{A})$ = 140 − (5 + 70 + 30) = 35.

One part of $n(C)$ now remains. This is $n(C \cap \tilde{A} \cap B)$. Since $n(C)$ = 90, we can subtract to find $n(C \cap \tilde{A} \cap \tilde{B})$. 90 − (35 + 5 + 35) = 15.

Last, we must fill in the number in the universal set which is not in any of the sets diagrammed. Adding all the diagrammed elements and subtracting from 250 (total universe) provides the answer,

$$250 - 15 - 35 - 15 - 35 - 30 - 70 - 5 = 45$$

We can now proceed to answer the questions by referring to the completed Venn diagram. The answer to **a** is 15; to **b** is 15; and to **c** is 45.

PARTITIONS

A set can be partitioned by setting up two or more subsets so that every element in the initial set is included in one and only one of the cells or subsets that make up the partition. Obviously, any set can be partitioned in a number of different ways.

EXAMPLE 12.2

If A is the set of automobiles on the road, partitions could be set up as shown in the following examples (and many other ways, too).

1 Chevrolets, Chryslers, Fords, etc., making sure that each is represented by a cell.
2 Red, White, Blue, Green, Black, etc., making sure that each color is represented by a cell.
3 Whitewall tires and blackwall tires.

EXAMPLE 12.3

If A is the set of all children in the world, two cells can be formed;

$$A_1 = \text{like ice cream}$$
$$A_2 = \text{do not like ice cream}$$

and $(A_1|A_2)$ is a valid partition of A.

CROSS PARTITIONS

If a set A is partitioned in two different manners, $(A_{11}|A_{12}| \cdots | A_{1m})$ and $(A_{21}|A_{22}| \cdots |A_{2n})$, then the set which has as its cells the intersection of each cell of one partition with each cell of the other $(A_{11} \cap A_{21}|A_{11} \cap A_{22}| \cdots |A_{11} \cap A_{2n}|A_{12} \cap A_{21}|A_{12} \cap A_{22}| \cdots| A_{1m} \cap A_{2n})$ is defined as the cross partition of A_{1i} and A_{2i}. The cross partition will include each element in the original set, and no element will be included more than once.

EXAMPLE 12.4

A group of 700 people are chosen and interviewed. Of these, 350 like hamburgers and 400 like hot dogs; 150 like both hamburgers and hot dogs. Find the cross partition suggested by this data.

One way of partitioning A is by the like or dislike displayed for hamburgers.

Let $\qquad\qquad\qquad A_1 = \text{likes hamburgers}$
then $\qquad\qquad\qquad \tilde{A}_1 = \text{does not like hamburgers}$

Thus $(A_1|\tilde{A}_1)$ is a partition of A; every person is again included, and each person is included in only one cell.

Another way to partition A is by the peoples' like or dislike for hot dogs.

Let $\qquad\qquad\qquad A_2 = \text{likes hot dogs}$
then $\qquad\qquad\qquad \tilde{A}_2 = \text{does not like hot dogs}$

Thus $(A_2|\tilde{A}_2)$ is a partition of A; every person is again included, and each person is included in only one cell.

The cross partition is defined as $(A_1 \cap A_2 | A_1 \cap \tilde{A}_2 | \tilde{A}_1 \cap A_2 | \tilde{A}_1 \cap \tilde{A}_2)$.   A Venn diagram (Figure 12.4) will be helpful for visualizing this cross partition.   To determine the number of people in each part of the Venn diagram, we begin with the intersection of A_1 and A_2.   This number is 150.   Next, we note that 350 like hamburgers and, therefore, must be within the A_1 set.   Since 150 are in the intersection, 200 must be in the part of A_1 not included in A_2.   Likewise, since 400 like hot dogs, 250 must be in the part of A_2 not included in A_1.   We have now accounted for 600 people.   The remaining 100 must be outside A_1 and A_2.

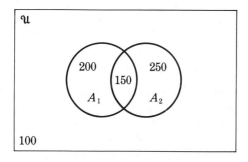

Figure 12.4

Now using the results portrayed by the Venn diagram, the cross partition can be written:

$$(150 | 200 | 250 | 100)$$

150 people like both hamburgers and hot dogs, 200 people like hamburgers but not hot dogs, 250 people like hot dogs but not hamburgers, 100 people do not like either hamburgers or hot dogs.

PERMUTATIONS

The number of possible permutations of objects or symbols is defined as the number of different arrangements of the objects or symbols. For example, if three letters were available, A, B, and C, and if we wished to find the number of permutations of groups of two of these numbers, we could list them as AB, AC, BA, BC, CA, and CB. Thus, there are six permutations possible. Note that AB is considered a different permutation from BA.

If we let n = number of items available (A, B, C in the example) and r = size of the group chosen (two in the example) then the number of permutations is given by the formula

$$n(n - 1)(n - 2) \cdot \cdot \cdot (n - r + 1)$$

This means that, beginning with n, successively smaller numbers are to be multiplied together until the term $(n - r + 1)$ is reached. This will be the last term.

EXAMPLE 12.5

Find the number of permutations of 10 objects, taken 5 at a time.

$$n = 26 \qquad r = 3 \qquad (n - r + 1) = 26 - 3 + 1 = 24$$
$$P = 26 \cdot 25 \cdot 24 = 15,600$$

EXAMPLE 12.6

How many three letter words can be made from the alphabet?

$$n = 26 \qquad r = 3 \qquad (n - r + 1) = 26 - 3 + 1 = 24$$
$$P = 26 \cdot 25 \cdot 24 = 15,000$$

COMBINATIONS

Combinations are different from permutations in that order does not distinguish one combination from another. Thus, AB and BA are identical in terms of combinations; they each represent the set with the two elements A and B. If n = number of items available and r = size of the group chosen, then the number of combinations $\binom{n}{r}$ is defined as

$$\binom{n}{r} = \frac{n!}{r!(n - r)!}$$

$n!$ is read "n factorial" and means $n(n - 1)(n - 2) \cdots 1$. Thus $5!$ is $5 \cdot 4 \cdot 3 \cdot 2 \cdot 1 = 120.$†

EXAMPLE 12.7

Find the number of combinations of 10 objects taken 5 at a time.

$$n = 10 \qquad r = 5$$

$$\binom{n}{r} = \binom{10}{5} = \frac{10!}{5!(10 - 5)!} = \frac{10!}{5!5!} = \frac{10 \cdot 9 \cdot 8 \cdot 7 \cdot 6 \cdot \cancel{5 \cdot 4 \cdot 3 \cdot 2 \cdot 1}}{5 \cdot 4 \cdot 3 \cdot 2 \cdot 1 \cdot \cancel{5 \cdot 4 \cdot 3 \cdot 2 \cdot 1}}$$

$$= \frac{\cancel{10} \cdot \cancel{9} \cdot \cancel{8} \cdot 7 \cdot 6}{\cancel{5} \cdot \cancel{4} \cdot \cancel{3} \cdot \cancel{2} \cdot 1} = 3 \cdot 2 \cdot 7 \cdot 6 = 252$$

EXAMPLE 12.8

How many different sets of two numbers can be chosen from the digits 0 through 4?

$$n = 5 \qquad r = 2$$

$$\binom{n}{r} = \binom{5}{2} = \frac{5!}{2!(5 - 2)!} = \frac{5!}{2!3!} = \frac{5 \cdot 4 \cdot \cancel{3 \cdot 2 \cdot 1}}{2 \cdot 1 \cdot \cancel{3 \cdot 2 \cdot 1}} = \frac{5 \cdot \cancel{4}}{\cancel{2} \cdot 1} = 5 \cdot 2 = 10$$

†$0! = 1$

PERMUTATIONS WITH IDENTICAL OBJECTS

Sometimes, the group from which items are to be selected includes a number of objects which are identical.   If we wish to find the number of permutations, but do not want to consider the interchange of two identical objects as different permutations, then another formula must be used.

Let n = number of objects in the group
         r_1 = number of objects of type 1 which are alike
         r_2 = number of objects of type 2 which are alike

then $P = \dfrac{n!}{r_1!r_2! \cdots r_n!}$

EXAMPLE 12.9

Find the number of permutations of the letters in the word *initiate*.

$$n = 8 \qquad r_1 = \text{number of } i\text{'s} = 3 \qquad r_2 = \text{number of } t\text{'s} = 2$$

$$P = \frac{8!}{3!2!} = \frac{\overset{4}{\cancel{8}} \cdot 7 \cdot \cancel{6} \cdot 5 \cdot 4 \cdot 3 \cdot 2 \cdot 1}{\cancel{3} \cdot \cancel{2} \cdot 1 \cdot \cancel{2} \cdot 1} = 4 \cdot 7 \cdot 5 \cdot 4 \cdot 3 \cdot 2 \cdot 1 = 3,360$$

ARRANGEMENT OF INDEPENDENT COLUMNS

If, instead of a general population of elements which may be chosen for any position, we adjust the situation so that a specified population of items is available for selection in each position, we encounter another type of counting problem.

If n_1 = number of elements available for the first position
       n_2 = number of elements available for the second position
       n_r = number of elements available for the rth position

then

$$\text{number of arrangements} = n_1 \cdot n_2 \cdots n_r$$

EXAMPLE 12.10

If five switches are to be operated, and each switch can be either open or closed, how many arrangements are possible?

   Note that with permutations the selection of an element for one position precluded its selection for another position in the same permutation.   The same applies to combinations.   In this situation, however, whether switch 1 is open or closed will have no effect on switch 2.   Since the columns are independent, the arrangement formula applies.

$$n_1 = 2 \qquad n_2 = 2 \qquad n_3 = 2 \qquad n_4 = 2 \qquad n_5 = 2$$

The arrangements are

$$2 \cdot 2 \cdot 2 \cdot 2 \cdot 2 = 2^5 = 32$$

EXAMPLE 12.11

If a product must pass through three departments in a specified order, and if any one of six machines can be used to process the product in department 1, and any one of four machines can be used to process the product in department 2, and any one of five machines can be used to process the product in department 3, how many different ways can the product be processed?

$$n_1 = 6 \qquad n_2 = 4 \qquad n_3 = 5$$

The arrangements are

$$6 \cdot 4 \cdot 5 = 120$$

EXAMPLE 12.12

If, in Example 12.11 above, the order of passage were not important, so that the product could go through in any manner, how many arrangements would be possible?

We have already noted that if the department order of processing were restricted to (1, 2, 3), 120 arrangements would be possible. If the order were (2, 3, 1),

$$4 \cdot 5 \cdot 6 = 120$$

arrangements would be possible. For any specific order of departments it can be determined that 120 arrangements are possible. The problem can be solved, then, by finding the number of permutations of the order of the three departments and multiplying by 120. The formula for permutations is $n(n - 1)(n - 2) \cdots (n - r + 1)$,

$$n = 3 \qquad r = 3$$
$$n - r + 1 = 3 - 3 + 1 = 1$$
$$P = 3 \cdot 2 \cdot 1 = 6$$

There are six different ways in which the product can be processed through three departments, and $6 \cdot 120 = 720$ different machine arrangements for a product.

PROBLEMS

1 If the universal set contains 37 items and 15 of these items are common to both of the sets within the universe, how many belong to the second if 25 belong to the first and 5 belong to neither?

2 Three hundred people were polled. One hundred fifty believed implicitly in Zen. One hundred disagreed entirely with the tenets of Zen. Fifty had no opinion about Zen. Of these 300, 135 had high IQ. The remainder had low IQ. Of those that disagreed with the tenets of Zen, 25 had low IQ. The believers included 115 with low IQ. Obtain the cross partition.

3 Five hundred cars were selected at random. Three hundred forty were red; 300 had whitewalls; 125 were Chevrolets; 10 of the Chevrolets had whitewalls and were not red; 15 were red Chevrolets with whitewalls; 40 of the red cars were not Chevrolets and did not have whitewalls; 300 of the cars were red and not Chevrolets.
   a How many of the cars were in none of the three classifications?
   b How many of the red cars were not Chevrolets and did not have whitewalls?
   c How many cars had exactly two of the distinguishing characteristics?

4 How many groups of seven can be selected from the first 10 letters of the alphabet?

5 How many groups of five can be selected from the set of single digits?

6 How many arrangements are possible with the letters in the alphabet (using them all)?

7 If 10 men are available, how many committees of five can be set up so that no two committees are identical?

8 How would Prob. 7 be solved if each committee had five specific officers?

9 If a plant has seven identical machines, and each part is run through two of the machines (the second for checking purposes), how many combinations of two machines could be used?   First assume that order is of no importance, and then solve the problem assuming that it matters which machine is used first.

10 How many ways can the letters in the word *intelligent* be arranged?

11 How many ways can the letters in the word *engineer* be arranged?

12 If a part must go through three departments, and the departments have five, seven, and three identical machines, respectively, how many combinations of machines would be possible for a part?

13 If an invoice must be prepared by one of four people, checked by one of three people, approved by two of three people, and paid by one of four people, how many combinations of people could handle an invoice?

13 PROBABILITY THEORY:
BASIC CONCEPTS

THE IMPORTANCE OF PROBABILITY IN
BUSINESS DECISION MAKING

Most business decisions must be made before every pertinent fact is known, if, for that matter, every fact is ever known. This means that most business decision making involves a degree of uncertainty. The successful decision maker is one who is able, either knowingly or subconsciously, to estimate the likelihood of uncertain facts or parameters in a situation and to weigh the likelihood of the occurrence of these events against the effects.

Probability theory enables the user to substitute numbers for hunches or guesses. The numbers are, of course, no more accurate than the hunch or guess on which they are based. However, the numbers are more flexible; they can be used to determine more precisely the consequences which would take place if the guesses were accurate, they can be readjusted in the light of additional information more precisely than can intuition, and large numbers of individual hunches can be grouped, weighed against one another, and combined to enable the decision maker to evaluate complex unknowns for which guesses are difficult.

SIMPLE EVENTS AND A SAMPLE SPACE

A simple event can be defined as a possible occurrence in a given situation. For example, the situation might be the tossing of a coin.

One simple event would be the appearance of a head.   Another simple event would be the appearance of a tail.

In a given situation, the sample space is defined as a listing of all the events which could possibly occur.   In the example above, where a coin was tossed, the sample space contains the two events, head and tail.   In more complicated situations the sample space may contain a large number of events, and sophisticated counting techniques might be necessary in order to find all the events which could occur.

EXAMPLE 13.1

Itemize the sample space of the numbers which could appear if two dice were rolled.

The simple events are

Table 13.1

Die 1	Die 2	Die 1	Die 2
1	1	4	1
1	2	4	2
1	3	4	3
1	4	4	4
1	5	4	5
1	6	4	6
2	1	5	1
2	2	5	2
2	3	5	3
2	4	5	4
2	5	5	5
2	6	5	6
3	1	6	1
3	2	6	2
3	3	6	3
3	4	6	4
3	5	6	5
3	6	6	6

Note that 2,3 is an entirely different event from 3,2.   Assume, for example, that die 1 is red and die 2 is green.   Note that there are 36 simple events in the sample space.

We could have used counting techniques to determine the number of items in the sample space.   Since die 1 can take on any of six values and die 2 can take on any of six values, and since the value of die 1 has no effect on the value of die 2, the formula to be used is the one for arrangements of independent columns. The formula is $n_1 \cdot n_2$, where n_1 and n_2 are the number of possible values of column 1 and column 2, respectively. Thus

$$6 \cdot 6 = 36 \qquad \text{arrangements}$$

EXAMPLE 13.2

If the situation under consideration is the drawing of three cards from a deck of 52, how many events are in the sample space, assuming an event is described as the three-card sequence held after the cards have been drawn?

Note that if the five of spades, three of hearts, and eight of clubs were drawn in the order listed, the hand will be the same as if the three of hearts, eight of clubs, and five of spades were drawn. Thus the events are not dependent on order. We are interested in the number of combinations of three items selected from a group of 52. The formula, it will be recalled, is

$$\binom{n}{r} = \frac{n!}{r!(n - r)!}$$

where n is the number of items in the group and r is the number of items in any one combination. Thus:

$$\binom{52}{3} = \frac{52!}{3!(52 - 3)!} = \frac{52!}{3!49!} = \frac{52 \cdot 51 \cdot 50}{3 \cdot 2 \cdot 1}$$
$$= 52 \cdot 17 \cdot 25$$
$$= 22{,}100$$

There are 22,100 simple events which comprise this sample space.

EXAMPLE 13.3

The Acme Manufacturing Company has five interchangeable machines. Every product is always put through two of the machines. This is a safety check which helps the foreman to determine when a machine is out of adjustment. If an event is described as the sequence of machines which a product might be put through for the initial and secondary trimming, how many events comprise the sample space?

Note that order is meaningful in this situation. A product put through machine 1 first and machine 2 second would be considered as having been sent through a different sequence from a product sent through machine 2 first and machine 1 second. Thus, this situation requires the permutation formula which is $n(n - 1)(n - 2) \cdots (n - r + 1)$, where n is the total number of possible alternatives and r is the number of alternatives to be included in one event. Thus $n = 5$, $r = 2$, and $(n - r + 1) = (5 - 2 + 1) = 4$. So

$$(5)(4) = 20$$

There are 20 possible sequences in the sample space.

COMPOSITE EVENTS

The sample space is the universal set of which all of the simple events are elements. Composite events are sets containing simple events.

There can be any number of composite events in a sample space, and, of course, one simple event will often be an element of more than one composite event. Thus the sample space may be comprised of all the pairs of numbers which might appear when two dice are thrown.

EXAMPLE 13.4

The composite event A is: the sum of the two dice is greater than 5.   Event B is: at least one of the numbers appearing is a 2.   Event C is: the number on the first die is the same as the number of the second.   Drawing a Venn diagram will help to illustrate this situation (Figure 13.1).   We can itemize all the simple events in the sample space and show which ones belong to sets A, B, and C.

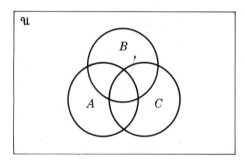

Figure 13.1

Table 13.2

Die 1	Die 2	A	B	C	Die 1	Die 2	A	B	C
1	1			x	4	1			
1	2		x		4	2	x	x	
1	3				4	3	x		
1	4				4	4	x		x
1	5	x			4	5	x		
1	6	x			4	6	x		
2	1		x		5	1	x		
2	2		x	x	5	2	x	x	
2	3		x		5	3	x		
2	4	x	x		5	4	x		
2	5	x	x		5	5	x		x
2	6	x	x		5	6	x		
3	1				6	1	x		
3	2		x		6	2	x	x	
3	3	x		x	6	3	x		
3	4	x			6	4	x		
3	5	x			6	5	x		
3	6	x			6	6	x		x

Thus, there are 36 events in the sample space. Twenty-six of these are in A, 11 are in B, and 6 are in C. In Venn diagram form, this can be shown as Figure 13.2. Note that some events are in set A only, while some are in A and B or A and C. The same is true for events in B and C.

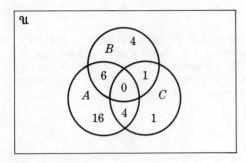

Figure 13.2

MUTUALLY EXCLUSIVE EVENTS

Two composite events, A and B, are mutually exclusive if

$$A \cap B = \varnothing$$

that is, if A and B have no simple events in common. Thus, if event A is described, in the case of our two dice, as, "the sum of the two dice is six or more," and if B is described as, "the sum of the two dice is three or less," no simple event will apply to both A and B concurrently. Thus $A \cap B = \varnothing$.

A set of events is exhaustive if every element in the sample space belongs to at least one event of the set. A set of events is mutually exclusive and exhaustive if each element in the sample space belongs to one and only one event of the set. For example, let's return to our two dice and define events A and B as before, that is $A = \text{Sum} \geq 6$ and $B = \text{Sum} \leq 3$. If we add event C, and define it as, "the sum equals 4 or 5," the three events, A, B, and C are mutually exclusive and exhaustive.

INDEPENDENT VERSUS DEPENDENT EVENTS

Two events are independent of one another if the occurrence of one of the events has no effect upon the likelihood of occurrence of the other event. Conversely, two events are dependent if the occurrence of one (or lack of occurrence) will affect the likelihood of occurrence of the other.

EXAMPLE 13.5

A manufacturing company has five departments, each with 10 employees. Define event A to be "the three men who are selected from department 1 and the five men who are selected from department 2, to serve on a committee." Define event B as "the employees in department 1 who are not serving on any committee and who eat lunch at home." Define event C as, "employees who eat lunch at home." Which events are dependent and which are independent?

A and B are dependent. Once the makeup of A is known, many elements of the sample space of B are eliminated.

A and C are independent unless selection for committees was based on or influenced by where the employees ate lunch.

B and C are dependent since the number who eat lunch at home (C) will be affected by the number in department 1 who eat lunch at home.

EXAMPLE 13.6

A company has found that three media are useful in selling its product, namely newspapers, magazines, and television. They have taken a poll of product users and have defined two sets as:

A = people who can read and bought the product
B = people who live in the metropolitan area and bought the product

If more people read in the metropolitan area than in the country at large, are these events dependent or independent?

They are dependent. Knowing what percentage of the people who read purchased the product would influence the prediction of how many people in the metropolitan area will buy the product.

PROBABILITY DEFINITION

Precisely speaking, the word "probability" refers to a number. It is a number between 0 and 1 which represents the likelihood of occurrence of a particular event. A probability of 0 indicates that the occurrence of the event is impossible or at least very unlikely. A probability of 1 indicates that the event is certain to occur, or almost certain.

Probabilities may be numbers determined after long and rigorous tests, or they may be based on quite logical theorems, i.e., the probability of a fair coin coming up heads is one-half. Probabilities determined in either of these manners are called *objective probabilities*. In contrast, *subjective probabilities* are numbers representing an opinion or guess as to the likelihood of a particular event's occurrence. In business decision making, most probability estimates are subjective, since long experimentation is usually impractical.

If a sample space is made up of n equally likely events, the probability associated with each event is $1/n$. The probability of a composite event is equal to the sum of the probabilities of the simple events which are its elements. The probability of all the simple events in a sample space must add up to 1.

PROBABILITY: UNION OF EVENTS

Let us define the symbol $P(A)$ as the probability connected with the occurrence of event A. Then $0 \leq P(A) \leq 1$, and

$$P(A) = P(a_1 + a_2 + \cdots a_n)$$

if $a_1, a_2, \cdots, a_n$ are all the elements in A.

$P(A \cup B)$ is the probability connected with the union of events A and B. $P(A \cup B)$ can also be written $P(A + B)$.

$$P(A \cup B) = P(A) + P(B) - P(A \cap B)$$

This can be most easily understood through a Venn diagram (Figure 13.3). The probability of the occurrence of either of two events is the sum of the probabilities of each of the elements in both of the sets. But some of the elements are in both of the sets and so will be counted twice when $P(A)$ and $P(B)$ are added. By subtracting $P(A \cap B)$, i.e., the probability connected with the events in the intersection of A and B, we will be adding the probability of each of the events in the two sets once and only once.

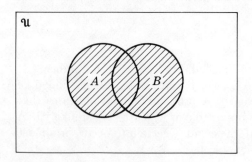

Figure 13.3

EXAMPLE 13.7

If
$$P(A) = .55$$
and
$$P(B) = .45$$
and
$$P(A \cap B) = .20$$
find $P(A \cup B)$

$$P(A \cup B) = .55 + .45 - .20 = .80$$

EXAMPLE 13.8

If A and B are mutually exclusive, and if $P(A) = .2$ and $P(B) = .1$, find $P(A \cup B)$.

$$P(A \cup B) = .2 + .1 - 0 = .3$$

since the intersection of two mutually exclusive events is zero.

EXAMPLE 13.9

What is $P(A \cup B)$ if A and B are mutually exclusive and exhaustive?

$$P(A \cup B) = 1.00$$

since the events are exhaustive.

EXAMPLE 13.10

If $P(A \cap B) = .6$, and if $P(A) = .7$, and if $P(A \cup B) = .9$, find $P(B)$.

$$P(A \cup B) = P(A) + P(B) - P(A \cap B)$$
$$P(B) = P(A \cup B) - P(A) + P(A \cap B)$$
$$P(B) = .9 - .7 + .6 = .8$$

JOINT PROBABILITY: INDEPENDENT EVENTS

The probability connected with the intersection of two events, written $P(A \cap B)$ or $P(AB)$, is the probability that the simple event occurring will be within both A and B. The term often used to describe the probability connected with the intersection of two events is joint probability. If the two events are independent, the joint probability can be determined by the equation:

$$P(AB) = P(A) \cdot P(B)$$

EXAMPLE 13.11

If A and B are independent and $P(A) = .4$ and $P(B) = .6$, find $P(AB)$.

$$P(AB) = (.4) \cdot (.6) = .24$$

CONDITIONAL PROBABILITY

Conditional probability is the probability associated with the occurrence of one event, given that another event has occurred. The symbol for conditional probability is $P(A|B)$ and is read "P of A given B." The equation for conditional probability is:

$$P(A|B) = \frac{P(A \cap B)}{P(B)}$$

EXAMPLE 13.12

If the joint probability of A and B is .5, and if $P(B) = .8$, find $P(A|B)$.

$$P(A|B) = \frac{.5}{.8} = .625$$

EXAMPLE 13.13

If A and B are mutually exclusive, what is $P(A|B)$?
Mutually exclusive indicates that the occurrence of B precludes the occurrence of A. Therefore

$$P(A|B) = 0$$

EXAMPLE 13.14

If A and B are independent, what is $P(A|B)$?
Independent indicates that the occurrence of B will have no effect on the likelihood of A occurring. Therefore, if A and B are independent,

$$P(A|B) = P(A)$$

JOINT PROBABILITY: DEPENDENT EVENTS

When two events, A and B, are dependent, joint probability is determined by the formula

$$P(AB) = P(A) \cdot P(B|A)$$
or $$P(AB) = P(B) \cdot P(A|B)$$

EXAMPLE 13.15

If A and B are dependent and if the probability of A occurring is .7 and if the probability of B occurring—given that A has occurred—is .9, find the joint probability, $P(AB)$.

$$P(AB) = .7(.9) = .63$$

BAYES' THEOREM

Bayes' theorem can be written as follows:

$$P(A_i|B) = \frac{P(B|A_i)P(A_i)}{P(B|A_1)P(A_1) + P(B|A_2)P(A_2) + \cdots + P(B|A_n)P(A_n)}$$

where $A_1, A_2, \ldots, A_n$ are mutually exclusive and exhaustive. The net effect of the formula is to convert from $P(B|A_i)$ to $P(A_i|B)$.

EXAMPLE 13.16

The Columbia Company is bringing out a new product. They estimate that the product has an 80-percent probability of being a large seller. A market test is to be conducted, and the management has estimated that the product will have a 10-percent chance of selling 2,000 units or less in the test if it is going to be successful. It will have a 95 percent chance of selling 2,000 or less units if it is not going to be a large seller. The survey is now complete. Less than 2,000 units were sold. What is the revised probability that the product will be a large seller?

Let $\quad A_1$ = probability of product being a large seller
$\quad\quad\quad A_2$ = probability of product not being a large seller

Note that A_1 and A_2 are mutually exclusive and exhaustive.

Let
$$B_1 = \text{sell more than 2,000 units in test}$$
$$B_2 = \text{sell 2,000 units or less in test}$$

Then
$$P(A_1|B_2) = \frac{P(B_2|A_1)P(A_1)}{P(B_2|A_1)P(A_1) + P(B_2|A_2)P(A_2)}$$

Since
$$P(A_1) = .80 \qquad P(B_2|A_1) = .10$$
$$P(A_2) = .20 \qquad P(B_2|A_2) = .95$$

Thus
$$P(A_1|B_2) = \frac{.10(.8)}{.10(.8) + .2(.95)} = \frac{.08}{.08 + .19} = \frac{.08}{.27} = .30$$

Note that the result of the test was to reduce the probability assigned to success from 80 to 30 percent.

PROBLEMS

1 Itemize the sample space for the flipping of three coins.

2 Itemize the sample space for the possible answers to five true-false questions.

3 How many events are in the following sample spaces:
  a flipping 10 coins
  b rolling three dice
  c selecting five cards from a deck without replacement
  d selecting five cards from a deck with replacement

4 How many events are in the following sample spaces:
  a selecting three workers from a group of five
  b getting a majority of votes from a group of 15 voters
  c selecting one of three machines to begin the processing of a product and one of five other machines to complete the processing of the product
  d selecting a committee chairman and two committee members from a group of 10 men

5 This question refers to the following table:

Number of Employees in the XYZ Company

Department		Experience				Totals
		Less than 1 yr	1–2 yrs	2–3 yrs	More than 3 yrs	
		B_1	B_2	B_3	B_4	
Control	A_1	5	10	15	25	55
Operations	A_2	8	5	3	1	17
Marketing	A_3	13	6	8	1	28
Totals		26	21	26	27	100

Find the probability of drawing an individual at random from this group, possessing the attributes described, and explain the meaning of each:

a $P(A_1)$

b $P(B_3)$

c $P(A_1 \cup A_2)$

d $P(A_3 \cup B_1)$

e $P(A_2 \cap B_1)$

f $P(B_2 \cap B_3)$

g $P(A_1|B_2)$

h $P(B_2|A_1 \cup B_4)$

i $P(B_3|A_1 \cap B_3)$

j $P(A_1 \cap A_2|B_1 \cap B_2)$

6 This question refers to the following table:

Employees Performance on a Vocational Achievement Test

		Grades				
		40% or less	40%–50%	50%–60%	60% or more	Totals
		B_1	B_2	B_3	B_4	
Control group	A_1	8	15	20	12	55
Specially trained group	A_2	3	2	15	35	55
Totals		11	17	35	47	110

Find the probability of drawing an individual at random from the group taking the achievement exam, with the following characteristics:

a $P(A_1)$

b $P(B_2)$

c $P(B_1 \cup B_2)$

d $P(A_1 \cup B_3)$

e $P(A_2 \cap B_1)$

f $P(B_3 \cap B_4)$

g $P(A_2|B_2)$

h $P(B_3|A_1 \cup B_1)$

i $P(B_4|A_1 \cap B_4)$

j $P(B_1 \cup B_3|A_1 \cap B_3)$

14 PROBABILITY DISTRIBUTIONS

INTRODUCTION

Probability distributions are tabular, graphical, or mathematical listings of all the events in a sample space along with the probabilities associated with each of these events. Sometimes exact probabilities are known for every event in a sample space. At other times estimates of the probable distribution of probabilities are all that are available. The probabilities of all the events constituting a probability distribution must add up to one.

DISCRETE VERSUS CONTINUOUS DISTRIBUTIONS

If there are a finite number of distinct events in a probability distribution, the distribution is considered discrete. Examples are: the number of workers who will be absent from a factory, the number of product A which will be sold this week, and the hair color of models applying for a job. A continuous distribution is one in which the number of events is infinite and the events are not distinct. Examples are: the ages of workers, the time necessary to complete a job, and the dimensions or measurements of a product. Note that if all the workers were between the ages of 35 and 36 there would still be an infinite number of possible ages. For example, one worker might be 35 years, 2 months, 3 days, 1 hour, and 10 minutes old.

It is often possible to estimate continuous distributions with discrete ones and vice versa. However, it is important to be able to distinguish between the two and to understand the reasons for treating the two types of data differently.

COMMONLY USED DISTRIBUTIONS VERSUS INDIVIDUALIZED MODELS

A number of distributions have been developed which often very closely describe natural phenomena and common types of situations. Often these formulas will closely conform to the data and probabilities of situations under investigation. The major advantage in using these distributions is that their characteristics are well known and their formulas and values are readily available.

Sometimes distributions will not be found which conform to a given situation, and one will have to develop a mathematical model to describe the situation. These models are often difficult and time consuming to build, but can often be tailor-made or at least more closely fitted to a particular situation.

MEAN—VARIANCE—STANDARD DEVIATION

The mean of a probability distribution, if the distribution is discrete, is

$$\bar{x} = \sum_{i=1}^{n} x_i P(x_i)$$

where $\bar{x}$ = mean of x
   x_i = ith event
   $P(x_i)$ = probability of the ith event
   n = number of events in the distribution
For a continuous distribution, the mean is

$$\bar{x} = \int_{a}^{b} xf(x) \, dx$$

where $f(x)$ is the probability function of the variable x and $f(x) = 0$ when $x < a$ or $x > b$.

The variance of a probability distribution is a measure of deviation of the events or variables from the mean value. For a discrete distribution, variance is determined by

$$V(x) \sum_{i=1}^{n} (x_i - \bar{x})^2 P(x_i)$$

For a continuous distribution, variance is determined by

$$V(x) = \int_a^b (x - \bar{x})^2 f(x) \, dx$$

Standard deviation, which is another measure of variance, is described by the formula,

$$\sigma = \sqrt{v(x)}, \text{ where } \sigma \text{ represents the standard deviation}$$

EXAMPLE 14.1

For the following table, find the mean, variance, and standard deviation.

Salary offer	Probability
$5,000	.6
6,000	.3
7,000	.1

$$\bar{x} = 5,000(.6) + 6,000(.3) + 7,000(.1) = 3,000 + 1,800 + 700 = \$5,500$$
$$V(x) = (5,000 - 5,500)^2(.6) + (6,000 - 5,500)^2(.3) + (7,000 - 5,500)^2(.1)$$
$$= (250,000)(.6) + (250,000)(.3) + (2,250,000)(.1)$$
$$= 150,000 + 75,000 + 225,000$$
$$= 450,000$$
$$\sigma = \sqrt{450,000} = 670.8$$

EXAMPLE 14.2

If the probability of the occurrence of x can be described by

$$f(x) = 0 \qquad\qquad x < 0$$
$$f(x) = \frac{3x - 5}{100} \qquad 0 \le x \le 10$$
$$f(x) = 0 \qquad\qquad x > 10$$

find the mean, variance, and standard deviation of the distribution.

$$\bar{x} = \int_0^{10} x \frac{3x - 5}{100} \, dx = \int_0^{10} \frac{3x^2 - 5x}{100} \, dx = \frac{3x^3}{300} - \frac{5x^2}{200} \Big|_0^{10}$$
$$= \frac{3(10)^3}{300} - \frac{5(10)^2}{200} - \left[\frac{3(0)^3}{300} - \frac{5(0)^2}{200} \right]$$
$$= 10 - 2.5 = 7.5$$

$$V(x) = \int_0^{10} (x - 7.5)^2 \frac{3x - 5}{100} \, dx = \int_0^{10} (x^2 - 15x + 56.25) \frac{3x - 5}{100} \, dx$$

$$= \int_0^{10} \frac{3x^3 - 45x^2 + 168.75x - 5x^2 + 75x - 281.25}{100} \, dx$$

$$= \int_0^{10} \frac{3x^3 - 50x^2 + 243.75x - 281.25}{100} \, dx$$

$$= \frac{3x^4/4 - 50x^3/3 + 243.75x^2/2 - 281.25x}{100} \Big|_0^{10}$$

$$= \frac{1}{100} \left[\frac{3(10)^4}{4} - \frac{50(10)^3}{3} + \frac{243.75(10)^2}{2} - 281.25(10) - 0 \right]$$

$$= \frac{1}{100} \left(7,500 - \frac{50,000}{3} + 12,187.50 - 2,812.50 \right)$$

$$= \frac{1}{100} \left(\frac{50,625}{3} - \frac{50,000}{3} \right) = \frac{1}{100} \cdot \frac{625}{3} = \frac{625}{300} = 2.08$$

$$\sigma = \sqrt{2.08} = 1.44$$

COMMON DISCRETE DISTRIBUTION: BINOMIAL

The binomial distribution describes discrete data of the two-possibility type, such as yes-no, either-or, or accept-reject. The necessary symbols are

p = probability of one of the two alternatives
q = probability of the other alternative
k = number of trials

The frequency function $f(x)$ is

$$f(x) = \binom{k}{x} p^x q^{k-x}$$

where x is the number of occurrences of the event associated with p and $f(x)$ is the probability of x occurring in k trials.

EXAMPLE 14.3

If the probability of a salesman successfully selling something to a customer can be represented by a binomial distribution with a mean of .7, and if the salesman makes three calls, find the probability distribution for the number of calls which are successful.

$$f(0) = \binom{3}{0} (.7)^0(.3)^{3-0} = \frac{3!}{0!3!} (1)(.3)^3 = 1(1)(.027) = .027$$

$$f(1) = \binom{3}{1} (.7)^1(.3)^{3-1} = \frac{3!}{1!2!} (.7)^1(.3)^2 = 3(.7)(.09) = .189$$

$$f(2) = \binom{3}{2} (.7)^2(.3)^{3-2} = \frac{3!}{2!1!} (.7)^2(.3)^1 = 3(.49)(.3) = .441$$

$$f(3) = \binom{3}{3} (.7)^3(.3)^{3-3} = \frac{3!}{3!0!} (.7)^3(.3)^0 = 1(.343)(1) = .343$$

Number of successes in three calls	Probability
0	.027
1	.189
2	.441
3	.343
	1.000

COMMON DISCRETE DISTRIBUTIONS: HYPERGEOMETRIC

The hypergeometric distribution is similar to the binomial.   It also is applicable to either-or situations.   The hypergeometric distribution applies to those situations where each trial depletes the population, i.e., where no replacement takes place.   The formula for probable frequency with the hypergeometric distribution is:

$$f(x) = \frac{\binom{a}{x}\binom{b}{n-x}}{\binom{a+b}{n}}$$

where a = number of one type of item in the set
b = number of other type of item in the set
n = number of items chosen
x = number of items of type "a" chosen

EXAMPLE 14.4

The Cavalier Electronics Company had decided several years ago that if the Research and Development Department of the company were to be successful, 40 percent of the projects which were begun during a year would be successful. Of last year's projects, 10 were begun and three were finished.   None of the three was successful.   What is the probability that this could happen and the Research and Development Department would still be working at the expected success rate?

Where a = number of successes = 40 percent of 10 = 4
b = number of failures = 60 percent of 10 = 6
n = number chosen = 3
x = number of successes chosen = 0

$$f(0) = \frac{\binom{4}{0}\binom{6}{3-0}}{\binom{4+6}{3}} = \frac{\left(\frac{4!}{0!4!}\right)\left(\frac{6!}{3!3!}\right)}{\frac{10!}{3!7!}} = \frac{1\left(\frac{6 \cdot 5 \cdot 4}{3 \cdot 2 \cdot 1}\right)}{\frac{10 \cdot 9 \cdot 8}{3 \cdot 2 \cdot 1}}$$

$$= \frac{\overset{2}{6 \cdot 5 \cdot 4}}{\underset{2 \cdot 3 \cdot 2}{10 \cdot 9 \cdot 8}} = \frac{1}{3 \cdot 2} = \frac{1}{6}$$

COMMON DISCRETE DISTRIBUTION: POISSON

The Poisson distribution describes phenomena where the number of possible events to the left of the mean is relatively few and where there are a large number of possible events to the right of the mean. This is very common in business situations where the mean number is 3, 7, or 15, and where it is impossible for a number less than 0 to occur, whereas it might be possible, although extremely unlikely, for numbers such as 200 or 500 to occur. The mean and variance of the Poisson distribution are identical and are usually represented by the Greek letter lambda. Thus

$$\lambda = \text{mean} = \text{variance}$$

The probability function for the number of occurrences x is

$$f(x) = \frac{\lambda^x e^{-\lambda}}{x!}$$

EXAMPLE 14.5

The average number of employees absent on any particular day is two and is generally well described by a Poisson distribution. Prepare a probability distribution for the number of absences on a given day.

Note that $\lambda = 2$ since this is the average or mean number of absences. Also from the table of e^{-x}, note that $e^{-2} = .135$.

$$f(0) = 2^0(.135) = \frac{1(.135)}{1} = .135$$

$$f(1) = \frac{2^1(.135)}{1!} = \frac{2(.135)}{1} = .270$$

$$f(2) = \frac{2^2(.135)}{2!} = \frac{4(.135)}{2.1} = .270$$

$$f(3) = \frac{2^3(.135)}{3!} = \frac{8(.135)}{6} = .180$$

$$f(4) = \frac{2^4(.135)}{4!} = \frac{16(.135)}{24} = .090$$

$$f(5) = \frac{2^5(.135)}{5!} = \frac{32(.135)}{120} = .036$$

$$f(6) = \frac{2^6(.135)}{6!} = \frac{64(.135)}{720} = .012$$

$$f(7) = \frac{2^7(.135)}{7!} = \frac{128(.135)}{5040} = .003$$

$$f(8) = \frac{2^8(.135)}{8!} = \frac{256(.135)}{40,320} = .001$$

The distribution, then, is

Table 14.1

Number of absences	Probability
0	.135
1	.270
2	.270
3	.180
4	.090
5	.036
6	.012
7	.003
8	.001

Note that a small probability occurs with 9 absences, 10, 11, even 50 or 500.   Since the total of the probabilities must sum to 1, and the distribution through eight sums to .997, .003 must represent the probability associated with $x \geq 9$.

CONTINUOUS DISTRIBUTIONS

A major conceptual difference exists between discrete and continuous probabilities.   When thinking in discrete terms, the probability associated with an event is meaningful.   With continuous events, however, where the number of possible events is infinite, the probability that a specific event will occur is practically zero.   For example, what is the probability that a man getting on the scale will weigh exactly 175.000003 pounds?   Obviously, even if the same man weighed between 175 and 175.5 the day before, the probability is practically zero that he will weigh 175.000003 on this day.

For this reason, continuous probability statements must be worded somewhat differently from discrete.   Instead of finding the probability that x equals some value, say a, we find the probability that x is less than or equal to a, or is greater than or equal to a.

PROBABILITY DENSITY FUNCTIONS

Continuous distributions are often shown in cumulative form for the reasons indicated above.   Thus, if x varies from 0 to 5, the cumulative distribution would show the probability of $x \leq 1$, $x \leq 2$, $x \leq 3$, $x \leq 4$, and $x \leq 5$.   Obviously, if x only varies between 0 and 5, the probability that $x \leq 5$ will be 1.

Let $F(x)$ be a function such that the derivative of $F(x)$ is greater than or equal to 0 for $a \leq x \leq b$.   Note that if $F'(x) \leq 0$, then $F(x)$ will either be increasing or will be remaining steady in the interval. $F(x)$ can then be defined as a cumulative probability function between a and b.   The derivative of $F(x)$, which we will denote as $f(x)$, is a probability density function.   The integral:

$$\int_a^b f(x) \, dx = 1$$

where $f(x)$ is a probability density function

$$\int_a^c f(x) \, dx = P(x \leq c) \qquad a \leq c \leq b$$
$$\int_c^d f(x) \, dx = P(c \leq x \leq d) \qquad a \leq c \leq d \leq b$$

If we envision a curve $f(x)$ bounding an area between a and b of 1, the $\int f(x) \, dx$ provides the area under any desired portion of the curve (Figures 14.1, 14.2, and 14.3).

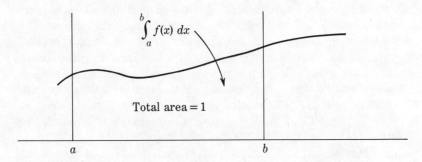

Figure 14.1

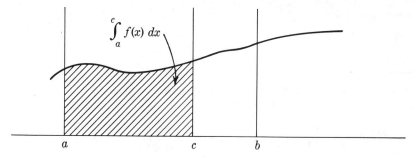

Figure 14.2

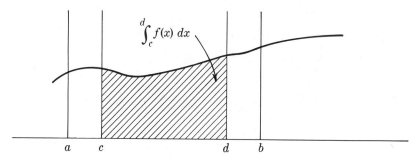

Figure 14.3

EXAMPLE 14.6

The probability density function for the number of hours necessary to complete a project is

$$f(x) = \frac{2(3x + 5)}{147} \qquad 5 \leq x \leq 8$$

What is the probability that from 6 to 7 hours will be required to complete the project?

$$\int_6^7 \frac{2(3x + 5)}{147} \, dx = \frac{2}{147} \int_6^7 3x + 5 \, dx = \frac{2}{147} \left(\frac{3x^2}{2} + 5x \right) \Big|_6^7$$

$$= \frac{2}{147} \left\{ \left[\frac{3(7)^2}{2} + 5(7) \right] - \left[\frac{3(6)^2}{2} + 5(6) \right] \right\}$$

$$= \frac{2}{147} \left(\frac{49}{2} \right) = \frac{49}{147}$$

$$= .33$$

EXAMPLE 14.7

The probability density function for net profit for 1965 is given by

$$f(x) = .028 \sin \frac{x}{50}$$

where x = thousands of dollars of profit

$$10 \leq x \leq 100$$

$$\frac{x}{50} \text{ is in radians}$$

Is the probability of a profit of 15,000 to 20,000 greater than or less than the probability of profits between 75,000 and 80,000?

$$\int_{15}^{20} .028 \sin \frac{x}{50} \, dx = .028 \int_{15}^{20} \sin \frac{x}{50} \, dx = .028 \left(\frac{1}{50}\right)\left(- \cos \frac{x}{50}\right) \Big|_{15}^{20}$$

$$= \frac{.028}{50}\left[- \cos \frac{20}{50} - \left(- \cos \frac{15}{50}\right)\right] = \frac{.028}{50}(- \cos .4 + \cos .3)$$

$$= \frac{.028}{50}(-.92106 + .95534)$$

$$= \frac{.028}{50}(.03428) = .000019$$

$$\int_{75}^{80} .028 \sin \frac{x}{50} \, dx = .028 \int_{75}^{80} \sin \frac{x}{50} \, dx = .028 \left(\frac{1}{50}\right)\left(- \cos \frac{x}{50}\right) \Big|_{75}^{80}$$

$$= \frac{.028}{50}\left[- \cos \frac{80}{50} - \left(- \cos \frac{75}{50}\right)\right] = \frac{.028}{50}(- \cos 1.6 + \cos 1.5)$$

$$= \frac{.028}{50}[-(-.02920) + .07074]$$

$$= \frac{.028}{50}(.09994)$$

$$= .000056$$

Therefore the probability is higher for 75,000 to 80,000 profit, although both are quite small.

EXAMPLE 14.8

In Example 14.2, for what value of x does the density function obtain a maximum?

$$f(x) = .028 \sin \frac{x}{50}$$

$$f'(x) = \left(\frac{1}{50}\right)(.028) \cos \frac{x}{50}$$

Setting the derivative equal to zero

$$\frac{.028}{50} \cos \frac{x}{50} = 0$$

$$\cos \frac{x}{50} = 0$$

Since the cos 1.5708 radians is equal to zero,

$$\frac{x}{50} = 1.5708$$

$$x = 78.54$$

$$f''(x) = \left(\frac{1}{50}\right)\left(\frac{1}{50}\right)(.028)\left(-\sin\frac{x}{50}\right)$$

$$f''(78.54) = \left(\frac{1}{50}\right)\left(\frac{1}{50}\right)(0.28)(-\sin 1.5708)$$

$$= \left(\frac{1}{50}\right)\left(\frac{1}{50}\right)(.028)(-1) = \frac{-.028}{2500}$$

Since the second derivative is negative, $f(78.54)$ must be a maximum.

USING INTEGRAL CALCULUS TO CONSTRUCT PROBABILITY DENSITY FUNCTIONS

If a function is known which will model the shape of a needed probability distribution over a range of x, integral calculus techniques can be used to convert the function to a probability density function over the desired range. If $g(x)$ is a function, and the range of x is $a \leq x \leq b$, integrate $g(x)$ over a range $a \leq x \leq b$. Multiply the inverse of the resulting number by $g(x)$ to find the probability density function $f(x)$.

EXAMPLE 14.9

If the function $3x^2 - 5x + 100$ will provide the right shape for a probability density function with $5 \leq x \leq 10$, determine the density function.

$$\int_5^{10} 3x^2 - 5x + 100 \, dx = x^3 - \frac{5x^2}{2} + 100x \Big|_5^{10}$$

$$= \left[(10)^3 - \frac{5(10)^2}{2} + 100(10)\right] - \left[(5)^3 - \frac{5(5)^2}{2} + 100(5)\right]$$

$$= 1000 - 250 + 1000 - 125 + \tfrac{125}{2} - 500$$

$$= \tfrac{2250}{2} + \tfrac{125}{2}$$

$$= \tfrac{2375}{2}$$

Therefore, the probability density function is

$$f(x) = \frac{2(3x^2 - 5x + 100)}{2375} \qquad 5 \leq x \leq 10$$

EXAMPLE 14.10

Find the probability density function for $(50 - x)/(100x - x^2)$, $1 \leq x \leq 5$.

$$\int_1^5 g(x) = \int_1^5 \frac{50 - x}{100x - x^2} \, dx$$

Let
$$u = 100x - x^2$$

then
$$du = 100 - 2x \, dx = 2(50 - x) \, dx$$

$$\int_1^5 g(x) = \frac{1}{2} \int_1^5 \frac{2(50 - x)}{100x - x^2}$$

$$dx = \frac{1}{2} \int_1^5 \frac{1}{u} \, du \Big|_{u \,=\, 100x - x^2}$$

$$= \tfrac{1}{2} \ln u \Big|_{u \,=\, 100x - x^2} \Big|_1^5$$

$$= \tfrac{1}{2}[\ln (100x - x)^2] \Big|_1^5$$

$$= \tfrac{1}{2}\{\ln [100(5) - 5^2]\} - \ln [100(1) - 1^2]$$

$$= \tfrac{1}{2}(\ln 475 - \ln 99)$$

$$= \tfrac{1}{2}(6.16331 - 4.59512)$$

$$= \tfrac{1}{2}(1.56819)$$

$$= .784095$$

$$\frac{1}{\int_1^5 g(x)} = \frac{1}{.784095} = 1.275$$

Thus, the probability density function is

$$f(x) = 1.275 \left(\frac{50 - x}{100x - x^2} \right)$$

NORMAL CURVE TABLES

One of the most frequently used distributions for continuous data is the normal curve. The normal curve is bell shaped and has two identifying parameters, the mean and the standard deviation. The curve is shaped so that 68 percent of the area is within ± 1 standard deviation from the mean, and 95 percent of the area is within ± 2 standard deviations.

Often, when developing a normal curve for a business situation, the mean can easily be estimated, but the standard deviation is harder to determine. It is often more convenient to ascertain the range which will include 50 percent of the expected results. This is easily converted to standard deviations by subtracting the mean from the upper limit of the 50–50 range (or the lower limit from the mean) and dividing by 667. Mathematically, if a is the lower end and b the upper end of the 50–50 range, the mean will be

$$\bar{x} = \frac{(a + b)}{2}$$

and the standard deviation will be

$$\sigma = \frac{(b - \bar{x})}{.667}$$

or

$$\sigma = \frac{(\bar{x} - a)}{.667}$$

When reading the normal curve table, remember that the curve is symmetric about the mean, and that 50 percent of the area under the curve lies on each side of the mean. To convert a value on the x scale of a particular normal curve to the general normal curve in the table, determine

$$z = \frac{(a - \bar{x})}{\sigma}$$

where a = a value on the x axis of a particular normal curve
$\bar{x}$ = the mean of the normal curve
σ = the standard deviation for the normal curve

If z is positive, the area is given directly in the table and represents the area illustrated in Figure 14.4.

To find the area between $-\infty$ and z, add .5000 to the value in the table. The resulting area is shown in Figure 14.5. To find the area to the right of z, subtract the tabled value from .500. The result will show the area in Figure 14.6. If z is negative, look up the same numerical value (positive) in the table. This will represent the area as shown in Figure 14.7. To find the area to the left of a negative z, subtract the tabled value for the same positive z from .5000. The resulting area is shown in Figure 14.8. The entire area to the right of a negative z is found by adding .5000 to the table value for the positive z. The area represented is shown in Figure 14.9.

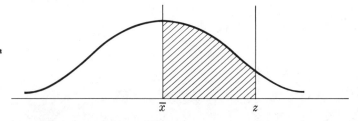

Figure 14.4 The area bounded by $x = \bar{x}$ and $x = z$, where $z > \bar{x}$

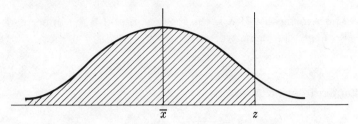

Figure 14.5 The area bounded by $x = -\infty$ and $x = z$, where $z > \bar{x}$

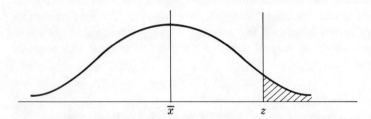

Figure 14.6 The area bounded by $x = z$ and $x = \infty$, where $z > \bar{x}$

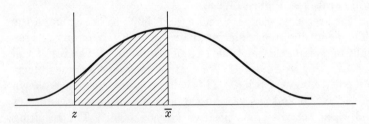

Figure 14.7 The area bounded by $x = z$ and $x = \bar{x}$, where $z < \bar{x}$

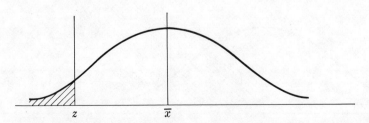

Figure 14.8 The area bounded by $x = -\infty$ and $x = z$, where $z < \bar{x}$

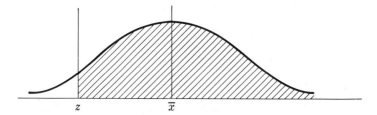

Figure 14.9 The area bounded by $x = z$ and $x = \infty$, where $z < \bar{x}$

EXAMPLE 14.11

If $\bar{x} = 10$ and $\sigma = 5$, find:

1 the probability of $x \geq 15$
2 the probability of $x \leq 14$
3 the probability of $6 \leq x \leq 12$
4 the probability of $x \leq 3$
5 the probability of $x \geq 4$

1 First compute

$$z = \frac{x - \bar{x}}{\sigma} = \frac{15 - 10}{5} = \frac{5}{5} = 1$$

the table value for $z = 1$ is .3413.   Since this represents the area between 10 and 15 (Figure 14.10), to find the area to the right of 15 we subtract this value from .5000. Thus $P(x \geq 15) = .5000 - .3413 = .1587.$

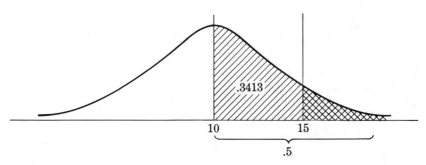

Figure 14.10

2 To find $P(x \leq 14)$, note that $z = (14 - 10)/5 = \frac{4}{5} = .8$.   The tabular value for $z = .8$ is .2881.   This value represents the area between 10 and 14 as shown in Figure 14.11. $P(x \leq 14) = .5000 + .2881 = .7881.$

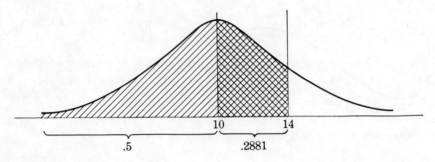

Figure 14.11

3   To find $P(6 \leq x \leq 12)$, the z value at 6 and 12 must be determined

$$z_6 = \frac{6 - 10}{5} = \frac{-4}{5} = -.8$$

Looking up .8 in the table, we note the area value is .2881.   Since z is negative, this represents the area shown in Figure 14.12.

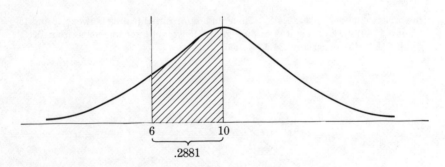

Figure 14.12

$$z_{12} = \frac{12 - 10}{5} = \frac{2}{5} = .4$$

The tabular value for .4 is .1554, and this represents the area shown in Figure 14.13. The area between 6 and 12 is found by adding the two areas together.   Thus

$$P(6 \leq x \leq 12) = .2881 + .1554 = .4435$$

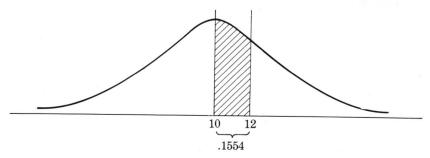

.1554

Figure 14.13

4 To find $P(x \leq 3)$, first compute z.

$$z = \frac{3 - 10}{5} = \frac{-7}{5} = -1.4$$

The area for $z = 1.4$ according to the table is .4192.   Since z is negative this represents the area from 3 to 10.   To find the area to the left of 3, subtract .4192 from
.5000.   Thus,

$$P(x \leq 3) = .5000 - .4192 = .0808$$

5 $x \geq 4$, $z = (4 - 10)/5 = -6/5 = -1.2$.   The table value for 1.2 is .3849.   This
gives the area from 4 to 10.   The area to the right of 10 = .5000, so

$$P(x \geq 4) = .3849 + .5000 = .8849$$

EXAMPLE 14.12

The Zileh Company estimates that maintenance expenditures for the coming year
have a 50–50 chance of being between $12,000 and $16,000, and they believe that
the probability distribution for maintenance expense can be closely approximated
by a normal curve.   If the probability of maintenance expense being in excess of
$20,000 is 10 percent or more, they have decided to purchase new equipment and
renovate the plant.   Should they purchase the new equipment?
   If the 50–50 estimate is $12,000 to $16,000, the mean estimate is $14,000, and
= (16,000 − 14,000)/.667 = 2,000/.667 = 3,000.   The z value for $20,000 is

$$\frac{(20,000 - 14,000)}{3,000} = \frac{6,000}{3,000} = 2$$

Looking up $z = 2$ in the table, we find .4773.
   This represents the area between $14,000 and $20,000.   To find the area to the
right of $20,000, we must subtract from .5000.   Thus,

$$P(x > 20,000) = .5000 - .4773 = .0227$$

This is less than 10 percent, so the new equipment should not be purchased.

PROBLEMS

1 Find the mean, variance, and standard deviation of the following probability distribution:

Number of repairs	Probability
0	.65
1	.25
2	.06
3	.03
4 or more	.01

2 Find the mean, variance, and standard deviation of the following probability distribution:

Dollar profit	Probability
10,000	.3
12,000	.4
14,000	.2
16,000	.1

3 Find the mean, variance, and standard deviation of the following density functions:

a $f(x) = .0004x^3 - .0012x$ $\quad 0 \leq x \leq 10$

b $f(x) = e^{-x}$ $\quad 0 \leq x \leq 100$

4 Find the mean, variance, and standard deviation of the following density functions:

a $f(x) = .09375x^2 - .125x$ $\quad 2 \leq x \leq 4$

b $f(x) = -.17657 \ln |x^2 - 5|$ $\quad 6 \leq x \leq 10$

5 The probability of a sample containing a required amount of a critical element is .7. Using the binomial distribution, develop a probability distribution for the number of successful samples which might be drawn out of four trials. What is the probability of three or more being successful? How about two or less?

6 Three-fourths of the employees of the Artisan Manufacturing Company are women. Develop a probability distribution for the number of women who might be elected to a committee of five members. What is the probability of two or more being elected? How about four or less?

7 The number of arrivals at the Glynn County Airport in a 15-minute interval follow a Poisson distribution with a mean of 3. Develop the probability distribution.

8 The number of machine breakdowns in a day at the Revere Company follows a Poisson distribution with a mean of 1. Develop the probability distribution.

9 Develop density functions out of the following functions:
   a $f(x) = 3x^2 - 4x + 5; 0 \leq x \leq 5$. Find the probability of $3 \leq x \leq 4$.
   b $f(x) = 2x^3 + 3x^2 - 25x; 0 \leq x \leq 10$. Find the probability of $2 \leq x \leq 5$.
   c $f(x) = 3e^{-4x}; 1 \leq x \leq 5$. Find the probability of $1 \leq x \leq 3$.
   d $f(x) = \ln|2x - 1|; 3 \leq x \leq 8$. Find the probability of $3 \leq x \leq 7$.

10 Develop density functions out of the following functions:
   a $f(x) = 5x^2 - 2x + 2; 0 \leq x \leq 2$. Find the probability of $0 \leq x \leq 1$.
   b $f(x) = x^3 - x; 2 \leq x \leq 5$. Find the probability of $2 \leq x \leq 3$.
   c $f(x) = 5e^{-6x}; 1 \leq x \leq 4$. Find the probability of $2 \leq x \leq 4$.
   d $f(x) = \ln|5x + 8|; 2 \leq x \leq 6$. Find the probability of $5 \leq x \leq 6$.

11 When is each of the functions in Prob. 9 at a maximum?

12 When is each of the functions in Prob. 10 at a maximum?

13 For a normal curve with $\bar{x} = 20$ and $\sigma = 10$, find:
   a $P(x \geq 25)$ **b** $P(x \leq 10)$
   c $P(22 \leq x \leq 35)$ **d** $P(5 \leq x \leq 25)$

14 For a normal curve with $\bar{x} = 50$ and $\sigma = 15$, find:
   a $P(x \geq 70)$ **b** $P(x \leq 20)$
   c $P(60 \leq x \leq 90)$ **d** $P(35 \leq x \leq 65)$

15 EXPECTED VALUE

DISCRETE DATA

Conditional value is defined as the gain (or loss) which will be experienced if a possible event comes to pass. Assume that a company is trying to decide whether to invest in a particular stock. They feel that the market may go up, remain the same, or fall. If the market goes up, they will profit by $1,000; if it remains steady they will neither gain nor lose; but if it goes down, they will lose $2,000. The $1,000, $0, and −$2,000 are conditional values. They are the estimated or known profits (or losses) that can be expected if a given condition comes to pass.

Assume, now, that we were able to assign probabilities for the likelihood of the market increasing, remaining steady, or decreasing, of .5, .3, and .2 respectively. The expected value for a strategy or decision is determined by adding the products of all the conditional values for the events which could occur if the strategy were followed and the corresponding probabilities. The expected value in our example is

$$E(S_1) = A_1 P(A_1) + A_2 P(A_2) + \cdots + A_n P(A_n)$$

where $A_1, A_2, \ldots, A_n$ are the conditional values for each possible event if S_1 is followed, and $P(A_1), P(A_2), \ldots, P(A_n)$ are the probabilities associated with the occurrence of each possible event.

Moving one step further, assume that the only other alternative the company wishes to consider in the above situations is buying bonds.

If bonds are purchased and the market goes up, the company estimates a conditional profit of \$800.   If the market remains steady or declines, it is expected to result in conditional values of \$0, and $-\$200$, respectively.

If we let
$$S_1 = \text{buy stock}$$
$$S_2 = \text{buy bonds}$$

then $E(S_1) = .5(1{,}000) + .3(0) + .2(-2{,}000) = 500 - 400 = \$100$

$$E(S_2) = .5(800) + .3(0) + .2(-200) = 400 - 40 = \$360$$

and strategy 2 would be preferable.

Perhaps it should be noted that decisions based on expected values, which have been determined using profit payoffs, implicitly assume that the strategist has a linear utility for money.   The assumption is made, for example, that one would be twice as happy to win \$1,000 as \$500 and would be indifferent if presented a strategy which was equilikely to profit him a thousand dollars or to lose him a thousand dollars. This assumption is not generally valid with widely divergent amounts of money or with losses which are great compared to the resources of the strategist.   However, the oversimplification of assuming a linear utility function for money, if used carefully, provides excellent decisions in a much less complicated manner than would be possible if complex utility functions had to be derived.

Returning to our example, observe that the conditional values can be put into matrix form and that this will allow us to portray the model more concisely and manipulate it more easily.   Thus, if each row represents a strategy, and each column an event, the matrix would appear as

	E_1	E_2	E_3
S_1	1,000	0	$-2{,}000$
S_2	800	0	-200

where E_1 = market increase
E_2 = market steady
E_3 = market decrease

The probabilities associated with each event can be portrayed by a vector

$$\mathbf{p} = \begin{pmatrix} .5 \\ .3 \\ .2 \end{pmatrix}$$

and the expected values of each strategy will be the vector resulting from the product $\mathbf{Ap}$.

$$\mathbf{Ap} = \begin{pmatrix} 1000 & 0 & -2.000 \\ 800 & 0 & -200 \end{pmatrix} \begin{pmatrix} .5 \\ .3 \\ .2 \end{pmatrix} = \begin{pmatrix} 100 \\ 360 \end{pmatrix}$$

EXAMPLE 15.1

Select the strategy with the highest expected value.

$$\begin{array}{cc} & E_1 \quad E_2 \\ \begin{array}{c} S_1 \\ S_2 \\ S_3 \end{array} & \begin{pmatrix} 10 & 100 \\ 25 & 70 \\ 5 & 200 \end{pmatrix} \end{array} \quad \begin{array}{c} E_1 \\ E_1 \end{array} \begin{pmatrix} .90 \\ .10 \end{pmatrix}$$

Multiplying the matrix and vector, we get

$$\mathbf{E(v)} = \begin{pmatrix} 10 & 100 \\ 25 & 70 \\ 5 & 200 \end{pmatrix} \begin{pmatrix} .90 \\ .10 \end{pmatrix} = \begin{pmatrix} 19.0 \\ 29.5 \\ 24.5 \end{pmatrix}$$

Strategy 2 has the highest expected value.

EXAMPLE 15.2

Conditional value $= \begin{pmatrix} 5 & 20 \\ 10 & 15 \end{pmatrix}$. A consulting firm has determined that the expected values are $\begin{pmatrix} 14 \\ 13 \end{pmatrix}$. What probability did they assign to each event?

Let
$$\mathbf{A} = \text{conditional-value matrix}$$
$$\mathbf{p} = \text{probability vector}$$
$$\mathbf{e} = \text{expected-value vector}$$
then
$$\mathbf{Ap} = \mathbf{e}$$
and
$$\mathbf{AA^{-1}p} = \mathbf{A^{-1}e}$$
$$\mathbf{Ip} = \mathbf{A^{-1}e}$$
$$\mathbf{p} = \mathbf{A^{-1}e}$$

The Gaussian method can be used to find $\mathbf{A^{-1}}$. The initial tableau is:

$$\begin{pmatrix} 5 & 20 & | & 1 & 0 \\ 10 & 15 & | & 0 & 1 \end{pmatrix}$$

Row 1 $\div$ 5 $\rightarrow$ Row 1
$$\begin{pmatrix} 1 & 4 & | & \frac{1}{5} & 0 \\ 10 & 15 & | & 0 & 1 \end{pmatrix}$$

Row 2 $-$ 10 Row 1 $\rightarrow$ Row 2
$$\begin{pmatrix} 1 & 4 & | & \frac{1}{5} & 0 \\ 0 & -25 & | & -2 & 1 \end{pmatrix}$$

Row 2 $\div$ -25 $\rightarrow$ Row 2
$$\begin{pmatrix} 1 & 4 & | & \frac{1}{5} & 0 \\ 0 & 1 & | & \frac{2}{25} & -\frac{1}{25} \end{pmatrix}$$

Row 1 $-$ 4 Row 2 $\rightarrow$ Row 1
$$\begin{pmatrix} 1 & 0 & | & -\frac{3}{25} & \frac{4}{25} \\ 0 & 1 & | & \frac{2}{25} & -\frac{1}{25} \end{pmatrix}$$

Thus
$$\mathbf{A}^{-1} = \begin{pmatrix} -\frac{3}{25} & \frac{4}{25} \\ \frac{2}{25} & -\frac{1}{25} \end{pmatrix}$$

and
$$\mathbf{p} = \mathbf{A}^{-1}\mathbf{e} = \begin{pmatrix} -\frac{3}{25} & \frac{4}{25} \\ \frac{2}{25} & -\frac{1}{25} \end{pmatrix} \begin{pmatrix} 14 \\ 13 \end{pmatrix} = \begin{pmatrix} \frac{10}{25} \\ \frac{15}{25} \end{pmatrix}$$

Thus the probabilities associated with events 1 and 2 were .4 and .6, respectively.

CONTINUOUS FORM

Instead of the situation in which a finite number of events could occur for any strategy, let us now consider the type of situation in which an infinite number of events are possible. For example, assume that a different conditional value would apply to each possible percentage point that a stock went up or down. This would be extremely difficult to represent in a matrix since many thousands of columns would be required, i.e., one for each possible percentage point.

The most efficient method for finding expected value in such a situation is with the use of integral calculus. Let us define a probability density function $f(x)$ which gives probabilities associated with the set of all possible conditional values connected with a specific strategy. This function will be constructed in such a manner that x represents all possible conditional values or payoffs for the given strategy. The expected value can be represented by the following integral:

$$\int_a^b xf(x)\,dx$$

where
$$f(x) = 0 \qquad x < a$$
$$0 \le f(x) \le 1 \qquad a \le x \le b$$
$$f(x) = 0 \qquad x > b$$
$$\int_a^b f(x)\,dx = 1$$

EXAMPLE 15.3

Two strategies are under consideration. Their probability density functions and range of conditional values are

$$S_1 = f(x) = \frac{x}{300} + \frac{1}{60} \qquad -10 \le x \le 20$$
$$S_2 = \frac{4x^4 + 200}{153x^3} \qquad -5 \le x \le 10$$

Which strategy has the greater expected value?

$$E(S_1) = \int_{-10}^{20} x \left(\frac{x}{300} + \frac{1}{60} \right) dx = \int_{-10}^{20} \frac{x^2}{300} + \frac{x}{60} \, dx$$

$$= \frac{1}{300} \int_{-10}^{20} x^2 \, dx + \frac{1}{60} \int_{-10}^{20} x \, dx$$

$$= \left(\frac{1}{300} \right) \left(\frac{1}{3} \right) x^3 \Big|_{-10}^{20} + \left(\frac{1}{60} \right) \left(\frac{1}{2} \right) x^2 \Big|_{-10}^{20}$$

$$= \frac{1}{900} [20^3 - (-10)^3] + \frac{1}{120} [20^2 - (-10)^2]$$

$$= \frac{1}{900} (8000 + 1000) + \frac{1}{120} (400 - 100)$$

$$= \frac{9000}{900} + \frac{300}{120} = 10 + 2\frac{1}{2} = 12.5$$

$$E(S_2) = \int_{-5}^{10} x \left(\frac{4x^4}{153x^3} + \frac{200}{153x^3} \right) dx = \int_{-5}^{10} \left(\frac{4x^5}{153x^3} + \frac{200x}{153^3} \right) dx$$

$$= \int_{-5}^{10} \frac{4x^5}{153x^3} \, dx + \int_{-5}^{10} \frac{200x}{153x^3} \, dx$$

$$= \frac{4}{153} \int_{-5}^{10} x^2 \, dx + \frac{200}{153} \int_{-5}^{10} \frac{1}{x^2}$$

$$= \left(\frac{4}{153} \right) \left(\frac{1}{3} \right) x^3 \Big|_{-5}^{10} + \frac{200}{153} (-1) \frac{1}{x} \Big|_{-5}^{10}$$

$$= \frac{4}{459} [10^3 - (-5)^3] - \frac{200}{153} (\frac{1}{10} - \frac{1}{5})$$

$$= \frac{4}{459} (1000 + 125) - \frac{200}{153} (\frac{1}{10} + \frac{2}{10})$$

$$= \frac{4}{459} (1125) - \frac{200}{153} (\frac{3}{10}) = \frac{4500}{459} - \frac{600}{1530}$$

$$= \frac{45,000}{4,590} - \frac{1,800}{4,590} = \frac{43,200}{4,590}$$

$$= 9.4$$

Thus $E(S_1) > E(S_2)$.

EXAMPLE 15.4

The Arnold Embalming Company wishes to evaluate two procedures for manufacturing caskets. Method 1 has a probability density function for cost of

$$f(x) = 2.071 \sin x \qquad 1.1 \leq x \leq 1.6$$

where x is in radians and represents cost in thousands of dollars.
Method 2 has a probability density function for cost of

$$g(x) = 6.410 \cos x \qquad 1 \leq x \leq 1.5$$

where x is defined as in method 1.
Which method provides the lowest expected cost?

$$E(S_1) = E[f(x)] = \int_{1.1}^{1.6} x(2.071 \sin x) \, dx = 2.071 \int_{1.1}^{1.6} x \sin x \, dx$$

Integration by parts will provide a method for integrating $x \sin x$.

Let $\qquad\qquad u = x \qquad$ and $\qquad dv = \sin x \, dx.$
then $\qquad\qquad du = dx \qquad$ and $\qquad v = - \cos x$

Now,

$$E(S_1) = 2.071 \left(-x \cos x - \int_{1.1}^{1.6} - \cos x \, dx \right)$$

$$= 2.071 \left(-x \cos x + \int_{1.1}^{1.6} \cos x \, dx \right)$$

$$= 2.071(-x \cos x + \sin x) \Big|_{1.1}^{1.6}$$

$$= 2.071[(-1.6 \cos 1.6 + \sin 1.6) - (-1.1 \cos 1.1 + \sin 1.1)]$$

$$= 2.071[-1.6(-.0292) + .9996 + 1.1(.4536) - .8912]$$

$$= 2.071(.0467 + .9996 + .4990 - .8912)$$

$$= 2.071(.6541) = 1.355$$

$$E(S_2) = E[g(x)] = \int_{1}^{1.5} x(6.410 \cos x) \, dx = 6.410 \int_{1}^{1.5} x \cos x \, dx$$

Let $\qquad\qquad u = x \qquad$ and $\qquad dv = \cos x \, dv$
then $\qquad\qquad du = dx \qquad$ and $\qquad v = \sin x$

Now

$$E(S_2) = 6.410(x \sin x - \int_{1}^{1.5} \sin x \, dx) = 6.410(x \sin x \cos x) \Big|_{1}^{1.5}$$

$$= 6.410[(1.5 \sin 1.5 + \cos 1.5) - (1 \sin 1 + \cos 1)]$$

$$= 6.410[1.5(.9975) + .0707 - .8415 - .5403]$$

$$= 6.410(1.4963 + .0707 - .8415 - .5403) = 6.410(.1852) = 1.187$$

Therefore $\qquad\qquad\qquad E(S_2) \leq E(S_1)$

EXPECTED VALUE OF PERFECT INFORMATION

If expected value is being used as the criterion in a decision situation, the strategy having the highest expected value or the lowest expected cost will be selected. Obviously, in a given situation, the strategy having the highest expected value will not necessarily be the most advantageous one. In the long run, the chances are good that the strategy having the highest expected value will be more advantageous than the alternate strategies available, but in the short run, this does not have to be the case. For example, assume the following situation.

$$\begin{array}{c} \quad E_1 \quad\quad E_2 \\ S_1 \begin{pmatrix} 8 & 100 \\ 20 & 30 \end{pmatrix} \quad \begin{array}{c} E_1 \\ E_2 \end{array} \begin{pmatrix} .5 \\ .5 \end{pmatrix} \\ S_2 \end{array}$$

The expected values are

$$\begin{pmatrix} 8 & 100 \\ 20 & 30 \end{pmatrix} \begin{pmatrix} .5 \\ .5 \end{pmatrix} = \begin{pmatrix} 54 \\ 25 \end{pmatrix}$$

S_1 has the higher expected value, and if the 50–50 probability is reasonably accurate, S_1 will yield more than S_2 in the long run. In the short run, however, E_1 could come to pass 1, 2, 3, 4, or ? times in a row, and each time the player would wish that he had played S_2.

Now let us assume that although E_1 and E_2 are equally likely to occur over the long run, there is a pattern, possibly a highly complex pattern, that is not evident. This means that by finding the pattern we could predict whether E_1 or E_2 would occur at a given time. Notice that *knowing* this pattern will not give us control over it. E_1 will still come about approximately half the time and E_2 the other half. However, since we know the pattern we can select the best strategy each time. Thus when E_1 is to come about, we will select S_2 and when E_2 is predicted we will pick S_1. The expected value under conditions of certainty, for this situation, could be defined as

$$E(\text{certainty}) = 20(.5) + 100(.5) = 10 + 50 = 60$$

since half the time when E_1 comes about we will receive 20 by selecting S_2 and the other half of the time when E_2 comes about we will receive 100 by selecting S_1. Now, observe that we could expect a payoff of 54 with no predicting system simply by selecting S_1 all the time. The perfect predicting system, in this situation is worth $60 - 54 = 6$ to us. This 6 can be identified as the *expected value of perfect information*, or EVPI.

$$\text{EVPI} = E(\text{certainty}) - E(S_i)$$

where $E(S_i) > E(S)$ for all S.

The EVPI establishes an upper bound for the worth of a perfect forecasting system. Since it would be highly unlikely to be able to develop a perfect system, a company should never contract to spend as much as the EVPI to develop a new predicting system. EVPI serves as an upper bound to help managements in estimating the worth of better predicting systems.

EXAMPLE 15.5

Assume four strategies and three possible events with the following conditional costs.

	E_1	E_2	E_3
S_1	5	10	20
S_2	15	40	0
S_3	5	5	50
S_4	20	10	10

The probabilities associated with the events are

$$\begin{array}{c} E_1 \\ E_2 \\ E_3 \end{array} \begin{pmatrix} .1 \\ .1 \\ .8 \end{pmatrix}$$

What is a perfect predicting system worth?

Let

$$A = \begin{pmatrix} 5 & 10 & 20 \\ 15 & 40 & 0 \\ 5 & 5 & 50 \\ 20 & 10 & 10 \end{pmatrix} \quad \text{and} \quad b = \begin{pmatrix} .1 \\ .1 \\ .8 \end{pmatrix}$$

then

$$Ab = \begin{pmatrix} 5 & 10 & 20 \\ 15 & 40 & 0 \\ 5 & 5 & 50 \\ 20 & 10 & 10 \end{pmatrix} \begin{pmatrix} .1 \\ .1 \\ .8 \end{pmatrix} = \begin{pmatrix} 17.5 \\ 5.5 \\ 41.0 \\ 11.0 \end{pmatrix}$$

Thus $E(S_2) = 5.5$ is the lowest expected cost.

Now, if we knew E_1 would occur, we would be indifferent to S_1 and S_3 and would have a cost of 5, for E_2 we would select S_3 for a cost of 5, and for E_3 we would select S_2 with a cost of 0.   Thus,

$$E(\text{certainty}) = .1(5) + .1(5) + .8(0) = .5 + .5 + 0 = 1$$
$$\text{EVPI} = 5.5 - 1 = 4.5$$

which is what a perfect predicting system would be worth.   Notice that the example deals with cost rather than profit, and, therefore, the goal is to minimize rather than maximize.

EXAMPLE 15.6

Conditional values and probabilities of events are given by the following data

$$\begin{array}{ccccc} & E_1 & E_2 & E_3 & E_4 \\ S_1 & \begin{pmatrix} 100 & 200 & 150 & 400 \\ S_2 & 20 & 30 & 40 & 1{,}000 \end{pmatrix} \end{array} \qquad \begin{array}{c} E_1 \\ E_2 \\ E_3 \\ E_4 \end{array} \begin{pmatrix} .2 \\ .1 \\ .3 \\ .4 \end{pmatrix}$$

What would a perfect prediction be worth?

$$A = \begin{pmatrix} 100 & 200 & 150 & 400 \\ 20 & 30 & 40 & 1{,}000 \end{pmatrix} \qquad b = \begin{pmatrix} .2 \\ .1 \\ .3 \\ .4 \end{pmatrix}$$

$$Ab = \begin{pmatrix} 100 & 200 & 150 & 400 \\ 20 & 30 & 40 & 1{,}000 \end{pmatrix} \begin{pmatrix} .2 \\ .1 \\ .3 \\ .4 \end{pmatrix} = \begin{pmatrix} 245 \\ 419 \end{pmatrix}$$

Thus $E(S_2) = 419$ and $E(S_2) > E(S_1)$.

Under conditions of certainty

Table 15.1

Event	Strategy	Value
E_1	S_1	100
E_2	S_1	200
E_3	S_1	150
E_4	S_2	1000

Thus if $\mathbf{c}$ = conditional values under certainty

$$\mathbf{c} = (100, 200, 150, 1000)$$

and $\qquad E(V \text{ certainty}) = \mathbf{cb} = (100, 200, 150, 1000)\begin{pmatrix} .2 \\ .1 \\ .3 \\ .4 \end{pmatrix} = 485$

and $\qquad\qquad\qquad\qquad$ EVPI = 485 − 419 = 66

PROBLEMS

1 Find the expected value of each strategy in the following situation:

Payoffs

		Events		
		E_1	E_2	E_3
Strategies	S_1	5	15	10
	S_2	−4	10	25
	S_3	−3	25	−10
	S_4	10	30	8

$$P(E_1) = .2$$
$$P(E_2) = .4$$
$$P(E_3) = .4$$

2 Find the expected value of each strategy in the following situation:

Payoffs

		Events				
		E_1	E_2	E_3	E_4	E_5
Strategies	S_1	20	50	20	80	−40
	S_2	100	10	30	30	−10
	S_3	40	10	60	30	−10

Event	Probability
1	.1
2	.1
3	.2
4	.3
5	.3

3 What is the expected value of perfect information in Prob. 1?

4 What is the expected value of perfect information in Prob. 2?

5 If the density function for sales of a product is

$$.0033x^2 - .0022x + .0006 \qquad 0 \le x \le 10$$

and if the profit function is $f(x) = 10x$, find the expected profit.

6 If the density function for number of complaints is

$$.1156e^{-.1x} \qquad 0 \le x \le 20$$

and if the cost function is $f(x) = 3x$, find the expected cost.

7 The Williams Company is faced with the problem of whether to make or buy part #1104 to be used in the manufacture of its widgets.   Estimated costs of manufacture are as follows:

Material	$1.00	
Direct labor	.50	
Variable overhead	.75	
Estimated fixed overhead	.75	based on 10,000 units

The purchase cost of the part is $4.00.   Estimates of demand for widgets is

$$5x - 2 \qquad 3 \le x \le 10$$

where x is in thousands of units
   If the decision is to make the part, the manufacture of zulus will have to be discontinued (space limitations).

Price per zulu	$2.00	
Material	.50	
Labor	1.00	
Overhead	.50	based on 15,000 units

Demand for zulus is modelled by

$$3x - 1 \qquad 6 \le x \le 15,000$$

Since zulus are not being manufactured at a profit, management thinks that this should not enter into the problem.   Should the company make or buy part #1104?

8

	Part A	Part B
Selling price per unit	$16.00	$6.00
Material per unit	4.00	2.00
Direct labor	8.00	2.00
Variable overhead	2.00	1.00
Fixed overhead	25% of direct labor at full capacity	25% of direct labor at full capacity

The plant can manufacture either 16,000 or 20,000 units of A or 80,000 or 100,000 units of B. They must produce either A or B, not both. Unsold units of A can be sold for salvage at $.05 each. Unsold units of B cannot be used. The plant could be sold for $1,000. Shut down costs are estimated at $1,500. The probability distribution for demand for part A is modelled by

$$x - 3 \qquad 14,000 \leq x \leq 20,000$$

where $x =$ thousands of units

and for part B

$$-x + 8 \qquad 30,000 \leq x \leq 80,000$$

where $x =$ thousands of units

An extra trim could be added to part B. The selling price would change to $7.00. Material cost would be increased $.50. Direct labor and variable overhead would each be expected to increase $.25. Demand, it is estimated, would be 10 percent higher.

Using expected value, determine the effects of each possible decision, and the corresponding opportunity costs.

PART 4

16 DIFFERENTIAL EQUATIONS

INTRODUCTION

Differential equations are equations which include derivatives of the dependent variable. $dy/dx = 3x^2$ is an example. In general, any equation in the general form $f(x,\ y,\ y',\ y'',\ \ldots,\ y^{[n]}) = 0$ is classified as an ordinary differential equation. An ordinary differential equation is one which has only one independent variable, whereas a partial differential equation is defined as one which has more than one independent variable.

Differential equations have a number of important business applications. The primary use, currently, is in situations where the data available is, at least partially, available in marginal form. The solution of most differential equations is exceedingly difficult. We will classify and demonstrate the method of solution of some of the easier forms. These forms alone will provide solutions for many business problems.

TERMINOLOGY AND CLASSIFICATION FOR DIFFERENTIAL EQUATIONS

The order of a differential equation is equal to the highest derivative included in the equation. Thus, if the fourth derivative is the highest derivative represented in a particular differential equation, the equation is said to be of the fourth order. The equation

$$(x - 2)y'' + (2x^2 - 5)y' = 10$$

is a differential equation of the second order since the highest derivative represented in the equation is y''.

The degree of a differential is equal to the highest power of the highest derivative. Thus $(x - 2)y''^5 + (x - 10) = 0$ is a second-order fifth-degree differential equation since the highest derivative is y'' and it is raised to the fifth power.

A linear differential equation is one where the dependent variables, i.e., the y variables, are raised to the first power only.

$$y' + (3x^2 - 4)y = 4x + 5$$

is a linear differential equation since the dependent variable, y, is raised only to the first power.

A differential equation with constant coefficients is one where the coefficients of the dependent variables are constants rather than functions of x and y. Thus, $y' + 7y = x^2 + 7x$ has the coefficients 1 and 7 for the dependent variables and is therefore a linear equation with constant coefficients.

The equation $F(x, y) + G(x, y)y' = 0$ is said to be homogeneous if $F(x, y)$ and $G(x, y)$ are of the same degree, and if $F(tx, ty) = t^n G(x, y)$ for all t and for any positive integer n.

We shall limit our text to the solution of the following types of problems:

1 Linear differential equations of first order
   a Homogeneous with constant coefficients
   b Nonhomogeneous with constant coefficients
   c Homogeneous
   d General case
2 Linear differential equations of second order
   a Homogeneous with constant coefficients
   b Nonhomogeneous with constant coefficients
3 Nonlinear differential equations of first order and first degree
   a Variables separable case
   b Homogeneous
   c Exact differential equations

FIRST-ORDER LINEAR DIFFERENTIAL EQUATIONS

Homogeneous linear differential equations of the first order with constant coefficients

Homogeneous linear differential equations of the first order with constant coefficients can be put in the following general form:

$$Y' + \alpha Y = 0$$

where α is any constant.

The general solution is given by

$$y = ke^{-\alpha x}$$

where k is a constant.

Evaluation of k for a particular case, i.e., where it is known that the equation passes through a particular point, will give the specific solution to the problem.

EXAMPLE 16.1

$$\frac{dy}{dx} + 3y = 0$$

Find the general solution.

$$\alpha = 3 \qquad y = ke^{-3x}$$

is the general solution. If the function passes through the point (1,2), then the particular solution is given by

$$2 = ke^{-3(1)}$$
$$2 = ke^{-3}$$
$$\frac{2}{e^{-3}} = k$$
$$k = \frac{2}{.05} = 40$$

So

$$y = 40e^{-3x}$$

is the particular solution.

EXAMPLE 16.2

Solve

$$8\frac{dy}{dx} = 32y$$

Putting this into homogeneous form, we obtain

$$8\frac{dy}{dx} = 32y$$

$$8\frac{dy}{dx} - 32y = 0$$

$$\frac{dy}{dx} - 4y = 0$$

then

$$\alpha = -4 \qquad \text{and} \qquad y = ke^{-(-4)x} = ke^{4x}$$

is the general solution. If the point (0,7) is passed through, the particular solution will be

$$7 = ke^{4(0)}$$
$$7 = ke^{0}$$
$$7 = k$$
$$y = 7e^{4x}$$

EXAMPLE 16.3

A company has noticed that the rate of change of selling expense is related to the change in new product innovations. Specifically, if y = selling expenses in thousands of dollars and x = number of new product innovations, the change in y per change in x is equal to $-\frac{1}{8}y$. Define selling expenses as a function of new product innovation, if it is known that when the number of new product innovations is four, selling expenses are $3,000.

The relationship described is $dy/dx = -\frac{1}{8}y$. This is a first-order linear differential equation with constant coefficients. It can be put in homogeneous form

$$\frac{dy}{dx} + \frac{1}{8}y = 0$$

when $\alpha = \frac{1}{8}$ and $y = ke^{-\frac{1}{8}x}$.

The particular solution can be found by letting $x = 4$ and $y = 3$. Thus

$$3 = ke^{-\frac{1}{8}(4)} = ke^{-\frac{1}{2}} = k(.607)$$
$$\frac{3}{.607} = k$$
$$k = 4.9$$

The solution, then, is

$$y = 4.9e^{-\frac{1}{8}x}$$

This equation will permit the estimation of selling expenses for different quantities of new product innovations. For example, if no product innovations were made in a particular period, selling expenses would be expected to be

$$y = 4.9e^{-\frac{1}{8}(0)}$$
$$= 4.9e^0$$
$$= 4.9$$
$$= \$4,900$$

On the other hand, if eight product innovations were made in the period, selling expenses would be reduced to

$$y = 4.9e^{-\frac{1}{8}(8)}$$
$$= 4.9e^{-1}$$
$$= 4.9(.368)$$
$$= 1.8$$
$$= \$1,800$$

Nonhomogeneous linear differential equations of the first order with constant coefficients

Nonhomogeneous linear differential equations of the first order with constant coefficients can be put into the following form:

$$Y' + \alpha Y = F(x)$$

Note that the difference between homogeneous and nonhomogeneous equations is that $F(x) = 0$ in the homogeneous case.

To solve the nonhomogeneous form, note that the solution will be

$$Y(x) = ke^{-\alpha x} + Y^*(x)$$

where $Y^*(x)$ is any particular solution to the original equation $Y' + \alpha Y = F(x)$. The steps to be taken for solution are as follows:

1 Solve the homogeneous form of the equation ($Y' + \alpha Y = 0$) according to the methods of the preceding section. This will yield $ke^{-\alpha x}$.

2 a If $F(x)$ is a polynomial of degree n, then let

$$Y^*(x) = a_0 x^n + a_1 x^{n-1} + \cdots + a_{n-1} x + a_n$$

The derivative of $Y^*(x) = dy^*/dx = na_0 x^{n-1} + (n-1)a_1 x^{n-2} + \cdots + a_{n-1}$. Substitute $Y^*(x)$ and dy^*/dx in the original equation in place of Y and Y', and solve for $a_0, a_1, \ldots, a_n$. The final answer for the general solution, then, will be: $y = ke^{-\alpha x} + Y^*(x)$ with the values of $a_0, a_1, \ldots, a_n$ substituted for the letters. Then, given any point (x,y), one can solve for k and find the particular solution.

b If $F(x)$ is in exponential form, such as $F(x) = ce^{bx}$, then let

$$Y^*(x) = \frac{c}{b + \alpha} e^{bx} \qquad b \neq -\alpha$$

The general solution will be

$$y = ke^{-\alpha x} + \frac{c}{b + \alpha} e^{bx}$$

A particular solution may be found for any value of x and y. If, in the equation

$$Y' + \alpha Y = ce^{bx} \qquad b = -\alpha$$

then let

$$Y^*(x) = cxe^{-\alpha x} \qquad \text{and} \qquad y = ke^{-\alpha x} + cxe^{-\alpha x}$$

c If $F(x)$ is in exponential form, such as $F(x) = cxe^{bx}$, let

$$Y^*(x) = \frac{c}{b + \alpha} xe^{bx} + \left[\frac{-c}{(b + \alpha)^2} \right] e^{bx}$$

The general solution will be

$$y = ke^{-\alpha x} + \frac{c}{b + \alpha} xe^{bx} + \left[\frac{-c}{(b + \alpha)^2} \right] e^{bx}$$

A particular solution may be found for any given point (x,y).

EXAMPLE 16.4

$$Y' - 4Y = 2x^3 + 4x^2 + 5x - 6$$

First, solving $Y' - 4Y = 0$, we note that $\alpha = -4$, and

$$y = ke^{-(-4)x} = ke^{4x}$$

Next, since we have a third degree polynomial, we set up

$$Y^*(x) = a_0x^3 + a_1x^2 + a_2x + a_3$$

Then

$$\frac{dy^*}{dx} = 3a_0x^2 + 2a_1x + a_2$$

$$3a_0x^2 + 2a_1x + a_2 - 4(a_0x^3 + a_1x^2 + a_2x + a_3) = 2x^3 + 4x^2 + 5x - 6$$

$$3a_0x^2 + 2a_1x + a_2 - 4a_0x^3 - 4a_1x^2 - 4a_2x - 4a_3 - 2x^3 - 4x^2 - 5x + 6 = 0$$

$$(-4a_0 - 2)x^3 + (3a_0 - 4a_1 - 4)x^2 + (2a_1 - 4a_2 - 5)x + (a_2 - 4a_3 + 6) = 0$$

Setting $-4a_0 - 2 = 0$; $3a_0 - 4a_1 - 4 = 0$; $2a_1 - 4a_2 - 5 = 0$; and $a_2 - 4a_3 + 6 = 0$, we can solve for a_0, a_1, a_2, and a_3.

$$-4a_0 - 2 = 0$$
$$-4a_0 = 2$$
$$a_0 = -\tfrac{2}{4} = -\tfrac{1}{2}$$

$$3a_0 - 4a_1 - 4 = 0$$
$$3(-\tfrac{1}{2}) - 4a_1 - 4 = 0$$
$$-\tfrac{3}{2} - 4a_1 - 4 = 0$$
$$-4a_1 = \tfrac{11}{2}$$
$$a_1 = -\tfrac{11}{8}$$

$$2a_1 - 4a_2 - 5 = 0$$
$$2(-\tfrac{11}{8}) - 4a_2 - 5 = 0$$
$$-\tfrac{22}{8} - 4a_2 - 5 = 0$$
$$-4a_2 = \tfrac{62}{8}$$
$$a_2 = -\tfrac{62}{32} = -\tfrac{31}{16}$$

$$a_2 - 4a_3 + 6 = 0$$
$$-\tfrac{31}{16} - 4a_3 + 6 = 0$$
$$-4a_3 = -\tfrac{65}{16}$$
$$a_3 = \tfrac{65}{64}$$

Thus,

$$Y^*(x) = -\tfrac{1}{2}x^3 - \tfrac{11}{8}x^2 - \tfrac{31}{16}x + \tfrac{65}{64}$$

and

$$y = ke^{4x} - \tfrac{1}{2}x^3 - \tfrac{11}{8}x^2 - \tfrac{31}{16}x + \tfrac{65}{64}$$

is the general solution to the problem.

If we knew that the solution passed through the point $(0,2)$ we could find k.

$$2 = ke^{4(0)} - \tfrac{1}{2}(0)^3 - \tfrac{11}{8}(0)^2 - \tfrac{31}{16}(0) + \tfrac{65}{64}$$

$$ke^0 = 2 - \tfrac{65}{64}$$

$$k = \tfrac{63}{64}$$

Thus, the particular solution would be

$$y = \tfrac{63}{64}e^{4x} - \tfrac{1}{2}x^3 - \tfrac{11}{8}x^2 - \tfrac{31}{16}x + \tfrac{65}{64}$$

EXAMPLE 16.5

$$Y' + 4x + 10 = -3Y + 10x^2 - 5$$

when $x = 0$, $Y = 3$. Find the particular solution.

Setting this problem up in general form we obtain

$$Y' + 3Y = 10x^2 - 4x - 15$$

Solving the homogeneous equation

$$Y' + 3Y = 0$$

we find $\alpha = 3$ and $y = ke^{-3x}$.

Letting

$$Y^*(x) = a_0x^2 + a_1x + a_2$$

then

$$\frac{dy^*}{dx} = 2a_0x + a_1$$

Substituting in the original equation

$$2a_0x + a_1 + 3(a_0x^2 + a_1x + a_2) = 10x^2 - 4x - 15$$

$$2a_0x + a_1 + 3a_0x^2 + 3a_1x + 3a_2 - 10x^2 + 4x + 15 = 0$$

$$(3a_0 - 10)x^2 + (2a_0 + 3a_1 + 4)x + (a_1 + 3a_2 + 15) = 0$$

Setting $3a_0 - 10 = 0$; $2a_0 + 3a_1 + 4 = 0$; and $a_1 + 3a_2 + 15 = 0$ and solving for a_0, a_1, and a_2, we obtain

$$3a_0 - 10 = 0$$
$$a_0 = \tfrac{10}{3}$$

$$2a_0 + 3a_1 + 4 = 0$$
$$2(\tfrac{10}{3}) + 3a_1 + 4 = 0$$
$$\tfrac{20}{3} + 3a_1 + 4 = 0$$
$$3a_1 = -\tfrac{32}{3}$$
$$a_1 = -\tfrac{32}{9}$$

$$a_1 + 3a_2 + 15 = 0$$
$$-\tfrac{32}{9} + 3a_2 + 15 = 0$$
$$3a_2 = -\tfrac{103}{9}$$
$$a_2 = -\tfrac{103}{27}$$

Thus,

$$Y^*(x) = \tfrac{10}{3}x^2 - \tfrac{32}{9}x - \tfrac{103}{27}$$

and

$$y = ke^{-3(0)} + \tfrac{10}{3}(0)^2 - \tfrac{32}{9}(0) - \tfrac{103}{27}$$

$$3 = k - \tfrac{103}{27}$$

$$k = \frac{-22}{27}$$

$$y = \frac{-22}{27}e^{-3x} + \frac{10}{3}x^2 - \frac{32}{9}x - \frac{103}{27}$$

EXAMPLE 16.6

Solve

$$Y' + 3Y = 4e^{2x}$$

if $Y = 2$ when $x = 0$.

First, solving the homogeneous equation

$$Y' + 3Y = 0$$

we note that $\alpha = 3$ and $y = ke^{-3x}$.

Since the right-hand side of the equation is in the exponential form ce^{bx}, with $c = 4$, and $b = 2$, we let

$$Y^*(x) + \frac{c}{b + \alpha} e^{bx} = \frac{4}{2 + 3} e^x = \frac{4}{5} e^x$$

and the general solution is

$$y = ke^{-3} + \tfrac{4}{5}e^{2x}$$

The particular solution passing through the point (0,2) is given by

$$2 = ke^{-2(0)} + \tfrac{4}{5}e^{2(0)} = k + \tfrac{4}{5}$$
$$k = 2 - \tfrac{4}{5}$$
$$k = \tfrac{6}{5}$$

and is

$$y = \tfrac{6}{5}e^{-3x} + \tfrac{4}{5}e^{2x}$$

EXAMPLE 16.7

Solve

$$Y' - \tfrac{1}{2}Y = 2xe^{-5x}$$

if it passes through the point (0,4).

First solving the homogeneous equation

$$Y' - \tfrac{1}{2}Y = 0$$

we note that $\alpha = -\tfrac{1}{2}$ and $y = ke^{-(-1/2)x} = ke^{x/2}$.

$2xe^{-5x}$ is in the exponential form cxe^{bx}, with $c = 2$ and $b = -5$. Thus,

$$Y^*(x) = \frac{c}{b + \alpha} xe^{bx} + \frac{-c^2}{(b + \alpha)^2} e^{bx}$$

$$= \frac{2}{-5 - \tfrac{1}{2}} xe^{-5x} = \frac{-2}{(-5 - \tfrac{1}{2})^2} e^{-5x}$$

$$= \frac{-4}{11} xe^{-5x} - \frac{8}{121} e^{-5x}$$

and

$$y = ke^{x/2} - \frac{4}{11} xe^{-5x} - \frac{8}{121} e^{-5x}$$

is the general solution.   The particular solution is given by solving

$$-4 = ke^{0/2} - \tfrac{4}{11}(0)e^{-5(0)} - \tfrac{8}{121}e^{-5(0)}$$

$$-4 = k - \tfrac{8}{121}$$

$$k = \frac{-476}{121}$$

and

$$y = \frac{-476}{121} e^{x/2} - \tfrac{4}{11}xe^{-5x} - \tfrac{8}{121}e^{-5x}$$

EXAMPLE 16.8

Solve

$$Y' + 3Y = 5e^{-3x}$$

if the function passes through the point (0,8). $5e^{-3x}$ is in the exponential form ce^{bx}, with $c = 5$ and $b = -3$. However, this is an example of the special case where $\alpha = -b$. The solution is therefore given by the equation $y = (cx + k)e^{-\alpha x}$. Substituting our values for α and c, we obtain $y = (5x + k)e^{-3x}$. This is the general solution. Substituting $x = 0$, $y = 8$, we can obtain the value of k for the particular solution.

$$8 = [5(0) + k]e^{-3(0)}$$
$$8 = (0 + k)1 = k$$

The particular solution, then, is

$$y = (5x + 8)e^{-3x}$$

Homogeneous linear differential equations of the first order: general case

Homogeneous linear equations of the first order can be put into the form

$$Y' + G(x)Y = 0$$

Note that this form is similar to the homogeneous form with constant coefficients. The only difference is that the constant α is replaced by a function of x.

The solution of differential equations in this form is based on the formula

$$y = ke^{-\int G(x)\, dx}$$

where k is an arbitrary constant. This is the general solution, of course. The particular solution may be found, as in the other types of equations discussed, by substituting a known value of x and y into the general equation and solving for k.

EXAMPLE 16.9

Find the solution to the equation

$$Y' + (3x^2 + 5x)Y = 0$$

passing through the point (0,4).

Note that $G(x) = 3x^2 + 5x$,

and

$$y = ke^{-\int 3x^2 + 5x\, dx}$$
$$y = ke^{-(x^3 + 5/2x^2)}$$
$$y = ke^{-x^3 - 5/2x^2}$$

Substituting $x = 0$, $y = 4$, we find

$$4 = ke^{-(0)^3 - 5/2(0)^2} = k$$

The solution, then, is

$$y = 4e^{-x^3 - 5/2x^2}$$

EXAMPLE 16.10

Solve

$$Y' - Y \sin x = 0$$

if the function passes through $(0, -10)$.

$$G(x) = - \sin x$$
$$y = ke^{-\int - \sin x \, dx}$$
$$y = ke^{- \cos x}$$

Substituting $x = 0$, $y = -10$, we find

$$-10 = ke^{- \cos 0}$$
$$-10 = ke^1$$
$$k = \frac{-10}{e}$$

The solution, then, is

$$y = \frac{-10}{e} e^{- \cos x} = -10e^{- \cos x - 1}$$

Linear differential equations of the first order: general case

Linear differential equations of the first order can always be put into the form

$$Y' + G(x)Y = F(x)$$

Note that this form is similar to the homogeneous equation in the preceding section. The only difference is that the zero is replaced by a function of x. The solution to the general case for first-order linear differential equations is given by the equation

$$y = \left[\int F(x)(e^{\int G(x) \, dx}) \, dx + k \right] e^{-\int G(x) \, dx}$$

where k is an arbitrary constant. This is the general solution. Using any point (x,y) through which the function is known to pass, the value of k and thus the particular solution, may be found. This formula is extremely difficult to evaluate for any but the simplest of differential equations of this type.

EXAMPLE 16.11

Solve

$$Y' + 2xY = x$$

First, we note that $F(x) = x$ and $G(x) = 2x$.

$$y = \left[\int x(e^{\int 2x \, dx}) \, dx + k \right] e^{-\int 2x \, dx}$$
$$= \left(\int xe^{x^2} \, dx + k \right) e^{-x^2}$$

To find $\int xe^{x^2} \, dx$, let $u = x^2$

then
$$du = 2x\,dx$$

$$\int xe^{x^2}\,dx = \tfrac{1}{2}\int 2xe^{x^2}\,dx$$

$$= \tfrac{1}{2}\int e^u\,du\,\Big|_{u=x^2}$$

$$= \tfrac{1}{2}e^u\,\Big|_{u=x^2}$$

$$= \tfrac{1}{2}e^{x^2}$$

Thus,

$$y = \left(\int xe^{x^2}\,dx + k\right)e^{-x^2}$$

$$= (\tfrac{1}{2}e^{x^2} + k)e^{-x^2}$$

$$= \frac{1}{2}\left(\frac{e^{x^2}}{e^{x^2}}\right) + \frac{k}{e^{x^2}}$$

$$= \tfrac{1}{2} + ke^{-x^2}$$

is the general solution.   If the function is known to pass through the point (0,5) we can find k and the particular solution by substitution.

$$5 = \tfrac{1}{2} + ke^{-(0)^2} = \tfrac{1}{2} + k(1)$$
$$\tfrac{9}{2} = k$$

and the particular solution will be

$$y = \tfrac{1}{2} + \tfrac{9}{2}e^{-x^2}$$

EXAMPLE 16.12

Solve

$$Y' + Y\sin x = \sin x$$

if the function passes through (0,4).   Note that $F(x) = \sin x$ and $G(x) = \sin x$. The solution is found by solving

$$y = \left[\int \sin x(e^{\int \sin x\,dx})\,dx + k\right]e^{-\int \sin x\,dx}$$

$$y = \left(\int \sin xe^{-\cos x}\,dx + k\right)e^{\cos x}$$

Let
$$u = -\cos x$$

then
$$du = \sin x\,dx$$

$$y = \left(\int e^u\,du\,\Big|_{u=-\cos x} + k\right)e^{\cos x}$$

$$y = \left(e^u\,\Big|_{u=-\cos x} + k\right)e^{\cos x}$$

$$y = (e^{-\cos x} + k)e^{\cos x}$$

$$y = 1 + ke^{\cos x}$$

is the general solution. Substituting $x = 0$ and $y = 4$, we find

$$4 = 1 + ke^{\cos 0} = 1 + ke^1$$
$$3 = ke$$
$$k = \frac{3}{e}$$
$$y = 1 + ke^{\cos x}$$
$$= 1 + 3^{\cos x - 1}$$

is the particular solution.

SECOND-ORDER LINEAR DIFFERENTIAL EQUATIONS

Homogeneous linear equations of the second order with constant coefficient

A second-order homogeneous linear equation with constant coefficients can be put into the form

$$Y'' + \alpha Y' + \beta Y = 0$$

where α and β are constants. The solution of any second-order linear equation will involve two arbitrary constants instead of one, and two points are necessary to set particular values of these two constants in order to find a particular solution.

The general solution will be found through the equation

$$y = k_1 e^{\lambda_1 x} + k_2 e^{\lambda_2 x}$$

where k_1 and k_2 are arbitrary constants and $\lambda_1 \neq \lambda_2$. The formulas for λ_1 and λ_2 are

$$\lambda_1 = \frac{-\alpha}{2} + \frac{\sqrt{\alpha^2 - 4\beta}}{2}$$

$$\lambda_2 = \frac{-\alpha}{2} - \frac{\sqrt{\alpha^2 - 4\beta}}{2}$$

We will only be interested in those cases where $\alpha^2 \geq 4\beta$ since otherwise this solution would involve imaginary numbers.

In this case, the two constants, k_1 and k_2, may be evaluated at the point where $x = 0$ by finding Y_0—the Y value where $x = 0$—and Y_0'—the derivative of the Y value when $x = 0$—by using the following formulas

$$k_1 = \frac{\lambda_2 Y_0 - Y_0'}{\lambda_2 - \lambda_1} \qquad k_2 = \frac{Y_0' - \lambda_1 Y_0}{\lambda_2 - \lambda_1}$$

In the case where $\lambda_1 = \lambda_2$, the solution can be found through the equation

$$y = k_1 e^{\lambda x} + k_2 x e^{\lambda x}$$

where $\lambda = \lambda_1 = \lambda_2 = -\alpha/2$

The constants k_1 and k_2 can be found where $\lambda_1 = \lambda_2$ by finding Y_0—the Y value when $x = 0$—and Y_0'—the value of the derivative of Y when $x = 0$—and by using the formulas

$$k_1 = Y_0 \qquad k_2 = Y_0' - \lambda k_1$$

EXAMPLE 16.13

Solve

$$Y'' + 5Y' - 8Y = 0$$

if $x = 0$, $Y = 6$, and $Y' = 3$. In this problem $\alpha = 5$ and $\beta = -8$. Thus, we can find

$$\lambda_1 = \frac{-5}{2} + \frac{\sqrt{(5)^2 - 4(-8)}}{2} = \frac{-5}{2} + \frac{\sqrt{57}}{2} = \frac{-5 + 7.55}{2}$$

$$= \frac{2.55}{2} = 1.27$$

$$\lambda_2 = \frac{-5}{2} - \frac{\sqrt{57}}{2} = \frac{-5 - 7.55}{2} = \frac{-12.55}{2} = -6.27$$

The general solution will be

$$y = k_1 e^{1.27x} + k_2 e^{-6.27x}$$

Solving for k_1 and k_2, given that $Y_0 = 6$, and $Y_0' = 3$, we obtain

$$k_1 = \frac{-6.27(6) - 3}{-6.27 - 1.27} = \frac{-37.62 - 3}{-7.54} = \frac{-40.62}{-7.54} = 5.39$$

$$k_2 = \frac{3 - (1.27)(6)}{-6.27 - 1.27} = \frac{3 - 7.62}{-7.54} = \frac{-4.62}{-7.54} = .6$$

The particular solution, then, is

$$y = 5.39 e^{1.27x} + .6 e^{-6.27x}$$

EXAMPLE 16.14

Solve

$$Y'' = 2Y - 10Y'$$

if $x = 0$, $Y = 1$, and $Y' = 2$. First, putting this equation into general form:

$$Y'' + 10Y' - 2Y = 0$$

Note that $\alpha = 10$ and $\beta = -2$.

$$\lambda_1 = \frac{-10}{2} + \frac{\sqrt{(10)^2 - 4(-2)}}{2} = -5 + \frac{\sqrt{108}}{2}$$

$$= -5 + \frac{10.4}{2} = -5 + 5.2 = .2$$

$$\lambda_2 = -5 - \frac{\sqrt{108}}{2} = -5 - \frac{10.4}{2} = -5 - 5.2 = -10.2$$

$$y = k_1 e^{.2x} + k_2 e^{-10.2x}$$

is the general solution. Solving for k_1 and k_2,

$$k_1 = \frac{(-10.2)(1) - 2}{-10.2 - .2} = \frac{-12.2}{-10.4} = 1.2$$

$$k_2 = \frac{2 - (.2)(1)}{-10.2 - .2} = \frac{1.8}{-10.4} = -.2$$

Thus, $y = 1.2e^{.2x} - .2e^{-10.2x}$ is the particular solution to the problem.

EXAMPLE 16.15

Solve

$$Y'' + 6Y' + 9Y = 0$$

if $x = 0$, $Y = 3$, and $Y' = 1$. This equation is already in general form.

$$\alpha = 6 \qquad \beta = 9$$

Note that $\alpha^2 = 4$:

$$(6)^2 = 4(9)$$
$$36 = 36$$

Therefore,

$$\lambda = \lambda_1 = \lambda_2 = \frac{-\alpha}{2} = -3$$

and the general solution is

$$y = k_1 e^{-3x} + k_2 x e^{-3x}$$

For the case mentioned in the problem where $Y_0 = 3$ and $Y'_0 = 1$, $k_1 = 3$ and $k_2 = 1 - -3(3) = 1 + 9 = 10$, and the particular solution is

$$y = 3e^{-3x} + 10xe^{-3x}$$

Nonhomogeneous linear equations of the second order with constant coefficients

In the nonhomogeneous case, the general equation becomes

$$Y'' + \alpha Y' + \beta Y = F(x)$$

The solution is found through the equation

$$y = k_1 e^{\lambda_1 x} + k_2 e^{\lambda_2 x} + Y^*(x)$$

where $\lambda_1 \neq \lambda_2$

and by

$$y = k_1 e^{\lambda x} + k_2 x e^{\lambda x} + Y^*(x)$$

where $\lambda_1 = \lambda_2$

Note that the first two terms are identical to the homogeneous solution and can be found by solving

$$Y'' + \alpha Y' + \beta Y = 0$$

The third term, $Y^*(x)$, is identical to the $Y^*(x)$ described in the section on first-order nonhomogeneous linear differential equations with constant coefficients, and can be found by following the methods outlined in that section, with the following adjustments.

In the exponential form $Y'' + \alpha Y' + \beta Y = ce^{bx}$,

$$Y^*(x) = \left(\frac{c}{b^2 + \alpha b + \beta} \right) e^{bx} \qquad b \neq \frac{\alpha \pm \sqrt{\alpha^2 - 4\beta}}{-2}$$

If, in the equation $Y'' + \alpha Y' + \beta Y = ce^{bx}$,

$$b = \frac{\alpha \pm \sqrt{\alpha^2 - 4\beta}}{-2}$$

then $Y^* = [c/(2b + \alpha)]xe^{bx}$.

In the exponential form $Y'' + \alpha Y' + \beta Y = cxe^{bx}$,

$$Y^*(x) = \left(\frac{c}{b^2 + \alpha b + \beta} \right) xe^{bx}$$

$$= \left[\frac{c(2b + \alpha)}{(b^2 + \alpha b + \beta)^2} \right] e^{bx}$$

$$b \neq \frac{\alpha \pm \sqrt{\alpha^2 - 4\beta}}{-2}$$

The particular solution, given a specific Y and Y' value for $x = 0$, is found by solving

$$k_1 = \frac{\lambda_2[Y_0 - Y^*(0)] - [Y_0' - dY^*(0)/dx]}{\lambda_2 - \lambda_1}$$

$$k_2 = \frac{\lambda_1[Y_0 - Y^*(0)] - [Y_0' - dY^*(0)/dx]}{\lambda_2 - \lambda_1}$$

when $\lambda_2 \neq \lambda_1$

When $\lambda_1 = \lambda_2$, k_1 and k_2 are found as follows

$$k_1 = Y_0 - Y^*(0)$$

$$k_2 = Y_0' - \frac{dy^*(0)}{dx} - \lambda k_1$$

EXAMPLE 16.16

Solve the differential equation

$$Y'' + 8Y' + 2Y = x^2 + 4$$

for the case when $Y = 2$, $Y' = 7$, $x = 0$.

First solving the homogeneous form

$$Y'' + 8Y' + 2Y = 0$$

we set $\alpha = 8$, and $\beta = 2$. Solving for λ_1 and λ_2 we find

$$\lambda_1 = \frac{-8}{2} + \frac{\sqrt{(8)^2 - 4(2)}}{2} = -4 + \frac{\sqrt{64 - 8}}{2} = -4 + \frac{\sqrt{56}}{2}$$

$$= -4 + \frac{7.5}{2} = -4 + 3.75 = -.25$$

$$\lambda_2 = -4 - \frac{\sqrt{56}}{2} = -4 - \frac{7.5}{2} = -4 - 3.75 = -7.75$$

The general solution to the homogeneous case, then, is

$$y = k_1 e^{-.25x} + k_2 e^{-7.75x}$$

and the solution to the problem will be

$$y = k_1 e^{-.25x} + k_2 e^{-7.75x} + Y^*(x)$$

The next step is to evaluate $Y^*(x)$. Since the right-hand side of our initial differential equation is a polynomial of the second degree, we let

$$Y^*(x) = a_0 x^2 + a_1 x + a_2$$

and the first derivative of $Y^*(x)$ will be $dY^*(x)/dx = 2a_0 x + a_1$. The second derivative of $Y^*(x)$ is $d^2 Y^*(x)/dx^2 = 2a_0$.

Substituting $Y^*(x)$ and its derivatives for Y, Y', and Y'' in the original equation allows us to solve for a_0, a_1, and a_2.

$$2a_0 + 8(2a_0 x + a_1) + 2(a_0 x^2 + a_1 x + a_2) = x^2 + 4$$

$$2a_0 + 16a_0 x + 8a_1 + 2a_0 x^2 + 2a_1 x + 2a_2 = x^2 + 4$$

$$2a_0 + 16a_0 x + 8a_1 + 2a_0 x^2 + 2a_1 x + 2a_2 - x^2 - 4 = 0$$

$$(2a_0 - 1)x^2 + (16a_0 + 2a_1)x + (2a_0 + 8a_1 + 2a_2 - 4) = 0$$

Setting each coefficient equal to zero,

$$2a_0 - 1 = 0$$
$$2a_0 = 1$$
$$a_0 = \tfrac{1}{2}$$

$$16_0a + 2a_1 = 0$$
$$16(\tfrac{1}{2}) + 2a_1 = 0$$
$$8 + 2a_1 = 0$$
$$2a_1 = -8$$
$$a_1 = -4$$

$$2a_0 + 8a_1 + 2a_2 - 4 = 0$$
$$2(\tfrac{1}{2}) + 8(-4) + 2a_2 - 4 = 0$$
$$1 - 32 + 2a_2 - 4 = 0$$
$$2a_2 = 35$$
$$a_2 = \tfrac{35}{2}$$

Thus,
$$Y^*(x) = \tfrac{1}{2}x^2 - 4x + \tfrac{35}{2}$$

and the general solution to the problem is

$$y = k_1 e^{-.25x} + k_2 e^{-7.75x} + \tfrac{1}{2}x^2 - 4x + \tfrac{35}{2}$$

To determine the particular solution, we must begin by evaluating $Y^*(0)$ and $dY^*(0)/dx$.

$$Y^*(0) = \tfrac{1}{2}(0)^2 - 4(0) + \tfrac{35}{2} = \tfrac{35}{2}$$

$$\frac{dY^*(0)}{dx} = 2(\tfrac{1}{2})(0) + (-4) = -4$$

Y_0 and Y_0' are given as 2 and 7 respectively. So

$$k_1 = \frac{\lambda_2[Y_0 - Y^*(0)] - [Y_0' - dY^*(0)/dx]}{\lambda_2 - \lambda_1}$$

$$= \frac{-7.75[2 - \tfrac{35}{2}] - [7 - (-4)]}{-7.75 - (-.25)} = \frac{-7.75(-\tfrac{31}{2}) - 11}{-7.5}$$

$$= \frac{120.1 - 11}{-7.5} = \frac{109.1}{-7.5} = -14.5$$

$$k_2 = \frac{\lambda_1[Y_0 - Y^*(0)] - [Y_0' - dY^*(0)/dx]}{\lambda_2 - \lambda_1}$$

$$= \frac{-.25(2 - \tfrac{35}{2}) - [7 - (-4)]}{-7.75 - (-.25)} = \frac{-.25(-\tfrac{31}{2}) - 11}{-7.5}$$

$$= \frac{3.9 - 11}{-7.5} = \frac{-7.1}{-7.5} = .95$$

The particular solution, then, is given by

$$y = -14.5e^{-.25x} + .95e^{-7.75x} + \tfrac{1}{2}x^2 - 4x + \tfrac{35}{2}$$

EXAMPLE 16.17

Solve the equation

$$Y'' - Y' + Y = 3e^{5x}$$

if $x = 0$, $Y = 3$, and $Y' = 2$.

The homogeneous form of this equation is $Y'' - 2Y' + Y = 0$, and $\alpha = -2$ and $\beta = 1$. Note that $\alpha^2 = 4\beta = 4$. The solution of the homogeneous form is found by defining $\lambda = -\alpha/2 = -(-\frac{2}{2}) = 1$. Then

$$y = k_1 e^x + k_2 x e^x$$

and the general solution will be given by

$$y = k_1 e^x + k_2 x e^x + Y^*(x)$$

To find $Y^*(x)$, note that the right-hand side of the equation is in the exponential form ce^{bx}. Therefore

$$Y^*(x) = \left(\frac{c}{b + \alpha}\right) e^{bx}$$

when $\alpha = -2$, $b = 5$, and $c = 3$. Thus,

$$Y^*(x) = \left[\frac{3}{5 + (-2)}\right] e^{5x} = e^{5x}$$

and the general solution may be rewritten as

$$y = k_1 e^x + k_2 x e^x + e^{5x}$$

Next, we can find $Y^*(0)$ and $dY^*(0)/dx$.

$$Y^*(x) = e^{5x} \qquad \frac{dY^*(x)}{dx} = 5e^{5x}$$

$$Y^*(0) = e^{5(0)} = 1 \qquad \frac{dY^*(0)}{dx} = 5e^{5(0)} = 5$$

Then, since Y_0 is given as 3, and Y_0' is given as 2,

$$k_1 = Y_0 - Y^*(0) = 3 - 1 = 2$$

and $\qquad k_2 = Y_0' - \dfrac{dY^*(0)}{dx} - \lambda k_1 = 2 - 5 - 1(2) = 2 - 5 - 2 = -5$

and the particular solution is

$$y = 2e^x - 5xe^x + e^{5x}$$

EXAMPLE 16.18

Solve the equation

$$Y'' + 3Y' - 10Y = 5e^{2x}$$

if $Y_0 = 3$, and $Y'_0 = 1$. The solution to the homogeneous equation is first obtained:
$\alpha = 3, \beta = -10$

$$\lambda_1 = -\frac{3}{2} + \frac{\sqrt{(3)^2 - 4(-10)}}{2} = -\frac{3}{2} + \frac{\sqrt{9 + 40}}{2}$$

$$= -\tfrac{3}{2} + \tfrac{7}{2} = 2$$

$$\lambda_2 = -\frac{3}{2} - \frac{\sqrt{9 + 40}}{2} = -\frac{3}{2} - \frac{7}{2} = -5$$

and
$$y = k_1 e^{2x} + k_2 e^{-5x} + Y^*(x)$$

Note that

$$b = \frac{\alpha - \sqrt{\alpha^2 - 4}}{-2} = \frac{3 - \sqrt{(3)^2 - 4(-10)}}{-2} = \frac{3 - \sqrt{49}}{-2}$$

$$= \frac{3 - 7}{-2} = 2$$

Therefore,

$$Y^*(x) = \left[\frac{5}{2(2) + 3}\right] x e^{2x} = \frac{5}{7} x e^{2x}$$

and
$$y = k_1 e^{2x} + k_2 e^{-5x} + \tfrac{5}{7} x e^{2x}$$

is the general solution to the problem.

$$Y^*(x) = \frac{5}{7} x e^{2x} \qquad \frac{dY^*(x)}{dx} = \frac{10}{7} x e^{2x} + \frac{5}{7} e^{2x}$$

$$Y^*(0) = \frac{5}{7}(0) e^{2(0)} = 0 \qquad \frac{dY^*(0)}{dx} = \frac{10}{7}(0) e^{2(0)} + \frac{5}{7} e^{2(0)}$$

$$= 0 + \frac{5}{7} = \frac{5}{7}$$

$$k_1 = \frac{-5(3 - 0) - (1 - \tfrac{5}{7})}{-5 - 2} = \frac{-5(3) - (\tfrac{2}{7})}{-7} = \frac{-15 - \tfrac{2}{7}}{-7} = \frac{107}{49} = 2.2$$

$$k_2 = \frac{2(3 - 0) - (1 - \tfrac{5}{7})}{-5 - 2} = \frac{2(3) - (\tfrac{2}{7})}{-7} = \frac{5\tfrac{5}{7}}{-7} = \frac{-40}{49} = .8$$

The particular solution is

$$y = 2.2 e^{2x} - .8 e^{-5x} + \tfrac{5}{7} x e^{2x}$$

NONLINEAR DIFFERENTIAL EQUATIONS OF THE FIRST ORDER AND FIRST DEGREE

The solution of most of the types of differential equations not already discussed is very difficult and beyond the scope of this text. Under this heading come most nonlinear differential equations. However, several special cases in the nonlinear type of problem are quite easily solved and we will investigate three of these. All are first-order and first-degree differential equations of the general form $Y' = f(x,y)$, where $f(x,y)$ is a function of the two variables x and y.

Variables separable case

The general equation $Y' = f(x,y)$ can be rewritten as follows:

$$\frac{dy}{dx} = f(x,y)$$

$$\frac{dy}{dx} - f(x,y) = 0$$

$$dy - f(x,y)\, dx = 0$$

If $f(x,y)$ can be divided by some function $G(y)$ so that

$$\frac{f(x,y)}{G(y)} = H(x)$$

then

$$\frac{1}{G(y)}\, dy - H(x)\, dx = 0$$

and since $G(y)$ is a function with only one variable y, and $H(x)$ is a function with only one variable x, the problem can be solved by integrating both sides of the equation. Thus

$$\int \frac{1}{G(y)}\, dy - \int H(x)\, dx = \int 0$$

$$\int \frac{1}{G(y)}\, dy - \int H(x)\, dx = C$$

where C is an arbitrary constant.

This method depends, then, on being able to separate $f(x,y)$ into two functions, each with one variable.

EXAMPLE 16.19

Solve

$$Y' = 3x^2y$$

if the function passes through the point (0,3). $Y' = 3x^2y$ can be rewritten as

$$\frac{dy}{dx} - 3x^2y = 0$$

Multiplying through by dx, we obtain

$$dy - 3x^2y\, dx = 0$$

Dividing through by y, we get

$$\frac{1}{y}\, dy - 3x^2\, dx = 0$$

We have now succeeded in separating the variables. The problem can now be solved by integration.

$$\int \frac{1}{y}\,dy - \int 3x^2\,dx = C$$

where C is an arbitrary constant.

In $y - x^3 = C$ would constitute a general solution to the problem. However, usually the solution needed will be in terms of y, so we can continue as follows:

$$\ln y = x^3 + C$$

If $x^3 + C$ is the natural log of y, then e^{x^3+C} must equal y by the definition of natural logs.

$$y = e^{x^3+C}$$

Since $e^{x^3+C} = e^x e^C$, $y = e^{x^3}e^C$. Note that e^C is an arbitrary constant if C is an arbitrary constant. So, letting $k = e^C$

$$y = ke^{x^3}$$

is a general solution to the problem.
Substituting (0,3) for x and y yields

$$3 = ke^{(0)^3} = k$$

So the particular solution is

$$y = 3e^{x^3}$$

EXAMPLE 16.20

Solve

$$Y' - 4x^3y^2 = y^2$$

if the function passes through (2,3). The equation can be put into the form

$$\frac{dy}{dx} - 4x^3y^2 - y^2 = 0$$

Multiplying through by dx, we obtain

$$dy - 4x^3y^2\,dx - y^2\,dx = 0$$

which becomes

$$dy - (4x^3 - 1)y^2\,dx = 0$$

Dividing through by y^2 gives

$$\frac{1}{y^2}\,dy - (4x^3 - 1)\,dx = 0$$

The variables are now separated. Thus,

$$\int \frac{1}{y^2}\,dy - \int 4x^3 - 1\,dx = C$$

where C equals an arbitrary constant. Integrating, we get

$$\frac{-1}{y} - (x^4 - x) = C$$

$$\frac{-1}{y} = x^4 - x + C$$

$$y = \frac{1}{x^4 - x + C}$$

is the general solution. Substituting (2,3) for x and y

$$3 = \frac{1}{(2)^4 - 2 + C} = \frac{1}{16 - 2 + C}$$

$$= \frac{1}{14 + C}$$

$$3(14 + C) = 1$$
$$42 + 3C = 1$$
$$3C = -41$$
$$C = -\frac{41}{3}$$

Thus,
$$y = \frac{-1}{(x^4 - x - 41)/3}$$

is the particular solution.

Differential equations with homogeneous coefficients

If a differential equation can be put into the form

$$f(x,y)\ dx + g(x,y)\ dy = 0$$

where $f(x,y)$ and $g(x,y)$ are each homogeneous of the same order, then a solution may be obtained by change of variable.

In order for $f(x,y)$ to be homogeneous

$$f(\lambda x, \lambda y) = \lambda^n f(x,y)$$

for any constant λ where n is the order.

If inspection discloses that the two functions are homogeneous of the same order, let

$$y = vx \qquad \text{and} \qquad dy = v\ dx + x\ dv$$

Then substitute vx for y and $v\ dx + x\ dv$ for dy to give:

$$f(x,vx)\ dx + g(x,vx)(v\ dx + x\ dv) = 0$$

Divide through by $g(x,vx)$

$$\frac{f(x,vx)}{g(x,vx)} \, dx + v \, dx + x \, dv = 0$$

The x's in $f(x,vx)/g(x,vx)$ will cancel, giving

$$\left(\frac{f(1,\ v)}{g(1,\ v)} + v\right) dx + x \, dv = 0$$

This can now be solved by the variables separable method.

EXAMPLE 16.21

Find the general solution for

$$y^2 - (xy - x^2)\,Y' = 0$$

This equation can be rewritten as

$$y^2 - (xy - x^2)\,\frac{dy}{dx} = 0$$

Multiplying through by dx

$$y^2 \, dx - (xy - x^2) \, dy = 0$$

Letting $f(x,y) = y^2$ and $g(x,y) = xy - x^2$, we can test for homogeneity.

$$f(\lambda x,\lambda y) = (\lambda y)^2 = \lambda^2 y^2$$

which is homogeneous of order two.

$$g(\lambda x,\lambda y) = \lambda x \lambda y - (\lambda x)^2 = \lambda^2 xy - \lambda^2 x^2 = \lambda^2(xy - x^2)$$

This is also homogeneous of order two. Therefore, both $f(x,y)$ and $g(x,y)$ are homogeneous of the same order.

Let $y = vx$, and $dy = v \, dx + x \, dv$,

$$f(x,vx) = (vx)^2 = v^2 x^2$$
$$g(x,vx) = x(vx) - x^2 = vx^2 - x^2$$

so that

$$v^2 x^2 \, dx - (vx^2 - x^2)(v \, dx + x \, dv) = 0$$

Dividing through by $g(x,vx)$ we obtain

$$\frac{v^2 x^2}{vx^2 - x^2} \, dx - v \, dx - x \, dv = 0$$

The x^2 cancels in the first term, giving

$$\frac{v^2}{v - 1} \, dx - v \, dx - x \, dv = 0$$

Factoring dx from the first two terms,

$$\frac{v^2}{(v - 1) - v} \, dx - x \, dv = 0$$

Simplifying,

$$\frac{v^2 - v(v - 1)}{v - 1} \, dx - x \, dv = 0$$

$$\frac{v^2 - v^2 + v}{v - 1} \, dx - x \, dv = 0$$

$$\frac{v}{v - 1} \, dx - x \, dv = 0$$

Now the equation can be multiplied by $1/x$ to give

$$\frac{1}{x} \frac{v}{v - 1} \, dx - dv = 0$$

and by $(v - 1)/v$ to give

$$\frac{1}{x} \, dx - \frac{v - 1}{v} \, dv = 0$$

The variables are now properly separated.
   Integrating, we obtain:

$$\int \frac{1}{x} \, dx - \int \frac{v - 1}{v} \, dv = C$$

where C is an arbitrary constant.

$$\int \frac{1}{x} \, dx - \left(\int \frac{v}{v} \, dv - \int \frac{1}{v} \, dv \right) = C$$

$$\ln x - (v - \ln v) = C$$
$$\ln x - v + \ln v = C$$

Substituting back $y/x = v$ gives:

$$\ln x - \frac{y}{x} + \ln \frac{y}{x} = C$$

Note that $\ln x + \ln y/x = \ln [x(y/x)] = \ln y$,

thus

$$\ln y - \frac{y}{x} = C$$

$$\ln y = \frac{y}{x} = C$$

$$y = e^{y/x+C} + e^{y/x}e^C$$

Let $k = e^C =$ an arbitrary constant.   Then,

$$y = ke^{y/x}$$
and
$$y - ke^{y/x} = 0$$

Solving in terms of y would prove difficult, so the solution can be left in this form.

EXAMPLE 16.22

Find the solution to

$$2xy \, Y' = -x^2 - y^2$$

which passes through the point (1,2).   Adding $x^2 + y^2$ to each side and converting Y' to dy/dx gives

$$x^2 + y^2 + 2xy\,\frac{dy}{dx} = 0$$

Multiplying through by dx,

$$x^2\,dx + y^2\,dx + 2xy\,dy = 0$$

Collecting the terms containing dx

$$(x^2 + y^2)\,dx + 2xy\,dy = 0$$

The equation is now in the form $f(x,y)\,dx + g(x,y)\,dy = 0$.   Next, we must determine whether $f(x,y)$ and $g(x,y)$ are homogeneous of the same order.

$$f(\lambda x,\lambda y) = (\lambda x)^2 + (\lambda y)^2 = \lambda^2 x^2 + \lambda^2 y^2 = \lambda^2(x^2 + y^2) = \lambda^2 f(x,y)$$
$$g(\lambda x,\lambda y) = 2(\lambda x)(\lambda y) = 2\lambda^2 xy = \lambda^2(2xy) = \lambda^2 g(x,y)$$

Therefore, the two functions are each homogeneous of order two.   Letting

$$y = vx \qquad \text{and} \qquad dy = v\,dx + x\,dv$$

the substitution can be made:

$$[x^2 + (vx)^2]\,dx + 2x(vx)(v\,dx + x\,dv) = 0$$
$$(x^2 + v^2x^2)\,dx + 2x^2v(v\,dx + x\,dv) = 0$$

Dividing by $2x^2v$,

$$\frac{\cancel{x^2}(1 + v^2)}{\cancel{x^2}2v}\,dx + v\,dx + x\,dv = 0$$

Collecting the dx terms

$$\frac{(1 + v^2) + v(2v)}{2v}\,dx + x\,dv = 0$$

$$\frac{1 + v^2 + 2v^2}{2v}\,dx + x\,dv = 0$$

$$\frac{1 + 3v^2}{2v}\,dx + x\,dv = 0$$

Multiplying by $1/x$ gives

$$\left(\frac{1}{x}\right)\left(\frac{1 + 3v^2}{2v}\right)dx + dv = 0$$

and multiplying by $2v/(1 + 3v^2)$ gives

$$\frac{1}{x}\,dx + \frac{2v}{1 + 3v^2}\,dv = 0$$

which can now be solved by integration.

$$\int \frac{1}{x}\,dx + \int \frac{2v}{1 + 3v^2}\,dv = C$$

where C is an arbitrary constant.

$$\ln x + \int \frac{2v}{1 + 3v^2}\,dv = C$$

Solution of this integral will be easiest by change of variable.   Let

$$u = 1 + 3v^2$$

then
$$du = 6v \, dv$$

Multiplying by 3 gives

$$3 \ln x + \int \frac{6v}{1 + 3v^2} \, dv = 3C$$

Substituting u and du,

$$3 \ln x + \int \frac{1}{u} \, du \Big|_{u = 1 + 3v^2} = 3C$$

$$3 \ln x + \ln u \Big|_{u = 1 + 3v^2} = 3C$$

$$3 \ln x + \ln (1 + 3v^2) = 3C$$

Since $a \ln x = \ln x^a$, we can write the above equation as

$$\ln x^3 + \ln (1 + 3v^2) = 3C$$

Since $\ln f(x) + \ln g(x) = \ln [f(x)g(x)]$, we can rewrite the equation as follows:

$$\ln [x^3(1 + 3v^2)] = 3C$$

Therefore

$$x^3(1 + 3v^2) = e^{3C}$$

by definition of natural logarithms.   Replacing v with y/x, we get:

$$x^3 \left[1 + 3 \left(\frac{y}{x} \right)^2 \right] = e^{3C}$$

$$x^3 + 3x^3 \frac{y^2}{x^2} = e^{3C}$$

$$x^3 + 3xy^2 = e^{3C}$$

Let $k = e^{3C} =$ any arbitrary constant.

$$x^3 + 3xy^2 = k$$

is the general solution.

The particular solution is found by letting $x = 1$ and $y = 2$, and by solving for k.

$$(1)^3 + 3(1)(2)^2 = k$$
$$1 + 12 = k$$
$$13 = k$$

$$x^3 + 3xy^2 = 13$$
$$3xy^2 = 13 - x^3$$
$$y^2 = \frac{13 - x^3}{3x}$$

$$y = \sqrt{\frac{13 - x^3}{3x}}$$

is the particular solution in terms of y.

Exact differential equations

A differential equation in the form

$$F(x,y) + G(x,y) Y' = 0$$

is called exact if

$$F_y(x,y) = G_x(x,y)$$

that is, if the partial derivative with respect to y of $F(x,y)$ is equal to the partial derivative with respect to x of $G(x,y)$.

The solution of an exact differential equation is given by the formula

$$\int F(x,y) \, dx + \int \left[G(x,y) - \int F_y(x,y) \, dx \, dy \right] = C$$

where C is an arbitrary constant.

EXAMPLE 16.23

Solve

$$\left(\tfrac{2}{5}x^5y^3 + \tfrac{5}{2}x^2y^2 \right) Y' = -\tfrac{1}{2}x^4y^4 - \tfrac{5}{3}xy^3$$

for the equation which passes through the point (2,5). Subtracting the right side of the equation from both sides gives

$$\left(\tfrac{1}{2}x^4y^4 + \tfrac{5}{3}xy^3 \right) + \left(\tfrac{2}{5}x^5y^3 + \tfrac{5}{2}x^2y^2 \right) Y' = 0$$

The partial derivative with respect to y of the first term is

$$F_y(x,y) = 2x^4y^3 + 5xy^2$$

and the partial derivative with respect to x of the coefficient of Y' is

$$G_x(x,y) = 2x^4y^3 + 5xy^2$$

Since these are identical, this is an exact differential equation and the solution is obtained as follows:

$$\int \tfrac{1}{2}x^4y^4 + \tfrac{5}{3}xy^3 \, dx + \int \left(\tfrac{2}{5}x^5y^3 + \tfrac{5}{2}x^2y^2 - \int 2x^4y^3 - 5xy^2 \, dx \right) dy = C$$

Integrating the innermost integral, noting that it is with respect to x, (that is, y is treated as a constant) gives

$$\int \tfrac{1}{2}x^4y^4 + \tfrac{5}{3}xy^3 \, dx + \int \left[\tfrac{2}{5}x^5y^3 + \tfrac{5}{2}x^2y^2 - \left(\tfrac{2}{5}x^5y^3 + \tfrac{5}{2}x^2y^2 \right) \right] dy = C$$

$$\int \tfrac{1}{2}x^4y^4 + \tfrac{5}{3}xy^3 \, dx + \int \tfrac{2}{5}x^5y^3 + \tfrac{5}{2}x^2y^2 - \tfrac{2}{5}x^5y^3 - \tfrac{5}{2}x^2y^2 \, dy = C$$

Now, integrating the other terms, noting that the first integral is with respect to the variable x and the second is with respect to the variable y, we get

$$\tfrac{1}{10}x^5y^4 + \tfrac{5}{6}x^2y^6 + \tfrac{2}{20}x^5y^4 + \tfrac{5}{6}x^2y^3 - \tfrac{2}{20}x^5y^4 - \tfrac{5}{4}x^2y^6 = C$$

Adding together similar terms gives the general solution

$$\tfrac{1}{10}x^5y^4 + \tfrac{5}{6}x^2y^3 = C$$

Substituting $x = 2$ and $y = 5$, we can compute C.

$$\tfrac{1}{10}(2)^5(5)^4 + \tfrac{5}{6}(2)^2(5)^3 = C$$
$$\tfrac{1}{10}(32)(625) + \tfrac{5}{6}(4)(125) = C$$
$$2,000 + 416\tfrac{2}{3} = 2,416\tfrac{2}{3} = C$$

The particular solution, then, is

$$\tfrac{1}{10}x^5y^4 + \tfrac{5}{6}x^2y^3 = 2,416\tfrac{2}{3}$$

EXAMPLE 16.24

Solve

$$(x \sin y - y)Y' = \cos y$$

for the equation which passes through the point (0,0).

First, the equation must be put in general form. Subtract $\cos y$ from each side.

$$- \cos y + (x \sin y - y)Y' = 0$$

Define $\qquad f(x,y) = - \cos y \qquad$ and $\qquad g(x,y) = x \sin y - y$

Note that $\qquad\qquad f_y(x,y) = -(- \sin y) = \sin y$
$$g_x(x,y) = \sin y$$

Since these derivatives are identical, this is an exact differential equation. The solution form is

$$\int - \cos y \, dx + \int \left(x \sin y - y - \int \sin y \, dx \right) dy = C$$

where C is an arbitrary constant.

Integrating the innermost integral with respect to the variable x gives

$$\int - \cos y \, dx + \int (x \sin y - y - x \sin y) \, dy = C$$

The other integrations can be performed next

$$-x \cos y + x(- \cos y) - \tfrac{1}{2}y^2 - x(- \cos y) = C$$

The general solution, then, is

$$-x \cos y - \tfrac{1}{2}y^2 = C$$

Substituting the point (0,0) for x and y, we obtain

$$-(0)(1) - \tfrac{1}{2}(0)^2 = C$$
$$0 = C$$

Thus, the particular solution is

$$-x \cos y - \tfrac{1}{2}y^2 = 0$$

17 THE CALCULUS OF FINITE DIFFERENCES

INTRODUCTION

Many similarities exist between calculus and finite differences, and between differential equations and difference equations. The major point of departure for the two branches of mathematics is in the type of data described. Calculus deals with continuous data or data which can be treated as continuous, while finite differences applies to discrete data. Thus, in calculus, the curve $f(x)$ was considered continuous or unbroken for all values of x within a certain range. "All values of x" is taken to mean not only integer values, such as 1 or 2, but also every value in between any two integers, such as 1.2 or 1.21315. Thus the dependent variable y or $f(x)$ was defined for x whether x was an integer, a fraction, or a decimal.

Finite differences deals with situations where the independent variable x is discrete, usually being defined only for integer values such as 1, 2, or 3. It applies in those cases where an x value of $\frac{2}{3}$ or 1.35 would be meaningless. The most common variable which occurs in business problems, and usually is best treated as discrete, is time. Thus, if the year is to be divided into quarters, and $x = 1$ means the first quarter, $x = 2$, the second quarter, and so on, $x = 1.371$ would not be particularly meaningful.

Finite differences and difference equations have a tremendous potential of business significance. We will cover a number of possible applications, and the reader will most assuredly be able to devise a large number of others.

FINITE DIFFERENCES: DEFINITION OF TERMS AND OPERATIONS

The term Δx, read "delta x," can be interpreted as a change in x. Since we are dealing with discrete variables, Δx means a one-unit increase in x. If $x = 3$, for example, $x + \Delta x = 4$. Graphically, Δx can be interpreted in the manner shown in Figure 17.1. The symbol Δ is called a *difference operator*.

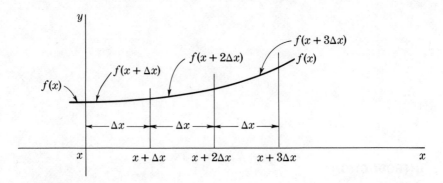

Figure 17.1

The operation Δy_x is defined mathematically as: $\Delta y_x = y_{x+1} - y_x$. This can be easily visualized graphically (Figure 17.2). Thus Δy_x means the height y, one unit to the right of x, minus the height at x.

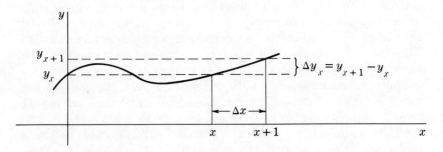

Figure 17.2

Δy is called the first difference. The second difference is defined as

$$\begin{aligned}
\Delta(\Delta y) = \Delta^2 y &= \Delta y_{x+\Delta x} - \Delta y_x \\
&= (y_{x+2\Delta x} - y_{x+\Delta x}) - (y_{x+\Delta x} - y_x) \\
&= y_{x+2\Delta x} - 2y_{x+\Delta x} + y_x
\end{aligned}$$

In a similar manner, the third difference is defined as

$$\Delta(\Delta^2 y) = \Delta^3 y = \Delta y_{x+2\Delta x} - \Delta 2 y_{x+\Delta x} + \Delta y_x$$
$$= (y_{x+3\Delta x} - y_{x+2\Delta x}) - 2(y_{x+2\Delta x} - y_{x+\Delta x}) + (y_{x+\Delta x} - y_x)$$
$$= y_{x+3\Delta x} - y_{x+2\Delta x} - 2y_{x+2\Delta x} + 2y_{x+\Delta x} + y_{x+\Delta x} - y_x$$
$$= y_{x+3\Delta x} - 3y_{x+2\Delta x} + 3y_{x+\Delta x} - y_x$$

By the same reasoning, higher differences can be defined by the general formula

$$\Delta^n y_x = (-1)^0 \binom{n}{0} y_{x+n\Delta x} + (-1)^1 \binom{n}{1} y_{x+(n-1)\Delta x} + \cdots$$
$$+ (-1)^{n-1} \binom{n}{n-1} y_{x+\Delta x} + (-1)^n y_x$$

where
$$\binom{n}{k} = \frac{n!}{k!(n-k)!}$$

where $k = 1, 2, \cdots, n$
$$\binom{n}{0} = 1$$
$$0! = 1$$

Another way to define $\Delta^n y_x$ is

$$\Delta^{n+1} y_x = \Delta^n y_{x+\Delta x} - \Delta^n y_x$$

EXAMPLE 17.1

If $y_x = x^2 + 4x - 8$, find Δy_x, Δy_{x+1}, and $\Delta^2 y_x$.

$$\Delta y_x = [(x+1)^2 + 4(x+1) - 8] - (x^2 + 4x - 8)$$
$$= \cancel{x^2} + 2x + 1 + \cancel{4x} + 4 - 8 - \cancel{x^2} - \cancel{4x} + \cancel{8}$$
$$= 2x + 5$$
$$\Delta y_{x+1} = 2(x+1) + 5 = 2x + 2 + 5 = 2x + 7$$
$$\Delta^2 y_x = (2x+7) - (2x+5) = \cancel{2x} + 7 - \cancel{2x} - 5 = 2$$

EXAMPLE 17.2

If $y_x = 4x + 5/x$, find Δy_x and $\Delta^3 \dot{y}_x$.

$$\Delta y_x = \left[4(x+1) + \frac{5}{x+1} \right] - \left[4x + \frac{5}{x} \right]$$
$$= \cancel{4x} + 4 + \frac{5}{x+1} - \cancel{4x} - \frac{5}{x}$$
$$= \frac{4x(x+1) + 5x - 5(x+1)}{x(x+1)} = \frac{4x^2 + 4x + \cancel{5x} - \cancel{5x} - 5}{x(x+1)}$$
$$= \frac{4x^2 + 4x - 5}{x^2 + x}$$

$$\Delta^3 y_x = \left[4(x+3) + \frac{5}{x+3} \right] - 3\left[4(x+2) + \frac{5}{x+2} \right] + 3\left[4(x+1) + \frac{5}{x+1} \right]$$
$$- \left[4x + \frac{5}{x} \right]$$

$$= \cancel{4x} + \cancel{12} + \frac{5}{x+3} - \cancel{12x} - \cancel{24} - \frac{15}{x+2} + \cancel{12x} + \cancel{12} + \frac{15}{x+1} - \cancel{4x} - \frac{5}{x}$$

$$= \frac{5}{x+3} - \frac{15}{x+2} + \frac{15}{x+1} - \frac{5}{x}$$

$$= \frac{5(x+2)(x+1)(x) - 15(x+3)(x+1)(x) + 15(x+3)(x+2)(x)}{(x+3)(x+2)(x+1)(x)}$$
$$\frac{- 5(x+3)(x+2)(x+1)}{}$$

$$= \frac{\cancel{5x^3} + \cancel{15x^2} + \cancel{10x} - \cancel{15x^3} - \cancel{60x^2} - \cancel{45x} + \cancel{15x^3} + \cancel{75x^2} + \cancel{90x}}{(x+3)(x+2)(x+1)(x)}$$
$$\frac{- \cancel{5x^3} - \cancel{30x^2} - \cancel{55x} - 30}{}$$

$$= \frac{-30}{x^4 + 6x^3 + 11x^2 + 6x}$$

BASIC DIFFERENCING FORMULAS

As in differential and integral calculus, a number of formulas are available for differencing operations. A few very simple rules are

$$\Delta k = 0 \qquad \text{where } k \text{ is a constant}$$
$$\Delta x = 1$$
$$\Delta kx = k\Delta x \qquad \text{where } k \text{ is a constant}$$

EXAMPLE 17.3

If $f(x) = 10$, find $\Delta f(x)$. Note that $f(x)$ in this case represents a constant. Therefore $\Delta f(x) = \Delta 10 = 0$.

EXAMPLE 17.4

If $f(x) = 7x$, find $\Delta f(x)$.
$$\Delta f(x) = \Delta 7x = 7\Delta x = 7(1) = 7$$

EXAMPLE 17.5

If $f(x) = -ex$, find $\Delta f(x)$.
$$\Delta f(x) = \Delta - ex = -e\Delta x = -e(1) = -e$$

A FORMULA FOR DIFFERENCING $n!/(n-r)!$

If we define

$$x_{\{r\}} = \frac{x!}{(x-r)!} = x(x-1)(x-2) \cdots (x-r+1)$$

(note that there are r factors in this sequence), a differencing formula is available which is analogous to the power formula in differential calculus.

$$\Delta x_{\{r\}} = rx_{\{r-1\}}$$

EXAMPLE 17.6

If $f(x) = x_{\{8\}}$, find $\Delta f(x)$.

$$\Delta f(x) = \Delta x_{\{8\}} = 8x_{\{7\}}$$

EXAMPLE 17.7

If $f(x) = x_{\{3\}}$, find $\Delta f(x)$ and $\Delta^2 f(x)$.

$$\Delta f(x) = \Delta x_{\{3\}} = 3x_{\{2\}}$$
$$\Delta^2 f(x) = \Delta 3x_{\{2\}} = 6x_{\{1\}} = 6x$$

EXAMPLE 17.8

If, in Example 17.7, x was assumed to be 7, show that the formulas for Δ and Δ^2 yield the correct numerical answer.

$$7_{\{3\}} = (7)(6)(5) = 210$$
$$8_{\{3\}} = (8)(7)(6) = 336$$
$$\Delta 7_{\{3\}} = 8_{\{3\}} - 7_{\{3\}} = 336 - 210 = 126$$

$$\Delta x_{\{3\}} = 3x_{\{2\}}$$
$$\Delta 7_{\{3\}} = 3(7)_{\{2\}} = 3(7)(6) = 126$$

Therefore, the formula Δ yields the same answer as would be found using the definition of Δ.

$$9_{\{3\}} = (9)(8)(7) = 504$$
$$\Delta 8_{\{3\}} = 9_{\{3\}} - 8_{\{3\}} = 504 - 336 = 168$$
$$\Delta^2 7_{\{3\}} = \Delta 8_{\{3\}} - \Delta 7_{\{3\}} = 168 - 126 = 42$$

$$\Delta^2 x_{\{3\}} = 6x$$
$$\Delta^2 7_{\{3\}} = 6(7) = 42$$

So, the formula for Δ^2 also yields the same answer as would be found using the definition.

A FORMULA FOR DIFFERENCING a^x

The formula for differencing a^x, where a is any constant, is

$$\Delta a^x = a^x(a - 1)$$

EXAMPLE 17.9

If $f(x) = 7^x$, find $\Delta f(x)$.

$$\Delta f(x) = \Delta 7^x = 7^x(7 - 1) = 7^x(6)$$

EXAMPLE 17.10

If $f(x) = 6e^x$, find $\Delta f(x)$.

$$\Delta f(x) = \Delta 6e^x = 6\Delta e^x = 6e^x(e - 1)$$

COMBINATION OF FUNCTIONS: SUMS AND DIFFERENCES

Exactly as with sums and differences in differential calculus, the formula for differencing the sum (or difference) of two functions is given by

$$\Delta[f(x) \pm g(x)] = \Delta f(x) \pm \Delta g(x)$$

EXAMPLE 17.11

Difference $f(x) = 8x + 8^x$.

$$\begin{aligned}
\Delta f(x) &= \Delta(8x + 8^x) = \Delta 8x + \Delta 8^x \\
&= 8\Delta x + 8^x(8 - 1) = 8 + 8^x(7)
\end{aligned}$$

EXAMPLE 17.12

If $f(x) = 4x_{\{3\}} + 5^x - 10x + 3$, find $\Delta f(4)$.

$$\begin{aligned}
\Delta f(x) &= \Delta(4x_{\{3\}} + 5^x - 10x + 3) \\
&= \Delta 4x_{\{3\}} + \Delta 5^x - \Delta 10x + \Delta 3 \\
&= 4\Delta x_{\{3\}} + \Delta 5^x - 10\Delta x + \Delta 3 \\
&= 4(3)x_{\{2\}} + 5^x(4) - 10(1) + 0 \\
&= 12x_{\{2\}} + 5^x(4) - 10 \\
\Delta f(4) &= 12(4)_{\{2\}} + 5^{(4)}(4) - 10 \\
&= 12(4)(3) + 625(4) - 10 \\
&= 144 + 2{,}500 - 10 \\
&= 2{,}634
\end{aligned}$$

COMBINATION OF FUNCTIONS: PRODUCTS

The formula for differencing the product of two functions is

$$\Delta[f(x)g(x)] = f(x + 1)\Delta g(x) + g(x)\Delta f(x)$$

EXAMPLE 17.13

If $f(x) = x8^x$, find $\Delta f(x)$.

$$\begin{aligned}
\Delta f(x) &= \Delta x8^x = (x + 1)\Delta(8^x) + 8^x \Delta x \\
&= (x + 1)(8^x)(7) + 8^x(1) \\
&= 8^x(7x + 7 + 1) = 8^x(7x + 8)
\end{aligned}$$

EXAMPLE 17.14

If $f(x) = x^2$, find $\Delta f(x)$.

$$\begin{aligned}
\Delta f(x) = \Delta x^2 = \Delta(x \cdot x) &= (x + 1)\Delta x + x\Delta x = (x + 1)(1) + x(1) \\
&= x + 1 + x = 2x + 1
\end{aligned}$$

EXAMPLE 17.15

If $f(x) = x^3$, find $\Delta f(x)$.

$$\Delta f(x) = \Delta x^3 = \Delta(x \cdot x^2) = (x + 1)\Delta x^2 + x^2\Delta x$$
$$= (x + 1)(2x + 1) + x^2(1)$$
$$= 2x^2 + 3x + 1 + x^2$$
$$= 3x^2 + 3x + 1$$

COMBINATION OF FUNCTIONS: QUOTIENTS

The formula for differencing the quotient of two functions is given by:

$$\Delta \frac{f(x)}{g(x)} = \frac{g(x)\Delta f(x) - f(x)\Delta g(x)}{g(x + 1)g(x)}$$

EXAMPLE 17.16

Difference $f(x) = x^2(3x + 5)$.

$$\Delta f(x) = \frac{(3x + 5)\Delta x^2 - x^2\Delta(3x + 5)}{[3(x + 1) + 5](3x + 5)}$$
$$= \frac{(3x + 5)(2x + 1) - x^2(3)}{(3x + 8)(3x + 5)}$$

EXAMPLE 17.17

If $f(x) = (2x + 5^x)^{-1}$, find $\Delta f(x)$.

$$\Delta f(x) = \Delta(2x + 5^x)^{-1}$$
$$= \Delta \frac{1}{2x + 5^x}$$
$$= \frac{(2x + 5^x)\Delta 1 - 1\Delta(2x + 5^x)}{[2(x + 1) + 5^{x+1}](2x + 5^x)}$$
$$= \frac{(2x + 5^x)0 - 2 - 5^x(4)}{(2x + 2 + 5^{x+1})(2x + 5^x)}$$
$$= \frac{-2 - 5^x(4)}{(2x + 2 + 5^{x+1})(2x + 5^x)}$$

MAXIMA: MINIMA

If we define a point of the function $f(x)$ as $f(\bar{x})$, $f(x)$ will have a local minimum $f(\bar{x})$ at $\bar{x}$ if

$$\Delta f(\bar{x} - 1) < 0 < \Delta f(\bar{x})$$

Furthermore, $f(\bar{x})$ will be an absolute minimum of $f(x)$ if, in addition to the above,

$$\Delta^2 f(x) \geq 0 \qquad \text{for all } x$$

Reversing the signs of the above inequalities will provide sufficient conditions for a maximum.

It should be noted that a function may obtain a maximum or minimum without all the above conditions; i.e., they are not necessary conditions. However, whenever these conditions are met, a maximum or minimum will exist for the point satisfying the conditions. Hence these conditions are sufficient.

EXAMPLE 17.18

Test $f(x) = x^2 - 5x_{\{2\}}$ for an absolute maximum.

In order for $f(x)$ to have a maximum at $\bar{x}$, $\Delta f(\bar{x}) < 0$ and $\Delta f(\bar{x} - 1) > 0$.

First solving for $\Delta f(x)$, we get

$$\begin{aligned}
\Delta f(x) &= \Delta(x^2 - 5x_{\{2\}}) \\
&= \Delta x^2 - \Delta 5x_{\{2\}} \\
&= \Delta x^2 - 5\Delta x_{\{2\}} \\
&= (2x + 1) - 5(2)x_{\{1\}} \\
&= 2x + 1 - 10x \\
&= -8x + 1
\end{aligned}$$

Then $\bar{x}$ must be an x which satisfies

$$\begin{aligned}
-8x + 1 &< 0 \\
-8x &< -1 \\
x &> \tfrac{1}{8}
\end{aligned}$$

(Note that when dividing by a negative number the direction of the inequality is reversed.)

Also, if $\Delta f(x) = -8x + 1$, then

$$\begin{aligned}
\Delta f(x - 1) &= -8(x - 1) + 1 \\
&= -8x + 8 + 1 \\
&= -8x + 9
\end{aligned}$$

Then $\bar{x}$ must also satisfy

$$\begin{aligned}
-8x + 9 &> 0 \\
-8x &> -9 \\
x &< \tfrac{9}{8}
\end{aligned}$$

We know, then, that $\tfrac{1}{8} < \bar{x} < \tfrac{9}{8}$. Since $\bar{x}$ must be an integer, the only number that will satisfy this inequality is $\bar{x} = 1$.

To prove that $\bar{x} = 1$ is an absolute maximum, we must ascertain that $\Delta^2 f(x) < 0$ for all x.

$$\begin{aligned}
\Delta^2 f(x) = \Delta[\Delta f(x)] &= \Delta(-8x + 1) \\
&= -8\Delta x + \Delta 1 \\
&= -8(1) + 0 \\
&= -8
\end{aligned}$$

$-8 < 0$ for all values of x. So, the equation $f(x) = x^2 - 5x_{\{2\}}$ has an absolute maximum when $x = 1$.

EXAMPLE 17.19

Solve for an absolute minimum $f(x) = 4x^2 - 32x + 100$.

$$\Delta f(x) = \Delta(4x^2 - 32x + 100)$$
$$= \Delta 4x^2 - \Delta 32x + \Delta 100$$
$$= 4\Delta x^2 - 32\Delta x + 0$$
$$= 4(2x + 1) - 32(1)$$
$$= 8x + 4 - 32$$
$$= 8x - 28$$

$$\Delta f(x - 1) = 8(x - 1) - 28$$
$$= 8x - 8 - 28$$
$$= 8x - 36$$

$$\Delta^2 f(x) = \Delta(8x - 28)$$
$$= \Delta 8x - \Delta 28$$
$$= 8\Delta x - 0$$
$$= 8(1) = 8$$

In order for $f(\bar{x})$ to be a minimum, $\Delta f(\bar{x} - 1) < 0$ and $\Delta f(\bar{x}) > 0$.

$$8x - 36 < 0 \qquad 8x - 28 > 0$$
$$8x < 36 \qquad 8x > 28$$
$$x < \tfrac{36}{8} \qquad x > \tfrac{28}{8}$$

Thus,
$$\tfrac{28}{8} < \bar{x} < \tfrac{36}{8}$$

and $\bar{x}$ must be an integer.

$$\tfrac{32}{8} = 4$$

will provide such a number

$$\tfrac{28}{8} < \tfrac{32}{8} < \tfrac{36}{8}$$

Thus $\bar{x} = 4$ is a minimum. Since $\Delta^2 f(x) = 8$, which is positive for all x, $\bar{x} = 4$ must be an absolute minimum.

ANTIDIFFERENCES AND SUMMATION OF SERIES

If we define $F(x)$ as the antidifference of $f(x)$ and say that $f(x) = \Delta F(x)$, this will enable us to quickly evaluate summations of numbers. Defining sigma,

$$\sum_{i=a}^{b} x_i$$

to mean $x_a + x_{a+1} + x_{a+2} + \cdots + x_b$, we can utilize a formula for summation

$$\sum_{i=a}^{b} f(x_i) = F(b + 1) - F(a)$$

where $F(x)$ is the antidifference of $f(x)$.

EXAMPLE 17.20

Solve

$$\sum_{i=2}^{5} 8^i(7)$$

Note that $f(x) = 8^i(7)$ is the difference of 8^i; that is, $\Delta 8^i = 8(8-1)$. Thus

$$\sum_{i=2}^{5} 8^i(7) = 8^i \Big|_{i=2}^{5+1}$$

$$= 8^6 - 8^2$$
$$= 262{,}144 - 64$$
$$= 262{,}080$$

EXAMPLE 17.21

Solve

$$\sum_{i=4}^{15} 2i + 1$$

Note that $\Delta x^2 = 2x + 1$.

Thus

$$\sum_{i=4}^{15} 2i + 1 = x^2 \Big|_{i=4}^{15+1}$$

$$= (16)^2 - (4)^2$$
$$= 256 - 16$$
$$= 240$$

EXAMPLE 17.22

Solve

$$\sum_{i=3}^{7} 3i_{\{2\}}$$

Note that $\Delta i_{\{3\}} = 3i_{\{2\}}$.

Thus

$$\sum_{i=3}^{7} 3i_{\{2\}} = i_{\{3\}} \Big|_{i=3}^{7+1}$$

$$= 8_{\{3\}} - 3_{\{3\}}$$
$$= (8 \cdot 7 \cdot 6) - (3 \cdot 2 \cdot 1)$$
$$= 336 - 6$$
$$= 330$$

18 DIFFERENCE EQUATIONS

TERMINOLOGY

A difference equation can be defined as an equation relating an independent variable x to a dependent variable y through the use of one or more finite differences of the function y.

The order of a difference equation is the difference between the largest difference shown in the equation and the smallest. Thus

$$y_{x+2} + 4y_{x+1} = 0$$

is a first-order difference equation, and

$$y_{x+5} + y_{x+4} + y_x = 0$$

is a fifth-order difference equation.

HOMOGENEOUS FIRST-ORDER LINEAR DIFFERENCE EQUATIONS WITH CONSTANT COEFFICIENTS

Homogeneous first-order linear difference equations with constant coefficients can be represented by the general equation

$$y_{x+1} - Ay_x = 0$$

where A is any constant.

Any difference equation which can be put into this form can be solved by the equation

$$y_x = CA^x$$

where C is an arbitrary constant. This is the general solution for the problem. The particular solution is given by substituting the initial value of y where $x = 0$, i.e., the value of y_0.

EXAMPLE 18.1

Solve

$$y_{x+1} - 7y_x = 0 \qquad y_0 = 5$$

Since this equation is of the form $y_{x+1} - Ay_x = 0$, we can solve it by the equation

$$y_x = CA^x = C \cdot 7^x$$

where C is an arbitrary constant. This is the general solution. The particular solution is found by substituting the initial value. Thus

$$5 = CA^0 = C \qquad \text{and} \qquad y_x = 5(7^x)$$

EXAMPLE 18.2

Solve

$$y_{x+1} = ey_x \qquad y_0 = 15$$

This equation can be put into homogeneous form by subtracting ey_x from each side. Thus

$$y_{x+1} - ey_x = 0$$

is the homogeneous form. Note that e is a constant. Therefore this is an equation with constant coefficients, and the solution is

$$y_x = Ce^x$$

Since the initial condition is $y_0 = 15$, the particular solution may be found as follows

$$15 = Ce^0 = C$$

Thus, the answer is $y_x = 15e^x$.

EXAMPLE 18.3

Solve

$$5y_x = 8y_{x+1} \qquad y_0 = 8$$

This equation must first be put into homogeneous form. Subtracting $8y_{x+1}$ from each side gives

$$-8y_{x+1} + 5y_x = 0$$

Now, dividing through by -8 puts the equation into general form.

$$y_{x+1} - \tfrac{5}{8}y_x = 0$$

The general solution is given as

$$y_x = C(\tfrac{5}{8})^x$$

where C is an arbitrary constant. The particular solution is obtained by solving

$$8 = C(\tfrac{5}{8})^0 = C$$

Thus, the solution is

$$y_x = 8(\tfrac{5}{8})^x$$

NONHOMOGENEOUS FIRST-ORDER LINEAR DIFFERENCE EQUATIONS WITH CONSTANT COEFFICIENTS

Nonhomogeneous first-order linear difference equations can be characterized by the general equation

$$y_{x+1} - Ay_x = g(x)$$

Case 1: $g(x) = B$

First let us solve the simplest case, that is, the case where $g(x)$ equals some constant B.   The solution to the equation $y_{x+1} - Ay_x = B$ is

$$y_x = CA^x + B\frac{1 - A^x}{1 - A} \qquad A \neq 1$$

where C is an arbitrary constant.
For the case where $A = 1$, the solution is

$$y_x = C + Bx \qquad A = 1$$

where C is an arbitrary constant.

Case 2: $g(x) = B^x$

When $g(x)$ is in the form B^x, where B is a constant, the solution will be given by:

$$y_x = CA^x + Y^*$$

where Y^* is computed as follows:

Let
$$y_x = kB^x \qquad B \neq A$$
$$y_x = kxB^x \qquad B = A$$

Substitute these values in the original equation and solve for k. Then kB^x (or kxB^x) will be Y^* and will complete the general solution.

Case 3: $g(x) = x^n$

When $g(x)$ is in the form x^n, where n is a constant, the solution is again:

$$y_x = CA^x + Y^*$$

In this situation Y^* is computed by letting

$$y_x = A_0 + A_1x + A_2x^2 + \cdots + A_nx^n$$

Substituting this for y_x in the original equation and solving A_0, A_1, A_2, . . . , A_n will provide Y^*.

$$Y^* = A_0 + A_1x + A_2x^2 + \cdots + A_nx^n$$

Case 4: $g(x) = B^x + x^n$

When $g(x)$ is in the form $B^x + x^n$, where B and n are constants, the solution form is again

$$y_x = CA^x + Y^*$$

where Y^* is computed by letting

$$y_x = kB^x + A_0 + A_1x + A_2x^2 + \cdots + A_nx^n \qquad B \neq A$$

or

$$y_x = kxB^x + A_0 + A_1x + A_2x^2 + \cdots + A_nx^n \qquad B = A$$

Solving for k, A_0, A_1, A_2, . . . , A_n,

$$Y^* = kxB^x + A_0 + A_1x + A_2x^2 + \cdots + A_nx^n$$

Case 5: $g(x) = B^x \cdot x^n$

When $g(x)$ is in the form $B^x \cdot x^n$, where B and n are constants, the form $y_x = CA^x + Y^*$ still applies. In this case Y^* is found by letting $y_x = B^x(A_0 + A_1x + A_2x^2 + \cdots + A_nx^n)$. Solving in the original equation for A_0, A_1, A_2, . . . , A_n,

$$Y^* = B^x(A_0 + A_1x + A_2x^2 + \cdots + A_nx^n)$$

EXAMPLE 18.4

Solve

$$y_{x+1} - 15y_x = 25 \qquad y_0 = 4$$

Note that $g(x) = B = 25$, and that $A = 15$. The solution form, then, is

$$y_x = C(15)^x + 25\left(\frac{1 - 15^x}{1 - 15}\right) \qquad \text{since } A \neq 1$$

Simplifying,

$$y_x = C(15)^x + \frac{25}{-14}(1 - 15^x)$$

$$y_x = C(15)^x - \frac{25}{14} + \frac{25}{14}(15)^x$$

$$y_x = (C + \tfrac{25}{14})15^x - \tfrac{25}{14}$$

The initial condition is

$$y_0 = 4$$

Therefore

$$4 = (C + \tfrac{25}{14})15^0 - \tfrac{25}{14}$$
$$4 = C + \tfrac{25}{14} - \tfrac{25}{14} = C$$

So the particular solution is

$$y_x = (4 + \tfrac{25}{14})15^x - \tfrac{25}{14}$$
$$y_x = (\tfrac{81}{14})15^x - \tfrac{25}{14}$$

EXAMPLE 18.5

Solve

$$y_{x+1} - y_x = 6 \qquad y_0 = 7$$

Note that $g(x) = B = 6$, and that $A = 1$. The solution form, then, is

$$y_x = C + B_x \qquad \text{since } A = 1$$

and
$$y_x = C + 6x$$

is the general solution.

The particular solution is found by solving

$$7 = C + 6(0) = C$$

and the answer, then, is

$$y_x = 7 + 6x$$

EXAMPLE 18.6

Solve

$$y_{x+1} - 5y_x = 8^x \qquad y_0 = 2$$

Note that $g(x) = B^x = 8^x$, and that $A = 5$. The solution form will be

$$y_x = CA^x - Y^*$$

or
$$y_x = C(5)^x + Y^*$$

Let
$$y_x = k8^x \qquad \text{since } B \neq A$$

Substituting in the original equation gives

$$k8^{x+1} - 5k8^x = 8^x$$

Factoring an 8^x on the left side gives

$$8^x(k8^1 - 5k) = 8^x$$
$$8^x(8k - 5k) = 8^x$$
$$8^x(3k) = 8^x$$

Dividing through by 8^x,

$$3k = 1$$
$$k = \tfrac{1}{3}$$

Thus,
$$Y^* = \tfrac{1}{3}(8)^x$$

and the general solution is

$$y_x = C(5)^x + \tfrac{1}{3}8^x$$

Noting that $y_0 = 2$, and, solving for C,

$$2 = C(5)^0 + \tfrac{1}{3}(8)^0 = C + \tfrac{1}{3}$$
$$C = 2 - \tfrac{1}{3} = \tfrac{5}{3}$$

The particular solution, then, is

$$y_x = \tfrac{5}{3}(5)^x + \tfrac{1}{3}(8)^x$$

EXAMPLE 18.7

Solve

$$y_{x+1} - 3y_x = 3^x \qquad y_0 = 8$$

Note that $g(x) = B^x = 3^x$, and that $A = 3$. Also note that $A = B = 3$. The solution form will be

$$y_x = CA^x + Y^* = C(3)^x + Y^*$$

To find Y^* let

$$y_x = kxB^x = kx(3)^x \qquad \text{since } A = B$$

Substituting in the original equation

$$k(x + 1)3^{x+1} - 3(kx)3^x = 3^x$$

Factoring 3^x from the left side,

$$3^x[k(x + 1)3^1 - 3kx] = 3^x$$
$$3^x(3kx + 3k - 3kx) = 3^x$$
$$3^x(3k) = 3^x$$

Dividing through by 3^x,

$$3k = 1$$
$$k = \tfrac{1}{3}$$

Thus, $Y^* = \tfrac{1}{3}x(3)^x$, and the general solution is

$$y_x = C(3)^x + \tfrac{1}{3}x(3)^x$$

Since the initial condition is $y_0 = 8$,

$$8 = C(3)^0 = \tfrac{1}{3}(0)(3)^0 = C$$

and the particular solution is

$$y_x = 8(3)^x + \tfrac{1}{3}x(3)^x$$

EXAMPLE 18.8

Solve

$$y_{x+1} - 4y_x = x^2 \qquad y_0 = 6$$

Note that $g(x) = x^n = x^2$, and that $A = 4$. The solution form will be

$$y_x = CA^x + Y^* = C(4)^x + Y^*$$

To find Y^*, let $y_x = A_0 + A_1 x + A_2 x^2$. Substituting in the original equation gives

$$A_0 + A_1(x + 1) + A_2(x + 1)^2 - 4(A_0 + A_1 x + A_2 x^2) = x^2$$
$$A_0 + A_1 x + A_1 + A_2(x^2 + 2x + 1) + 4A_0 - 4A_1 x - 4A_2 x^2 = x^2$$
$$A_0 + A_1 x + A_1 + A_2 x^2 + 2A_2 x + A_2 + 4A_0 - 4A_1 x - 4A_2 x^2 - x^2 = 0$$
$$(A_2 - 4A_2 - 1)x^2 + (A_1 + 2A_2 - 4A_1)x + (A_0 + A_1 + A_2 + 4A_0) = 0$$
$$(-3A_2 - 1)x^2 + (-3A_1 + 2A_2)x + (5A_0 + A_1 + A_2) = 0$$

Setting each of the coefficients of x equal to 0, gives

$$-3A_2 - 1 = 0$$
$$-3A_2 = 1$$
$$A_2 = -\tfrac{1}{3}$$

$$-3A_1 + 2A_2 = 0$$
$$-3A_1 + 2(-\tfrac{1}{3}) = 0$$
$$-3A_1 - \tfrac{2}{3} = 0$$
$$-3A_1 = \tfrac{2}{3}$$
$$A_1 = -\tfrac{2}{9}$$

$$5A_0 + A_1 + A_2 = 0$$
$$5A_0 + (-\tfrac{1}{3}) + (-\tfrac{2}{9}) = 0$$
$$5A_0 - \tfrac{1}{3} - \tfrac{2}{9} = 0$$
$$5A_0 - \tfrac{5}{9} = 0$$
$$5A_0 = \tfrac{5}{9}$$
$$A_0 = \tfrac{1}{9}$$

Then $Y^* = \tfrac{1}{9} - \tfrac{2}{9}x - \tfrac{1}{3}x^2$, and the general solution is:

$$y_x = C4^x + \tfrac{1}{9} - \tfrac{2}{9}x - \tfrac{1}{3}x^2$$

Since $y_0 = 6$

$$6 = C4^0 + \tfrac{1}{9} - \tfrac{2}{9}(0) - \tfrac{1}{3}(0)^2 = C + \tfrac{1}{9}$$
$$C = 6 - \tfrac{1}{9} = \tfrac{53}{9}$$

and

$$y_x = \tfrac{53}{9}(4)^x + \tfrac{1}{9} - \tfrac{2}{9}x = \tfrac{1}{3}x^2$$

which is the particular solution.

EXAMPLE 18.9

Solve

$$y_{x+1} - 3y_x = 4^x + x^3 \qquad y_0 = 2$$

Note that $g(x) = B^x + x^n = 4^x + x^3$, and that $A = 3$. The solution form will be

$$y_x = CA^x + Y^* = C(3)^x + Y^*$$

To find Y^*, let

$$y_x = k4^x + A_0 + A_1x + A_2x^2 + A_3x^3 \qquad \text{since } A \neq B$$

Substituting in the original equation,

$$k4^{x+1} + A_0 + A_1(x + 1) + A_2(x + 1)^2 + A_3(x + 1)^3$$
$$- 3(k4^x + A_0 + A_1x + A_2x^2 + A_3x^3) = 4^x + x^3$$

Simplifying,

$$k4^{x+1} + A_0 + A_1x + A_1 + A_2(x^2 + 2x + 1) + A_3(x^3 + 3x^2 + 3x + 1)$$
$$- 3k4^x - 3A_0 - 3A_1x - 3A_2x^2 - 3A_3x^3 = 4^x + x^3$$

$$k4^{x+1} + A_0 + A_1x + A_1 + A_2x^2 + 2A_2x + A_2 + A_3x^3 + 3A_3x^2 + 3A_3x$$
$$+ A_3 - 3k4^x - 3A_0 - 3A_1x - 3A_2x^2 - 3A_3x^3 - 4^x - x^3 = 0$$

$$4^x(4k - 3k - 1) + x^3(A_3 - 3A_3 - 1) + x^2(A_2 + 3A_3 - 3A_2)$$
$$+ x(A_1 + 2A_2 + 3A_3 - 3A_1) + (A_0 + A_1 + A_2 + A_3 - 3A_0) = 0$$

Then, setting each coefficient of x equal to 0 gives

$$4k - 3k - 1 = 0$$
$$k = 1$$

$$A_3 - 3A_3 - 1 = 0$$
$$-2A_3 = 1$$
$$A_3 = -\tfrac{1}{2}$$

$$A_2 + 3A_3 - 3A_2 = 0$$
$$-2A_2 + 3(-\tfrac{1}{2}) = 0$$
$$-2A_2 = \tfrac{3}{2}$$
$$A_2 = -\tfrac{3}{4}$$

$$A_1 + 2A_2 + 3A_3 - 3A_1 = 0$$
$$-2A_1 + 2(-\tfrac{3}{4}) + 3(-\tfrac{1}{2}) = 0$$
$$-2A_1 = \tfrac{6}{4} + \tfrac{3}{2} = 3$$
$$A_1 = -\tfrac{3}{2}$$

$$A_0 + A_1 + A_2 + A_3 - 3A_0 = 0$$
$$-2A_0 - \tfrac{3}{2} - \tfrac{3}{4} - \tfrac{1}{2} = 0$$
$$-2A_0 = \tfrac{3}{2} + \tfrac{3}{4} + \tfrac{1}{2} = \tfrac{11}{4}$$
$$A_0 = -\tfrac{11}{8}$$

Then,
$$Y^* = 4^x - \tfrac{11}{8} - \tfrac{3}{2}x - \tfrac{3}{4}x^2 - \tfrac{1}{2}x^3$$

and the general solution is

$$y_x = C(3)^x + 4^x - \tfrac{11}{8} - \tfrac{3}{2}x - \tfrac{3}{4}x^2 - \tfrac{1}{2}x^3$$

Since $y_0 = 2$,

$$2 = C(3)^0 + 4^0 - \tfrac{11}{8} - \tfrac{3}{2}(0) - \tfrac{3}{4}(0)^2 - \tfrac{1}{2}(0)^3$$
$$2 = C + 1 - \tfrac{11}{8}$$
$$C = 2 - 1 + \tfrac{11}{8} = \tfrac{19}{8}$$

and the particular solution is

$$y_x = \tfrac{19}{8}(3)^x + 4^x - \tfrac{11}{8} - \tfrac{3}{2}x - \tfrac{3}{4}x^2 - \tfrac{1}{2}x^3$$

EXAMPLE 18.10

Solve

$$y_{x+1} - 8y_x = 5^x \cdot x^2 \qquad y_0 = 5$$

Note that $g(x) = B^x \cdot x^n = 5^x \cdot x^2$, and that $A = 8$. The general solution form is given by

$$y_x = CA^x + Y^* = C(8)^x + Y^*$$

To find Y^*, let $y_x = 5^x(A_0 + A_1x + A_2x^2)$. Substituting in the original equation,

$$5^{x+1}[A_0 + A_1(x + 1) + A_2(x + 1)^2] - 8[5^x(A_0 + A_1x + A_2x^2)] = 5^x \cdot x^2$$

$$5^{x+1}[A_0 + A_1x + A_1 + A_2(x^2 + 2x + 1)] - 8(A_05^x + A_1x5^x + A_2x^25^x) = 5^x \cdot x^2$$

$$5^{x+1}(A_0 + A_1x + A_1 + A_2x^2 + 2A_2x + A_2)$$
$$- 8A_05^x - 8A_1x5^x - 8A_2x^25^x = 5^x \cdot x^2$$

$$A_05^{x+1} + A_1x5^{x+1} + A_15^{x+1} + A_2x^25^{x+1} + 2A_2x5^{x+1} + A_25^{x+1}$$
$$- 8A_05^x - 8A_1x5^x - 8A_2x^25^x - x^25^x = 0$$

Grouping the coefficients of x^0, x^1, and x^2 and factoring 5^x, we obtain:

$$x^2 5^x(A_2 5^1 - 8A_2 - 1) + x5^x(A_1 5^1 + 2A_2 5^1 - 8A_1)$$
$$+ 5^x(A_0 5^1 + A_1 5^1 + A_2 5^1 - 8A_0) = 0$$

Setting each coefficient equal to 0, we can solve for A_0, A_1, and A_2.

$$5A_2 - 8A_2 - 1 = 0$$
$$-3A_2 = 1$$
$$A_2 = -\tfrac{1}{3}$$
$$5A_1 + 2 \cdot 5A_2 - 8A_1 = 0$$
$$-3A_1 + 10(-\tfrac{1}{3}) = 0$$
$$-3A_1 = \tfrac{10}{3}$$
$$A_1 = -\tfrac{10}{9}$$
$$5A_0 + 5A_1 + 5A_2 - 8A_0 = 0$$
$$-3A_0 + 5(-\tfrac{10}{9}) + 5(-\tfrac{1}{3}) = 0$$
$$-3A_0 = \tfrac{50}{9} + \tfrac{5}{3} = \tfrac{65}{9}$$
$$A_0 = -\tfrac{65}{27}$$

Thus $Y^* = 5^x(-\tfrac{65}{27} - \tfrac{10}{9}x - \tfrac{1}{3}x^2)$ and the general solution to the problem is

$$y_x = C(8)^x + 5^x(-\tfrac{65}{27} - \tfrac{10}{9}x - \tfrac{1}{3}x^2)$$

Since $y = 5$,

$$5 = C(8)^0 + 5^0[-\tfrac{65}{27} - \tfrac{10}{9}(0) - \tfrac{1}{3}(0)^2]$$
$$5 = C - \tfrac{65}{27}$$
$$C = 5 + \tfrac{65}{27} = \tfrac{200}{27}$$

The particular solution, then, is

$$y_x = \tfrac{200}{27}(8)^x + 5^x(-\tfrac{65}{27} - \tfrac{10}{9}x - \tfrac{1}{3}x^2)$$

HOMOGENEOUS SECOND-ORDER LINEAR DIFFERENCE EQUATIONS WITH CONSTANT COEFFICIENTS

Homogeneous second-order linear difference equations with constant coefficients are of the general form

$$y_{x+2} + A_1 y_{x+1} + A_2 y_x = 0$$

where A_1 and A_2 are constants. For solving equations in this form, we define two constants B_1 and B_2 as

$$B_1 = \frac{-A_1 + \sqrt{A_1^2 - 4A_2}}{2}$$

$$B = \frac{-A_1 - \sqrt{A_1^2 - 4A_2}}{2}$$

The solution depends on the form of B_1 and B_2, specifically on whether they can be classified as

1 real, distinct, and unequal
2 equal
3 numbers of the form $A + bi$, where $i = \sqrt{-1}$

The particular solution for second-order linear difference equations requires the knowledge of the y value for two consecutive x values. The general solution form includes two arbitrary constants. With the two consecutive y values, two equations can be set up and solved simultaneously to find the values of the two constants.

Case 1: B_1 and B_2 are real and distinct

When B_1 and B_2 are real and distinct, i.e., do not include $\sqrt{-1}$ as a part of the number, the solution is

$$y_x = C_1 B_1{}^x + C_2 B_2{}^x \qquad B_1 \neq B_2$$

Case 2: B_1 and B_2 are real, distinct, and equal

The solution form when B_1 and B_2 are equal is

$$y_x = C_1 B^x + C_2 x B^x$$

Case 3: B_1 and B_2 are in the form $A + bi$

If, in solving for B_1 and B_2, the number within the square root turns out to be negative, the form of B_1 and B_2 is said to be complex since the square root of a negative number is imaginary.

Let us define

$$B_1 = a + bi \qquad i = \sqrt{-1}$$
$$B_2 = a - bi \qquad i = \sqrt{-1}$$

Also, let us define $c = \sqrt{a^2 + b^2}$, and $\theta = \tan^{-1} a/b$. The general solution will be:

$$y_x = c^x(k_1 \cos \theta x + k_2 \sin \theta x)$$

where k_1 and k_2 are arbitrary constants.

EXAMPLE 18.11

Solve

$$y_{x+2} - 5y_{x+1} + 6y_x = 0 \qquad y_0 = 2, \text{ and}$$
$$y_1 = 5$$

Note that this equation is in the form

$$y_{x+2} + A_1 y_{x+1} + A_2 y_x = 0$$

where $A_1 = -5$ and $A_2 = 6$.

$$B_1 = \frac{-(-5) + \sqrt{(-5)^2 - 4(6)}}{2} = \frac{5 + \sqrt{25 - 24}}{2}$$

$$= \frac{5 + \sqrt{1}}{2} = \frac{5 + 1}{2} = 3$$

$$B_2 = \frac{-(-5) - \sqrt{(-5)^2 - 4(6)}}{2} = \frac{5 - \sqrt{25 - 24}}{2}$$

$$= \frac{5 - \sqrt{1}}{2} = \frac{5 - 1}{2} = 2$$

Thus, B_1 and B_2 are real and unequal.   The solution form then is

$$y_x = C_1 3^x + C_2 2^x$$

Since $y_0 = 2$,

$$2 = C_1(3)^0 + C_2(2)^0$$
$$2 = C_1 + C_2$$

and since $y_1 = 5$,

$$5 = C_1(3)^1 + C_2(2)^1$$
$$5 = 3C_1 + 2C_2$$

Using the Cramer method for solving for C_1 and C_2, let

$$\mathbf{A} = \begin{pmatrix} 1 & 1 \\ 3 & 2 \end{pmatrix} \quad \text{and} \quad \mathbf{b} = \begin{pmatrix} 2 \\ 5 \end{pmatrix}$$

Then

$$|A| = \begin{vmatrix} 1 & 1 \\ 3 & 2 \end{vmatrix} = 2 - 3 = -1$$

and

$$C_1 = \frac{\begin{vmatrix} 2 & 1 \\ 5 & 2 \end{vmatrix}}{-1} = \frac{4 - 5}{-1} = 1$$

and

$$C_2 = \frac{\begin{vmatrix} 1 & 2 \\ 3 & 5 \end{vmatrix}}{-1} = \frac{5 - 6}{-1} = 1$$

and the particular solution is

$$y_x = 3^x + 2^x$$

EXAMPLE 18.12

Solve

$$y_{x+2} + 16y_{x+1} + 100y_x = 0 \qquad \begin{aligned} y_0 &= 2 \text{ and} \\ y_1 &= 12 \end{aligned}$$

Note that this equation is in homogeneous form with $A_1 = 16$ and $A_2 = 100$. Solving for B_1 and B_2, we find that

$$B = \frac{-16 + \sqrt{(16)^2 - 4(100)}}{2} = -8 + \frac{\sqrt{256 - 400}}{2}$$

$$= -8 + \frac{\sqrt{-144}}{2} = -8 + \frac{12\sqrt{-1}}{2} = -8 + 6i$$

$$B_2 = \frac{-16 - \sqrt{(16)^2 - 4(100)}}{2} = -8 - \frac{\sqrt{-144}}{2}$$

$$= -8 - \frac{12\sqrt{-1}}{2} = -8 - 6i$$

Since B_1 and B_2 are complex numbers of the form $a \pm bi$, we note that $a = -8$ and $b = 6$.

Then,

$$C = \sqrt{(-8)^2 + (6)^2} = \sqrt{64 + 36} = \sqrt{100} = 10$$

and

$$\theta = \tan^{-1} - \tfrac{8}{6} = \tan^{-1} - 1.3333$$

This is equivalent to saying $\tan \theta = -1.3333$. In the table we note that

$$\tan \theta = 1.3333$$

when $\theta = 53°$. Since $\tan \theta = -1.333$, $\theta = 180° - 53° = 127°$.† The general solution, then, is

$$y_x = 10^x(k_1 \cos 127°x + k_2 \sin 127°x)$$

where k_1 and k_2 are arbitrary constants.

Since $y_0 = 2$,

$$2 = 10°[k_1 \cos 127°(0) + k_2 \sin 127°(0)]$$
$$2 = 1[k_1 \cos 0 + k_2 \sin 0]$$
$$2 = k_1(1) + k_2(0)$$
$$2 = k_1$$

and, since $y_1 = 12$,

$$12 = 10^1[k_1 \cos 127°(1) + k_2 \sin 127°(1)]$$
$$12 = 10[k_1 \cos 127° + k_2 \sin 127°]$$

Since

$$\cos 127° = -\cos 180° - 127° = -\cos 53°$$

and

$$\sin 127° = \sin 180° - 127° = \sin 53°$$
$$12 = 10(-k_1 \cos 53° + k_2 \sin 53°)$$
$$12 = 10[-k_1(.60) + k_2(.80)]$$
$$12 = -6k_1 + 8k_2$$

Since $k_1 = 2$,

$$12 = -6(2) + 8k_2$$
$$12 = -12 + 8k_2$$
$$24 = 8k_2$$
$$k_2 = 3$$

† The tangent is positive in the first quadrant (0°–90°) and negative in the second (91°–180°). To find θ when $\tan \theta$ is negative find the positive θ and subtract from 180°.

The particular solution, then, is

$$y_x = 10^x(2 \cos 127°x + 3 \sin 127°x)$$

This might be more conveniently put into radians. Since $127° = 2.217$ radians,

$$y_x = 10^x(2 \cos 2.217x + 3 \sin 2.217x)$$

would also be the solution.

NONHOMOGENEOUS SECOND-ORDER LINEAR DIFFERENCE EQUATIONS WITH CONSTANT COEFFICIENTS

Nonhomogeneous second-order linear difference equations with constant coefficients are of the general form

$$y_{x+2} + A_1y_{x+1} + A_2y_x = g(x)$$

where A_1 and A_2 are constants. The method of handling is almost identical to the method for handling nonhomogeneous first-order constant coefficient equations. If B_1 and B_2 are real and unequal, the solution will be

$$y_x = C_1B_1{}^x + C_2B_2{}^x + Y^*$$

If B_1 and B_2 are real and equal, the solution will be

$$y_x = C_1B^x + C_2xB^x + Y^*$$

and if B_1 and B_2 are complex numbers, the solution will be

$$y_x = C^x(C_1 \cos \theta x + C_2 \sin \theta x) + Y^*$$

The computation of Y^* depends upon the form of $g(x)$.

Case 1: $g(x) = B^x$

If the original equation is

$$y_{x+2} + A_1y_{x+1} + A_2y_x = B^x$$

to find Y^* we substitute in the original equation: $y_x = kB^x$, unless CB^x is already in the homogeneous solution. If CB^x is in the homogeneous solution, substitute $y_x = kxB^x$ in the original equation. If CxB^x is also in the homogeneous solution, substitute $y_x = kx^2B^x$. In any of the three mentioned situations the value of k will be found, and $Y^* = kB^x$ or kxB^x or kx^2B^x according to which substitution was necessary.

EXAMPLE 18.13

Solve

$$y_{x+2} - 8y_{x+1} + 15y_x = 4^x \qquad \begin{array}{l} y_0 = 3 \\ y_1 = 8 \end{array}$$

The homogeneous solution is found by determining B_1 and B_2.

$$B_1 = \frac{-(-8) + \sqrt{(-8)^2 - 4(15)}}{2} = \frac{8 + \sqrt{64 - 60}}{2}$$

$$= 4 + \frac{\sqrt{4}}{2} = 4 + \frac{2}{2} = 5$$

$$B_2 = \frac{-(-8) - \sqrt{(-8)^2 - 4(15)}}{2} = \frac{8 - \sqrt{64 - 60}}{2}$$

$$= 4 - \frac{\sqrt{4}}{2} = 4 - \frac{2}{2} = 3$$

The solution form is

$$y_x = C_1 5^x + C_2 3^x + Y^*$$

To find Y^* substitute

$$y_x = k4^x$$

in the original equation.   Thus

$$k4^{x+2} - 8k4^{x+1} + 15k4^x = 4^x$$

Factoring out a 4^x on the left side gives

$$4^x(k4^2 - 8k4^1 + 15k) = 4^x$$
$$4^x(16k - 32k + 15k) = 4^x$$
$$4^x(-k) = 4^x$$

Dividing through by 4^x gives

$$-k = 1$$
$$k = -1$$

Thus $Y^* = -(4)^x$, and the general solution will be

$$y_x = C_1 5^x + C_2 3^x - 4^x$$

Since $y_0 = 3$,

$$3 = C_1 5^0 + C_2 3^0 - 4^0$$
$$3 = C_1 + C_2 - 1$$
$$4 = C_1 + C_2$$

and since $y_1 = 8$

$$8 = C_1 5^1 + C_2 3^1 = 4^1$$
$$12 = 5C_1 + 3C_2$$

Using the Cramer method and solving for C_1 and C_2 gives

$$A = \begin{pmatrix} 1 & 1 \\ 5 & 3 \end{pmatrix} \qquad b = \begin{pmatrix} 8 \\ 12 \end{pmatrix}$$

$$|A| = \begin{vmatrix} 1 & 1 \\ 5 & 3 \end{vmatrix} = 3 - 5 = -2$$

$$C_1 = \frac{\begin{vmatrix} 8 & 1 \\ 12 & 3 \end{vmatrix}}{-2} = \frac{24 - 12}{-2} = \frac{+12}{-2} = -6$$

$$C_2 = \frac{\begin{vmatrix} 1 & 8 \\ 5 & 12 \end{vmatrix}}{-2} = \frac{12 - 40}{-2} = \frac{-28}{-2} = +14$$

The particular solution, then, is

$$y_x = -6(5^x) + 14(3^x) - 4^x$$

EXAMPLE 18.14

Solve

$$y_{x+2} - 2y_{x+1} - 8y_x = 4^x \qquad \begin{array}{l} y_0 = 5 \\ y_1 = 2 \end{array}$$

First solving for B_1 and B_2, we get

$$B_1 = \frac{-(-2) + \sqrt{(-2)^2 - 4(-8)}}{2} = \frac{2 + \sqrt{4 + 32}}{2}$$

$$= \frac{2 + \sqrt{36}}{2} = \frac{2 + 6}{2} = 4$$

$$B_2 = \frac{-(-2) - \sqrt{(-2)^2 - 4(-8)}}{2} = \frac{2 - \sqrt{4 + 32}}{2}$$

$$= \frac{2 - \sqrt{36}}{2} = \frac{2 - 6}{2} = -2$$

The solution form, then, is $y_x = C_1 4^x + C_2(-2)^x + Y^*$. We cannot let $y_x = k4^x$ since $C_1 4^x$ is already in the homogeneous solution, so to find Y^*, let $y_x = kx4^x$. Then

$$k(x + 2)4^{x+2} - 2[k(x + 1)4^{x+1}] - 8(kx4^x) = 4^x$$

and

$$(kx + 2k)4^{x+2} - (2kx + 2k)4^{x+1} - 8kx4^x = 4^x$$

Factoring 4^x on the left side of the equation gives

$$4^x[(kx + 2k)4^2 - (2kx + 2k)4^1 - 8kx] = 4^x$$
$$4^x(16kx + 32k - 8kx - 8k - 8kx) = 4^x$$
$$4^x(24k) = 4^x$$

Dividing through by 4^x we find that

$$24k = 1$$
$$k = \tfrac{1}{24}$$

so, $Y^* = \tfrac{1}{24}x4^x$, and the general solution is

$$y_x = C_1 4^x + C_2(-2)^x + \tfrac{1}{24}x4^x$$

Since $y_0 = 5$,

$$5 = C_1 4^0 + C_2(-2)^0 + \tfrac{1}{24}(0)4^0$$
$$5 = C_1 + C_2$$

and since $y_1 = 2$

$$2 = C_1 4^1 + C_2(-2)^1 + \tfrac{1}{24}(1)4^1$$
$$2 = 4C_1 - 2C_2 + \tfrac{1}{24}(4)$$
$$2 - \tfrac{1}{6} = 4C_1 - 2C_2$$
$$\tfrac{11}{6} = 4C_1 - 2C_2$$
$$1.83 = 4C_1 - 2C_2$$

Using the Cramer method,

$$A = \begin{pmatrix} 1 & 1 \\ 4 & -2 \end{pmatrix} \qquad b = \begin{pmatrix} 5 \\ 1.83 \end{pmatrix}$$

$$|A| = \begin{vmatrix} 1 & 1 \\ 4 & -2 \end{vmatrix} = -2 - 4 = -6$$

$$C_1 = \frac{\begin{vmatrix} 5 & 1 \\ 1.83 & -2 \end{vmatrix}}{-6} = \frac{-10 - 1.83}{-6} = \frac{-11.83}{-6} = 1.97$$

$$C_2 = \frac{\begin{vmatrix} 1 & 5 \\ 4 & 1.83 \end{vmatrix}}{-6} = \frac{1.83 - 20}{-6} = \frac{-18.17}{-6} = 3.03$$

The particular solution, then, is

$$y_x = 1.97(4)^x + 3.03(-2)^x + \tfrac{1}{24}x(4)^x$$

EXAMPLE 18.15

Solve

$$y_{x+2} - 6y_{x+1} + 9y_x = 3^x \qquad \begin{aligned} y_0 &= 5 \\ y_1 &= 10 \end{aligned}$$

Solving for B_1 and B_2, we obtain

$$B_1 = \frac{-(-6) + \sqrt{(-6)^2 - 4(9)}}{2} = \frac{6 + \sqrt{36 - 36}}{2}$$

$$= \tfrac{6}{2} = 3$$

$$B_2 = \frac{-(-6) - \sqrt{(-6)^2 - 4(9)}}{2} = \frac{6 - \sqrt{36 - 36}}{2}$$

$$= \tfrac{6}{2} = 3$$

Since $B_1 = B_2 = 3$, the solution form will be

$$y_x = C_1 3^x + C_2 x 3^x + Y^*$$

To find Y^* we note that y_x cannot equal $k3^x$ or $kx3^x$ since terms of the homogeneous equations already include 3^x and $x3^x$. Therefore, let $y_x = kx^2 3^x$. Then, substituting, in the original equation,

$$[k(x + 2)^2 3^{x+2}] - 6[k(x + 1)^2 3^{x+1}] + 9(kx^2 3^x) = 3^x$$
$$[k(x^2 + 4x + 4)3^{x+2}] - 6[k(x^2 + 2x + 1)3^{x+1}] + 9kx^2 3^x = 3^x$$
$$(kx^2 + 4kx + 4k)3^{x+2} - (6kx^2 + 12kx + 6k)3^{x+1} + 9kx^2 3^x = 3^x$$

Factoring 3^x on the left side, gives

$$3^x[(kx^2 + 4kx + 4k)3^2 - (6kx^2 + 12kx + 6k)3^1 + 9kx^2] = 3^x$$
$$3^x(9kx^2 + 36kx + 36k - 18kx^2 - 36kx - 18k + 9kx^2) = 3^x$$
$$3^x(36k - 18k) = 3^x$$

Dividing through by 3^x gives

$$36k - 18k = 1$$
$$18k = 1$$
$$k = \tfrac{1}{18}$$

So, $Y^* = \frac{1}{18}x^2(3^x)$, and the general solution is

$$y_x = C_1 3^x + C_2 x 3^x + \frac{1}{18}x^2 3^x$$

Since $y_0 = 5$,

$$5 = C_1 3^0 + C_2(0)3^0 + \frac{1}{18}(0)^2 3^0$$
$$5 = C_1$$

and since $y_1 = 10$,

$$10 = C_1(3)^1 + C_2(1)3^1 + \frac{1}{18}(1)^2 3^1$$
$$10 = 3C_1 + 3C_2 + \frac{1}{6}$$
$$10 = 3(5) + 3C_2 + \frac{1}{6}$$
$$-\frac{31}{6} = 3C_2$$
$$-\frac{31}{18} = C_2$$

So, the particular solution is $y_x = 5(3)^x - \frac{31}{18}x(3)^x + \frac{1}{18}x^3(3)^x$.

Case 2: $g(x) = x^n$

This case is solved identically as in the first-order analogous situation.

EXAMPLE 18.16

Solve

$$y_{x+2} - 11y_{x+1} + 28y_x = x^2 \qquad \begin{matrix} y_0 = 3 \\ y_1 = 20 \end{matrix}$$

First solve for B_1 and B_2.

$$B_1 = \frac{-(-11) + \sqrt{(-11)^2 - 4(28)}}{2} = \frac{11 + \sqrt{121 - 112}}{2}$$

$$= \frac{11 + \sqrt{9}}{2} = \frac{11 + 3}{2} = 7$$

$$B_2 = \frac{-(-11) - \sqrt{(-11)^2 - 4(28)}}{2} = \frac{11 - \sqrt{121 - 112}}{2}$$

$$= \frac{11 - \sqrt{9}}{2} = \frac{11 - 3}{2} = 4$$

The solution form, then, is

$$y_x = C_1 7^x + C_2 4^x + Y^*$$

To find Y^*, let $y_x = A_0 + A_1 x + A_2 x^2$. Then, substituting in the original equation

$$[A_0 + A_1(x + 2) + A_2(x + 2)^2] - 11[A_0 + A_1(x + 1) + A_2(x + 1)^2]$$
$$+ 28(A_0 + A_1 x + A_2 x^2) = x^2$$

$$[A_0 + A_1(x + 2) + A_2(x^2 + 4x + 4)] - 11[A_0 + A_1(x + 1) + A_2(x^2 + 2x + 1)]$$
$$+ 28(A_0 + A_1 x + A_2 x^2) = x$$

$$A_0 + A_1 x + 2A_1 + A_2 x^2 + 4A_2 x + 4A_2 - 11A_0 - 11A_1 x - 11A_1 - 11A_2 x^2$$
$$- 22A_2 x - 11A_2 + 28A_0 + 28A_1 x + 28A_2 x^2 - x^2 = 0$$

And, collecting terms as coefficients of powers of x,

$$x^2(A_2 - 11A_2 + 28A_2 - 1) + x(A_1 + 4A_2 - 11A_1 - 22A_2 + 28A_1)$$
$$+ (A_0 + 2A_1 + 4A_2 - 11A_1 - 11A_2 + 28A_0) = 0$$

Then, setting each coefficient equal to 0, we can solve for A_0, A_1, and A_2. Thus:

$$A_2 - 11A_2 + 28A_2 - 1 = 0$$
$$18A_2 = 1$$
$$A_2 = \tfrac{1}{18}$$
$$A_1 + 4A_2 - 11A_1 - 22A_2 + 28A_1 = 0$$
$$18A_1 = 18A_2$$
$$18A_1 = 18(\tfrac{1}{18}) = 1$$
$$A_1 = \tfrac{1}{18}$$
$$A_0 + 2A_1 + 4A_2 - 11A_1 - 11A_2 + 28A_0 = 0$$
$$29A_0 = 9A_1 + 7A_2$$
$$29A_0 = 9(\tfrac{1}{18}) + 7(\tfrac{1}{18}) = \tfrac{16}{18}$$
$$A_0 = \tfrac{16}{522} = \tfrac{8}{261}$$
$$Y^* = \tfrac{8}{261} + \tfrac{1}{18}x + \tfrac{1}{18}x^2$$

And the general solution is

$$y_x = C_1 7^x + C_2 4^x + \tfrac{8}{261} + \tfrac{1}{18}x + \tfrac{1}{18}x^2$$

Since $y_0 = 3$,

$$3 = C_1 7^0 + C_2 4^0 + \tfrac{8}{261} + \tfrac{1}{18}(0) + \tfrac{1}{18}(0)^2$$
$$3 = C_1 + C_2 + \tfrac{8}{261}$$
$$C_1 + C_2 = \tfrac{775}{261} = 2.97$$

Since $y_1 = 20$,

$$20 = C_1 7^1 + C_2 4^1 + \tfrac{8}{261} + \tfrac{1}{18}(1) + \tfrac{1}{18}(1)^2$$
$$20 = 7C_1 + 4C_2 + \tfrac{8}{261} + \tfrac{1}{18} + \tfrac{1}{18}$$
$$7C_1 + 4C_2 = 20 - \tfrac{8}{261} - \tfrac{1}{18} - \tfrac{1}{18}$$
$$7C_1 + 4C_2 = \frac{10{,}440}{522} - \frac{16}{522} - \frac{29}{522} - \frac{29}{522}$$
$$7C_1 + 4C_2 = \frac{10{,}366}{522} = 19.86$$

Using the Cramer method,

$$\mathbf{A} = \begin{pmatrix} 1 & 1 \\ 7 & 4 \end{pmatrix} \qquad \mathbf{b} = \begin{pmatrix} 2.97 \\ 19.86 \end{pmatrix}$$

$$|A| = \begin{vmatrix} 1 & 1 \\ 7 & 4 \end{vmatrix} = 4 - 7 = -3$$

$$C = \frac{\begin{vmatrix} 2.97 & 1 \\ 19.86 & 4 \end{vmatrix}}{-3} = \frac{11.88 - 19.86}{-3} = \frac{-7.98}{-3} = 2.66$$

$$C_2 = \frac{\begin{vmatrix} 1 & 2.97 \\ 7 & 19.86 \end{vmatrix}}{-3} = \frac{19.86 - 20.79}{-3} = \frac{-.93}{-3} = .31$$

Thus, the particular solution is

$$y_x = 2.66(7^x) + .31(4)^x + \tfrac{8}{261} + \tfrac{1}{18}x + \tfrac{1}{18}x^2$$

Case 3: $g(x) = B^x + x^n$

In the case where $g(x) = B^x + x^n$, Y^* is found by substituting

$$y_x = A_0 + A_1x + A_2x^2 + \cdots + A_nx^n + kB^x$$

in the original equation, unless the homogeneous equation has a constant term. If one of the B's for the homogeneous equation is 1, meaning that one term of the homogeneous solution is $C_1(1)^x = C_1$ (or C_2), then substitute

$$y_x = A_0x + A_1x^2 + A_2x^3 + \cdots + A_nx^{n+1} + kB^x$$

Also, if the homogeneous solution contains a CB^x, change the last term of the y_x substitution to kxB^x or kx^2B^x as required.

EXAMPLE 18.17

Solve

$$y_{x+2} - 2y_{x+1} - 15y_x = 5^x + 3x \qquad \begin{aligned} y_0 &= 2 \\ y_1 &= 4 \end{aligned}$$

First, solving for B_1 and B_2

$$B_1 = \frac{-(-2) + \sqrt{(-2)^2 - 4(-15)}}{2} = \frac{+2 + \sqrt{4 + 60}}{2} = \frac{2 + \sqrt{64}}{2} = \frac{2 + 8}{2} = 5$$

$$B_2 = \frac{-(-2) - \sqrt{(-2)^2 - 4(-15)}}{2} = \frac{2 - \sqrt{4 + 60}}{2} = \frac{2 - \sqrt{64}}{2} = \frac{2 - 8}{2} = -3$$

The solution form then, is $y_x = C_1 5^x + C_2(-3)^x + Y^*$. Since there is a 5^x term in the homogeneous solution, let $y_x = A_0 + A_1x + kx5^x$. Substituting in the original equation gives

$$[A_0 + A_1(x + 2) + k(x + 2)5^{x+2}] - 2[A_0 + A_1(x + 1) + k(x + 1)5^{x+1}]$$
$$- 15(A_0 + A_1x + kx5^x) = 5^x + 3x$$

$$A_0 + A_1x + 2A_1 + (kx + 2k)5^{x+2} - 2A_0 - 2A_1x - 2A_1 + (-2kx - 2k)5^{x+1}$$
$$- 15A_0 - 15A_1x - 15kx5^x - 5^x - 3x = 0$$

$$-16A_0 - 16A_1x - 3x + 5^x[(kx + 2k)5^2 - (2kx + 2k)5 - 15kx - 1] = 0$$

$$-16A_0 - 16A_1x - 3x + 5^x(25kx + 50k - 10kx - 10k - 15kx - 1) = 0$$

$$-16A_0 - 16A_1x - 3x + 5^x(40k - 1) = 0$$

$$(-16A_0) - x(16A_1 - 3) + 5^x(40k - 1) = 0$$

Setting each coefficient equal to 0 gives

$$-16A_0 = 0$$
$$A_0 = 0$$

$$16A_1 - 3 = 0$$
$$A_1 = \tfrac{3}{16}$$

$$40k - 1 = 0$$
$$k = \tfrac{1}{40}$$

$$Y^* = \tfrac{3}{16}x + \tfrac{1}{40}(5^x)$$
$$y_x = C_1 5^x + C_2(-3)^x + \tfrac{3}{16}x + \tfrac{1}{40}(5^x)$$

Since $y_0 = 2$,

$$2 = C_1 5^0 + C_2(-3)^0 + \tfrac{3}{16}(0) + \tfrac{1}{40}(5^0)$$
$$2 = C_1 + C_2 + \tfrac{1}{40}$$
$$C_1 + C_2 = \tfrac{79}{40} = 1.975$$

And since $y_1 = 4$,

$$4 = C_1 5^1 + C_2(-3)^1 + \tfrac{3}{16}(1) + \tfrac{1}{40}(5^1)$$
$$4 = 5C_1 - 3C_2 + \tfrac{3}{16} + \tfrac{5}{40}$$
$$5C_1 - 3C_2 = \tfrac{320}{80} - \tfrac{15}{80} - \tfrac{10}{80} = \tfrac{295}{80} = 3.688$$

Using the Cramer method,

$$\mathbf{A} = \begin{pmatrix} 1 & 1 \\ 5 & -3 \end{pmatrix} \qquad \mathbf{b} = \begin{pmatrix} 1.975 \\ 3.688 \end{pmatrix}$$

$$|A| = \begin{vmatrix} 1 & 1 \\ 5 & -3 \end{vmatrix} = -3 - 5 = -8$$

$$C_1 = \frac{\begin{vmatrix} 1.975 & 1 \\ 3.688 & -3 \end{vmatrix}}{-8} = \frac{-5.925 - 3.688}{-8} = \frac{-9.613}{-8} = 1.2$$

$$C_2 = \frac{\begin{vmatrix} 1 & 1.975 \\ 5 & 3.688 \end{vmatrix}}{-8} = \frac{3.688 - 9.875}{-8} = \frac{-6.187}{-8} = .77$$

So, the particular solution is,

$$y_x = 1.2(5^x) + .77(-3^x) + \tfrac{3}{16}x + \tfrac{1}{40}(5^x)$$

EXAMPLE 18.18

Solve

$$y_{x+2} + 2y_{x+1} - 3y_x = x^2 + 4^x \qquad \begin{aligned} y_0 &= 1 \\ y_1 &= 5 \end{aligned}$$

First, solving for B_1 and B_2, we obtain

$$B_1 = \frac{-2 + \sqrt{(2)^2 - 4(-3)}}{2} = \frac{-2 + \sqrt{4 + 12}}{2} = \frac{-2 + \sqrt{16}}{2} = \frac{-2 + 4}{2} = 1$$

$$B_2 = \frac{-2 - \sqrt{(2)^2 - 4(-3)}}{2} = \frac{-2 - \sqrt{4 + 12}}{2} = \frac{-2 - \sqrt{16}}{2} = \frac{-2 - 4}{2} = -3$$

The solution form, then, is $y_x = C_1 + C_2(-3)^x + Y^*$. Since the homogeneous equation includes a constant term, let $y_x = A_0x + A_1x^2 + A_2x^3 + k4^x$. Substituting in the original equation,

$$[A_0(x+2) + A_1(x+2)^2 + A_2(x+2)^3 + k4^{x+2}] + 2[A_0(x+1) + A_1(x+1)^2$$
$$+ A_2(x+1)^3 + k4^{x+1}] - 3(A_0x + A_1x^2 + A_2x^3 + k4^x) = x^2 + 4x$$

$$A_0(x+2) + A_1(x^2 + 2x + 4) + A_2(x^3 + 4x^2 + 8x + 8) + k4^{x+2}$$
$$+ 2[A_0(x+1) + A_1(x^2 + 2x + 1) + A_2(x^3 + 3x^2 + 3x + 1) + k4^{x+1}]$$
$$-3(A_0x + A_1x^2 + A_2x^3) + k4^x = x^2 + 4x$$

$$A_0x + 2A_0 + A_1x^2 + 2A_1x + 4A_1 + A_2x^3 + 4A_2x^2 + 8A_2x + 8A_2$$
$$+ k4^{x+2} + 2A_0x + 2A_0 + 2A_1x^2 + 4A_1x + 2A_1 + 2A_2x^3 + 6A_2x^2 + 6A_2x$$
$$+ 2A_2 + 2k4^{x+1} - 3A_0x - 3A_1x^2 - 3A_2x^3 - 3k4^x - x^2 - 4^x = 0$$

$$x^2(A_1 + 4A_2 + 2A_1 + 6A_2 - 3A_1 - 1) + x(A_0 + 2A_1 + 8A_2 + 2A_0 + 4A_1$$
$$+ 6A_2 - 3A_0) + (2A_0 + 4A_1 + 8A_2 + 2A_0 + 2A_1 + 2A_2)$$
$$+ 4(k4^2 + 2k4^1 - 3k - 1) = 0$$

Setting the coefficients of x equal to 0, we get

$$A_1 + 4A_2 + 2A_1 + 6A_2 - 3A_1 - 1 = 0$$
$$10A_2 = +1$$
$$A_2 = \tfrac{1}{10}$$

$$A_0 + 2A_1 + 8A_2 + 2A_0 + 4A_1 + 6A_2 - 3A_0 = 0$$
$$6A_1 + 14A_2 = 0$$
$$6A_1 = -14(\tfrac{1}{10})$$
$$A_1 = -\tfrac{14}{60} = -\tfrac{7}{30}$$

$$2A_0 + 4A_1 + 8A_2 + 2A_0 + 2A_1 + 2A_2 = 0$$
$$4A_0 = -6A_1 - 10A_2$$
$$4A_0 = -6(\tfrac{1}{10}) - 10(-\tfrac{7}{30}) = -\tfrac{6}{10} + \tfrac{70}{30} = \tfrac{52}{30} = \tfrac{26}{15}$$
$$A_0 = \tfrac{26}{60} = \tfrac{13}{30}$$

$$k4^2 + 2k4^1 - 3k - 1 = 0$$
$$16k + 8k - 3k - 1 = 0$$
$$21k = 1$$
$$k = \tfrac{1}{21}$$

$$Y^* = \tfrac{13}{30}x - \tfrac{7}{30}x^2 + \tfrac{1}{10}x^3 + \tfrac{1}{21}(4)^x$$
$$y_x = C_1 + C_2(-3)^x + \tfrac{13}{30}x - \tfrac{7}{30}x^2 + \tfrac{1}{10}x^3 + \tfrac{1}{21}(4)^x$$

Since $y_0 = 1$,

$$1 = C_1 + C_2(-3)^0 + \tfrac{13}{30}(0) - \tfrac{7}{30}(0)^2 + \tfrac{1}{10}(0)^3 + \tfrac{1}{4}(4)^0$$
$$1 = C_1 + C_2 + \tfrac{1}{21}$$
$$C_1 + C_2 = 1 - \tfrac{1}{21} = \tfrac{20}{21} = .95$$

And since $y_1 = 5$,

$$5 = C_1 + C_2(-3)^1 + \tfrac{13}{30}(1) - \tfrac{7}{30}(1)^2 + \tfrac{1}{10}(1)^3 + \tfrac{1}{21}(4)^1$$
$$5 = C_1 - 3C_2 + \tfrac{13}{30} - \tfrac{7}{30} = \tfrac{1}{10} + \tfrac{4}{21}$$
$$C_1 - 3C_2 = 5 - \tfrac{13}{30} + \tfrac{7}{30} - \tfrac{1}{10} - \tfrac{4}{21} = \tfrac{1050}{210} - \tfrac{91}{210} + \tfrac{49}{210} - \tfrac{21}{210} - \tfrac{40}{210}$$
$$C_1 - 3C_2 = \tfrac{947}{210} = 4.51$$

Using the Cramer method,

$$\mathbf{A} = \begin{pmatrix} 1 & 1 \\ 1 & -3 \end{pmatrix} \qquad \mathbf{b} = \begin{pmatrix} .95 \\ 4.51 \end{pmatrix}$$

$$|A| = \begin{vmatrix} 1 & 1 \\ 1 & -3 \end{vmatrix} = -3 - 1 = -4$$

$$C_1 = \frac{\begin{vmatrix} .95 & 1 \\ 4.51 & -3 \end{vmatrix}}{-4} = \frac{-2.85 - 4.51}{-4} = \frac{-7.36}{-4} = 1.84$$

$$C_2 = \frac{\begin{vmatrix} 1 & .95 \\ 1 & 4.51 \end{vmatrix}}{-4} = \frac{4.51 - .95}{-4} = \frac{3.56}{-4} = -.89$$

The particular solution, then, is

$$y_x = 1.84 - .89(-3)^x + \tfrac{13}{30}x - \tfrac{7}{30}x^2 + \tfrac{1}{10}x^3 + \tfrac{1}{4}(4)^x$$

Case 4: $g(x) = B^x \cdot x^n$

The method used when the equation is in the form

$$y_{x+2} + A_1 y_{x+1} + A_2 y_x = B^x \cdot x^n$$

is identical with the analogous first-order method. Let

$$y_x = B^x(A_0 + A_1 x + A_2 x^2 + \cdots + A_n x^n)$$

and solve for A_0, A_1, A_2, $\ldots$, A_n in the original equation.

EXAMPLE 18.19

Solve

$$y_{x+2} + 4y_{x+1} - 32y_x = 8^x \cdot (x^2) \qquad y_0 = 5$$
$$y_1 = 6$$

First solve for B_1 and B_2.

$$B_1 = \frac{-4 + \sqrt{(4)^2 - 4(-32)}}{2} = \frac{-4 + \sqrt{16 + 128}}{2} = \frac{-4 + \sqrt{144}}{2}$$

$$= \frac{-4 + 12}{2} = \frac{8}{2} = 4$$

$$B_2 = \frac{-4 - \sqrt{(4)^2 - 4(-32)}}{2} = \frac{-4 - \sqrt{16 + 128}}{2} = \frac{-4 - \sqrt{144}}{2}$$

$$= \frac{-4 - 12}{2} = \frac{-16}{2} = -8$$

The solution form, then, is $y_x = C_1 4^x + C_2(-8)^x + Y^*$. To find Y^* let

$$y_x = 8^x(A_0 + A_1 x + A_2 x^2)$$

Substituting in the original equation, we get

$$8^{x+2}[A_0 + A_1(x + 2) + A_2(x + 2)^2] + 4(8^{x+1})[A_0 + A_1(x + 1) + A_2(x + 1)^2]$$
$$- 32(8^x)(A_0 + A_1x + A_2x^2) = 8^x \cdot x^2$$

$$8^{x+2}[A_0 + A_1(x + 2) + A_2(x^2 + 4x + 4)] + 4(8^{x+1})[A_0 + A_1(x + 1)$$
$$+ A_2(x^2 + 2x + 1)] - 32(8^x)(A_0 + A_1x + A_2x^2) = 8^x \cdot x^2$$

$$8^{x+2}(A_0 + A_1x + 2A_1 + A_2x^2 + 4A_2x + 4A_2) + 8^{x+1}(4A_0 + 4A_1x + 4A_1$$
$$+ 4A_2x^2 + 8A_2x + 4A_2) - 8^x(32A_0 + 32A_1x + 32A_2x^2) = 8^x \cdot x^2$$

$$8^x[8^2(A_0 + A_1x + 2A_1 + A_2x^2 + 4A_2x + 4A_2) + 8(4A_0 + 4A_1x + 4A_1 + 4A_2x^2$$
$$+ 8A_2x + 4A_2) - (32A_0 + 32A_1x + 32A_2x^2)] = 8^x \cdot x^2$$

$$8^x(64A_0 + 64A_1x + 128A_1 + 64A_2x^2 + 256A_2x + 256A_2 + 32A_0 + 32A_1x$$
$$+ 32A_1 + 32A_2x^2 + 64A_2x + 32A_2 - 32A_0 - 32A_1x - 32A_2x^2) = 8^x \cdot x^2$$

$$8^x[x^2(64A_2 + 32A_2 - 32A_2) + x(64A_1 + 256A_2 + 32A_1 + 64A_2 - 32A_1)$$
$$+ (64A_0 + 128A_1 + 256A_2 + 32A_0 + 32A_1 + 32A_2 - 32A_0)] = 8^x \cdot x^2$$

$$8^x[x^2(64A_2) + x(64A_1 + 320A_2) + (64A_0 + 160A_1 + 288A_2)] = 8^x \cdot x^2$$

Dividing through by 8^x, we get

$$x^2(64A_2) + x(64A_1 + 320A_2) + (64A_0 + 160A_1 + 288A_2) = x^2$$
$$x^2(64A_2 - 1) + x(64A_1 + 320A_2) + (64A_0 + 160A_1 + 288A_2) = 0$$

Setting the coefficients equal to 0, we get

$$64A_2 - 1 = 0$$
$$64A_2 = 1$$
$$A_2 = \tfrac{1}{64}$$

$$64A_1 + 320A_2 = 0$$
$$64A_1 = -320A_2$$
$$64A_1 = -320(\tfrac{1}{64}) = -5$$
$$A_1 = -\tfrac{5}{64}$$

$$64A_0 + 160A_1 + 288A_2 = 0$$
$$64A_0 = -160A_1 = 288A_2$$
$$64A_0 = -160(-\tfrac{5}{64}) - 288(\tfrac{1}{64}) = \tfrac{800}{64} - \tfrac{288}{64} = \tfrac{512}{64} = 8$$
$$A_0 = \tfrac{8}{64} = \tfrac{1}{8}$$

$$Y^* = 8^x(\tfrac{1}{8} - \tfrac{5}{64}x + \tfrac{1}{64}x^2)$$

And the general solution is

$$y_x = C_1 4^x + C_2(-8)^x + 8^x(\tfrac{1}{8} - \tfrac{5}{64}x + \tfrac{1}{64}x^2)$$

Since $y_0 = 5$,

$$5 = C_1 4^0 + C_2(-8)^0 + 8^0[\tfrac{1}{8} - \tfrac{5}{64}(0) + \tfrac{1}{64}(0)^2]$$
$$5 = C_1 + C_2 + \tfrac{1}{8}$$
$$C_1 + C_2 = \tfrac{39}{8} = 4.88$$

And since $y_1 = 6$,

$$6 = C_1 4^1 + C_2(-8)^1 + 8^1[\tfrac{1}{8} - \tfrac{5}{64}(1) + \tfrac{1}{64}(1)^2]$$
$$6 = 4C_1 - 8C_2 + 1 - \tfrac{40}{64} + \tfrac{8}{64}$$
$$4C_1 - 8C_2 = 6 - 1 + \tfrac{32}{64} = 5\tfrac{1}{2} = 5.50$$

Using the Cramer method,

$$A = \begin{pmatrix} 1 & 1 \\ 4 & -8 \end{pmatrix} \qquad b = \begin{pmatrix} 4.88 \\ 5.50 \end{pmatrix}$$

$$|A| = \begin{vmatrix} 1 & 1 \\ 4 & -8 \end{vmatrix} = -8 - 4 = -12$$

$$C_1 = \frac{\begin{vmatrix} 4.88 & 1 \\ 5.50 & -8 \end{vmatrix}}{-12} = \frac{-39.04 - 5.50}{-12} = \frac{-44.54}{-12} = 3.71$$

$$C_2 = \frac{\begin{vmatrix} 1 & 4.88 \\ 4 & 5.50 \end{vmatrix}}{-12} = \frac{5.50 - 19.52}{-12} = \frac{-14.02}{-12} = 1.17$$

And the particular solution is

$$3.71(4^x) + 1.17(-8)^x + 8^x(\tfrac{1}{8} - \tfrac{5}{64}x + \tfrac{1}{64}x^2)$$

HIGHER-ORDER LINEAR DIFFERENCE EQUATIONS

Higher-order linear difference equations are solved in exactly the same manner as the second-order equations. Three consecutive y values are necessary for a particular solution.

EXAMPLE 18.20

Solve

$$y_{x+3} + 6y_{x+2} + 11y_{x+1} + 6y_x = 0 \qquad \begin{aligned} y_0 &= 2 \\ y_1 &= 5 \\ y_2 &= 9 \end{aligned}$$

Factoring $(x^3 + 6x^2 + 11x + 6)$, we find the three factors

$$(x + 1)(x + 2)(x + 3)$$

Therefore, $B_1 = -1$, $B_2 = -2$, and $B_3 = -3$, and the solution is

$$y_x = C_1(-1)^x + C_2(-2)^x + C_3(-3)^x$$

Since $y_0 = 2$,

$$2 = C_1(-1)^0 + C_2(-2)^0 + C_3(-3)^0$$
$$2 = C_1 + C_2 + C_3$$

and since $y_1 = 5$,

$$5 = C_1(-1)^1 + C_2(-2)^1 + C_3(-3)^1$$
$$5 = -C_1 - 2C_2 - 3C_3$$

and since $y_2 = 9$,

$$9 = C_1(-1)^2 + C_2(-2)^2 + C_3(-3)^2$$
$$9 = C_1 + 4C_2 + 9C_3$$

Using the Cramer method,

$$A = \begin{pmatrix} 1 & 1 & 1 \\ -1 & -2 & -3 \\ 1 & 4 & 9 \end{pmatrix} \qquad b = \begin{pmatrix} 2 \\ 5 \\ 9 \end{pmatrix}$$

$$|A| = \begin{vmatrix} 1 & 1 & 1 \\ -1 & -2 & -3 \\ 1 & 4 & 9 \end{vmatrix} = \begin{vmatrix} 1 & 1 & 1 \\ 0 & -1 & -2 \\ 0 & 3 & 8 \end{vmatrix} = 1 \begin{vmatrix} -1 & -2 \\ 3 & 8 \end{vmatrix}$$

$$= -8 - (-6) = -8 + 6 = -2$$

$$C_1 = \frac{\begin{vmatrix} 2 & 1 & 1 \\ 5 & -2 & -3 \\ 9 & 4 & 9 \end{vmatrix}}{-2} = \frac{\begin{vmatrix} 0 & 0 & 1 \\ 11 & 1 & -3 \\ -9 & -5 & 9 \end{vmatrix}}{-2} = 1 \frac{\begin{vmatrix} 11 & 1 \\ -9 & 5 \end{vmatrix}}{-2}$$

$$= \frac{-55 - (-9)}{-2} = \frac{-55 + 9}{-2} = \frac{-46}{-2} = 23$$

$$C_2 = \frac{\begin{vmatrix} 1 & 2 & 1 \\ -1 & 5 & -3 \\ 1 & 9 & 9 \end{vmatrix}}{-2} = \frac{\begin{vmatrix} 1 & 2 & 1 \\ 0 & 7 & -2 \\ 0 & 7 & 8 \end{vmatrix}}{-2} = 1 \frac{\begin{vmatrix} 7 & -2 \\ 7 & 8 \end{vmatrix}}{-2}$$

$$= \frac{56 - (-14)}{-2} = \frac{56 + 14}{-2} = \frac{70}{-2} = -35$$

$$C_3 = \frac{\begin{vmatrix} 1 & 1 & 2 \\ -1 & -2 & 5 \\ 1 & 4 & 9 \end{vmatrix}}{-2} = \frac{\begin{vmatrix} 1 & 1 & 2 \\ 0 & -1 & 7 \\ 0 & 3 & 7 \end{vmatrix}}{-2} = 1 \frac{\begin{vmatrix} -1 & 7 \\ 3 & 7 \end{vmatrix}}{-2} = \frac{-7 - 21}{-2} = \frac{-28}{-2} = 14$$

The particular solution, then, is

$$y_x = 23(-1)^x - 35(-2)^x + 14(-3)^x$$

APPENDIX A

TABLE OF INTEGRALS

1 $\displaystyle\int x^n dx = \frac{1}{n+1} x^n + 1 + C \qquad n \neq -1$

2 $\displaystyle\int \frac{1}{x} dx = \ln |x| + C$

3 $\displaystyle\int \frac{1}{x^2 - a^2} dx = \frac{1}{2a} \ln \left| \frac{x-a}{x+a} \right| + C$

4 $\displaystyle\int x^m (ax+b)^n \, dx = \frac{1}{a(m+n+1)}$
$$\left[x^m(ax+b)^{n+1} - mb \int x^{m-1}(ax+b)^n \, dx \right] \qquad m > 0$$
$$m + n + 1 \neq 0$$

5 $\displaystyle\int \frac{1}{(ax+b)(cx+d)} dx = \frac{1}{bc-ad} \ln \left| \frac{cx+d}{ax+b} \right| + C \qquad bc - ad \neq 0$

6 $\displaystyle\int \frac{1}{(ax+b)(cx+d)} dx = \frac{1}{bc-ad} \left(\frac{b}{a} \ln |ax+b| - \frac{d}{c} \ln |cx+d| \right) + C$
$$bc - ad \neq 0$$

7 $\displaystyle\int \frac{1}{(ax+b)^2(cx+d)} dx = \frac{1}{bc-ad} \left(\frac{1}{ax+b} + \frac{c}{bc-ad} \ln \left| \frac{cx+d}{ax+b} \right| \right) + C$
$$bc - ad \neq 0$$

8 $\displaystyle\int \frac{x}{(ax+b)^2(cx+d)} dx$
$$= -\frac{1}{bc-ad} \left[\frac{b}{a(ax+b)} + \frac{d}{bc-ad} \ln \left| \frac{cx+d}{ax+b} \right| \right] + C \qquad bc - ad \neq 0$$

9 $\displaystyle\int x \sqrt{ax+b} \, dx = \frac{2}{15a^2} (3ax - 2b)(ax+b)^{\frac{3}{2}} + C$

10 $\displaystyle\int x^n \sqrt{ax+b} \, dx$
$$= \frac{2}{a(2n+3)} \left[x^n(ax+b)^{\frac{3}{2}} - nb \int x^{n-1} \sqrt{ax+b} \, dx \right] \qquad n \neq -\frac{3}{2}$$

11 $\displaystyle\int \frac{x}{\sqrt{ax+b}}\,dx = \frac{2}{3a^2}\,(ax-2b)\,\sqrt{ax+b}+C$

12 $\displaystyle\int \frac{x^n}{\sqrt{ax+b}}\,dx = \frac{2}{a(2n+1)}\left(x^n ax+b - nb\int \frac{x^{n-1}}{\sqrt{ax+b}}\,dx\right)$

13 $\displaystyle\frac{x^n}{x\sqrt{ax+b}}\,dx = \frac{1}{\sqrt{b}}\ln\left|\frac{\sqrt{ax+b}-\sqrt{b}}{\sqrt{ax+b}+\sqrt{b}}\right| + C \qquad b>0$

14 $\displaystyle\int \frac{1}{x^n\sqrt{ax+b}}\,dx = -\frac{1}{b(n-1)}\frac{\sqrt{ax+b}}{x^{n-1}}$
$$-\frac{(2n-3)a}{(2n-2)b}\int \frac{1}{x^{n-1}\sqrt{ax+b}}\,dx \qquad n\neq 1$$

15 $\displaystyle\int \frac{\sqrt{ax+b}}{x}\,dx = 2\sqrt{ax+b}+b\int \frac{1}{x\sqrt{ax+b}}\,dx$

16 $\displaystyle\int \sqrt{x^2\pm a^2}\,dx = \frac{x}{2}\sqrt{x^2\pm a^2}\pm\frac{a^2}{2}\ln|x+\sqrt{x^2\pm a^2}| + C$

17 $\displaystyle\int \frac{1}{\sqrt{x^2\pm a^2}}\,dx = \ln|x+\sqrt{x^2 a^2}| + C$

18 $\displaystyle\int x^2\sqrt{x^2\pm a^2}\,dx = \frac{x}{8}(2x^2\pm a^2)\sqrt{x^2\pm a^2}-\frac{a^4}{8}\ln|x+\sqrt{x^3\pm a^2}| + C$

19 $\displaystyle\int \frac{x^2}{\sqrt{x^2\pm a^2}}\,dx = \frac{x}{2}\sqrt{x^2\pm a^2}\pm a^2\frac{a^2}{2}\ln|x+\sqrt{x^2\pm a^2}| + C$

20 $\displaystyle\int (x^2\pm a^2)^{\frac{3}{2}}\,dx = x(x^2\pm a^2)^{\frac{3}{2}}-3\int x^2\sqrt{x^2\pm a^2}\,dx$

21 $\displaystyle\int \frac{1}{(x^2\pm a^2)^{\frac{3}{2}}}\,dx = \frac{\pm x}{a^2\sqrt{x^2\pm a^2}} + C$

22 $\displaystyle\int \frac{x^2}{(x^2\pm a^2)^{\frac{3}{2}}}\,dx = -\frac{x}{\sqrt{x^2\pm a^2}} + \ln|x+\sqrt{x^2\pm a^2}| + C$

23 $\displaystyle\int \frac{1}{x^2\sqrt{x^2\pm a^2}}\,dx = \pm\frac{\sqrt{x^2\pm a^2}}{a^2 x} + C$

24 $\displaystyle\int \frac{\sqrt{x^2\pm a^2}}{x^2}\,dx = -\frac{\sqrt{x^2\pm a^2}}{x} + \ln|x+\sqrt{x^2\pm a^2}| + C$

25 $\displaystyle\int \frac{\sqrt{x^2\pm a^2}}{x}\,dx = \sqrt{x^2\pm a^2} + a^2\frac{1}{x\sqrt{x^2\pm a^2}}\,dx$

26 $\displaystyle\int \frac{1}{x\sqrt{x^2+a^2}}\,dx = \frac{1}{a}\ln\left|\frac{a+\sqrt{x^2+a^2}}{x}\right| + C$

27 $\displaystyle\int x^2\sqrt{a^2-x^2}\,dx = -\frac{x}{4}(a^2-x^2)^{\frac{3}{2}}+\frac{a^2}{4}\int \sqrt{a^2-x^2}\,dx$

28 $\displaystyle\int (a^2-x^2)^{\frac{3}{2}}\,dx = \frac{x}{4}(a^2-x^2)^{\frac{3}{2}}+\frac{3a^2}{4}\int \sqrt{a^2-x^2}\,dx$

29 $\displaystyle\int \frac{1}{(a^2-x^2)^{\frac{3}{2}}}\,dx = \frac{x}{a^2\sqrt{a^2-x^2}} + C$

30 $\displaystyle\int \frac{x^2}{(a^2 - x^2)^{\frac{3}{2}}}\, dx = \frac{x}{\sqrt{a^2 - x^2}} - \sin^{-1}\frac{x}{a} + C$

31 $\displaystyle\int \frac{1}{x\sqrt{a^2 - x^2}}\, dx = -\frac{1}{a}\ln\left|\frac{a + \sqrt{a^2 - x^2}}{x}\right| + C$

32 $\displaystyle\int \frac{1}{x^2\sqrt{a^2 - x^2}}\, dx = -\frac{\sqrt{a^2 - x^2}}{a^2 x} + C$

33 $\displaystyle\int \frac{\sqrt{a^2 - x^2}}{x}\, dx = \sqrt{a^2 - x^2} - a\ln\left|\frac{a + \sqrt{a^2 - x^2}}{x}\right| + C$

34 $\displaystyle\int \frac{1}{(x^2 + a^2)^n}\, dx = \frac{1}{2(n-1)a^2}\frac{x}{(x^2 + a^2)^{n-1}} + (2n - 3)\frac{1}{(x^2 + a^2)^{n-1}}\, dx$

$$n \neq 1$$

35 $\displaystyle\int \sin x\, dx = -\cos x + C$

36 $\displaystyle\int \sin^2 x\, dx = \frac{x}{2} - \frac{1}{4}\sin 2x + C$

37 $\displaystyle\int \sin^n x\, dx = -\frac{1}{n}\sin^{n-1} x\cos x + \frac{n-1}{n}\int \sin^{n-2} x\, dx \qquad n \geq 2$

38 $\displaystyle\int x^2 \sin x\, dx = \sin x - x\cos x + C$

39 $\displaystyle\int x^n \sin x\, dx = -x^n \cos x + nx^{n-1}\sin x - n(n-1)\int x^{n-2}\sin x\, dx$

40 $\displaystyle\int \cos x\, dx = \sin x + C$

41 $\displaystyle\int \cos^2 x\, dx = \frac{x}{2} + \frac{1}{4}\sin 2x + C$

42 $\displaystyle\int \cos^n x\, dx = \frac{1}{n}\sin x\cos^{n-1} x + \frac{n-1}{n}\int \cos^{n-2} x\, dx \qquad n \geq 2$

43 $\displaystyle\int x\cos x\, dx = \cos x + x\sin x + C$

44 $\displaystyle\int x^2 \cos x\, dx = 2x\cos x + (x^2 - 2)\sin x + C$

45 $\displaystyle\int x^n \cos x\, dx = x^n \sin x + nx^{n-1}\cos x - n(n-1)\int x^{n-2}\cos x\, dx$

46 $\displaystyle\int \sin x\cos x\, dx = \frac{1}{2}\sin^2 x + C$

47 $\displaystyle\int \sin^2 x\cos^2 x\, dx = \frac{x}{8} - \frac{1}{32}\sin 4x + C$

48 $\displaystyle\int \sin^m x\cos^n x\, dx$

$$= \begin{cases} \dfrac{1}{m+n}\left[-\sin^{m-1} x\cos^{n+1} x + (m-1)\displaystyle\int \sin^{m-2} x\cos^n x\, dx\right] \\[2ex] \dfrac{1}{m+n}\left[\sin^{m+1} x\cos^{n-1} x + (n-1)\displaystyle\int \sin^m x\cos^{n-2} x\, dx\right] \end{cases}$$

$$m \neq -n$$

49 $\displaystyle\int \tan x \, dx = \ln |\sec x| + C$

50 $\displaystyle\int \tan^2 x \, dx = \tan x - x + C$

51 $\displaystyle\int \tan^n x \, dx = \frac{1}{n-1} \tan^{n-1} - \int \tan^{n-2} x \, dx \qquad n \geq 2$

52 $\displaystyle\int \cot x \, dx = \ln |\sin x| + C$

53 $\displaystyle\int \cot^2 x \, dx = \cot x - x + C$

54 $\displaystyle\int \cot^n x \, dx = -\frac{1}{n-1} \cot^{n-1} x - \int \cot^{n-2} x \, dx \qquad n \geq 2$

55 $\displaystyle\int \sec x \, dx = \ln |\sec x + \tan x| + C$

56 $\displaystyle\int \sec^2 x \, dx = \tan x + C$

57 $\displaystyle\int \sec^n x \, dx = \frac{1}{n-1} \left(\sec^{n-2} x \tan x + (n-2) \int \sec^{n-2} x \, dx \right) \qquad n \geq 2$

58 $\displaystyle\int \csc x \, dx = \ln |\csc x - \cot x| + C$

59 $\displaystyle\int \csc^2 x \, dx = -\cot x + C$

60 $\displaystyle\int \csc^n x \, dx = \frac{1}{n-1} \left[-\csc^{n-2} x \cot x + (n-1) \int \csc^{n-2} x \, dx \right]$
$$n \geq 2$$

61 $\displaystyle\int \sec x \tan x \, dx = \sec x + C$

62 $\displaystyle\int \csc x \cot x \, dx = -\csc x + C$

63 $\displaystyle\int e^{az} \, dx = \frac{1}{a^e} az + C$

64 $\displaystyle\int x e^{az} \, dx = \frac{1}{a^2} (ax - 1) e^{az} + C$

65 $\displaystyle\int x^n e^{az} \, dx = \frac{x^n}{a} e^{az} - \frac{n}{a} \int x^{n-1} e^{az} \, dx$

66 $\displaystyle\int e^{az} \sin bx \, dx = \frac{1}{a^2 + b^2} (a \sin bx = b \cos bx) e^{az} + C$

67 $\displaystyle\int e^{az} \cos bx \, dx = \frac{1}{a^2 + b^2} (a \cos bx + b \sin bx) e^{az} + C$

68 $\displaystyle\int \ln |x| \, dx = x \ln |x| - x + C$

69 $\displaystyle\int \ln^n |x| \, dx = x \ln^n |x| - n \int \ln^{n-1} |x| \, dx$

70 $\displaystyle\int x^n \ln |x| \, dx = \frac{x^{n+1}}{n+1} \left(\ln |x| - \frac{1}{n+1} \right) + C \qquad n \neq -1$

71 $\displaystyle\int \frac{\ln^n |x|}{x} \, dx = \frac{1}{n+1} \ln^{n+1} x + C \qquad n \neq -1$

72 $\displaystyle\int \frac{1}{x \ln |x|} \, dx = \ln | \ln |x| | + C$

73 $\displaystyle\int x^m \ln^n |x| \, dx = \frac{1}{m+1} \left(x^{m+1} \ln^n |x| - n \int x^m \ln^{n-1} |x| \, dx \right) \qquad m \neq -1$

APPENDIX B

TABLE OF RANDOM DIGITS

62	33	26	16	80	45	60	11	14	10	95
32	27	07	36	07	51	24	51	79	89	73
53	13	55	38	58	59	88	97	54	14	10
15	57	12	10	14	21	88	26	49	81	76
90	06	18	44	32	53	23	83	01	30	30
78	87	35	20	96	43	84	26	34	91	64
67	21	76	33	50	25	83	92	12	06	76
75	12	86	73	58	07	44	39	52	38	79
38	15	51	00	13	42	99	66	02	79	54
62	90	52	84	77	27	08	02	73	43	28
62	06	76	50	03	10	55	23	64	05	05
24	20	14	85	88	45	10	93	72	88	71
08	32	98	94	07	72	93	85	79	10	75
38	80	22	02	53	53	86	60	42	04	53
88	54	42	06	87	98	35	85	29	48	29
74	17	76	37	13	04	07	74	21	19	30
47	70	33	24	03	54	97	77	46	44	80
00	04	43	18	66	79	94	77	24	21	90
49	12	72	07	34	45	99	27	72	95	14
49	52	85	66	60	44	38	68	88	11	80
26	04	33	46	09	52	68	07	97	06	57
54	13	58	18	24	76	15	54	55	95	52
10	96	46	92	42	43	97	60	49	04	91
29	10	45	65	04	26	11	04	96	67	24
30	34	25	20	57	27	40	48	73	51	92

TABLE OF RANDOM DIGITS *(Continued)*

74	60	47	21	29	68	02	02	37	03	31
02	76	70	90	30	86	38	45	94	30	38
91	16	92	53	56	16	02	75	50	95	98
41	40	01	74	91	62	48	51	84	08	32
91	00	52	43	48	85	27	55	26	89	62
68	76	83	20	37	90	57	16	00	11	66
86	22	98	12	22	08	07	52	74	95	80
55	59	33	82	43	90	49	37	38	44	59
08	39	54	16	49	36	47	95	93	13	30
06	40	78	78	89	62	02	67	74	17	33
77	59	56	78	06	83	52	91	05	70	74
15	06	51	29	16	93	58	05	77	09	51
12	44	95	92	63	16	29	56	24	29	48
42	32	17	55	85	74	94	44	67	16	94
55	13	08	27	01	50	15	29	39	39	43

APPENDIX C

TABLE OF AREAS FROM MEAN TO DISTANCES z FROM MEAN FOR NORMAL PROBABILITY DISTRIBUTION

z	.00	.01	.02	.03	.04	.05	.06	.07	.08	.09
0.0	.0000	.0040	.0080	.0120	.0160	.0199	.0239	.0279	.0319	.0359
0.1	.0398	.0438	.0478	.0517	.0557	.0596	.0636	.0675	.0714	.0753
0.2	.0793	.0832	.0871	.0910	.0948	.0987	.1026	.1064	.1103	.1141
0.3	.1179	.1217	.1255	.1293	.1331	.1368	.1406	.1443	.1480	.1517
0.4	.1554	.1591	.1628	.1664	.1700	.1736	.1772	.1808	.1844	.1879
0.5	.1915	.1950	.1985	.2019	.2054	.2088	.2123	.2157	.2190	.2224
0.6	.2257	.2291	.2324	.2357	.2389	.2422	.2454	.2486	.2518	.2549
0.7	.2580	.2612	.2642	.2673	.2704	.2734	.2764	.2794	.2823	.2852
0.8	.2881	.2910	.2939	.2967	.2995	.3023	.3051	.3078	.3106	.3133
0.9	.3159	.3186	.3212	.3238	.3264	.3289	.3315	.3340	.3365	.3389
1.0	.3413	.3438	.3461	.3485	.3508	.3531	.3554	.3577	.3599	.3621
1.1	.3643	.3665	.3686	.3708	.3729	.3749	.3770	.3790	.3810	.3830
1.2	.3849	.3869	.3888	.3907	.3925	.3944	.3962	.3980	.3997	.4015
1.3	.4032	.4049	.4066	.4082	.4099	.4115	.4131	.4147	.4162	.4177
1.4	.4192	.4207	.4222	.4236	.4251	.4265	.4279	.4292	.4306	.4319
1.5	.4332	.4345	.4357	.4370	.4382	.4394	.4406	.4418	.4429	.4441
1.6	.4452	.4463	.4474	.4484	.4495	.4505	.4515	.4525	.4535	.4545
1.7	.4554	.4564	.4573	.4582	.4591	.4599	.4608	.4616	.4625	.4633
1.8	.4641	.4649	.4656	.4664	.4671	.4678	.4686	.4693	.4699	.4706
1.9	.4713	.4719	.4726	.4732	.4738	.4744	.4750	.4756	.4761	.4767
2.0	.4772	.4778	.4783	.4788	.4793	.4798	.4803	.4808	.4812	.4817
2.1	.4821	.4826	.4830	.4834	.4838	.4842	.4846	.4850	.4854	.4857
2.2	.4861	.4864	.4868	.4871	.4875	.4878	.4881	.4884	.4887	.4890
2.3	.4893	.4896	.4898	.4901	.4904	.4906	.4909	.4911	.4913	.4916
2.4	.4918	.4920	.4922	.4925	.4927	.4929	.4931	.4932	.4934	.4936
2.5	.4938	.4940	.4941	.4943	.4945	.4946	.4948	.4949	.4951	.4952
2.6	.4953	.4955	.4956	.4957	.4959	.4960	.4961	.4962	.4963	.4964
2.7	.4965	.4966	.4967	.4968	.4969	.4970	.4971	.4972	.4973	.4974
2.8	.4974	.4975	.4976	.4977	.4977	.4978	.4979	.4979	.4980	.4981
2.9	.4981	.4982	.4982	.4983	.4984	.4984	.4985	.4985	.4986	.4986
3.0	.49865	.4987	.4987	.4988	.4988	.4989	.4989	.4989	.4990	.4990
4.0	.4999683									

APPENDIX D

TABLE OF VALUES AND COMMON LOGARITHMS OF EXPONENTIAL AND HYPERBOLIC FUNCTIONS*

x	e^x	e^{-x}	x	e^x	e^{-x}
0.00	1.0000	1.00000	0.25	1.2840	.77880
0.01	1.0101	0.99005	0.26	1.2969	.77105
0.02	1.0202	.98020	0.27	1.3100	.76338
0.03	1.0305	.97045	0.28	1.3231	.75578
0.04	1.0408	.96079	0.29	1.3364	.74826
0.05	1.0513	.95123	0.30	1.3499	.74082
0.06	1.0618	.94176	0.31	1.3634	.73345
0.07	1.0725	.93239	0.32	1.3771	.72615
0.08	1.0833	.92312	0.33	1.3910	.71892
0.09	1.0942	.91393	0.34	1.4049	.71177
0.10	1.1052	.90484	0.35	1.4191	.70469
0.11	1.1163	.89583	0.36	1.4333	.69768
0.12	1.1275	.88692	0.37	1.4477	.69073
0.13	1.1388	.87809	0.38	1.4623	.68386
0.14	1.1503	.86936	0.39	1.4770	.67706
0.15	1.1618	.86071	0.40	1.4918	.67032
0.16	1.1735	.85214	0.41	1.5068	.66365
0.17	1.1853	.84366	0.42	1.5220	.65705
0.18	1.1972	.83527	0.43	1.5373	.65051
0.19	1.2092	.82696	0.44	1.5527	.64404
0.20	1.2214	.81873	0.45	1.5683	.63763
0.21	1.2337	.81058	0.46	1.5841	.63128
0.22	1.2461	.80252	0.47	1.6000	.62500
0.23	1.2586	.79453	0.48	1.6161	.61878
0.24	1.2712	.78663	0.49	1.6323	.61263

* Abridged by the author.

TABLE OF VALUES AND COMMON LOGARITHMS OF
EXPONENTIAL AND HYPERBOLIC FUNCTIONS (*Continued*)

x	e^x	e^{-x}	x	e^x	e^{-x}
0.50	1.6487	.60653	0.90	2.4596	.40657
0.51	1.6653	.60050	0.91	2.4843	.40252
0.52	1.6820	.59452	0.92	2.5093	.39852
0.53	1.6989	.58860	0.93	2.5345	.39455
0.54	1.7160	.58275	0.94	2.5600	.39063
0.55	1.7333	.57695	0.95	2.5857	.38674
0.56	1.7507	.57121	0.96	2.6117	.38289
0.57	1.7683	.56553	0.97	2.6379	.37908
0.58	1.7860	.55990	0.98	2.6645	.37531
0.59	1.8040	.55433	0.99	2.6912	.37158
0.60	1.8221	.54881	1.00	2.7183	.36788
0.61	1.8404	.54335	1.01	2.7456	.36422
0.62	1.8589	.53794	1.02	2.7732	.36060
0.63	1.8776	.53259	1.03	2.8011	.35701
0.64	1.8965	.52729	1.04	2.8292	.35345
0.65	1.9155	.52205	1.05	2.8577	.34994
0.66	1.9348	.51685	1.06	2.8864	.34646
0.67	1.9542	.51171	1.07	2.9154	.34301
0.68	1.9739	.50662	1.08	2.9447	.33960
0.69	1.9937	.50158	1.09	2.9743	.33622
0.70	2.0138	.49659	1.10	3.0042	.33287
0.71	2.0340	.49164	1.11	3.0344	.32956
0.72	2.0544	.48675	1.12	3.0649	.32628
0.73	2.0751	.48191	1.13	3.0957	.32303
0.74	2.0959	.47711	1.14	3.1268	.31982
0.75	2.1170	.47237	1.15	3.1582	.31664
0.76	2.1383	.46767	1.16	3.1899	.31349
0.77	2.1598	.46301	1.17	3.2220	.31037
0.78	2.1815	.45841	1.18	3.2544	.30728
0.79	2.2034	.45384	1.19	3.2871	.30422
0.80	2.2255	.44933	1.20	3.3201	.30119
0.81	2.2479	.44486	1.21	3.3535	.29820
0.82	2.2705	.44043	1.22	3.3872	.29523
0.83	2.2933	.43605	1.23	3.4212	.29229
0.84	2.3164	.43171	1.24	3.4556	.28938
0.85	2.3396	.42741	1.25	3.4903	.28650
0.86	2.3632	.42316	1.26	3.5254	.28365
0.87	2.3869	.41895	1.27	3.5609	.28083
0.88	2.4109	.41478	1.28	3.5966	.27804
0.89	2.4351	.41066	1.29	3.6328	.27527

TABLE OF VALUES AND COMMON LOGARITHMS OF
EXPONENTIAL AND HYPERBOLIC FUNCTIONS (*Continued*)

x	e^x	e^{-x}	x	e^x	e^{-x}
1.30	3.6693	.27253	1.70	5.4739	.18268
1.31	3.7062	.26982	1.71	5.5290	.18087
1.32	3.7434	.26714	1.72	5.5845	.17907
1.33	3.7810	.26448	1.73	5.6407	.17728
1.34	3.8190	.26185	1.74	5.6973	.17552
1.35	3.8574	.25924	1.75	5.7546	.17377
1.36	3.8962	.25666	1.76	5.8124	.17204
1.37	3.9354	.25411	1.77	5.8709	.17033
1.38	3.9749	.25158	1.78	5.9299	.16864
1.39	4.0149	.24908	1.79	5.9895	.16696
1.40	4.0552	.24660	1.80	6.0496	.16530
1.41	4.0960	.24414	1.81	6.1104	.16365
1.42	4.1371	.24171	1.82	6.1719	.16203
1.43	4.1787	.23931	1.83	6.2339	.16041
1.44	4.2207	.23693	1.84	6.2965	.15882
1.45	4.2631	.23457	1.85	6.3598	.15724
1.46	4.3060	.23224	1.86	6.4237	.15567
1.47	4.3492	.22993	1.87	6.4883	.15412
1.48	4.3929	.22764	1.88	6.5535	.15259
1.49	4.4371	.22537	1.89	6.6194	.15107
1.50	4.4817	.22313	1.90	6.6859	.14957
1.51	4.5267	.22091	1.91	6.7531	.14808
1.52	4.5722	.21871	1.92	6.8210	.14661
1.53	4.6182	.21654	1.93	6.8895	.14515
1.54	4.6646	.21438	1.94	6.9588	.14370
1.55	4.7115	.21225	1.95	7.0287	.14227
1.56	4.7588	.21014	1.96	7.0993	.14086
1.57	4.8066	.20805	1.97	7.1707	.13946
1.58	4.8550	.20598	1.98	7.2427	.13807
1.59	4.9037	.20393	1.99	7.3155	.13670
1.60	4.9530	.20190	2.00	7.3891	.13534
1.61	5.0028	.19989	2.01	7.4633	.13399
1.62	5.0531	.19790	2.02	7.5383	.13266
1.63	5.1039	.19593	2.03	7.6141	.13134
1.64	5.1552	.19398	2.04	7.6906	.13003
1.65	5.2070	.19205	2.05	7.7679	.12873
1.66	5.2593	.19014	2.06	7.8460	.12745
1.67	5.3122	.18825	2.07	7.9248	.12619
1.68	5.3656	.18637	2.08	8.0045	.12493
1.69	5.4195	.18452	2.09	8.0849	.12369

TABLE OF VALUES AND COMMON LOGARITHMS OF
EXPONENTIAL AND HYPERBOLIC FUNCTIONS (*Continued*)

x	e^x	e^{-x}	x	e^x	e^{-x}
2.10	8.1662	.12246	2.50	12.182	.08208
2.11	8.2482	.12124	2.51	12.305	.08127
2.12	8.3311	.12003	2.52	12.429	.08046
2.13	8.4149	.11884	2.53	12.554	.07966
2.14	8.4994	.11765	2.54	12.680	.07887
2.15	8.5849	.11648	2.55	12.807	.07808
2.16	8.6711	.11533	2.56	12.936	.07730
2.17	8.7583	.11418	2.57	13.066	.07654
2.18	8.8463	.11304	2.58	13.197	.07577
2.19	8.9352	.11192	2.59	13.330	.07502
2.20	9.0250	.11080	2.60	13.464	.07427
2.21	9.1157	.10970	2.61	13.599	.07353
2.22	9.2073	.10861	2.62	13.736	.07280
2.23	9.2999	.10753	2.63	13.874	.07208
2.24	9.3933	.10646	2.64	14.013	.07136
2.25	9.4877	.10540	2.65	14.154	.07065
2.26	9.5831	.10435	2.66	14.296	.06995
2.27	9.6794	.10331	2.67	14.440	.06925
2.28	9.7767	.10228	2.68	14.585	.06856
2.29	9.8749	.10127	2.69	14.732	.06788
2.30	9.9742	.10026	2.70	14.880	.06721
2.31	10.074	.09926	2.71	15.029	.06654
2.32	10.176	.09827	2.72	15.180	.06587
2.33	10.278	.09730	2.73	15.333	.06522
2.34	10.381	.09633	2.74	15.487	.06457
2.35	10.486	.09537	2.75	15.643	.06393
2.36	10.591	.09442	2.76	15.800	.06329
2.37	10.697	.09348	2.77	15.959	.06266
2.38	10.805	.09255	2.78	16.119	.06204
2.39	10.913	.09163	2.79	16.281	.06142
2.40	11.023	.09072	2.80	16.445	.06081
2.41	11.134	.08982	2.81	16.610	.06020
2.42	11.246	.08892	2.82	16.777	.05961
2.43	11.359	.08804	2.83	16.945	.05901
2.44	11.473	.08716	2.84	17.116	.05843
2.45	11.588	.08629	2.85	17.288	.05784
2.46	11.705	.08543	2.86	17.462	.05727
2.47	11.822	.08458	2.87	17.637	.05670
2.48	11.941	.08374	2.88	17.814	.05613
2.49	12.061	.08291	2.89	17.993	.05558

TABLE OF VALUES AND COMMON LOGARITHMS OF
EXPONENTIAL AND HYPERBOLIC FUNCTIONS (*Continued*)

x	e^x	e^{-x}	x	e^x	e^{-x}
2.90	18.174	.05502	4.00	54.598	.01832
2.91	18.357	.05448	4.10	60.340	.01657
2.92	18.541	.05393	4.20	66.686	.01500
2.93	18.728	.05340	4.30	73.700	.01357
2.94	18.916	.05287	4.40	81.451	.01227
2.95	19.106	.05234	4.50	90.017	.01111
2.96	19.298	.05182	4.60	99.484	.01005
2.97	19.492	.05130	4.70	109.95	.00910
2.98	19.688	.05079	4.80	121.51	.00823
2.99	19.886	.05029	4.90	134.29	.00745
3.00	20.086	.04979	5.00	148.41	.00674
3.05	21.115	.04736	5.10	164.02	.00610
3.10	22.198	.04505	5.20	181.27	.00552
3.15	23.336	.04285	5.30	200.34	.00499
3.20	24.533	.04076	5.40	221.41	.00452
3.25	25.790	.03877	5.50	244.69	.00409
3.30	27.113	.03688	5.60	270.43	.00370
3.35	28.503	.03508	5.70	298.87	.00335
3.40	29.964	.03337	5.80	330.30	.00303
3.45	31.500	.03175	5.90	365.04	.00274
3.50	33.115	.03020	6.00	403.43	.00248
3.55	34.813	.02872	6.25	518.01	.00193
3.60	36.598	.02732	6.50	665.14	.00150
3.65	38.475	.02599	6.75	854.06	.00117
3.70	40.447	.02472	7.00	1096.6	.00091
3.75	42.521	.02352	7.50	1808.0	.00055
3.80	44.701	.02237	8.00	2981.0	.00034
3.85	46.993	.02128	8.50	4914.8	.00020
3.90	49.402	.02024	9.00	8103.1	.00012
3.95	51.935	.01925	9.50	13360.	.00007
			10.00	22026.	.00005

APPENDIX E

TABLE OF NATURAL LOGARITHMS OF NUMBERS

0.00 to 5.99 † ‡
(Base $e = 2.718$ . . .)

N		0	1	2	3	4	5	6	7	8	9
0.0			5.395	6.088	6.493	6.781	7.004	7.187	7.341	7.474	7.592
0.1		7.697	7.793	7.880	7.960	8.034	8.103	8.167	8.228	8.285	8.339
0.2		8.391	8.439	8.486	8.530	8.573	8.614	8.653	8.691	8.727	8.762
0.3		8.796	8.829	8.861	8.891	8.921	8.950	8.978	9.006	9.032	9.058
0.4		9.084	9.108	9.132	9.156	9.179	9.201	9.223	9.245	9.266	9.287
0.5		9.307	9.327	9.346	9.365	9.384	9.402	9.420	9.438	9.455	9.472
0.6		9.489	9.506	9.522	9.538	9.554	9.569	9.584	9.600	9.614	9.629
0.7		9.643	9.658	9.671	9.685	9.699	9.712	9.720	9.739	9.752	9.764
0.8		9.777	9.789	9.802	9.814	9.826	9.837	9.849	9.861	9.872	9.883
0.9		9.895	9.906	9.917	9.927	9.938	9.949	9.959	9.970	9.980	9.990
1.0	0.0	0000	0995	1980	2956	3922	4879	5827	6766	7696	8618
1.1		9531	*0436	*1333	*2222	*3103	*3976	*4842	*5700	*6551	*7395
1.2	0.1	8232	9062	9885	*0701	*1511	*2314	*3111	*3902	*4686	*5464
1.3	0.2	6236	7003	7763	8518	9267	*0010	*0748	*1481	*2208	*2930
1.4	0.3	3647	4359	5066	5767	6464	7156	7844	8526	9204	9878
1.5	0.4	0547	1211	1871	2527	3178	3825	4469	5108	5742	6373
1.6		7000	7623	8243	8858	9470	*0078	*0682	*1282	*1879	*2473
1.7	0.5	3063	3649	4232	4812	5389	5962	6531	7098	7661	8222
1.8		8779	9333	9884	*0432	*0977	*1519	*2058	*2594	*3127	*3658
1.9	0.6	4185	4710	5233	5752	6269	6783	7294	7803	8310	8813
2.0		9315	9813	*0310	*0804	*1295	*1784	*2271	*2755	*3237	*3716
2.1	0.7	4195	4669	5142	5612	6081	6547	7011	7473	7932	8390
2.2		8846	9299	9751	*0200	*0648	*1093	*1536	*1978	*2418	*2855
2.3	0.8	3291	3725	4157	4587	5015	5442	5866	6289	6710	7129
2.4		7547	7963	8377	8789	9200	9609	*0016	*0422	*0826	*1228

[* Applicable preceding digits are listed at the beginning of the next row.]
† $\log_e 0.10 = 7.69741\ 49070 - 10$
‡ Entries in (this table) are values of $\log_e N$ for the indicated values of N .

TABLE OF NATURAL LOGARITHMS OF NUMBERS (*Continued*)

		0	1	2	3	4	5	6	7	8	9
2.5	0.9	1629	2028	2426	2822	3216	3509	4001	4391	4779	5166
2.6		5551	5935	6317	6698	7078	7456	7833	8208	8583	8954
2.7		9325	9695	*0063	*0430	*0796	*1160	*1523	*1885	*2245	*2604
2.8	1.0	2962	3318	3674	4028	4380	4732	5082	5431	5779	6126
2.9		6471	6815	7158	7500	7841	8181	8519	8856	9192	9527
3.0		9861	*0194	*0526	*0856	*1186	*1514	*1841	*2168	*2493	*2817
3.1	1.1	3140	3462	3783	4103	4422	4740	5057	5373	5688	6002
3.2		6315	6627	6938	7248	7557	7865	8173	8479	8784	9089
3.3		9392	9695	9996	*0297	*0597	*0896	*1194	*1491	*1788	*2083
3.4	1.2	2378	2671	2964	3256	3547	3837	4127	4415	4703	4990
3.5		5276	5562	5846	6130	6413	6695	6976	7257	7536	7815
3.6		8093	8371	8647	8923	9198	9473	9746	*0019	*0291	*0563
3.7	1.3	0833	1103	1372	1641	1909	2176	2442	2708	2972	3237
3.8		3500	3763	4025	4286	4547	4807	5067	5325	5584	5841
3.9		6098	6354	6609	6864	7118	7372	7624	7877	8128	8379
4.0		8629	8879	9128	9377	9624	9872	*0118	*0364	*0610	*0854
4.1	1.4	1099	1342	1585	1828	2070	2311	2552	2792	3031	3270
4.2		3508	3746	3984	4220	4456	4692	4927	5161	5395	5629
4.3		5862	6094	6326	6557	6787	7018	7247	7476	7705	7933
4.4		8160	8387	8614	8840	9065	9290	9515	9739	9962	*0185
4.5	1.5	0408	0630	0851	1072	1293	1513	1732	1951	2170	2388
4.6		2606	2823	3039	3256	3471	3687	3902	4116	4330	4543
4.7		4756	4969	5181	5393	5604	5814	6025	6235	6444	6653
4.8		6862	7070	7277	7485	7691	7898	8104	8309	8515	8719
4.9		8924	9127	9331	9534	9737	9939	*0141	*0342	*0543	*0744
5.0	1.6	0944	1144	1343	1542	1741	1939	2137	2334	2531	2728
5.1		2924	3120	3315	3511	3705	3900	4094	4287	4481	4673
5.2		4866	5058	5250	5441	5632	5823	6013	6203	6393	6582
5.3		6771	6959	7147	7335	7523	7710	7896	8083	8269	8455
5.4		8640	8825	9010	9194	9378	9562	9745	9928	*0111	*0293
5.5	1.7	0475	0656	0838	1019	1199	1380	1560	1740	1919	2098
5.6		2277	2455	2633	2811	2988	3166	3342	3519	3695	3871
5.7		4047	4222	4397	4572	4746	4920	5094	5267	5440	5613
5.8		5786	5958	6130	6302	6473	6644	6815	6985	7156	7326
5.9		7495	7665	7834	8002	8171	8339	8507	8675	8842	9009

[* Applicable preceding digits are listed at the beginning of the next row.]

TABLE OF NATURAL LOGARITHMS OF NUMBERS (*Continued*)

6.00 to 10.09

N		0	1	2	3	4	5	6	7	8	9
6.0	1.7	9176	9342	9509	9675	9840	*0006	*0171	*0336	*0500	*0665
6.1	1.8	0829	0993	1156	1319	1482	1645	1808	1970	2132	2294
6.2		2455	2616	2777	2938	3098	3258	3418	3578	3737	3896
6.3		4055	4214	4372	4530	4688	4845	5003	5160	5317	5473
6.4		5630	5786	5942	6097	6253	6408	6563	6718	6872	7026
6.5		7180	7334	7487	7641	7794	7947	8099	8251	8403	8555
6.6		8707	8858	9010	9160	9311	9462	9612	9762	9912	*0061
6.7	1.9	0211	0360	0509	0658	0806	0954	1102	1250	1398	1545
6.8		1692	1839	1986	2132	2279	2425	2571	2716	2862	3007
6.9		3152	3297	3442	3586	3730	3874	4018	4162	4305	4448
7.0		4591	4734	4876	5019	5161	5303	5445	5586	5727	5869
7.1		6009	6150	6291	6431	6571	6711	6851	6991	7130	7269
7.2		7408	7547	7685	7824	7962	8100	8238	8376	8513	8650
7.3		8787	8924	9061	9198	9334	9470	9606	9742	9877	*0013
7.4	2.0	0148	0283	0418	0553	0687	0821	0956	1089	1223	1357
7.5		1490	1624	1757	1890	2022	2155	2287	2419	2551	2683
7.6		2815	2946	3078	3209	3340	3471	3601	3732	3862	3992
7.7		4122	4252	4381	4511	4640	4769	4898	5027	5156	5284
7.8		5412	5540	5668	5796	5924	6051	6179	6306	6433	6560
7.9		6686	6813	6939	7065	7191	7317	7443	7568	7694	7819
8.0		7944	8069	8194	8318	8443	8567	8691	8815	8939	9063
8.1		9186	9310	9433	9556	9679	9802	9924	*0047	*0169	*0291
8.2	2.1	0413	0535	0657	0779	0900	1021	1142	1263	1384	1505
8.3		1626	1746	1866	1986	2106	2226	2346	2465	2585	2704
8.4		2823	2942	3061	3180	3298	3417	3535	3653	3771	3889
8.5		4007	4124	4242	4359	4476	4593	4710	4827	4943	5060
8.6		5176	5292	5409	5524	5640	5756	5871	5987	6102	6217
8.7		6332	6447	6562	6677	6791	6905	7020	7134	7248	7361
8.8		7475	7589	7702	7816	7929	8042	8155	8267	8380	8493
8.9		8605	8717	8830	8942	9054	9165	9277	9389	9500	9611
9.0		9722	9834	9944	*0055	*0166	*0276	*0387	*0497	*0607	*0717
9.1	2.2	0827	0937	1047	1157	1266	1375	1485	1594	1703	1812
9.2		1920	2029	2138	2246	2354	2462	2570	2678	2786	2894
9.3		3001	3109	3216	3324	3431	3538	3645	3751	3858	3965
9.4		4071	4177	4284	4390	4496	4601	4707	4813	4918	5024

[* Applicable preceding digits are listed at the beginning of the next row.]

TABLE OF NATURAL LOGARITHMS OF NUMBERS (*Continued*)

9.5		5129	5234	5339	5444	5549	5654	5759	5863	5968	6072
9.6		6176	6280	6384	6488	6592	6696	6799	6903	7006	7109
9.7		7213	7316	7419	7521	7624	7727	7829	7932	8034	8136
9.8		8238	8340	8442	8544	8646	8747	8849	8950	9051	9152
9.9		9253	9354	9455	9556	9657	9757	9858	9958	*0058	*0158
10.0	2.3	0259	0358	0458	0558	0658	0757	0857	0956	1055	1154

10 to 99 †

N	0	1	2	3	4	5	6	7	8	9
1	2.30259	39790	48491	56495	63906	70805	77259	83321	89037	94444
2	99573	*04452	*09104	*13549	*17805	*21888	*25810	*29584	*33220	*36730
3	3.40120	43399	46574	49651	52636	55535	58352	61092	63759	66356
4	68888	71357	73767	76120	78419	80666	82864	85015	87120	89182
5	91202	93183	95124	97029	98898	*00733	*02535	*04305	*06044	*07754
6	4.09434	11087	12713	14313	15888	17439	18965	20469	21951	23411
7	24850	26268	27667	29046	30407	31749	33073	34381	35671	36945
8	38203	39445	40672	41884	43082	44265	45435	46591	47734	48864
9	49981	51086	52179	53260	54329	55388	56435	57471	58497	59512

100 to 609 ‡

N		0	1	2	3	4	5	6	7	8	9
10	4.6	0517	1512	2497	3473	4439	5396	6344	7283	8213	9135
11	4.7	0048	0953	1850	2739	3620	4493	5359	6217	7068	7912
12		8749	9579	*0402	*1218	*2028	*2831	*3628	*4419	*5203	*5981
13	4.8	6753	7520	8280	9035	9784	*0527	*1265	*1998	*2725	*3447
14	4.9	4164	4876	5583	6284	6981	7673	8361	9043	9721	0395
15	5.0	1064	1728	2388	3044	3695	4343	4986	5625	6260	6890
16		7517	8140	8760	9375	9987	*0595	*1199	*1799	*2396	*2990
17	5.1	3580	4166	4749	5329	5906	6479	7048	7615	8178	8739
18		9296	9850	*0401	*0949	*1494	*2036	*2575	*3111	*3644	*4175
19	5.2	4702	5227	5750	6269	6786	7300	7811	8320	8827	9330
20		9832	*0330	*0827	*1321	*1812	*2301	*2788	*3272	*3754	*4233
21	5.3	4711	5186	5659	6129	6598	7064	7528	7990	8450	8907
22		9363	9816	*0268	*0717	*1165	*1610	*2053	*2495	*2935	*3372
23	5.4	3808	4242	4674	5104	5532	5959	6383	6806	7227	7646
24		8064	8480	8894	9306	9717	*0126	*0533	*0939	*1343	*1745
25	5.5	2146	2545	2943	3339	3733	4126	4518	4908	5296	5683
26		6068	6452	6834	7215	7595	7973	8350	8725	9099	9471
27		9842	*0212	*0580	*0947	*1313	*1677	*2040	*2402	*2762	*3121
28	5.6	3479	3835	4191	4545	4897	5249	5599	5948	6296	6643
29		6988	7332	7675	8017	8358	8698	9036	9373	9709	*0044

[* Applicable preceding digits are listed at the beginning of the next row.]
† $\log_e 10 = 2.30258\ 50930$
‡ $\log_e 100 = 4.60517\ 10860$

TABLE OF NATURAL LOGARITHMS OF NUMBERS (*Continued*)

		0	1	2	3	4	5	6	7	8	9
30	5.7	0378	0711	1043	1373	1703	2031	2359	2685	3010	3334
31		3657	3979	4300	4620	4939	5257	5574	5890	6205	6519
32		6832	7144	7455	7765	8074	8383	8690	8996	9301	9606
33		9909	*0212	*0513	*0814	*1114	*1413	*1711	*2008	*2305	*2600
34	5.8	2895	3188	3481	3773	4064	4354	4644	4932	5220	5507
35		5793	6079	6363	6647	6930	7212	7493	7774	8053	8332
36		8610	8888	9164	9440	9715	9990	*0263	*0536	*0808	*1080
37	5.9	1350	1620	1889	2158	2426	2693	2959	3225	3489	3754
38		4017	4280	4542	4803	5064	5324	5584	5842	6101	6358
39		6615	6871	7126	7381	7635	7889	8141	8394	8645	8896
40		9146	9396	9645	9894	*0141	*0389	*0635	*0881	*1127	*1372
41	6.0	1616	1859	2102	2345	2587	2828	3069	3309	3548	3787
42		4025	4263	4501	4737	4973	5209	5444	5678	5912	6146
43		6379	6611	6843	7074	7304	7535	7764	7993	8222	8450
44		8677	8904	9131	9357	9582	9807	*0032	*0256	*0479	*0702
45	6.1	0925	1147	1368	1589	1810	2030	2249	2468	2687	2905
46		3123	3340	3556	3773	3988	4204	4419	4633	4847	5060
47		5273	5486	5598	5910	6121	6331	6542	6752	6961	7170
48		7379	7587	7794	8002	8208	8415	8621	8826	9032	9236
49		9441	9644	9848	*0051	*0254	*0456	*0658	*0859	*1060	*1261
50	6.2	1461	1661	1860	2059	2258	2456	2654	2851	3048	3245
51		3441	3637	3832	4028	4222	4417	4611	4804	4998	5190
52		5383	5575	5767	5958	6149	6340	6530	6720	6910	7099
53		7288	7476	7664	7852	8040	8227	8413	8600	8786	8972
54		9157	9342	9527	9711	9895	*0079	*0262	*0445	*0628	*0810
55	6.3	0992	1173	1355	1536	1716	1897	2077	2257	2436	2615
56		2794	2972	3150	3328	3505	3683	3859	4036	4212	4388
57		4563	4739	4914	5089	5263	5437	5611	5784	5957	6130
58		6304	6475	6647	6819	6990	7161	7332	7502	7673	7843
59		8012	8182	8351	8519	8688	8856	9024	9192	9359	9526
60		9693	9859	*0026	*0192	*0357	*0523	*0688	*0853	*1017	*1182

600 to 1109†

N		0	1	2	3	4	5	6	7	8	9
60	6.3	9693	9859	*0026	*0192	*0357	*0523	*0688	*0853	*1017	*1182
61	6.4	1346	1510	1673	1836	1999	2162	2325	2487	2649	2811
62		2972	3133	3294	3455	3615	3775	3935	4095	4254	4413
63		4572	4731	4889	5047	5205	5362	5520	5677	5834	5990
64		6147	6303	6459	6614	6770	6925	7080	7235	7389	7543

[* Applicable preceding digits are listed at the beginning of the next row.]
† $\log_e 1000 = 6.90775$ 52790

TABLE OF NATURAL LOGARITHMS OF NUMBERS (*Continued*)

65		7697	7851	8004	8158	8311	8464	8616	8768	8920	9072
66		9224	9375	9527	9677	9828	9979	*0129	*0279	*0429	*0578
67	6.5	0728	0877	1026	1175	1323	1471	1619	1767	1915	2062
68		2209	2356	2503	2649	2796	2942	3088	3233	3379	3524
69		3669	3814	3959	4103	4247	4391	4535	4679	4822	4965
70		5108	5251	5393	5536	5678	5820	5962	6103	6244	6386
71		6526	6667	6808	6948	7088	7228	7368	7508	7647	7786
72		7925	8064	8203	8341	8479	8617	8755	8893	9030	9167
73		9304	9441	9578	9715	9851	9987	*0123	*0259	*0394	*0530
74	6.6	0665	0800	0935	1070	1204	1338	1473	1607	1740	1874
75		2007	2141	2274	2407	2539	2672	2804	2936	3068	3200
76		3332	3463	3595	3726	3875	3988	4118	4249	4379	4509
77		4639	4769	4898	5028	5157	5286	5415	5544	5673	5801
78		5929	6058	6185	6313	6441	6568	6696	6823	6950	7077
79		7203	7330	7456	7582	7708	7834	7960	8085	8211	8336
80		8461	8586	8711	8835	8960	9084	9208	9332	9456	9580
81		9703	9827	9950	*0073	*0196	*0319	*0441	*0564	*0686	*0808
82	6.7	0930	1052	1174	1296	1417	1538	1659	1780	1901	2022
83		2143	2263	2383	2503	2623	2743	2863	2982	3102	3221
84		3340	3459	3578	3697	3815	3934	4052	4170	4288	4406
85		4524	4641	4759	4876	4993	5110	5227	5344	5460	5577
86		5693	5809	5926	6041	6157	6273	6388	6504	6619	6734
87		6849	6964	7079	7194	7308	7422	7537	7651	7765	7878
88		7992	8106	8219	8333	8446	8559	8672	8784	8897	9010
89		9122	9234	9347	9459	9571	9682	9794	9906	*0017	*0128
90	6.8	0239	0351	0461	0572	0683	0793	0904	1014	1124	1235
91		1344	1454	1564	1674	1783	1892	2002	2111	2220	2329
92		2437	2546	2655	2763	2871	2979	3087	3195	3303	3411
93		3518	3626	3733	3841	3948	4055	4162	4268	4375	4482
94		4588	4694	4801	4907	5013	5118	5224	5330	5435	5541
95		5646	5751	5857	5961	6066	6171	6276	6380	6485	6589
96		6693	6797	6901	7005	7109	7213	7318	7420	7523	7626
97		7730	7833	7936	8038	8141	8244	8346	8449	8551	8653
98		8755	8857	8959	9061	9163	9264	9366	9467	9568	9669
99		9770	9871	9972	*0073	*0174	*0274	*0375	*0475	*0575	*0675
100	6.9	0776	0875	0975	1075	1175	1274	1374	1473	1572	1672
101		1771	1870	1968	2067	2166	2264	2363	2461	2560	2658
102		2756	2854	2952	3049	3147	3245	3342	3440	3537	3634
103		3731	3828	3925	4022	4119	4216	4312	4409	4505	4601
104		4698	4794	4890	4986	5081	5177	5273	5368	5464	5559

[* Applicable preceding digits are listed at the beginning of the next row.]

TABLE OF NATURAL LOGARITHMS OF NUMBERS (*Continued*)

105		5655	5750	5845	5940	6035	6130	6224	6319	6414	6508
106		6602	6697	6791	6885	6979	7073	7167	7261	7354	7448
107		7541	7635	7728	7821	7915	8008	8101	8193	8286	8379
108		8472	8564	8657	8749	8841	8934	9026	9118	9210	9302
109		9393	9485	9577	9668	9760	9851	9942	*0033	*0125	*0216
110	7.0	0307	0397	0488	0579	0670	0760	0851	0941	1031	1121

To find the logarithm of a number which is 10 (or $\frac{1}{10}$) times a number whose logarithm is given, add to (or subtract from) the given logarithm the logarithm of 10.

[* Applicable preceding digits are listed at the beginning of the next row.]

APPENDIX F

TABLE OF TRIGONOMETRIC FUNCTIONS IN RADIAN MEASURE†

Rad	Sin	Tan	Cot	Cos	Rad	Sin	Tan	Cot	Cos
.00	.0000	.0000	......	1.0000	.25	.2474	.2553	3.916	.9689
.01	.0100	.0100	99.997	1.0000	.26	.2571	.2660	3.759	.9664
.02	.0200	.0200	49.993	.9998	.27	.2667	.2768	3.613	.9638
.03	.0300	.0300	33.323	.9996	.28	.2764	.2876	3.478	.9611
.04	.0400	.0400	24.987	.9992	.29	.2860	.2984	3.351	.9582
.05	.0500	.0500	19.983	.9988	.30	.2955	.3093	3.233	.9553
.06	.0600	.0601	16.647	.9982	.31	.3051	.3203	3.122	.9523
.07	.0699	.0701	14.262	.9976	.32	.3146	.3314	3.018	.9492
.08	.0799	.0802	12.473	.9968	.33	.3240	.3425	2.920	.9460
.09	.0899	.0902	11.081	.9960	.34	.3335	.3537	2.827	.9428
.10	.0998	.1003	9.967	.9950	.35	.3429	.3650	2.740	.9394
.11	.1098	.1104	9.054	.9940	.36	.3523	.3764	2.657	.9359
.12	.1197	.1206	8.293	.9928	.37	.3616	.3879	2.578	.9323
.13	.1296	.1307	7.649	.9916	.38	.3709	.3994	2.504	.9287
.14	.1395	.1409	7.096	.9902	.39	.3802	.4111	2.433	.9249
.15	.1494	.1511	6.617	.9888	.40	.3894	.4228	2.365	.9211
.16	.1593	.1614	6.197	.9872	.41	.3986	.4346	2.301	.9171
.17	.1692	.1717	5.826	.9856	.42	.4078	.4466	2.239	.9131
.18	.1790	.1820	5.495	.9838	.43	.4169	.4586	2.180	.9090
.19	.1889	.1923	5.200	.9820	.44	.4259	.4708	2.124	.9048
.20	.1987	.2027	4.933	.9801	.45	.4350	.4831	2.070	.9004
.21	.2085	.2131	4.692	.9780	.46	.4439	.4954	2.018	.8961
.22	.2182	.2236	4.472	.9759	.47	.4529	.5080	1.969	.8916
.23	.2280	.2341	4.271	.9737	.48	.4618	.5206	1.921	.8870
.24	.2377	.2447	4.086	.9713	.49	.4706	.5334	1.875	.8823

TABLE OF TRIGONOMETRIC FUNCTIONS IN RADIAN MEASURE†
(*Continued*)

Rad	Sin	Tan	Cot	Cos	Rad	Sin	Tan	Cot	Cos
.50	.4794	.5463	1.830	.8776	.90	.7833	1.260	.7936	.6216
.51	.4882	.5594	1.788	.8727	.91	.7895	1.286	.7774	.6137
.52	.4969	.5726	1.747	.8678	.92	.7956	1.313	.7615	.6058
.53	.5055	.5859	1.707	.8628	.93	.8016	1.341	.7458	.5978
.54	.5141	.5994	1.668	.8577	.94	.8076	1.369	.7303	.5898
.55	.5227	.6131	1.631	.8525	.95	.8134	1.398	.7151	.5817
.56	.5312	.6269	1.595	.8473	.96	.8192	1.428	.7001	.5735
.57	.5396	.6410	1.560	.8419	.97	.8249	1.459	.6853	.5653
.58	.5480	.6552	1.526	.8365	.98	.8305	1.491	.6707	.5570
.59	.5564	.6696	1.494	.8309	.99	.8360	1.524	.6563	.5487
.60	.5646	.6841	1.462	.8253	1.00	.8415	1.557	.6421	.5403
.61	.5729	.6989	1.431	.8196	1.01	.8468	1.592	.6281	.5319
.62	.5810	.7139	1.401	.8139	1.02	.8521	1.628	.6142	.5234
.63	.5891	.7291	1.372	.8080	1.03	.8573	1.665	.6005	.5148
.64	.5972	.7445	1.343	.8021	1.04	.8624	1.704	.5870	.5062
.65	.6052	.7602	1.315	.7961	1.05	.8674	1.743	.5736	.4976
.66	.6131	.7761	1.288	.7900	1.06	.8724	1.784	.5604	.4889
.67	.6210	.7923	1.262	.7838	1.07	.8772	1.827	.5473	.4801
.68	.6288	.8087	1.237	.7776	1.08	.8820	1.871	.5344	.4713
.69	.6365	.8253	1.212	.7712	1.09	.8866	1.917	.5216	.4625
.70	.6442	.8423	1.187	.7648	1.10	.8912	1.965	.5090	.4536
.71	.6518	.8595	1.163	.7584	1.11	.8957	2.014	.4964	.4447
.72	.6594	.8771	1.140	.7518	1.12	.9001	2.066	.4840	.4357
.73	.6669	.8949	1.117	.7452	1.13	.9044	2.120	.4718	.4267
.74	.6743	.9131	1.095	.7385	1.14	.9086	2.176	.4596	.4176
.75	.6816	.9316	1.073	.7317	1.15	.9128	2.234	.4475	.4085
.76	.6889	.9505	1.052	.7248	1.16	.9168	2.296	.4356	.3993
.77	.6961	.9697	1.031	.7179	1.17	.9208	2.360	.4237	.3902
.78	.7033	.9893	1.011	.7109	1.18	.9246	2.427	.4120	.3809
.79	.7104	1.009	.9908	.7038	1.19	.9284	2.498	.4003	.3717
.80	.7174	1.030	.9712	.6967	1.20	.9320	2.572	.3888	.3624
.81	.7243	1.050	.9520	.6895	1.21	.9356	2.650	.3773	.3530
.82	.7311	1.072	.9331	.6822	1.22	.9391	2.733	.3659	.3436
.83	.7379	1.093	.9146	.6749	1.23	.9425	2.820	.3546	.3342
.84	.7446	1.116	.8964	.6675	1.24	.9458	2.912	.3434	.3248
.85	.7513	1.138	.8785	.6600	1.25	.9490	3.010	.3323	.3153
.86	.7578	1.162	.8609	.6524	1.26	.9521	3.113	.3212	.3058
.87	.7643	1.185	.8437	.6448	1.27	.9551	3.224	.3102	.2963
.88	.7707	1.210	.8267	.6372	1.28	.9580	3.341	.2993	.2867
.89	.7771	1.235	.8100	.6294	1.29	.9608	3.467	.2884	.2771

TABLE OF TRIGONOMETRIC FUNCTIONS IN RADIAN MEASURE†
(*Continued*)

Rad	Sin	Tan	Cot	Cos	Rad	Sin	Tan	Cot	Cos
1.30	.9636	3.602	.2776	.2675	1.45	.9927	8.238	.1214	.1205
1.31	.9662	3.747	.2669	.2579	1.46	.9939	8.989	.1113	.1106
1.32	.9687	3.903	.2562	.2482	1.47	.9949	9.887	.1011	.1006
1.33	.9711	4.072	.2456	.2385	1.48	.9959	10.983	.0910	.0907
1.34	.9735	4.256	.2350	.2288	1.49	.9967	12.350	.0810	.0807
1.35	.9757	4.455	.2245	.2190	1.50	.9975	14.101	.0709	.0707
1.36	.9779	4.673	.2140	.2092	1.51	.9982	16.428	.0609	.0608
1.37	.9799	4.913	.2035	.1994	1.52	.9987	19.670	.0508	.0508
1.38	.9819	5.177	.1931	.1896	1.53	.9992	24.498	.0408	.0408
1.39	.9837	5.471	.1828	.1798	1.54	.9995	32.461	.0308	.0308
1.40	.9854	5.798	.1725	.1700	1.55	.9998	48.078	.0208	.0208
1.41	.9871	6.165	.1622	.1601	1.56	.9999	92.620	.0108	.0108
1.42	.9887	6.581	.1519	.1502	1.57	1.0000	1255.8	.0008	.0008
1.43	.9901	7.055	.1417	.1403	1.58	1.0000	−108.65	−.0092	−.0092
1.44	.9915	7.602	.1315	.1304	1.59	.9998	−52.067	−.0192	−.0192
					1.60	.9996	−34.233	−.0292	−.0292

† π radians $= 180°$, $\pi = 3.14159$ 26536
  1 radian $= 57°17'44''$ .80625 $= .29577$ 95131
  $1° = 0.01745$ 32925   19943 radian $= 60' = 3600''$

INDEX